TAKING SIDES

Clashing Views on

Psychological Issues

FIFTEENTH EDITION

Selected, Edited, and with Introductions by

Brent Slife
Brigham Young University

Higher Education

Boston   Burr Ridge, IL   Dubuque, IA   New York   San Francisco   St. Louis
Bangkok   Bogotá   Caracas   Kuala Lumpur   Lisbon   London   Madrid   Mexico City
Milan   Montreal   New Delhi   Santiago   Seoul   Singapore   Sydney   Taipei   Toronto

Higher Education

TAKING SIDES: CLASHING VIEWS ON PSYCHOLOGICAL ISSUES, FIFTEENTH EDITION

Published by McGraw-Hill, a business unit of The McGraw-Hill Companies, Inc., 1221 Avenue of the Americas, New York, NY 10020. Copyright © 2008 by The McGraw-Hill Companies, Inc. All rights reserved. Previous edition(s) 1980–2006. No part of this publication may be reproduced or distributed in any form or by any means, or stored in a database or retrieval system, without the prior written consent of The McGraw-Hill Companies, Inc., including, but not limited to, in any network or other electronic storage or transmission, or broadcast for distance learning.

Some ancillaries, including electronic and print components, may not be available to customers outside the United States.

Taking Sides® is a registered trademark of the McGraw-Hill Companies, Inc.
Taking Sides is published by the **Contemporary Learning Series** group within the McGraw-Hill Higher Education division.

 This book is printed on recycled, acid-free paper containing 10% postconsumer waste.

1 2 3 4 5 6 7 8 9 0 DOC/DOC 0 9 8 7

MHID: 0-07-351510-8
ISBN: 978-0-07-351510-6
ISSN: 1098-5409

Managing Editor: *Larry Loeppke*
Production Manager: *Faye Schilling*
Senior Developmental Editor: *Jill Peter*
Editorial Assistant: *Nancy Meissner*
Production Service Assistant: *Rita Hingtgen*
Permissions Coordinator: *Lori Church*
Senior Marketing Manager: *Julie Keck*
Marketing Communications Specialist: *Mary Klein*
Marketing Coordinator: *Alice Link*
Project Manager: *Jane Mohr*
Design Specialist: *Tara McDermott*
Senior Administrative Assistant: *DeAnna Dausener*
Senior Operations Manager: *Pat Koch Krieger*
Cover Graphics: *Maggie Lytle*

Compositor: Hurix Systems Private Limited
Cover Image: Brand X

Library of Congress Cataloging-in-Publication Data
Main entry under title:
Taking sides: clashing views on psychological issues/selected, edited, and with introductions by Brent Slife—15th ed.

Includes bibliographical references.
1. Psychology. 2. Human behavior. I. Slife, Brent, *comp.*
150

www.mhhe.com

TAKING SIDES

Clashing Views on

Psychological Issues

FIFTEENTH EDITION

Preface

Critical thinking skills are a significant component of a meaningful education, and this book is specifically designed to stimulate critical thinking and initiate lively and informed dialogue on psychological issues. In this book I present 36 selections, arranged in pro and con pairs, that address a total of 18 different controversial issues in psychology. The opposing views demonstrate that even experts can derive conflicting conclusions and opinions from the same body of information.

A dialogue approach to learning is certainly not new. The ancient Greek philosopher Socrates engaged in it with his students some 2,400 years ago. His point-counterpoint procedure was termed a *dialectic*. Although Socrates and his companions hoped eventually to know the "truth" by this method, they did not see the dialectic as having a predetermined end. There were no right answers to know or facts to memorize. The emphasis in this learning method is on how to evaluate information—on developing reasoning skills.

It is in this dialectical spirit that *Taking Sides: Clashing Views on Psychological Issues* was originally compiled, and it has guided me through this 15th edition as well. To encourage and stimulate discussion and to focus the debates in this volume, each issue is expressed in terms of a single question and answered with two points of view. But certainly the reader should not feel confined to adopt only one or the other of the positions presented. There are positions that fall between the views expressed or totally outside them, and I encourage you to fashion your own conclusions.

Some of the questions raised in this volume go to the very heart of what psychology as a discipline is all about and the methods and manner in which psychologists work. Others address newly emerging concerns. In choosing readings I was guided by the following criteria: the readings had to be understandable to newcomers to psychology; they had to have academic substance; and they had to express markedly different points of view.

Plan of the book Each issue in this volume has an issue *introduction*, which defines each author's position and sets the stage for debate. Also provided is a set of point-counterpoint statements that pertain to the issue and that should help to get the dialogue off the ground. Each issue concludes with *challenge questions* to provoke further examination of the issue. The introduction and challenge questions are designed to assist the reader in achieving a critical and informed view on important psychological issues. Also, at the beginning of each part is a list of Internet site addresses (URLs) that should prove useful as starting points for further research. At the back of the book is a listing of all the *contributors to this volume*, which gives information on the psychologists, psychiatrists, philosophers, professors, and social critics whose views are debated here.

In the interest of space, the reference lists of many of the original articles have been omitted or severely curtailed. Although I welcome further scholarly investigations in these issues, I assume that readers who engage in such investigation will want to look up the original articles (with the original reference lists) anyway. Furthermore, many of the articles have been heavily edited.

Changes to this edition   This edition entails considerable revision. There are eight completely new issues: *Are Traditional Empirical Methods Sufficient to Provide Evidence for Psychological Practice?* (Issue 2); *Do Women and Men Communicate Differently?* (Issue 5); *Do Brain Deficiencies Determine Learning Disabilities?* (Issue 6); *Does the Environment Influence Human Development More than Genes?* (Issue 7); *Does Research Show That Homosexual Parenting Has No Negative Effects?* (Issue 9); *Is the Theory of Multiple Intelligences Valid?* (Issue 11); *Does Low Self-Esteem Lead to Antisocial Behavior?* (Issue 14); and *Can Sex Be Addictive?* (Issue 18). In addition, three issues have had one side replaced: *Are Humans Naturally Violent?* (Issue 4); *Does the Divorce of Parents Harm Their Children?* (Issue 8); and *Should Psychologists Be Able to Prescribe Drugs?* (Issue 15). This serves to bring the debates up to date, and totals 21 new selections.

A word to the instructor   An *Instructor's Resource Guide With Test Questions* (multiple-choice and essay) is available through the publisher for the instructor using *Taking Sides* in the classroom. A general guidebook, *Using Taking Sides in the Classroom,* which discusses methods and techniques for integrating the pro-con approach into any classroom setting, is also available. An online version of *Using Taking Sides in the Classroom* and a correspondence service for *Taking Sides* adopters can be found at http://www.mhcls.com/usingts/.

   Taking Sides: Clashing Views in Psychological Issues is only one title in the Taking Sides series. If you are interested in seeing the table of contents for any of the other titles, please visit the Taking Sides Web site at http://www.mhcls.com/takingsides/.

Acknowledgments   In working on this revision I received useful suggestions from many of the users of the previous edition, and I was able to incorporate many of their recommendations for new issues and new readings.

   In addition, special thanks to the McGraw-Hill staff for their support and perspective.

Brent Slife
Brigham Young University

Correlation Guide

The Taking Sides series presents current issues in a debate-style format designed to stimulate student interest and develop critical thinking skills. Each issue is thoughtfully framed with an issue summary, an issue introduction with points and counterpoints, and challenge questions. The pro and con essays—selected for their liveliness and substance—represent the arguments of leading scholars and commentators in their fields.

Taking Sides: Clashing Views in Psychological Issues, 15/e is an easy-to-use reader that presents issues on important topics in Psychology. For more information on Taking Sides and other McGraw-Hill Contemporary Learning Series titles, visit www.mhcls.com.

This convenient guide matches the units in *Taking Sides: Psychological Issues*, 15/e with the corresponding chapters in three of our best-selling McGraw-Hill Psychology textbooks by Robert S. Feldman and Michael W. Passer.

Taking Sides: Psychology, 15/e	Essentials of Understanding Psychology, 7/e	Understanding Psychology, 8/e	Psychology: The Science of Mind and Behavior, 4/e
Issue 1. Should Animal Research in Psychology Be Eliminated?	Chapter 1: Introduction to Psychology (Module 4—Research Challenges: Exploring the Process	Chapter 2: Psychological Research (Module 6—Critical Research Issues)	Chapter 2: Studying Behavior Scientifically
Issue 2. Are Traditional Scientific Methods Sufficient to Provide Evidence for Psychological Practice	Chapter 1: Introduction to Psychology (Module 1—Psychologists at Work and Module 3—Research in Psychology)	Chapter 1: Introduction to Psychology (Module 1—Psychologists at Work) Chapter 2: Psychological Research (Module 4—The Scientific Method)	Chapter 2: Studying Behavior Scientifically Chapter 15: Treatment of Psychological Disorders
Issue 3. Classic Dialogue: Was Stanley Milgram's Study of Obedience Unethical?	Chapter 14: Social Psychology (Module 44—Social Influence)	Chapter 17: Social Psychology (Module 55—Social Influence)	Chapter 16: Social Thinking and Behavior
Issue 4. Are Humans Naturally Violent?	Chapter 1: Introduction to Psychology (Module 2—A Science Evolves: The Past, the Present, and the Future) Chapter 5: Learning (Module 17—Cognitive-Social Approaches to Learning)	Chapter 1: Introduction to Psychology (Module 2—Science Evolves: The Past, the Present, and the Future) Chapter 6: Learning (Module 19—Cognitive Approaches to Learning)	Chapter 6: Learning and Adaptation: The Role of Experience Chapter 16: Social Thinking and Behavior

Taking Sides: Psychology, 15/e	Essentials of Understanding Psychology, 7/e	Understanding Psychology, 8/e	Psychology: The Science of Mind and Behavior, 4/e
Issue 5. Do Women and Men Communicate Differently?	Chapter 2: Neuroscience and Behavior (Module 7—The Brain)	Chapter 11: Sexuality and Gender (Module 33—Gender and Sex)	Chapter 11: Development Over the Life Span
Issue 6. Do Brain Deficiencies Determine Learning Disabilities?	Chapter 2: Neuroscience and Behavior (Module 5—Neurons: The Basic Elements of Behavior; Module 6—The Nervous System and the Endocrine System: Communicating Within the Body; Module 7—The Brain)	Chapter 3: Neuroscience and Behavior (Module 7— Neurons: The Basic Elements of Behavior; Module 8—The Nervous System and the Endocrine System: Communicating Within the Body; Module 9—The Brain)	Chapter 6: Learning and Adaptation: The Role of Experience
Issue 7. Does the Environment Influence Human Development More than Genes?	Chapter 1: Introduction to Psychology (Module 1—Psychologists at Work and Module 2—A Science Evolves: The Past, the Present, and the Future) Chapter 9: Development (Module 27—Nature, Nurture, and Prenatal Development)	Chapter 1: Introduction to Psychology (Module 1—Psychologists at Work; Module 2—Science Evolves: The Past, the Present, and the Future) Chapter 12: Development (Module 37— Nature and Nurture: The Enduring Development Issue)	Chapter 11: Development over the Life Span
Issue 8. Does the Divorce of Parents Harm Their Children?	Chapter 9: Development (Module 30—Adulthood)	Chapter 12: Development (Module—Adulthood)	Chapter 11: Development Over the Life Span
Issue 9. Does Research Show That Homosexual Parenting Has No Negative Effects?	Chapter 8: Motivation and Emotion (Module 25—Human Needs and Motivation: Eat, Drink, and Be Daring)	Chapter 11: Sexuality and Gender (Module 35—The Diversity of Sexual Behavior)	Chapter 10: Motivation and Emotion
Issue 10. Are Human Activities Determined?	Chapter 1: Introduction to Psychology (Module 2—A Science Evolves: The Past, the Present, and the Future) Chapter 10: Personality (Module 32—Trait, Learning, Biological, Evolutionary, and Humanistic Approaches to Personality)	Chapter 1: Introduction to Psychology (Module 2— A Science Evolves: The Past, the Present, and the Future Module 3—Psychology's Key Issues and Controversies) Chapter 13: Personality (Module 43—Trait, Learning, Biological, Evolutionary, and Humanistic Approaches to Personality)	Chapter 10: Motivation and Emotion

Taking Sides: Psychology, 15/e	Essentials of Understanding Psychology, 7/e	Understanding Psychology, 8/e	Psychology: The Science of Mind and Behavior, 4/e
Issue 11. Is the Theory of Multiple Intelligences Valid?	Chapter 7: Thinking, Language, and Intelligence (Module 23—Intelligence)	Chapter 9: Intelligence (Module 26—What is Intelligence?)	Chapter 9: Intelligence
Issue 12. Does ADHD Exist?	Chapter 12: Psychological Disorders (Module 38—The Major Psychological Disorders)	Chapter 15: Psychological Disorders (Module 49—The Major Psychological Disorders)	Chapter 14: Psychological Disorders
Issue 13. Does Taking Antidepressants Lead to Suicide?	Chapter 2: Neuroscience and Behavior (Module 5—Neurons: The Basic Elements of Behavior) Chapter 13: Treatment of Psychological Disorders (Module 42—Biomedical Therapy: Biological Approaches to Treatment)	Chapter 3: Neuroscience and Behavior (Module 7—Neurons: The Basic Elements of Behavior Chapter 16: Treatment of Psychological Disorders (Module 53—Biomedical Therapy: Biological Approaches to Treatment	Chapter 15: Treatment of Psychological Disorders
Issue 14. Does Low Self-Esteem Produce Anti-Social Behavior?	Chapter 10: Personality (Module 32—Trait, Learning, Biological, Evolutionary, and Humanistic Approaches to Personality) Chapter 11: Health Psychology: Stress, Coping, and Well-Being (Module 36—Promoting Health and Wellness)	Chapter 14: Health Psychology: Stress, Coping, and Well-Being (Module 47—Promoting Health and Wellness) Chapter 17: Social Psychology (Module 57—Positive and Negative Social Behavior	Chapter 12: Personality
Issue 15. Should Psychologists Be Able to Prescribe Drugs?	Chapter 13: Treatment of Psychological Disorders (Module 42—Biomedical Therapy: Biological Approaches to Treatment)	Chapter 1: Introduction to Psychology (Module 1—Psychologists at Work) Chapter 16: Treatment of Psychological Disorders (Module 53—Biomedical Therapy: Biological Approaches to Treatment	Chapter 15: Treatment of Psychological Disorders
Issue 16. Is Treating Homosexuality Ethical?	Chapter 8: Motivation and Emotion (Module 25—Human Needs and Motivation: Eat, Drink, and Be Daring)	Chapter 11: Sexuality and Gender (Module 35—The Diversity of Sexual Behavior)	Chapter 10: Motivation and Emotion

Taking Sides: Psychology, 15/e	Essentials of Understanding Psychology, 7/e	Understanding Psychology, 8/e	Psychology: The Science of Mind and Behavior, 4/e
Issue 17. Do Video Games Lead to Violence?	Chapter 1: Introduction to Psychology (Module 2—A Science Evolves: The Past, the Present, and the Future)	Chapter 1: Introduction to Psychology (Module 2—A Science Evolves: The Past, the Present, and the Future)	Chapter 16: Social Thinking and Behavior
	Chapter 5: Learning (Module 17—Cognitive-Social Approaches to Learning)	Chapter 6: Learning (Module 19—Cognitive Approaches to Learning)	
Issue 18. Can Sex Be Addictive?	Chapter 8: Motivation and Emotion (Module 24—Explaining Motivation; Module 25—Human Needs and Motivation: Eat, Drink, and Be Daring; Module 36—Understanding Emotional Experiences)	Chapter 11: Sexuality and Gender (Module 33—Gender and Sex; Module 34—Understanding Human Sexual Response: The Facts of Life; Module 35—The Diversity of Sexual Behavior; Module 36—Sexual Difficulties: When Sex Goes Wrong)	Chapter 10: Motivation and Emotion

Contents In Brief

Contents

psychologist Stanley Milgram, in response to Baumrind's accusations, asserts that the study was well designed, the stress caused to participants could not have been anticipated, and the participants' anguish dissipated after a thorough debriefing.

Field researcher Michael L. Wilson and biological anthropologist Richard Wrangham argue that humans are innately violent because their closest non human relatives—chimpanzees—are themselves violent and aggressive. Biological anthropologist Robert W. Sussman asserts that neither humans nor chimpanzees are inherently violent, but culture and upbringing are significantly involved in the violence evident in both species.

University professor and communication researcher Julia T. Wood explains how communication styles differ in men and women by examining gender roles in typical childhood games, men's and women's communication practices, and common misunderstandings between the sexes. Professors and researchers Laura L. Winn and Donald L. Rubin describe an empirical study aimed at understanding social roles and argue that these contextual factors, not biological sex, play the defining role in communication styles.

Sally and Bennett Shaywitz, codirectors of the National Institute of Child Health and Human Development, suggest that reading disabilities stem from "brain glitches". Educational psychologist Gerald Coles believes that learning "disabilities" come from myriad sources, and each source needs to be considered when diagnosing and treating disabilities.

UNIT 4   COGNITIVE PROCESSES   183

Psychologists John A. Bargh and Tanya L. Chartrand assert that people are controlled not by their purposeful choices and intentions but by the environment through automatic cognitive processes. In response, psychologist Amy Fisher Smith agrees that people do, in fact, have automatic behaviors but she believes these behaviors can be explained by mental processes akin to a free will.

Psychologist Howard Gardner argues for the validity of his theory of multiple intelligences because it both reflects the data collected about intelligent human behavior and explains why people excel in some areas but fail in others. Educational philosopher John White believes that Gardner cannot prove the existence of multiple types of intelligence and argues that people who are generally able to adapt well will excel in whatever field they choose.

UNIT 5   MENTAL HEALTH   229

Psychiatry professor Russell A. Barkley claims that current scientific evidence, particularly evidence provided by heritability and neuro-imaging studies points unarguably toward ADHD's validity and existence. Psychiatrist Sami Timimi claims the current ADHD epidemic is the result of unrealistic expectations for today's children and the pharmaceutical companies' desire to sell more drugs.

Psychiatrist David Healy and statistician Chris Whitaker argue that psychological research reveals a significant number of suicidal acts by individuals taking antidepressants and, thus, recommend stricter controls on these drugs. In response, psychiatrist Yvon D. Lapierre maintains that the research on suicidality and antidepressants is unconvincing, recommending that conclusions from these findings should be severely limited.

Psychologist M. Brent Donnellan and his colleagues describe empirical investigations that show low self-esteem as highly predictive of many externalizing problems, including antisocial behavior. Social psychologist Roy Baumeister and his associates review self-esteem studies to argue that low self-esteem generally has little influence on negative outcomes such as antisocial behavior.

Psychologists Patrick H. DeLeon and Debra Lina Dunivin assert that granting prescription authority to psychologists will improve the quality of psychological care because they will be able to treat a patient's mind and body. Psychologist William Robiner and his colleagues object to the idea of giving psychologists prescription privileges because psychologists do not receive the same rigorous medical training as those who can prescribe medicine.

Psychologist Christopher Rosik affirms that a therapist can ethically assist a patient in changing his or her sexual orientation as long as it is the patient's desire to do so. Psychologist Robert-Jay Green voices concern with sexual orientation therapy on the grounds that any attempt to sexually reorient a patient implies a moral disapproval of homosexuality.

UNIT 7   SOCIAL PSYCHOLOGY   347

Developmental psychologist Douglas A. Gentile, and department of psychology chair Craig A. Anderson assert that violent video games cause several physiological and psychological changes in children that lead to aggressive and violent behavior. Cheryl K. Olson, a professor of psychiatry, contends that further research is needed because there is so little current evidence of a substantial connection between exposure to violent video games and serious real-life violence.

Sexual addiction expert Patrick J. Carnes argues not only that sex can be addictive but that sex can be as addictive as drugs, alcohol, or any other chemical substance. Sex therapists Lawrence A. Siegel and Richard M. Siegel believe that while some sexual behaviors might be dysfunctional, calling those behaviors "addictive" confuses a moralistic ideology with a scientific fact.

Introduction

Why does psychology need a *Taking Sides* book? "Taking sides" implies that there are "controversial psychological issues," as the book title states. But how can there be controversial issues in a discipline that considers itself a science? Controversial issues would seem inherent in such disciplines as philosophy and religion, but wouldn't the issues of psychology be resolved by science, by finding out what is true and false through psychology's empirical methods? If so, are the "controversial issues" presented in this book only *temporary* issues waiting for empirical resolution? And if they are only temporary, why learn or argue about them? Why "take a side?"

As this introduction will argue, there are all sorts of reasons and opportunities to take a side in psychology. Scientific findings are not only decided by data—the information produced by scientific research—scientific findings are also decided by theoretical allegiances, industry loyalties, and philosophical assumptions that are not themselves driven or resolved by data. These allegiances and assumptions allow for and even spawn controversial issues. Indeed, they form what some call the "disguised ideologies" of science (Bernstein, 1983; Richardson, Fowers, & Guignon, 1999), implicit worldviews or philosophies that guide what variables to select for research, what methods to use in these investigations, and what sense to make of the resulting data. As we will see, these are just a few of the many places in psychological research where the researcher's bias or ideology, and thus "controversial issues," can come into play.

Some may hold that the problem of bias only affects the "soft" sciences. They may believe that "hard" sciences, such as physics and chemistry, have essentially eliminated biases and ideologies. However, as we will show, both soft and hard sciences are subject to these ideologies and controversial issues. Indeed, one of the recent conclusions of physics is that the observer's "frame of reference" always affects what is observed (Einstein, 1990; Heisenberg, 1958; Wolf, 1981). In this introduction, we will point to dramatic examples of systematic biases in both types of sciences, showing how some of the most important research—research about health treatment—is substantially driven by factors outside the data per se.

Even so, some scientists will argue that these biases are miscarriages of science, that science conducted correctly would have no systematic ideologies. As we will attempt to describe, however, nothing could be further from the truth, because the scientific method is itself based on a philosophy. It is itself based on a broad ideology in this sense. This is not to say that science is *only* bias or that science is worthless. Indeed, we will argue that science is one of the best tools we have for helping to resolve controversial issues. The main point of this introduction is that ideologies, biases, and "issues" are *never* avoided entirely and, indeed, play a *necessary* role in science. We believe this role is all the more reason to become aware of psychology's controversial issues, think them through, and, yes, even take a well-reasoned and well-informed "side."

Allegiance Effects in the Soft Sciences

There are many examples of systematic bias in psychology (Slife, Reber, & Richardson, 2005), but Luborsky's theoretical (or ideological) "allegiance" is surely one of the more striking and significant (Luborsky, Diguer, Seligman, et al., 1999; Luborsky & Barrett, in press). It is striking because theoretical allegiance is such an impressive predictor of psychological research, forecasting an unprecedented two-thirds of the variability in treatment outcomes, with correlations as high as .85 (Luborsky & Barrett, in press). We say unprecedented because correlations in psychology are rarely this high. Theoretical allegiance is also significant because it concerns the pivotal question: which psychological treatment is best? In other words, this particular systematic bias is involved in deciding what actually works in psychology.

The term *allegiance* refers to a person's conscious or unconscious loyalty or commitment to a particular ideal, philosophy, or organization. In research on psychotherapy, Luborsky views theoretical allegiance as the degree of a researcher's loyalty to a specific theory of behavior change. The most common theories of psychotherapy, and thus types of theoretical loyalty, are the broad categories of dynamic, cognitive, behavioral, and pharmacological. Luborsky and Barrett (in press) essentially showed that a researcher's preference for one of these broad categories—as rated most accurately through reprints, self-ratings, and colleague ratings—correlates with the therapy found to be the best in the researcher's comparison of several therapies. In other words, whatever therapies or ideas that researchers favor *before* the investigation is, with few exceptions, what the researchers "find" their results favoring *after* investigation.

Luborsky found this correlation through "meta-analyses." Instead of a conventional analysis of one particular study, meta-analysis is usually an analysis of many studies—an analysis of many conventional analyses. To understand what Luborsky's meta-analysis means, consider an example. Let us say that a particular researcher favors a certain theoretical approach, such as behavioral, and sets up a study comparing behavioral and pharmacological therapies. Luborsky's analysis indicates that this study will probably favor behavioral therapies over pharmacological, even though the two might *really* be equivalent in effectiveness. According to Luborsky, "treatment benefits, as evidenced in comparative trials, are so influenced by the researcher's theoretical allegiance that in many comparisons differences between treatments lessen or become negligible when the influence of allegiance is considered" (Luborsky & Barrett, in press, p. 355).

Therefore, if we know the theoretical orientation of the researcher, we can predict with considerable accuracy the outcome of an empirical comparison among the various treatment approaches—without even making the comparison! Theoretical allegiance, in this sense, is a clear bias or ideology that is not being corrected by what is really happening in the treatment comparison.

Theoretical allegiances are occurring in spite of the controls instituted for subjective biases in these elaborate research designs. Although Luborsky believes that such allegiances *should* be controlled, conventional scientific methods are not currently doing so. In short, there are "controversial issues" that are not *currently* being resolved by the data. Also, as we will see (in the "What Is Happening?" section below), scientific research is conducted in a way that will never eliminate or resolve *all* the controversial issues.

Allegiance Effects in the Hard Sciences

Is this also true in the hard sciences, or do they avoid the ideas and ideologies that lead to controversial issues? As mentioned, physics has long recognized Heisenberg's (1958) "uncertainty principle" and Einstein's (1990) relativity of the "inertial frame of reference" as just two of the ways in which the observer is assumed to have an important impact on the observed (Bohm, 1980; Wolf, 1981). However, there are also similar meta-analyses to Luborsky's in the hard sciences. Findings in medicine, for example, parallel those we have just described in psychology. Here, *theoretical* allegiance is less of an issue, but *industry* allegiance is widely acknowledged as a potent bias in medical research (Bhandari et al., 2004; Kjaergard & Als-Nielson, 2002; Lexchin et al., 2003). Industry allegiance refers to the high correlations between the industry sponsor of research and the pro-industry outcome of this research.

Healy (1999), for instance, suggests that much of our current conception of the effectiveness of antidepressants is molded more by the marketing imperatives of the pharmaceutical industry than by the scientific findings. There is certainly no dispute that the pharmaceutical industry is the largest funder of medical research in North America, and this, as Valenstein (1998) notes, is "overwhelmingly true" for research on psychiatric drugs (p. 187). Indeed, Valenstein (1998) claims that these companies are unlikely to fund researchers who have been negative about drug effectiveness. Still, it is one thing to point to this industry's massive funding efforts and profit motives, and quite another to claim that industry allegiance biases investigators. Is there evidence for this latter claim?

In fact, editorials in five different prestigious medical journals have all pointed to evidence that pharmaceutical funding has tainted the objectivity of these studies (Greenberg, 2001). Freemantle, Anderson, and Young (2000), for example, have recently shown in a meta-analysis of comparative studies that a sponsor's funding is the best predictor of whether studies will show the sponsor's drug to be effective. Similarly, Friedberg et al. (1999) have shown empirically that company-supported studies are more likely to report efficacy for the company's product than are independent studies of the same product. Bhandari et al. (2004) even report this effect for surgical interventions. Stern and Simes (1997) also found considerable evidence that studies which do not reflect positively on antidepressants are less likely to be published. Moncrieff (2001) reports that the problem of publication bias is even more pronounced with recent SSRI antidepressants, because the majority of trials have been conducted by the pharmaceutical industry, which has no obligation to publish negative results and may see little advantage in doing so.

What Is Happening?

What is happening in the soft and hard sciences to produce these "allegiance" effects, either theoretical or industrial? There are issues, such as allegiance, that data never seem to determine or decide definitively. This suggests that some issues require old-fashioned discussion and debate among those in the discipline. It also indicates that scientific experiments alone will not always suffice. Why? Why can't data alone decide all the discipline's "controversial issues?" One of the primary reasons is a concept called *underdetermination*. Underdetermination means that research data never *completely* determine the interpretation made of that data (Curd & Cover, 1998; Slife & Williams, 1995). The researcher always has a limited choice (within the parameters of the data) about which interpretation to use.

To begin to understand why this is true, consider that any set of data is meaningless without some interpretive framework for that data. In other words, a researcher must *add to* the data his or her own organization or interpretation for the results of any study to be meaningful findings. Even a quick scan of a (typical) data set reveals a bewildering array of numbers, especially if this scan lacks the researcher's explanation as to what specific categories of data and statistical results *mean* (or how they should be interpreted). (For an example, see Slife & Williams, 1995, pp. 5–6.) Researchers will often claim to "see" meanings in their data, but this is not because the data *inherently* "mean" something. This is because the researcher *already* has an interpretive framework, consciously or unconsciously, for the data in mind.

It is important to recognize that the interpretation selected must "fit" the data for the interpretation to be viable. In other words, not just any interpretation will do; meaningful interpretations must make sense of *all* the data. Nevertheless, more than one interpretation of all the data is always possible, with some potentially dramatic differences in these interpretations. This is what "underdetermination" means. (Please see Curd & Cover, 1999 and Slife & Williams, 1995, pp. 185–187 for the more technical considerations of this conception.) In this sense, a study's "findings" are never *merely* the data, because the data are not meaningful findings until the researcher organizes or interprets the data, allowing for systems of ideas, and thus "controversial issues," to enter the research picture.

Actually, data interpretation is just one of the many places where biases can creep into scientific research. Consider how researchers have all sorts of "subjective" choice-points in their studies: first—what to study (what variables are crucial); second—how to study the variables (what operationalization and method design to use); third—how to analyze the study (what assumptions are met and statistics used); fourth—what the statistical results really mean (what interpretation to use); and fifth—what limits the study has (what study problems might impede certain interpretations). These choice-points mean that subjective factors, such as allegiance, are inevitably part of any research study. Researchers, knowingly or unknowingly, are favoring their own ideologies through the decisions they make at these choice-points. Part of the purpose of *Taking Sides* books, then, is to reveal and discuss these ideologies, and help students to become aware of their impact on the discipline.

Science as Ideology

Many scientists will want to argue that influential ideological factors are not a necessary part of science—that the allegiance effects of psychology and medicine are examples of bad research. They may believe that good science occurs when all the systematic biases, and thus disguised ideologies, have been eliminated or controlled. However, as mentioned earlier, science itself is based on a broad ideology (or philosophy) about how science should be conducted. Moreover, this broad ideology could not itself have been scientifically derived because one would need the ideology (before its derivation) to conduct the scientific investigations to derive it. In short, *there is no empirical evidence for the philosophy of empiricism that underlies the scientific method.* Some may claim that this philosophy has been successful, but this is only a claim or an opinion, not a scientific fact. Even if we were to endorse this claim, which we would, it does not minimize the broad ideology of this philosophy of science, along with the biases and values it promotes.

Perhaps the most obvious bias or value of the philosophy of empiricism is the observability value. Because this philosophy assumes that sensory experience is the only really knowable experience, traditional science has based its doctrine of knowing on the sensory experience of vision or observability. For many students, this valuing of observability will not seem like a value (Slife, in press). These students may have unknowingly (no pun intended) accepted this philosophy as their own, without critically examining it. In this case, the doctrine of observability will seem more like an axiom than a value.

To be a value rather than an axiom, observability must indicate not only what particular things have merit or worth but also what alternative things *could* be valued (Slife, in press). Regarding the worth issue, it is probably obvious that traditional empiricism values, and thus selects, observable phenomena as having more merit or worth than nonobservable phenomena for scientific purposes. Perhaps the bigger hurdle for appreciating the value-ladenness of observability is understanding the possibility of alternatives—in this sense, the possibility of knowing *non*observables. Here, we could ask the empiricists if their doctrine of observability is itself observable. In other words, is the idea that "only the sensory can be known" *itself* observable? And if it is not, how then do we know that this idea is correct? Given that empiricists do not observe this idea, and given that they hold it to be correct, there must be other ways of knowing things than observability.

We can at this point describe other philosophies (or epistemologies) of knowing that assert that many unobservable experiences are knowable, such as the feelings we have for someone or the thoughts we have about something. With the feelings of love, for example, we can surely observe someone who is "in love" hugging and kissing or any specified observable factor (in research, these are called *operationalizations*). However, we would rarely assume that the feeling of love and these observables are identical. Hugs and kisses can occur without this feeling, and this feeling can occur without hugs and kisses. Therefore, studies of hugs and kisses (or any specified observable) are *not* studies of love. At the risk of noting the obvious, studies of observables are not studies of nonobservables. They may be studies of observables that are associated with nonobservables, but then if we cannot know the nonobservable, how can we know what is associated with them?

For this reason, traditional scientific methods selectively attend to, and thus value, one particular aspect of the world—observables over nonobservables. Indeed, this is part of the reason qualitative research methods were formulated and have become increasingly popular in psychology and other disciplines. They claim that they can investigate nonobservable experiences that are not strictly observable, such as meaning and emotion (cf. Denzin & Lincoln, 2000). If this is true, knowing nonobservables is possible, and the value-ladenness of only attending to observables is clear. Again, some may insist that only observables can be known, but this insistence is not itself a scientific claim because it cannot be decided through scientific observation (Slife, Wiggins, & Graham, 2005). It is a philosophical claim about how knowing occurs, and is thus subject to comparison with other philosophical claims about knowing (other epistemologies).

Observability is not the only value of traditional scientific methods. Many of the customs and traditions of how one conducts and is supposed to conduct research originate from similarly unproven values and assumptions, including reductionism (Yanchar, 2005), instrumentalism (Richardson, 2005), naturalism (Richards & Bergin, 2005), and positivism (Slife & Williams, 1995). Indeed, there is an entire special issue of the journal *Counseling and Values* (in press) that deals with the values and assumptions of psychology's scientific methods, which are the hidden roots of some of today's "controversial issues."

The lesson here is that many values and unproven ideas are *inherent* in the system of science itself. Before a method is even formulated, the persons formulating the method must make assumptions about the world in which the method would be successful. The world cannot be known through the method, because the method has not been invented yet. Consequently, the assumptions and values used for its formulation have to be speculations and guesswork to some degree—in short, values and assumptions that are not themselves scientifically proven (Slife, in press). Again, this does not make science wrong or bad. Indeed, these scientific values and assumptions have made science what it is, including any perceived effectiveness it has.

Still, the perceived effectiveness of the scientific enterprise does not mean that we can forget about these values. They are still unproven values, after all, and as such they can be problematic or helpful, depending on the context in which they are used. As we described, they may be useful for observable aspects of the world but not so useful for nonobservable aspects of the world. In this sense, there will always be "controversial issues" in any scientific enterprise, hard or soft. Some will be resolved by data, but some will require other means of examination and debate.

Application to the Issues of This Book

The issues of this book are a wide assortment of both types: "empirical questions," which are primarily decided by research, and "philosophical questions," which are primarily decided by discussion and consensus or theoretical examination in relation to disciplinary values. Psychologists typically have the most skills in resolving empirical or research issues. They have been trained since their undergraduate days with multiple courses, such as "Research Methods" and "Statistics," all in support of resolving empirical or research questions.

Psychologists are rarely as adept at philosophical questions, even though these questions pervade the discipline (as we have shown). Indeed, many psychologists may despair at such questions because they associate philosophy with irresolvable issues—issues that seem interminable. We have sympathy for this attitude, yet we need to be careful not to "throw the baby out with the bath water." In other words, just because there are seemingly interminable problems in philosophy does not mean that decisions and judgments cannot be made about the philosophical issues of a discipline such as psychology.[1] Many decisions and judgments have, of course, already been made. Otherwise, we would not have a philosophy that guides our science or a set of values that guide our ethics. As the issues of this book indicate, however, not all of these values and assumptions have been decided. Moreover, there is a case to be made that even the decided values should be continually explicated and reevaluated, as new research arenas and topics come to the fore.

Let us close this introduction, then, by pointing explicitly to how such philosophical issues may rear their ugly heads in a discipline such as psychology, and thus in this book. One way to categorize these issues is in terms of the *production* of research and the *outcome* of research. The first involves the many ways in which controversial ideas can enter the conducting of psychological investigations, whereas the second entails the many ways in which controversial ideas can enter the interpretation of a study's data or a program of research.

In the first case, controversial issues can arise when researchers have an allegiance or agenda in formulating and conducting their programs of research. This agenda does not have to be conscious, because loyalties can be influential—political or sociological, theoretical or organizational—whether or not they are known or articulated. For example, in the homosexual parenting issue of this *Taking Sides* edition, one author accuses researchers of a liberal agenda in conducting the investigations (Issue 9). We make no judgment here about the validity of this particular accusation. However, there is no doubt that such agendas can infiltrate these studies. They can influence what researchers consider important to study, how they design the study, how they operationalize the variables involved, and how they analyze the study. All these phases of a study, as we have described above, are choice-points for researchers that allow for agendas to be revealed and loyalties to be identified. It would thus be important for students of "controversial issues" to try to discern these loyalties and agendas in the production of data. That is the reason there is often no substitute for studying the studies themselves.

Controversial issues can also result from interpretations of the existing data and studies. Perhaps the most striking example of this involves two sets of scholars—each well-trained and each looking at essentially the same data—coming to dramatically different conclusions. For example, the authors

---

[1]Likewise, we should not "throw out" the achievements of science just because it is not totally objective.

of each side of the divorce issue (Issues 8) basically consider the same data. First, as we have noted, they can interpret the same data in two different ways (through the "underdetermination" of the data). Second, these interpretive frameworks can also lead researchers to weigh different sets of data differently. While one set of investigators views certain studies as pivotal, another set considers the same studies deeply problematic, and thus gives them far less weight. In both cases, the interpretive framework of the researchers is part of the reason they "take the side" they do. There is no doubt that the data of the studies are important. Nevertheless, there is also no doubt that the sides taken and the interpretations made are not solely data-driven.

Conclusion

The bottom line is that no science will avoid controversial issues. As long as humans are involved *as* scientists, allegiances and biases will be a factor. There are just too many choice-points for a scientist's ideologies, known or unknown, to seep into the methods employed. Truth be told, human beings are also the inventors and formulators of the methods of science. This means not only that these methods embody the biases and assumptions of the original inventors but also that subsequent changes in the philosophies that guide science will also stem from biased humans. In this sense, we will never be rid of controversial issues. Our job, then, is to expose them, discuss them, and take a well-informed "side" with respect to them.

References

Bernstein, R. J. (1983). *Beyond objectivism and relativism*. Philadelphia: University of Pennsylvania Press.

Bhandari, M. et al. (2004). Association between industry fundings and statistically significant pro-industry findings in medical and surgical randomized trials. *Journal of the Canadian Medical Association, 170*, 477–480.

Bohm, D. (1980). *Wholeness and the implicate order*. London: Routledge & Kegan Paul.

Curd, M., & Cover, J. A. (1998). *Philosophy of science: The central issues*. New York: W. W. Norton & Company.

Denzin, N. K., & Lincoln, Y. S. (Eds.). (2000). *Handbook of qualitative methods*. Thousand Oaks, CA: Sage.

Einstein, A. (1961/1990). Relativity: The special and general theory. Translated by Robert W. Larson. In M. Adler (Ed.), *Great books of the Western world*. Chicago: University of Chicago Press.

Freemantle, N., Anderson, I. M., & Young, P. (2000). Predictive value of pharmacological activity for the relative efficacy of antidepressant drugs: Meta-regression analysis. *British Journal of Psychiatry, 177*, 292–302.

Friedberg, M., Saffran, B., Stinson, T. J., Nelson, W., & Bennett, C. L. (1999). Evaluation of conflict of interest in economic analyses of new drugs used in oncology. *Journal of the American Medical Association, 282*, 1453–1457.

Introduction

Why does psychology need a *Taking Sides* book? "Taking sides" implies that there are "controversial psychological issues," as the book title states. But how can there be controversial issues in a discipline that considers itself a science? Controversial issues would seem inherent in such disciplines as philosophy and religion, but wouldn't the issues of psychology be resolved by science, by finding out what is true and false through psychology's empirical methods? If so, are the "controversial issues" presented in this book only *temporary* issues waiting for empirical resolution? And if they are only temporary, why learn or argue about them? Why "take a side?"

As this introduction will argue, there are all sorts of reasons and opportunities to take a side in psychology. Scientific findings are not only decided by data—the information produced by scientific research—scientific findings are also decided by theoretical allegiances, industry loyalties, and philosophical assumptions that are not themselves driven or resolved by data. These allegiances and assumptions allow for and even spawn controversial issues. Indeed, they form what some call the "disguised ideologies" of science (Bernstein, 1983; Richardson, Fowers, & Guignon, 1999), implicit worldviews or philosophies that guide what variables to select for research, what methods to use in these investigations, and what sense to make of the resulting data. As we will see, these are just a few of the many places in psychological research where the researcher's bias or ideology, and thus "controversial issues," can come into play.

Some may hold that the problem of bias only affects the "soft" sciences. They may believe that "hard" sciences, such as physics and chemistry, have essentially eliminated biases and ideologies. However, as we will show, both soft and hard sciences are subject to these ideologies and controversial issues. Indeed, one of the recent conclusions of physics is that the observer's "frame of reference" always affects what is observed (Einstein, 1990; Heisenberg, 1958; Wolf, 1981). In this introduction, we will point to dramatic examples of systematic biases in both types of sciences, showing how some of the most important research—research about health treatment—is substantially driven by factors outside the data per se.

Even so, some scientists will argue that these biases are miscarriages of science, that science conducted correctly would have no systematic ideologies. As we will attempt to describe, however, nothing could be further from the truth, because the scientific method is itself based on a philosophy. It is itself based on a broad ideology in this sense. This is not to say that science is *only* bias or that science is worthless. Indeed, we will argue that science is one of the best tools we have for helping to resolve controversial issues. The main point of this introduction is that ideologies, biases, and "issues" are *never* avoided entirely and, indeed, play a *necessary* role in science. We believe this role is all the more reason to become aware of psychology's controversial issues, think them through, and, yes, even take a well-reasoned and well-informed "side."

Allegiance Effects in the Soft Sciences

There are many examples of systematic bias in psychology (Slife, Reber, & Richardson, 2005), but Luborsky's theoretical (or ideological) "allegiance" is surely one of the more striking and significant (Luborsky, Diguer, Seligman, et al., 1999; Luborsky & Barrett, in press). It is striking because theoretical allegiance is such an impressive predictor of psychological research, forecasting an unprecedented two-thirds of the variability in treatment outcomes, with correlations as high as .85 (Luborsky & Barrett, in press). We say unprecedented because correlations in psychology are rarely this high. Theoretical allegiance is also significant because it concerns the pivotal question: which psychological treatment is best? In other words, this particular systematic bias is involved in deciding what actually works in psychology.

The term *allegiance* refers to a person's conscious or unconscious loyalty or commitment to a particular ideal, philosophy, or organization. In research on psychotherapy, Luborsky views theoretical allegiance as the degree of a researcher's loyalty to a specific theory of behavior change. The most common theories of psychotherapy, and thus types of theoretical loyalty, are the broad categories of dynamic, cognitive, behavioral, and pharmacological. Luborsky and Barrett (in press) essentially showed that a researcher's preference for one of these broad categories—as rated most accurately through reprints, self-ratings, and colleague ratings—correlates with the therapy found to be the best in the researcher's comparison of several therapies. In other words, whatever therapies or ideas that researchers favor *before* the investigation is, with few exceptions, what the researchers "find" their results favoring *after* investigation.

Luborsky found this correlation through "meta-analyses." Instead of a conventional analysis of one particular study, meta-analysis is usually an analysis of many studies—an analysis of many conventional analyses. To understand what Luborsky's meta-analysis means, consider an example. Let us say that a particular researcher favors a certain theoretical approach, such as behavioral, and sets up a study comparing behavioral and pharmacological therapies. Luborsky's analysis indicates that this study will probably favor behavioral therapies over pharmacological, even though the two might *really* be equivalent in effectiveness. According to Luborsky, "treatment benefits, as evidenced in comparative trials, are so influenced by the researcher's theoretical allegiance that in many comparisons differences between treatments lessen or become negligible when the influence of allegiance is considered" (Luborsky & Barrett, in press, p. 355).

Therefore, if we know the theoretical orientation of the researcher, we can predict with considerable accuracy the outcome of an empirical comparison among the various treatment approaches—without even making the comparison! Theoretical allegiance, in this sense, is a clear bias or ideology that is not being corrected by what is really happening in the treatment comparison.

Greenberg, R. P., Bornstein, R. F., Greenberg, M. D., & Fisher, S. (1992). A meta-analysis of antidepressant outcome under "blinder" conditions. *Journal of Consulting & Clinical Psychology, 60*, 664–669.

Healy, D. (1999). The three faces of the antidepressants: A critical commentary on the clinical-economic context of diagnoses. *Journal of Nervous and Mental Disorder, 187*, 174–180.

Heiman, G. W. (1995). *Research methods in psychology*. Boston: Houghton-Mifflin.

Heisenberg, W. (1958). *Physics and philosophy: The revolution of modern science*. New York: Harper Books.

Kjaergard, L. L., & Als-Nielson, B. (2002). Association between competing interests and authors' concluions: Epidemiological study of randomised clinical trials published in the *BMJ. British Journal of Medicine, 325*, 249–253.

Lexchin, J., Bero, L. A., Djulbegovic, B., & Clark, O. (2003). Pharmaceutical industry sponsorship and research outcome and quality: systematic review. *British Medical Journal, 326*, 1167–1170.

Luborsky, L. B., & Barrett, M. S. (in press). Theoretical allegiance.

Luborsky, L., Diguer, L., Seligman, D. A., Rosenthal, R., Krause, E. D., Johnson, S., Halperin, G., Bishop, M., Berman, J. S., & Schweizer, E. (1999). The researcher's own therapy allegiances: A "wild card" in comparisons of treatment efficacy. *Clinical Psychology: Science and Practice, 6*, 95–132.

Moncrieff, J. (2001). Are antidepressants overrated? A review of methodological problems in antidepressant trials. *The Journal of Nervous and Mental Disease, 189*, 288–295.

Richards, P. S., & Bergin, A. E. (2005). *A spiritual strategy for counseling and psychotherapy* (2nd ed.). Washington, D.C.: American Psychological Association.

Richardson, F. (2005). Psychotherapy and modern dilemmas. In B. Slife, J. Reber, & F. Richardson, (Eds.), *Critical thinking about psychology: Hidden assumptions and plausible alternatives* (pp. 17–38). Washington, D.C.: American Psychological Association Press.

Richardson, F., Fowers, B., & Guignon, C. (1999). *Re-envisioning psychology: Moral dimensions of theory and practice*. San Francisco, CA: Jossey-Bass.

Slife, B. D. (in press). A primer of the values implicit in counseling research. *Counseling and Values*.

Slife, B. D., Reber, J., & Richardson, F. (2005). *Critical thinking about psychology: Hidden assumptions and plausible alternatives*. 295 pages. Washington, D.C.: American Psychological Association Press.

Slife, B. D., Wiggins, B. J., & Graham, J. T. (2005). Avoiding an EST monopoly: Toward a pluralism of methods and philosophies. *Journal of Contemporary Psychotherapy, 35*, 83–97.

Slife, B. D., & Williams, R. N. (1995). *What's behind the research? Discovering hidden assumptions in the behavioral sciences*. Thousand Oaks, CA: Sage.

Stern, J. M., & Simes, R. J. (1997). Publication bias: Evidence of delayed publication in a cohort study of clinical research projects. *British Medical Journal, 315*, 640–645.

Valenstein, E. S. (1998). *Blaming the brain: The truth about drugs and mental health*. New York: Free Press.

Wolf, F. A. (1981). *Taking the quantum leap*. San Francisco: Harper-Row.

Yanchar, S. (2005). A contextualist alternative to cognitive psychology. In B. Slife, J. Reber, & F. Richardson (Eds.), *Critical thinking about psychology: Hidden assumptions and plausible alternatives* (pp. 171–186). Washington, D.C.: American Psychological Association Press.

Internet References . . .

Resisting Authority: A Personal Account of the Milgram Obedience Experiments

This site contains information on Stanley Milgram's study of obedience as well as the personal account of one of the participants in the study.

`http://www.jewishcurrents.org/2004-jan-dimow.htm`

Animal Research in Psychology

This site contains information published by the APA regarding the use of animals in psychological research.

`http://www.apa.org/SCIENCE/animal2.html`

Legal, Ethical, and Professional Issues in Psychoanalysis and Psychotherapy

This site's home page offers a wealth of information about different research issues in psychology. This particular link provides access to different papers that discuss the empirically supported treatment (EST) movement.

`http://www.academyprojects.org/est.htm`

Research Issues

*R*esearch methods allow psychologists to investigate their ideas and subject matter. However, the way that they conduct their research is sometimes the subject of controversy. For example, researchers have a responsibility to act ethically toward the participants in their studies. To this end, animals are often used to test experimental procedures before they are applied to humans. Is this right? Should animals be experimented upon—and sometimes subjected to pain or even killed—in the service of psychological investigation? What about the research ethics of subjecting humans to emotional pain? In a well known, "classic" experiment conducted by Stanley Milgram, human participants complained of the emotional pain they experienced in following the experimenters' instructions. Should we avoid both physical and emotional pain when dealing with research participants? Would this restrict psychological researchers too much as they attempt to help the broader population with their studies? What about studies of psychotherapy in this regard? Here, there are not only issues of ethics but also issues of the adequacy of the methods used to gauge the effectiveness of different therapy strategies. Normally, traditional scientific methods are understood as "objective," and thus free of biases. But is this strictly true? If not, what effect do these biases have on psychology's quest for evidence-based practices?

- Should Animal Research in Psychology Be Eliminated?

- Are Traditional Scientific Methods Sufficient to Provide Evidence for Psychological Practice?

- Classic Dialogue: Was Stanley Milgram's Study of Obedience Unethical?

ISSUE 1

Should Animal Research in Psychology Be Eliminated?

YES: Peter Singer, from *Animal Liberation* (Ecco, 2002)

NO: R. G. Frey, from "Justifying Animal Experimentation: The Starting Point," in Ellen Frankel Paul and Jeffrey Paul, eds., *Why Animal Experimentation Matters: The Use of Animals in Medical Research* (Transaction, 2001)

ISSUE SUMMARY

YES: Bioethicist Peter Singer asserts that to engage in animal research is to commit speciesism (similar to racism), often without any important research findings at all.

NO: Professor of philosophy R. G. Frey expresses support but ultimately argues that animals should be used for research because their quality of life is lower than that of most humans.

Many students assume that psychologists deal with humans exclusively. Psychotherapy, for example, is rarely thought to be relevant to animals. However, a large portion of psychological research does involve animals of all types—monkeys, pigeons, rats, dogs, etc. Psychologists often believe they need animals to perform the experiments that cannot be ethically conducted with humans. These experiments illuminate or test concepts that could be helpful to humans, such as in psychotherapy and education. Also, many psychologists are interested in the animals themselves. Understanding the behaviors and functioning of such animals is itself a goal of many researchers.

The problem is that many such experiments entail a treatment of animals that some might regard as harmful or painful. Indeed, this harm or pain is often the primary reason that animals are used instead of humans; no one would reasonably allow what happens to the animals to happen to humans. Researchers have shocked animals with electrical current, subjected them to painful situations, and injected them with harmful drugs, to name but a few of the research practices to which some people have objected. Why is this treatment of animals in research permitted? Why would researchers subject animals to situations and treatments that they would never condone with humans?

Peter Singer is often credited with first sensitizing people to these types of issues. A bioethicist of considerable notoriety, Singer penned a book in 1975 entitled *Animal Liberation* that formalized the arguments against the subjugation of animals to psychological and medical research. In the following selection from his 2002 update of this book, he continues to press the arguments he originally formulated. For example, Singer describes in some detail many different types of animal research in psychology but finds none that justifies the suffering of the animals involved. He also continues to refute the notion that lower animals are absolutely different from higher animals (humans). Consequently, when animals are subjected to harmful procedures, they are unjustifiably discriminated against (speciesism) in the same way that other races might be unjustifiably discriminated against (racism).

In the second selection, R. G. Frey replies with perhaps a surprising tack. Although he agrees with Singer that animals cannot be absolutely differentiated from humans, Frey argues that animals generally (though not without exception) have a lower quality of life than humans. He then brings to bear a second argument with respect to the consequences of animal experiments. He regards such consequences as almost indisputably positive and beneficial, especially for medical research. Also, Frey notes, university and government committees do attempt to safeguard the use of animals in psychological research, looking specifically at whether or not the significance of the studies proposed is substantial enough to warrant the animals used. The reason that so much animal research is approved, Frey concludes, is that the benefits clearly outweigh the quality of life of the animals involved.

POINT	COUNTERPOINT
• Lower and higher animals (humans) do not absolutely differ on any factor relevant to their suffering in psychological experimentation.	• Lower and higher animals do differ in their quality of life, which justifies the use of animals in experiments of significance.
• Many psychological experiments using animals are conducted for insignificant reasons.	• Animal-use committees specifically examine for significance.
• The members of many animal-use committees are biased toward the use of animals in questionable experiments.	• There is no reason to suspect that the members of these committees have unchangeable biases in favor of animal use.
• Experimenters are trained to ignore the suffering of animals.	• The benefits of much research is rarely disputed.

YES

Peter Singer

Animal Liberation

Most human beings are speciesists. The following [descriptions] show that ordinary human beings—not a few exceptionally cruel or heartless humans, but the overwhelming majority of humans—take an active part in, acquiesce in, and allow their taxes to pay for practices that require the sacrifice of the most important interests of members of other species in order to promote the most trivial interests of our own species. . . .

⌦

Many of the most painful experiments are performed in the field of psychology. To give some idea of the numbers of animals experimented on in psychology laboratories, consider that during 1986 the National Institute of Mental Health [NIMH] funded 350 experiments on animals. The NIMH is just one source of federal funding for psychological experimentation. The agency spent over $11 million on experiments that involved direct manipulation of the brain, over $5 million on experiments that studied the effects drugs have on behavior, almost $3 million on learning and memory experiments, and over $2 million on experiments involving sleep deprivation, stress, fear, and anxiety. This government agency spent more than $30 million dollars on animal experiments in one year.

One of the most common ways of experimenting in the field of psychology is to apply electric shocks to animals. This may be done with the aim of finding out how animals react to various kinds of punishment or to train animals to perform different tasks. In the first edition of [my] book I described experiments conducted in the late Sixties and early Seventies in which experimenters gave electric shocks to animals. Here is just one example from that period:

O. S. Ray and R. J. Barrett, working in the psychology research unit of the Veterans Administration Hospital, Pittsburgh, gave electric shocks to the feet of 1,042 mice. They then caused convulsions by giving more intense shocks through cup-shaped electrodes applied to the animals' eyes or through clips attached to their ears. They reported that unfortunately some of the mice who "successfully completed Day One training were found sick or dead prior to testing on Day Two."

Now, nearly twenty years later, . . . experimenters are still dreaming up trifling new variations to try out on animals: W. A. Hillex and M. R. Denny of

From *Ecco* by Peter Singer, pp. 9, 42–47, 69–70, 81–83, 85–87. Copyright © 2002 by Peter Singer. Reprinted by permission.

the University of California at San Diego placed rats in a maze and gave them electric shocks if, after one incorrect choice, on their next trial they failed to choose which way to go within three seconds. They concluded that the "results are clearly reminiscent of the early work on fixation and regression in the rat, in which the animals were typically shocked in the stem of the T-maze just preceding the choice point. . . ." (In other words, giving the rats electric shocks at the point in the maze at which they had to choose, rather than before that point—the novel feature of this particular experiment—made no significant difference.) The experimenters then go on to cite work done in 1933, 1935, and other years up to 1985. . . .

Experiments in conditioning have been going on for over eighty-five years. A report compiled in 1982 by the New York group United Action for Animals found 1,425 papers on "classical conditioning experiments" on animals. Ironically, the futility of much of this research is grimly revealed by a paper published by a group of experimenters at the University of Wisconsin. Susan Mineka and her colleagues subjected 140 rats to shocks that could be escaped and also subjected them to shocks that could not be escaped in order to compare the levels of fear generated by such different kinds of shocks. Here is the stated rationale for their work:

> Over the past 15 years an enormous amount of research has been directed toward understanding the differential behavior and physiological effects that stem from exposure to controllable as opposed to uncontrollable aversive elements. The general conclusion has been that exposure to uncontrollable aversive events is considerably more stressful for the organism than is exposure to controllable aversive events.

After subjecting their rats to various intensities of electric shock, sometimes allowing them the possibility of escape and sometimes not, the experimenters were unable to determine what mechanisms could be considered correct in accounting for their results. Nonetheless, they said that they believed their results to be important because "they raise some question about the validity of the conclusions of the hundreds of experiments conducted over the past 15 years or so."

In other words, fifteen years of giving electric shocks to animals may not have produced valid results. But in the bizarre world of psychological animal experiments, this finding serves as justification for yet more experiments giving inescapable electric shock to yet more animals so that "valid" results can finally be produced—and remember, these "valid results" will still only apply to the behavior of trapped animals subjected to inescapable electric shock.

An equally sad tale of futility is that of experiments designed to produce what is known as "learned helplessness"—supposedly a model of depression in human beings. In 1953 R. Solomon, L. Kamin, and L. Wynne, experimenters at Harvard University, placed forty dogs in a device called a "shuttlebox," which consists of a box divided into two compartments, separated by a barrier. Initially the barrier was set at the height of the dog's back. Hundreds of intense electric shocks were delivered to the dogs' feet through a grid floor. At first the dogs could escape the shock if they learned to jump the barrier into the other compartment. In an attempt to "discourage" one dog from jumping, the experimenters forced the dog to jump one hundred times onto a grid floor in the other compartment that also delivered a shock to the dog's feet. They said that as the dog jumped he gave a "sharp anticipatory yip which turned into a yelp when he landed on the electrified grid." They then blocked the passage between the compartments with a piece of plate glass and tested the dog again. The dog "jumped forward and smashed his head against the glass." The dogs began by showing symptoms such as "defecation, urination, yelping and shrieking, trembling, attacking the apparatus, and so on; but after ten or twelve days of trials dogs who were prevented from escaping shock ceased to resist. The experimenters reported themselves "impressed" by this, and concluded that a combination of the plate glass barrier and foot shock was "very effective" in eliminating jumping by dogs.

This study showed that it was possible to induce a state of hopelessness and despair by repeated administration of severe inescapable shock. Such "learned helplessness" studies were further refined in the 1960s. One prominent experimenter was Martin Seligman of the University of Pennsylvania. He electrically shocked dogs through a steel grid floor with such intensity and persistence that the dogs stopped trying to escape and "learned" to be helpless. In one study, written with colleagues Steven Maier and James Geer, Seligman describes his work as follows:

> When a normal, naive dog receives escape/avoidance training in a shuttle-box, the following behavior typically occurs: at the onset of electric shock the dog runs frantically about, defecating, urinating, and howling until it scrambles over the barrier and so escapes from shock. On the next trial the dog, running and howling, crosses the barrier more quickly, and so on, until efficient avoidance emerges.

Seligman altered this pattern by strapping dogs in harnesses and giving them shocks from which they had no means of escape. When the dogs were then placed in the original shuttlebox situation from which escape was possible, he found that

> such a dog reacts initially to shock in the shuttlebox in the same manner as the naive dog. However in dramatic contrast to the naive dog it soon stops running and remains silent until shock terminates. The dog does not cross the barrier and escape from shock. Rather it seems to "give up" and passively "accept" the shock. On succeeding trials the dog continues to fail to make escape movements and thus takes 50 seconds of severe, pulsating shock on each trial. . . . A dog previously exposed to inescapable shock . . . may take unlimited shock without escaping or avoiding at all.

In the 1980s, psychologists have continued to carry out these "learned helplessness" experiments. At Temple University in Philadelphia, Philip Bersh and three other experimenters trained rats to recognize a warning light that alerted them to a shock that would be delivered within five seconds. Once they understood the warning, the rats could avoid the shock by moving into the safe compartment. After the rats had learned this avoidance behavior, the experimenters walled off the safe chamber and subjected them to prolonged periods of inescapable shock. Predictably, they found that even after escape was possible, the rats were unable to relearn the escape behavior quickly. . . .

⋅✦⋅

How can these things happen? How can people who are not sadists spend their working days driving monkeys into lifelong depression, heating dogs to death, or turning cats into drug addicts? How can they then remove their white coats, wash their hands, and go home to dinner with their families? How can taxpayers allow their money to be used to support these experiments? How did students carry on protests against injustice, discrimination, and oppression of all kinds, no matter how far from home, while ignoring the cruelties that were—and still are—being carried out on their own campuses?

The answer to these questions lies in the unquestioned acceptance of speciesism. We tolerate cruelties inflicted on members of other species that would outrage us if performed on members of our own species. Speciesism allows researchers to regard the animals they experiment on as items of equipment, laboratory tools rather than living, suffering creatures. In fact, on grant applications to government funding agencies, animals are listed as "supplies" alongside test tubes and recording instruments.

In addition to the general attitude of speciesism that experimenters share with other citizens, some special factors also help to make possible the experiments I have described. Foremost among these is the immense respect that people still have for scientists. Although the advent of nuclear weapons and environmental pollution has made us realize that science and technology are not as beneficial as they might appear at first glance, most people still tend to be in awe of anyone who wears a white coat and has a Ph.D. In a well-known series of experiments Stanley Milgram, a Harvard psychologist, demonstrated that ordinary people will obey the directions of a white-coated researcher to administer what appears to be (but in fact is not) electric shock to a human subject as "punishment" for failing to answer questions correctly, and they will continue to do this even when the human subject cries out and pretends to be in great pain. If this can happen when the participants believe they are inflicting pain on a human being, how much easier is it for students to push aside their initial qualms when their professors instruct them to perform experiments on animals? What Alice Heim has rightly called the "indoctrination" of the student is a gradual process, beginning with the dissection of frogs in school biology classes. When the future medical students, psychology students, or veterinarians reach the university and find that to complete the course of studies on which they have set their hearts they must experiment on living animals, it is difficult for them to refuse to do so, especially since they know that what they are being asked to do is standard practice. Those students who have refused to engage in such studies have found themselves failing their courses and are often forced to leave their chosen field of study.

The pressure to conform does not let up when students receive their degrees. If they go on to graduate degrees in fields in which experiments on animals are usual, they will be encouraged to devise their own experiments and write them up for their Ph.D. dissertations. Naturally, if this is how students are educated they will tend to continue in the same manner when they become professors, and they will, in turn, train their own students in the same manner. . . .

When are experiments on animals justifiable? Upon learning of the nature of many of the experiments carried out, some people react by saying that all experiments on animals should be prohibited immediately. But if we make our demands as absolute as this, the experimenters have a ready reply: Would we be prepared to let thousands of humans die if they could be saved by a single experiment on a single animal?

This question is, of course, purely hypothetical. There has never been and never could be a single experiment that saved thousands of lives. The way to reply to this hypothetical question is to pose another: Would the experimenters be prepared to carry out their experiment on a human orphan under six months old if that were the only way to save thousands of lives?

If the experimenters would not be prepared to use a human infant then their readiness to use nonhuman animals reveals an unjustifiable form of discrimination on the basis of species, since adult apes, monkeys, dogs, cats, rats, and other animals are more aware of what is happening to them, more self-directing, and, so far as we can tell, at least as sensitive to pain as a human infant. (I have specified that the human infant be an orphan, to avoid the complications of the feelings of parents. Specifying the case in this way is, if anything, overgenerous to those defending the use of nonhuman animals in experiments, since mammals intended for experimental use are usually separated from their mothers at an early age, when the separation causes distress for both mother and young.)

So far as we know, human infants possess no morally relevant characteristic to a higher degree than adult nonhuman animals, unless we are to count the infants' potential as a characteristic that makes it wrong to experiment on them. Whether this characteristic should count is controversial—if we count it, we shall have to condemn abortion along with experiments on infants, since the potential of the infant and the fetus is the same. To avoid the complexities of this issue, however, we can alter our original question a little and assume that the infant is one with irreversible brain damage so severe as to rule out any mental development beyond the level of a six-month-old infant. There are, unfortunately, many such human beings, locked away in special wards throughout the country, some of them long since abandoned by their parents and other relatives, and, sadly, sometimes unloved by anyone else. Despite their mental deficiencies, the anatomy and physiology of these infants are in nearly all respects identical with those of normal humans. If, therefore, we were to force-feed them with large quantities of floor polish or drip concentrated solutions of cosmetics into their eyes, we would have a much more reliable indication of the safety of these products for humans than we now get by attempting to extrapolate the results of tests on a variety of other species. The LD50 tests, the Draize eye tests, the radiation experiments, the heatstroke experiments, and many others described [elsewhere] could have told us more about human reactions to the experimental situation if they had been carried out on severely brain-damaged humans instead of dogs or rabbits.

So whenever experimenters claim that their experiments are important enough to justify the use of animals, we should ask them whether they would be prepared to use a brain-damaged human being at a similar mental level to the animals they are planning to use. I cannot imagine that anyone would seriously propose carrying out the experiments described [here] on brain-damaged human beings. Occasionally it has become known that medical experiments have been performed on human beings without their consent; one case did concern institutionalized intellectually disabled children, who were given hepatitis. When such harmful experiments on human beings become known, they usually lead to an outcry against the experimenters, and rightly so. They are, very often, a further example of the arrogance of the research worker who justifies everything on the grounds of increasing knowledge. But if the experimenter claims that the experiment is important enough to justify inflicting suffering on animals, why is it not important enough to justify inflicting suffering on humans at the same mental level? What difference is there between the two? Only that one is a member of our species and the other is not? But to appeal to that difference is to reveal a bias no more defensible than racism or any other form of arbitrary discrimination. . . .

We have still not answered the question of when an experiment might be justifiable. It will not do to say "Never!" Putting morality in such black-and-white terms is appealing, because it eliminates the need to think about particular cases; but in extreme circumstances, such absolutist answers always break down. Torturing a human being is almost always wrong, but it is not absolutely wrong. If torture were the only way in which we could discover the location of a nuclear bomb hidden in a New York City basement and timed to go off within the hour, then torture would be justifiable. Similarly, if a single experiment could cure a disease like leukemia, that experiment would be justifiable. But in actual life the benefits are always more remote, and more often than not they are nonexistent. So how do we decide when an experiment is justifiable?

We have seen that experimenters reveal a bias in favor of their own species whenever they carry out experiments on nonhumans for purposes that they would not think justified them in using human beings, even brain-damaged ones. This principle gives us a guide toward an answer to our question. Since a speciesist bias, like a racist bias, is unjustifiable, an experiment cannot be justifiable unless the experiment is so important that the use of a brain-damaged human would also be justifiable.

This is not an absolutist principle. I do not believe that it could never be justifiable to experiment on a brain-damaged human. If it really were possible to save several lives by an experiment that would take just one life, and there were no other way those lives could be saved, it would be right to do the experiment. But this would be an extremely rare case. Certainly none of the experiments described in this [selection] could pass this test. Admittedly, as with any dividing line, there would be a gray area where it was difficult to decide if an experiment could be justified. But we need not get distracted by such considerations now. As this [selection] has shown, we are in the midst of an emergency in which appalling suffering is being inflicted on millions of animals for purposes that on any impartial view are obviously inadequate to justify the suffering. When we have ceased to carry out all those experiments, then there will be time enough to discuss what to do about the remaining ones which are claimed to be essential to save lives or prevent greater suffering.

In the United States, where the present lack of control over experimentation allows the kinds of experiments described in the preceding pages, a minimal first step would be a requirement that no experiment be conducted without prior approval from an ethics committee that includes animal welfare representatives and is authorized to refuse approval to experiments when it does not consider that the potential benefits outweigh the harm to the animals. . . . [S]ystems of this kind already exist in countries such as Australia and Sweden and are accepted as fair and reasonable by the scientific community there. [However], such a system falls far short of the ideal. The animal welfare representatives on such committees come from groups that hold a spectrum of views, but, for obvious reasons, those who receive and accept invitations to join animal experimentation ethics committees tend to come from the less radical groups within the movement. They may not themselves regard the interests of nonhuman animals as entitled to equal consideration with the interests of humans; or if they do hold such a position, they may find it impossible to put it into practice when judging applications to perform animal experiments, because they would be unable to persuade other members of the committee. Instead, they are likely to insist on proper consideration of alternatives, genuine efforts to minimize pain, and a clear demonstration of significant potential benefits, sufficiently important to outweigh any pain or suffering that cannot be eliminated from the experiment. An animal experimentation ethics committee operating today would almost inevitably apply these standards in a speciesist manner, weighing animal suffering more lightly than potential comparable human benefit; even so, an emphasis on such standards would eliminate many painful experiments now permitted and would reduce the suffering caused by others.

In a society that is fundamentally speciesist, there is no quick solution to such difficulties with ethics committees. For this reason some Animal Liberationists will have nothing to do with them. Instead they demand the total and immediate elimination of all animal experimentation. Such demands have been put forward many times during the last century and a half of antivivisection activity, but they have shown no sign of winning over the majority of voters in any country. Meanwhile the number of animals suffering in laboratories continued to grow, until . . . recent breakthroughs. . . . These breakthroughs resulted from the work of people who found a way around the "all or nothing" mentality that had effectively meant "nothing" as far as the animals were concerned.

R. G. Frey

Justifying Animal Experimentation: The Starting Point

Introduction

If the use of animals in scientific and medical research is justified, it seems reasonably clear that it is justified by the benefits that this research confers upon humans. The benefits involved here are understood to include such things as advances in knowledge as well as things more commonly regarded as benefits, such as improvements in disease diagnosis and treatment. Even were we to concede in a particular case that we may be unclear whether something is a benefit or whether the extreme costs we propose to exact from some animal are worth an envisaged benefit, some version of this *argument from benefit* appears to underlie all attempts to justify animal experimentation in science and medicine. This is not to ignore the fact that many of our efforts in fact benefit animals themselves, but I take it that no one would dispute the claim that the vast bulk of research has human benefit, not animal benefit, as its goal. Moreover, we must not think only of the short term: much research does not lead to immediate benefit. Often, it is only later, when the results of the research are put together with the results of other pieces of research (usually done by other researchers), that their long-term import can be detected. More often than not, science and medicine work by accretion rather than by individual instances of dramatic breakthrough.

Benefit and Abolitionism

The argument from benefit is a consequentialist argument: it maintains that the consequences of engaging in animal research provide clear benefits to humans that offset the costs to animals involved in the research. This is an empirical argument and so could be refuted by showing that the benefits of research are not all that we take them to be. This is not the place to undertake an examination of the costs and benefits of the myriad uses that we make of animals in science and medicine, nor am I the person to undertake such an examination. Instead, I want to look at another aspect of the argument from benefit. Therefore, I shall simply assume that, either in the short or long term (or both), the benefits of research are substantive, an assumption that is quite compatible with it also being true that some alleged benefits of research are spurious.

I myself accept some version of the argument from benefit, as do, I think, most people. Those who favor the abolition of animal experiments may dispute that the benefits of these experiments are all that substantial, but I often encounter in argument "abolitionists" who do not dispute this fact. They simply maintain that human gain can never be used to justify animal loss, while conceding that many human advances in medicine have come at the cost of animal suffering and loss of animal life.

There is another position, the *3R approach,* that shares some of the abolitionists' concerns about animal research, but still accepts the argument from benefit, at least at our current state of scientific knowledge. Those who favor the 3R approach to animal research usually support a pro-research position, suitably qualified. The 3R approach seeks (1) to *refine* experiments in order to diminish animal suffering and/or loss of life; (2) to *reduce* the number of animals used and the number of experiments performed to obtain or confirm a particular result; and, ultimately, (3) to *replace* animal subjects with nonanimal models or replace "higher" animals with "lower" ones. In fact, the 3R approach typically is thought today to help define a humane research position, even if and when adopting the approach might require that some piece of research be curtailed on the ground that it is incompatible with one strand or more of the 3R approach.

A humane research position is not an abolitionist position. While abolitionists may themselves be concerned with refinement, reduction, and replacement in animal experimentation, so long as present practices continue, abolitionists cannot be satisfied. They will still object that the 3R approach permits animal research to continue.

Moreover, an abolitionist will not be concerned with exactly how far along a piece of research is, or how likely we are to be able to come up with a nonanimal model for conducting this research in the immediate future. The thought that we may be able to replace animal models with nonanimal models for studying certain diseases is a pro-research thought, if it is also held that this replacement must await the development of nonanimal models for these diseases. Abolitionists reject this conditional approach because it would hold replacement hostage to scientific advances that may lie a considerable period into the future.

If an abolitionist had the opportunity to shut down all animal research now—whatever the potential for human benefit, however far along the research, and whatever the state of development of nonanimal models—I take it that the abolitionist would do so. Why a complete shutdown now? Why not a progressive shutdown over a much longer period, during which some experiments would be allowed to run their course, realize some benefit, or evolve into a nonanimal model? The abolitionist's reason is that a progressive shutdown of animal research would perpetuate animal suffering and/or loss of life. Therefore, a progressive shutdown, while it may appeal to those of a more practical disposition, is not typically proposed by abolitionists.

While it is obvious that abolitionists oppose the argument from benefit, it is not evident that many others do so. It is ironic, to say the least, that abolitionism has received so much attention in the media of late at the very time that scientific and medical research seems on the threshold of revolutionary discoveries that will greatly alleviate human suffering. Genetic research involving animals promises new treatments for diseases that previously were thought to be intractable defects in the human condition. AIDS research proceeds apace, with animal research playing a crucial role. One aspect of genetic engineering that is likely to have an impact in the near future involves transforming animals to become carriers of human organs for human transplants. Cross-species transplants—xenografts—that should result from these efforts will benefit the thousands of people who die each year while waiting on queues for human organs. Cloning of animals is another scientific breakthrough that holds out the prospect of genetic replacement as the solution to some presently incurable medical disorders. An enormous amount of genetic engineering in animals is presently underway with the goal of advancing human health care (quite apart from any genetic engineering in animals that has to do with food or meat-eating).

With the prospect of such remarkable discoveries on the horizon, I do not think it likely that very many people will embrace abolitionism. The benefits, real and potential, of animal research appear too considerable for us to turn away from them. Yet, lab break-ins, disturbances, and assaults upon scientists by abolitionist fringe groups are already of grave concern to researchers, and these incidents may increase. It is unlikely that such acts will win many converts to the abolitionist cause. In fact, it seems likely that acts of intimidation may well alienate moderates who strive for observance of the 3R approach, who otherwise might see themselves as allies of the abolitionists on some policy proposals. On the whole, then, I doubt that abolitionism is going to capture the day. The argument from benefit will continue to predominate.

Animals or Humans?

The argument from benefit requires closer philosophical scrutiny. For example, with many uses of the argument, the individual who bears the costs is also the individual who benefits; this is not true in the case of animal experimentation. Yet there are plenty of instances in which we impose costs on some to benefit others, as in the cases of conscription or the progressive income tax.

The feature of the argument from benefit that I want to discuss is this: Whatever benefits animal experimentation is thought to hold in store for us, those very same benefits could be obtained through experimenting upon humans instead of animals. Indeed, given that problems exist because scientists must extrapolate from animal models to humans, one might hold that there are good scientific reasons for preferring human subjects.

Accordingly, any reliance upon the argument from benefit, however hedged and qualified that reliance may be, has to be accompanied by a further argument establishing that while we may use animals as means to the ends of scientific and medical inquiry, we may not use humans to these ends. I do not mean that we may never use humans as research subjects; obviously, a good deal of research involves experiments on humans. I mean, rather, that we may not do to humans all the things that we presently do to animals. For example, we may not induce amyotrophic lateral sclerosis in a perfectly healthy human in order to study the pathology of the disease. Furthermore, we may not do this even if the human in question were to consent to be treated in this way.

The argument from benefit, then, needs to be supplemented by a further argument, one that strikes a deeper note than any obvious appeal to discernible benefit. This further argument must answer the question: what justifies using animals in science and medicine in ways that would be considered improper to use humans, even humans who consented to the treatment? This question can be asked regardless of whether the research is applied or pure (that is, whether or not the research has practical use), whether the techniques involved in it are invasive or noninvasive, or whether it involves pain or is entirely painless. In fact, what this question is asking of us is how we distinguish the human from the animal case. I have discussed this issue in a number of other places. In this essay, I want to distill from these other discussions how it is that this issue of separating humans from animals forms the starting point of any justification of animal experimentation.

The Appeal to Similarity

The appeal to similarity between ourselves and animals (or, in any event, the "higher" animals) has come to be thought of as one important barrier to animal experimentation. . . .

An Assumption About Humans

It is true, of course, that the appeal to similarity depends upon a crucial assumption, an assumption that those who make use of the appeal nevertheless seem justified in making. This is the assumption (which might be called the *characteristics claim*) that, for any characteristic around which one formulates the appeal, humans will be found who (1) lack the characteristic altogether, (2) lack it to a degree such that they are not protected from being used in scientific/medical experiments, or (3) lack it to a degree such that some animals have it to a greater degree. For example, it seems undeniably true that chimps give evidence of being more intelligent than many severely mentally subnormal humans, more sentient than anencephalic infants (infants born without a brain), and more able to direct their lives than humans in the final stages of Alzheimer's disease or senile dementia. Indeed, depending upon the characteristics selected and the humans under consideration, many animals, of many different species, will display levels of the characteristics higher than those found in some humans.

The only characteristic that seems unquestionably to favor humans, no matter what their condition or quality of life, is that of having had two human parents (in the near future, cloning may well call this characteristic into question). It is unclear, however, why this characteristic would be relevant. Having human parents could matter in one sense, at least if they objected to what was to be done to their offspring, but it is hard to see why having human parents matters in any deeper sense. The nature of one's parentage says nothing about one's present quality of life; one's intelligence; one's capacity for pain, distress, and suffering; one's ability to direct one's own life; etc. These characteristics seem more like the things that could serve to distinguish a human life as something that may not be treated in the way that we presently treat animal lives. This is because these characteristics say something not about what produced a life, but rather about the life being lived, about the nature and quality of that life. Thus, while it is true that anencephalic infants have human parents, the nature and quality of their lives nevertheless seem, by all reasonable standards, to be far worse than the lives of numerous ordinary animals. The same seems true of people in the final throes of AIDS, Alzheimer's disease, Lou Gehrig's disease, Huntington's disease, and so on.

In short, the appeal to similarity depends upon an assumption that, though it can be overturned, nevertheless appears to be very plausible. If we pick any characteristic around which to formulate the appeal, we seem inevitably doomed to come across some humans who lack that characteristic and some animals who, to a greater or lesser degree, have it. The result is a dilemma of a painful, unhappy kind: either we use humans as well as animals in order to obtain the benefits of research—since some humans fall outside the class of those having the relevant characteristic—or we use neither humans nor these animals that possess the characteristic and fall into the class of the protected. Given this dilemma, the case for opposing experimentation in science and medicine that uses the typical animal subjects is stronger than usually imagined, and it is salutary to be aware of this. However, if the benefits of scientific/medical research are everything we think them to be, then we can see how the first option, allowing the use of some humans as well as animals, is bound to seem the lesser of the two evils to some people. Those to whom this occurs are not Hitlers in the making; rather, they are simply those who employ the argument from benefit but are unable to separate human cases from animal cases in a morally significant way. . . .

Use and Quality of Life

I have argued elsewhere that . . . animals are indeed members of the moral community, they have moral standing in their own right, and their lives do indeed have significant value (though not the value of normal adult human life). If it is thought that the argument in favor of experimentation starts by denying animals moral standing or by denying that their lives have value, then I think that this strategy must be rejected. I see no way of denying either proposition. How, then, does the argument for experimentation get underway?

. . . [I]n our secular age, our problem is that we can find nothing that ensures that all human life (whatever its condition and quality), but no animal life (whatever its condition and quality), falls into the preferred class of nonuse. Secular attempts to replace God as the guarantor of the preferred status of humans have not proved successful. They inevitably involve us, yet again, in the search for some magical characteristic that can both separate humans from animals and be a plausible candidate upon which to hang a difference in treatment.

Suppose one can save either one's faithful dog, who has rendered long and valuable service, or some human whom one does not know. If one saves the dog, has one done something wrong? Is there a sense in which one *must* prefer human beings over animals, if one is to be moral? Suppose further that the human being suffers from a series of terrible maladies that give him a very low quality of life and a prognosis of a much-reduced life span: must one still prefer him to the dog? What if the human were an anencephalic infant? In these latter two cases, the questions seem to be asking us for the characteristic or set of characteristics upon which we can decide which life to save, whether human or animal, in circumstances in which it may be the dog, rather than the human, who best exemplifies that characteristic or set of characteristics.

Our central problem should now be obvious. Suppose someone were to claim that all human lives, whatever their condition or quality, possess equal worth. This comforting thought, which encapsulates the claim that two lives of massively different quality are nevertheless of the same worth, lies, I am sure, at the base of many attempts to provide a secular analog to the religious claim that all human lives are equal in the eyes of God. But if not in its condition or quality, in what does the worth of a life consist? How do we assess and recognize the worth of a life? What criteria do we use to determine such worth?

It is obvious that not all human lives are of the same quality: no one in the final stages of amyotrophic lateral sclerosis or pancreatic cancer would say otherwise. From the Judeo-Christian perspective, however, such lives are equal in worth to ordinary human lives because they are held to be equal in the eyes of God. If God is taken out of this picture, then what underpins the claim that all human lives are of equal worth? The notion of worth here does not pick out any actual features of the lives in question. Rather, what we are left with is simply the *quality* of the lives being lived, whether human or animal, and the implicit recognition that, in some cases, an animal will have a higher quality of life than a human. . . .

Experience and Quality of Life

As far as I can see, then, defending animal experimentation by means of the argument from benefit, which I think most people want to do, leaves us with a problem not about animals, but about humans. If there is nothing that shows that humans always, without exception, have a higher quality of life than any animal, then the cost of permitting experiments upon animals may have to be a preparedness to envisage similar uses of humans. For it seems inevitable, given that we know of nothing that always gives human life a higher quality, that on some occasions an animal will have a higher quality of life than a human to whom it is compared. To avoid the conclusion that humans may be used we might be forced to accept one of two claims: that we just do not know what an animal's quality of life is, or that animals have no quality of life whatsoever.

The claim of not knowing what an animal's quality of life is, while an important claim, does not seem to be a decisive refutation of the human-use conclusion. It might simply dictate that we should make greater efforts to learn about the quality of life of the animal. To say that we can never really know what it is like to be a rat is not to say that we can never know a good deal about what a better quality of life is like for a rat. Indeed, veterinary textbooks are filled with discussions of subjects that directly refer to or imply something about the inner states of animals. Difficulty is not the same thing as impossibility, and in the case of the higher primates, I think that we have already begun to overcome the difficulties of assessing quality of life. Moreover, to say that we do not know what an animal's quality of life is may well be taken as a reason for *not* using the animal, on the basis of some "play-safe" principle. The second claim then becomes crucial. But the claim that animals do not have a quality of life seems to me to be simply false.

Animals are *experiential subjects,* with an unfolding series of experiences that, depending upon their quality, can make an animal's life go well or badly. A creature of this sort has a welfare that can be enhanced or diminished by what we do to it; with this being the case, such a creature has a quality of life. To deny that rats, rodents, rabbits, and chimps are experiential subjects is to deny that they have subjective experiences at all. It is to deny that their lives are lived, just as ours are, in terms of unfolding sets of experiences, of a kind such that what we do to these animals can affect the quality of those experiences. Today, however, it is increasingly the case that scientific journals, peer review committees, Institutional Animal Care and Use Committees, and government funding agencies demand that it be clearly stated what sorts of techniques will be used on research animals and what sorts of impacts these techniques are likely to have on them. The scientists involved do this regularly. It cannot be the case, therefore, that these groups and scientists think that they are dealing with nonexperiential creatures, creatures that do not register anything at all with respect to what is done to them. So I doubt very much whether any party to the experimentation debate will argue that animals do not have a quality of life. . . .

Conclusion: Experimentation and the Argument From Benefit

How is my argument a pro-research position? I accept some version of the argument from benefit and hold that the benefits of scientific/medical research are sizable. I accept that animals may be used in such research. I believe that I have deployed arguments that show that normal adult human lives have a higher quality than animal lives. Animals, then, will remain the creatures of preferred use. However, I have not been able to find an argument that ensures always and inevitably that all human lives will exceed all animal lives in value; hence, I have not been able to come up with an argument that ensures that humans can never be used in experiments. When a human life is of lower quality than an animal life, it will not be right to use the animal rather than the human.

Mine is not a position that advocates the use of humans in experiments. Indeed, the adverse side effects of any such use, especially on those humans who are the weakest among us, are likely to be considerable, and my position would be strongly sensitive to these concerns. Yet however sensitive to these side effects we may be, the fact remains that the argument from benefit, if the benefits in question are all that science and medicine would have us believe and are as desired by the public as the media suggests, seems to demand that we proceed with experimentation and obtain the benefits. My doubt about the argument from benefit, then, is precisely this: I want to realize the benefits, just as other people do, but I can see no way of doing so without it coming into plain view that some humans will be put at risk as potential experimental subjects. In other words, I have found nothing to take the place that God played in the traditional argument: nothing to provide the comforting assurance that humans are the preferred creatures on Earth whose lives are the only ones that are morally considerable and valuable.

I am well aware, of course, that most people will find this starting point for the justification of animal experimentation to be very unpalatable. But I know of nothing that enables us to avoid it if we rely upon the argument from benefit. Failing to find some justification for why it is that the preferred class of nonuse includes any and all humans but no animals, my position is ineluctable, however unappealing it might be.

Finding my view extremely distasteful, many may respond by renewing the search for what makes us unique, for what confers on us the preferred status that we enjoyed under the traditional argument. But how, exactly, will they do this? As far as I can see, their only recourse is to generate yet more abstractions in the search for one that gives us the desired result. It remains to be seen whether or not the next generation of abstractions will be any more tenable than their predecessors.

Some will conclude that my position vis-à-vis impaired humans is so objectionable that my argument is tantamount to a rejection of animal experimentation. I don't see it that way. For me, the crucial question is: will we decide to forgo the benefits that scientific and medical research promise? It is hard to imagine that we will. Hence, we are faced with the problem over humans.

Notice another ploy that might be tried to evade my argument, and how it too goes astray. It might be argued that there are not enough anencephalic infants, or enough people in the final throes of devastating illnesses, to provide anything like the total number of research subjects that we can presently find in the animal kingdom. But the issue posed by my position is not about replacement of animals by humans; instead, it is about our need to come to terms with the issue of human use. It is a moral question, not a practical one. If we are going to use animals, the argument that I have raised in this essay seems to require that we at least be prepared to use certain humans as well, depending upon their respective qualities of life. Can we bring ourselves to do this?

One final ploy might be devised. It might be said that if a quality-of-life argument lands us at my unpalatable conclusion, then I have inadvertently discredited quality of life as the determiner of the value of a life. Yet every hospital in the land uses quality-of-life considerations in making all kinds of judgments, including life-or-death judgments. Hospitals use such consider-ations constantly in human health care, including situations in which they decide who will receive treatment and of what sort, who will be saved, and who left to nature's course. If quality-of-life is ubiquitous in making health care decisions for humans, how can it be sundered from medicine's bedrock—experimentation? Clearly, it cannot.

CHALLENGE QUESTIONS

Should Animal Research in Psychology Be Eliminated?

1. Read Singer's book and discuss why it has been so effective in galvanizing support for eliminating animal research.
2. Frey's article is part of an anthology of chapters that support the use of animals in scientific research. Read two other chapters from the book, and report what other arguments are used to justify animal experimentation.
3. Why might some people distinguish between medical and psychological research regarding the justification of animal research? Are there subject matter and philosophy of science differences between the two disciplines? Support your answer.
4. Do you agree with Frey's argument that animals cannot be distinguished from humans absolutely (i.e., without some exceptions)? Why, or why not?
5. Do you find Frey's emphasis on quality of life pertinent to the debate over animal research? What is this quality, and how might it be relevant to committees that approve the use of animals for experimentation?

ISSUE 2

Are Traditional Empirical Methods Sufficient to Provide Evidence for Psychological Practice?

YES: APA Presidential Task Force on Evidence-Based Practice, from "Evidence-Based Practice in Psychology," *American Psychologist* (2006)

NO: Brent D. Slife and Dennis Wendt, from "The Next Step in the Evidence-Based Practice Movement," APA Convention Presentation (2006)

ISSUE SUMMARY

YES: The APA Presidential Task Force on Evidence-Based Practice assumes that a variety of traditional empirical methods is sufficient to provide evidence for psychological practices.

NO: Psychologist Brent D. Slife and researcher Dennis C. Wendt contend that traditional empirical methods are guided by a single philosophy that limits the diversity of methods.

Imagine that one of your family members needs to see a therapist for a severe depression. Of the two therapists available, the first therapist's practices are supported by evidence obtained through traditional scientific methods. The second therapist's practices are not. The latter's practices could be equally effective or even more effective than the first therapist's practices, but we do not know. Which therapist would you choose for this member of your family?

Most people would readily choose therapists who have scientific evidence for their interventions. They think of psychotherapy much like they think of medicine, with treatments that have stood the test of science. Just as physicians can provide evidence that pain relievers actually relieve pain, so too psychologists hope to provide evidence that their practices deliver their desired results. Because not all psychological treatments come with evidence to support their use, some psychologists worry that some treatments could actually do more harm than good. It is with this potential harm in mind that many psychologists banded together to establish empirically supported treatments (ESTs). The goal was to establish a list of ESTs for specific psychological disorders. Those involved in this movement (various task forces from different divisions of the American Psychological Association) initially stressed the use of randomized clinical (or controlled) trials (RCTs)—a specific type of research design—to be sure that the scientific examination of these treatments was rigorous and thorough.

In the first article of this issue, however, the APA Presidential Task Force on Evidence-Based Practice questions whether too much emphasis has been placed on RCT research designs. This Task Force affirms the need for empirically based evidence in psychology but tries to reframe the notion of evidence-based practice so that a diversity of empirical methods, including correlational and even case study methods, are considered important for producing evidence. The Task Force calls for objectivity in gathering all forms of evidence. In fact, it still considers RCTs the most rigorous type of objective method. However, it also acknowledges that other empirical approaches to gathering information and evidence can and do have their place in deciding psychology's evidence-based practices.

In the second selection, psychologist Brent D. Slife and researcher Dennis Wendt applaud the APA Task Force for taking important steps in the right direction. Nevertheless, they argue that the Task Force's statement is "ultimately and fundamentally inadequate." The Task Force correctly champions the objectivity and diversity of methods and evidence, in their view, but they contend that the Task Force is not objective and diverse enough. They claim that just as the EST movement restricted the gathering of evidence to a single method (RCTs), the Task Force's suggestions assume, but never justify, that evidence-based practice should be restricted to a single *epistemology* of method. They acknowledge that many psychologists view this empirical epistemology as not affecting the outcome of research, but they note that most practices that are considered evidence-based fit the biases of the philosophy of empiricism.

POINT	COUNTERPOINT
• Psychological treatments should be supported by evidence.	• Not all psychologists agree on what qualifies as evidence.
• Evidence should include RCTs as well as other imperical methods.	• Traditional empirical methods are not the only methods by which evidence can be obtained.
• Evidence ought to be both objective and diverse.	• Including only the "empirical" is neither objective nor diverse.
• Evidence should not be limited to a single method (RCT).	• Evidence should not be limited to a single method*ology*.

YES

Report of the 2005 Presidential Task Force on Evidence-Based Practice[1]

From the very first conceptions of applied psychology as articulated by Lightner Witmer, who formed the first psychological clinic in 1896, psychologists have been deeply and uniquely associated with an evidence-based approach to patient care. As Witmer pointed out, "the pure and the applied sciences advance in a single front. What retards the progress of one retards the progress of the other; what fosters one fosters the other." As early as 1947 the idea that doctoral psychologists should be trained as both scientists and practitioners became the American Psychological Association (APA) policy. Early practitioners such as Frederick C. Thorne articulated the methods by which psychological practitioners integrate science into their practice by . . . "increasing the application of the experimental approach to the individual case into the clinician's own experience." Thus, psychologists have been on the forefront of the development of evidence-based practice for decades.

Evidence-based practice in psychology is therefore consistent with the past twenty years of work in evidence-based medicine, which advocated for improved patient outcomes by informing clinical practice with relevant research. Sackett and colleagues describe evidence-based medicine as "the conscientious, explicit, and judicious use of current best evidence in making decisions about the care of individual patients." The use and misuse of evidence-based principles in the practice of health care has affected the dissemination of health care funds, but not always to the benefit of the patient. Therefore, psychologists, whose training is grounded in empirical methods, have an important role to play in the continuing development of evidence-based practice and its focus on improving patient care.

One approach to implementing evidence-based practice in health care systems has been through the development of guidelines for best practice. During the early part of the evidence-based practice movement, APA recognized the

[1]This document was received by the American Psychological Association (APA) Council of Representatives during its meeting of August, 2005. The report represents the conclusions of the Task Force and does not represent the official policy of the American Psychological Association. The Task Force wishes to thank John R. Weisz, PhD, ABPP for his assistance in drafting portions of this report related to children and youth. The Task Force also thanks James Mitchell and Omar Rehman, APA Professional Development interns, for their assistance throughout the work of the Task Force.

importance of a comprehensive approach to the conceptualization of guidelines. APA also recognized the risk that guidelines might be used inappropriately by commercial health care organizations not intimately familiar with the scientific basis of practice to dictate specific forms of treatment and restrict patient access to care. In 1992, APA formed a joint task force of the Board of Scientific Affairs (BSA), the Board of Professional Affairs (BPA), and the Committee for the Advancement of Professional Practice (CAPP). The document developed by this task force—the *Template for Developing Guidelines: Interventions for Mental Disorders and Psychosocial Aspects of Physical Disorders* (Template)—was approved by the APA Council of Representatives in 1995 (APA, 1995). The Template described the variety of evidence that should be considered in developing guidelines, and cautioned that any emerging clinical practice guidelines should be based on careful systematic weighing of research data and clinical expertise. . . .

Although the goal was to identify treatments with evidence for efficacy comparable to the evidence for the efficacy of medications, and hence to highlight the contribution of psychological treatments, the Division 12 Task Force report sparked a decade of both enthusiasm and controversy. The report increased recognition of demonstrably effective psychological treatments among the public, policymakers, and training programs. At the same time, many psychologists raised concerns about the exclusive focus on brief, manualized treatments; the emphasis on specific treatment effects as opposed to common factors that account for much of the variance in outcomes across disorders; and the applicability to a diverse range of patients varying in comorbidity, personality, race, ethnicity, and culture.

In response, several groups of psychologists, including other divisions of APA, offered additional frameworks for integrating the available research evidence. In 1999, APA Division 29 (Psychotherapy) established a task force to identify, operationalize, and disseminate information on empirically supported therapy relationships, given the powerful association between outcome and aspects of the therapeutic relationship such as the therapeutic alliance. Division 17 (Counseling Psychology) also undertook an examination of empirically supported treatments in counseling psychology. The Society of Behavioral Medicine, which is not a part of APA but which has significantly overlapping membership, has recently published criteria for examining the evidence base for behavioral medicine interventions. As of this writing, we are aware that task forces have been appointed to examine related issues by a large number of APA divisions concerned with practice issues. . . .

Definition

Based on its review of the literature and its deliberations, the Task Force agreed on the following definition:

> Evidence-based practice in psychology (EBPP) is the integration of the best available research with clinical expertise in the context of patient characteristics, culture, and preferences.

This definition of EBPP closely parallels the definition of evidence-based practice adopted by the Institute of Medicine as adapted from Sackett and colleagues: "Evidence-based practice is the integration of best research evidence with clinical expertise and patient values." Psychology builds on the IOM definition by deepening the examination of clinical expertise and broadening the consideration of patient characteristics. The purpose of EBPP is to promote effective psychological practice and enhance public health by applying empirically supported principles of psychological assessment, case formulation, therapeutic relationship, and intervention.

Psychological practice entails many types of interventions, in multiple settings, for a wide variety of potential patients. In this document, *intervention* refers to all direct services rendered by health care psychologists, including assessment, diagnosis, prevention, treatment, psychotherapy, and consultation. As is the case with most discussions of evidence-based practice, we focus on treatment. The same general principles apply to psychological assessment, which is essential to effective treatment. The *settings* include but are not limited to hospitals, clinics, independent practices, schools, military, public health, rehabilitation institutes, primary care, counseling centers, and nursing homes.

To be consistent with discussions of evidence-based practice in other areas of health care, we use the term *patient* in this document to refer to the child, adolescent, adult, older adult, couple, family, group, organization, community, or other populations receiving psychological services. However, we recognize that in many situations there are important and valid reasons for using such terms as *client, consumer,* or *person* in place of *patient* to describe the recipients of services. Further, psychologists target a variety of problems, including but not restricted to mental health, academic, vocational, relational, health, community, and other problems, in their professional practice.

It is important to clarify the relation between EBPP and ESTs (empirically supported treatments). EBPP is the more comprehensive concept. ESTs start with a treatment and ask whether it works for a certain disorder or problem under specified circumstances. EBPP starts with the patient and asks what research evidence (including relevant results from RCTs) will assist the psychologist to achieve the best outcome. In addition, ESTs are specific psychological treatments that have been shown to be efficacious in controlled clinical trials, whereas EBPP encompasses a broader range of clinical activities (e.g., psychological assessment, case formulation, therapy relationships). As such, EBPP articulates a decision making process for integrating multiple streams of research evidence, including but not limited to RCTs, into the intervention process.

The following sections explore in greater detail the three major components of this definition—best available research, clinical expertise, and patient characteristics—and their integration.

Best Available Research Evidence

A sizeable body of scientific evidence drawn from a variety of research designs and methodologies attests to the effectiveness of psychological practices.

The research literature on the effect of psychological interventions indicates that these interventions are safe and effective for a large number of children and youth, adults and older adults across a wide range of psychological, addictive, health, and relational problems. More recent research indicates that compared to alternative approaches, such as medications, psychological treatments are particularly enduring. Further, research demonstrates that psychotherapy can and often does pay for itself in terms of medical costs offset, increased productivity, and life satisfaction.

Psychologists possess distinctive strengths in designing, conducting, and interpreting research studies that can guide evidence-based practice. Moreover, psychology—as a science and as a profession—is distinctive in combining scientific commitment with an emphasis on human relationships and individual differences. As such, psychology can help develop, broaden, and improve the research base for evidence-based practice.

There is broad consensus that psychological practice needs to be based on evidence, and that research needs to balance internal and external validity. Research will not always address all practice needs. Major issues in integrating research in day to day practice include: a) the relative weight to place on different research methods; b) the representativeness of research samples; c) whether research results should guide practice at the level of principles of change, intervention strategies, or specific protocols; d) the generalizability and transportability of treatments supported in controlled research to clinical practice settings; e) the extent to which judgments can be made about treatments of choice when the number and duration of treatments tested has been limited; and f) the degree to which the results of efficacy and effectiveness research can be generalized from primarily white samples to minority and marginalized populations. Nevertheless, research on practice has made progress in investigating these issues and is providing research evidence that is more responsive to day-to-day practice. There is sufficient consensus to move forward with the principles of EBPP.

Meta-analytic investigations since the 1970s have shown that most therapeutic practices in widespread clinical use are generally effective for treating a range of problems. In fact, the effect sizes for psychological interventions for children, adults and older adults rival, or exceed, those of widely accepted medical treatments. It is important not to assume that interventions that have not yet been studied in controlled trials are ineffective. Specific interventions that have not been subjected to systematic empirical testing for specific problems cannot be assumed to be either effective or ineffective; they are simply untested to date. Nonetheless, good practice and science call for the timely testing of psychological practices in a way that adequately operationalizes them using appropriate scientific methodology. Widely used psychological practices as well as innovations developed in the field or laboratory should be rigorously evaluated and barriers to conducting this research should be identified and addressed.

Multiple Types of Research Evidence

Best research evidence refers to scientific results related to intervention strategies, assessment, clinical problems, and patient populations in laboratory and field settings as well as to clinically relevant results of basic research in psychology and related fields. APA endorses multiple types of research evidence (e.g., efficacy, effectiveness, cost-effectiveness, cost-benefit, epidemiological, treatment utilization studies) that contribute to effective psychological practice.

Multiple research designs contribute to evidence-based practice, and different research designs are better suited to address different types of questions. These include:

- Clinical observation (including individual case studies) and basic psychological science are valuable sources of innovations and hypotheses (the context of scientific discovery).
- Qualitative research can be used to describe the subjective lived experience of people, including participants in psychotherapy.
- Systematic case studies are particularly useful when aggregated as in the form of practice research networks for comparing individual patients to others with similar characteristics.
- Single case experimental designs are particularly useful for establishing causal relationships in the context of an individual.
- Public health and ethnographic research are especially useful for tracking the availability, utilization, and acceptance of mental health treatments as well as suggesting ways of altering them to maximize their utility in a given social context.
- Process-outcome studies are especially valuable for identifying mechanisms of change.
- Studies of interventions as delivered in naturalistic settings (effectiveness research) are well suited for assessing the ecological validity of treatments.
- Randomized clinical trials and their logical equivalents (efficacy research) are the standard for drawing causal inferences about the effects of interventions (context of scientific verification).
- Meta-analysis is a systematic means to synthesize results from multiple studies, test hypotheses, and quantitatively estimate the size of effects.

With respect to evaluating research on specific interventions, current APA policy identifies two widely accepted dimensions. As stated in the *Criteria for Evaluating Treatment Guidelines*, "The first dimension is *treatment efficacy*, the systematic and scientific evaluation of whether a treatment works. The second dimension is *clinical utility*, the applicability, feasibility, and usefulness of the intervention in the local or specific setting where it is to be offered. This dimension also includes determination of the generalizability of an intervention whose efficacy has been established." Types of research evidence with regard to intervention research in ascending order as to their contribution to conclusions about efficacy include: clinical opinion, observation, and consensus among recognized experts representing the range of use in the field (Criterion 2.1); systematized clinical observation (Criterion 2.2); and sophisticated empirical methodologies, including quasi experiments and randomized controlled experiments or their logical equivalents (Criterion 2.3). Among sophisticated empirical methodologies, "randomized controlled experiments represent a more stringent way to evaluate treatment efficacy because they are the most effective way to rule out threats to internal validity in a single experiment."

Evidence on clinical utility is also crucial. As per established APA policy, at a minimum this includes attention to generality of effects across varying and diverse patients, therapists and settings and the interaction of these factors, the robustness of treatments across various modes of delivery, the feasibility with which treatments can be delivered to patients in real world settings, and the cost associated with treatments.

Evidence-based practice requires that psychologists recognize the strengths and limitations of evidence obtained from different types of research. Research has shown that the treatment method, the individual psychologist, the treatment relationship, and the patient are all vital contributors to the success of psychological practice. Comprehensive evidence-based practice will consider all of these determinants and their optimal combinations. Psychological practice is a complex relational and technical enterprise that requires clinical and research attention to multiple, interacting sources of treatment effectiveness. There remain many disorders, problem constellations, and clinical situations for which empirical data are sparse. In such instances, clinicians use their best clinical judgment and knowledge of the best available research evidence to develop coherent treatment strategies. Researchers and practitioners should join together to ensure that the research available on psychological practice is both clinically relevant and internally valid. . . .

Clinical Expertise[2]

Clinical expertise is essential for identifying and integrating the best research evidence with clinical data (e.g., information about the patient obtained over the course of treatment) in the context of the patient's characteristics and preferences to deliver services that have the highest probability of achieving the goals of therapy. Psychologists are trained as scientists as well as practitioners. An advantage of psychological training is that it fosters a clinical expertise informed by scientific expertise, allowing the psychologist to understand and integrate scientific literature as well as to frame and test hypotheses and interventions in practice as a "local clinical scientist."

Cognitive scientists have found consistent evidence of enduring and significant differences between experts and novices undertaking complex tasks in several domains. Experts recognize meaningful patterns and disregard irrelevant information, acquire extensive knowledge and organize it in ways that reflect a deep understanding of their domain, organize their knowledge using functional rather than descriptive features, retrieve knowledge relevant to the task at hand fluidly and automatically, adapt to new situations, self-monitor their knowledge and performance, know when their knowledge is

---

[2]As it is used in this report, clinical expertise refers to competence attained by psychologists through education, training, and experience resulting in effective practice; clinical expertise is not meant to refer to extraordinary performance that might characterize an elite group (e.g., the top two percent) of clinicians.

inadequate, continue to learn, and generally attain outcomes commensurate with their expertise.

However, experts are not infallible. All humans are prone to errors and biases. Some of these stem from cognitive strategies and heuristics that are generally adaptive and efficient. Others stem from emotional reactions, which generally guide adaptive behavior as well but can also lead to biased or motivated reasoning. Whenever psychologists involved in research or practice move from observations to inferences and generalizations, there is inherent risk for idiosyncratic interpretations, overgeneralizations, confirmatory biases, and similar errors in judgment. Integral to clinical expertise is an awareness of the limits of one's knowledge and skills and attention to the heuristics and biases—both cognitive and affective—that can affect clinical judgment. Mechanisms such as consultation and systematic feedback from the patient can mitigate some of these biases.

The individual therapist has a substantial impact on outcomes, both in clinical trials and in practice settings. The fact that treatment outcomes are systematically related to the provider of the treatment (above and beyond the type of treatment) provides strong evidence for the importance of understanding expertise in clinical practice as a way of enhancing patient outcomes. . . .

Patient Characteristics, Culture, and Preferences

Normative data on "what works for whom" provide essential guides to effective practice. Nevertheless, psychological services are most likely to be effective when responsive to the patient's specific problems, strengths, personality, sociocultural context, and preferences. Psychology's long history of studying individual differences and developmental change, and its growing empirical literature related to human diversity (including culture[3] and psychotherapy), place it in a strong position to identify effective ways of integrating research and clinical expertise with an understanding of patient characteristics essential to EBPP. EBPP involves consideration of patients' values, religious beliefs, worldviews, goals, and preferences for treatment with the psychologist's experience and understanding of the available research.

Several questions frame current debates about the role of patient characteristics in EBPP. The first regards the extent to which cross-diagnostic patient characteristics, such as personality traits or constellations, moderate the impact of empirically tested interventions. A second, related question concerns the extent to which social factors and cultural differences necessitate different forms of

---

[3]Culture, in this context, is understood to encompass a broad array of phenomena (such as shared values, history, knowledge, rituals, and customs) that often result in a shared sense of identity. Racial and ethnic groups may have a shared culture, but those personal characteristics are not the only characteristics that define cultural groups (e.g. deaf culture, inner-city culture). Culture is a multifaceted construct, and cultural factors cannot be understood in isolation from social, class and personal characteristics that make each patient unique.

treatment or whether interventions widely tested in majority populations can be readily adapted for patients with different ethnic or sociocultural backgrounds. A third question concerns maximizing the extent to which widely used interventions adequately attend to developmental considerations, both for children and adolescents and for older adults. A fourth question is the extent to which variable clinical presentations, such as comorbidity and polysymptomatic presentations, moderate the impact of interventions. Underlying all of these questions is the issue of how best to approach the treatment of patients whose characteristics (e.g., gender, gender identity, ethnicity, race, social class, disability status, sexual orientation) and problems (e.g., comorbidity) may differ from those of samples studied in research. This is a matter of active discussion in the field and there is increasing research attention to the generalizability and transportability of psychological interventions.

Available data indicate that a variety of patient-related variables influence outcomes, many of which are cross-diagnostic characteristics such as functional status, readiness to change, and level of social support. Other patient characteristics are essential to consider in forming and maintaining a treatment relationship and in implementing specific interventions. These include but are not limited to a) variations in presenting problems or disorders, etiology, concurrent symptoms or syndromes, and behavior; b) chronological age, developmental status, developmental history, and life stage; c) sociocultural and familial factors (e.g., gender, gender identity, ethnicity, race, social class, religion, disability status, family structure, and sexual orientation); d) current environmental context, stressors (e.g., unemployment or recent life event), and social factors (e.g., institutional racism and health care disparities); and e) personal preferences, values, and preferences related to treatment (e.g., goals, beliefs, worldviews, and treatment expectations). Available research on both patient matching and treatment failures in clinical trials of even highly efficacious interventions suggests that different strategies and relationships may prove better suited for different populations.

Many presenting symptoms—for example depression, anxiety, school failure, bingeing and purging—are similar across patients. However, symptoms or disorders that are phenotypically similar are often heterogeneous with respect to etiology, prognosis, and the psychological processes that create or maintain them. Moreover, most patients present with multiple symptoms or syndromes rather than a single, discrete disorder. The presence of concurrent conditions may moderate treatment response, and interventions intended to treat one symptom often affect others. An emerging body of research also suggests that personality variables underlie many psychiatric syndromes and account for a substantial part of the comorbidity among syndromes widely documented in research. Psychologists must attend to the individual person to make the complex choices necessary to conceptualize, prioritize, and treat multiple symptoms. It is important to know the person who has the disorder in addition to knowing the disorder the person has.

EBPP also requires attention to factors related to the patient's development and life-stage. An enormous body of research exists on developmental processes (e.g., attachment, socialization, and cognitive, social-cognitive, gender, moral, and emotional development) that are essential in understanding adult psychopathology and particularly in treating children, adolescents, families, and older adults.

Evidence-based practice in psychology requires attention to many other patient characteristics, such as gender, gender identity, culture, ethnicity, race, age, family context, religious beliefs, and sexual orientation. These variables shape personality, values, worldviews, relationships, psychopathology, and attitudes toward treatment. A wide range of relevant research literature can inform psychological practice, including ethnography, cross-cultural psychology, psychological anthropology, and cultural psychotherapy. Culture influences not only the nature and expression of psychopathology but also the patient's understanding of psychological and physical health and illness. Cultural values and beliefs and social factors such as implicit racial biases also influence patterns of seeking, using, and receiving help; presentation and reporting of symptoms, fears and expectations about treatment; and desired outcomes. Psychologists also understand and reflect upon the ways their own characteristics, values, and context interact with those of the patient.

Race as a social construct is a way of grouping people into categories on the basis of perceived physical attributes, ancestry, and other factors. Race is also more broadly associated with power, status, and opportunity. In Western cultures, European or white "race" confers advantage and opportunity, even as improved social attitudes and public policies have reinforced social equality. Race is thus an interpersonal and political process with significant implications for clinical practice and health care quality. Patients and clinicians may "belong" to racial groups, as they choose to self-identify, but the importance of race in clinical practice is relational, rather than solely a patient or clinician attribute. Considerable evidence from many fields suggests that racial power differentials between clinicians and their patients, as well as systemic biases and implicit stereotypes based on race or ethnicity, contribute to the inequitable care that patients of color receive across health care services. Clinicians must carefully consider the impact of race, ethnicity, and culture on the treatment process, relationship, and outcome.

The patient's social and environmental context, including recent and chronic stressors, is also important in case formulation and treatment planning. Sociocultural and familial factors, social class, and broader social, economic, and situational factors (e.g., unemployment, family disruption, lack of insurance, recent losses, prejudice, or immigration status) can have an enormous influence on mental health, adaptive functioning, treatment seeking, and patient resources (psychological, social, and financial).

Psychotherapy is a collaborative enterprise, in which patients and clinicians negotiate ways of working together that are mutually agreeable and likely to lead to positive outcomes. Thus, patient values and preferences (e.g., goals, beliefs, and preferred modes of treatment) are a central component of EBPP. Patients can have strong preferences for types of treatment and desired outcomes, and these preferences are influenced by both their cultural context and individual factors. One role of the psychologist is to ensure that patients understand the costs and benefits of different practices and choices.

Evidence-based practice in psychology seeks to maximize patient choice among effective alternative interventions. Effective practice requires balancing patient preferences and the psychologist's judgment, based on available evidence and clinical expertise, to determine the most appropriate treatment. . . .

Conclusions

Evidence-based practice in psychology is the integration of the best available research with clinical expertise in the context of patient characteristics, culture, and preferences. The purpose of EBPP is to promote effective psychological practice and enhance public health by applying empirically supported principles of psychological assessment, case formulation, therapeutic relationship, and intervention. Much has been learned over the past century from basic and applied psychological research as well as from observations and hypotheses developed in clinical practice. Many strategies for working with patients have emerged and been refined through the kind of trial and error and clinical hypothesis generation and testing that constitute the most scientific aspect of clinical practice. Yet clinical hypothesis testing has its limits, hence the need to integrate clinical expertise with best available research.

Perhaps the central message of this task force report, and one of the most heartening aspects of the process that led to it, is the consensus achieved among a diverse group of scientists, clinicians, and scientist-clinicians from multiple perspectives that EBPP requires an appreciation of the value of multiple sources of scientific evidence. In a given clinical circumstance, psychologists of good faith and good judgment may disagree about how best to weight different forms of evidence; over time, we presume that systematic and broad empirical inquiry—in the laboratory and in the clinic—will point the way toward best practice in integrating best evidence. What this document reflects, however, is a reassertion of what psychologists have known for a century: that the scientific method is a way of thinking and observing systematically and is the best tool we have for learning about what works for whom.

Clinical decisions should be made in collaboration with the patient, based on the best clinically relevant evidence, and with consideration for the probable costs, benefits, and available resources and options. It is the treating psychologist who makes the ultimate judgment regarding a particular intervention or treatment plan. The involvement of an active, informed patient is generally crucial to the success of psychological services. Treatment decisions should never be made by untrained persons unfamiliar with the specifics of the case.

The treating psychologist determines the applicability of research conclusions to a particular patient. Individual patients may require decisions and interventions not directly addressed by the available research. The application of research evidence to a given patient always involves probabilistic inferences. Therefore, ongoing monitoring of patient progress and adjustment of treatment as needed are essential to EBPP.

Moreover, psychologists must attend to a range of outcomes that may sometimes suggest one strategy and sometimes another and to the strengths and limitations of available research vis-à-vis these different ways of measuring success. Psychological outcomes may include not only symptom relief and prevention of future symptomatic episodes but also quality of life, adaptive functioning in work and relationships, ability to make satisfying life choices, personality change, and other goals arrived at in collaboration between patient and clinician.

EBPP is a means to enhance the delivery of services to patients within an atmosphere of mutual respect, open communication, and collaboration among all stakeholders, including practitioners, researchers, patients, health care managers, and policy-makers. Our goal in this document, and in the deliberations of the Task Force that led to it, was to set both an agenda and a tone for the next steps in the evolution of EBPP.

**Brent D. Slife and
Dennis C. Wendt**

 **NO**

The Next Step in the Evidence-Based Practice Movement

Nearly everyone agrees that psychological practice should be informed by evidence (Westen & Bradley, 2005, p. 266; Norcross, Beutler, & Levant, 2006, p. 7). However, there is considerable disagreement about what qualifies as evidence (e.g., Reed, 2006; Kihlstrom, 2006; Messer, 2006; Westen, 2006; Stirman & DeRubeis, 2006). This disagreement is not a simple scientific dispute to be resolved in the laboratory, but rather a "culture war" between different worldviews (Messer, 2004, p. 580). As Carol Tavris (2003) put it, this "war" involves "deeply held beliefs, political passions, views of human nature and the nature of knowledge, and—as all wars ultimately involve—money, territory, and livelihoods" (as qtd. in Norcross et al., p. 8).

How does one address a cultural battle of deeply held worldviews and political passions? We believe the approaches that have tried to address it so far in psychology have been well-intended and even headed in the right direction, but are ultimately and fundamentally inadequate. We will first describe what we consider the two major steps in this regard, beginning with the empirically supported treatment (EST) movement, which still has considerable energy in the discipline, and then moving to the "common factors" approach, which recently culminated in a policy regarding evidence-based practice (EBP) in psychology from the American Psychological Association (APA, 2006). We specifically focus on the latter, extolling its goals, but noting their distinct lack of fulfillment. We then offer what seems to us the logical extension of these first two steps—what could be called "objective methodological pluralism" in the spirit of one of our discipline's founding parents, William James (1902/1985; 1907/1975).

The First Step: The EST Movement

Psychology's first step in addressing this evidence controversy involved a succession of APA Division 12 (Clinical) task forces. Beginning in 1993, these task forces have "constructed and elaborated a list of empirically supported, manualized psychological interventions for specific disorders" (Norcross et al., 2006, p. 5). In other words, this first step assumed that the battle of worldviews would be resolved through rigorous scientific evidence.

"Rigorous evidence," in this case, was idealized as the randomized clinical (or controlled) trial (RCT), widely esteemed as the gold standard of evidence in medicine. The advantages of this step were obvious. Third-party payers were familiar with this gold standard from medicine, and many psychologists believed that an EST list would provide a clear-cut index of "proven" treatments, not to mention greater respect from medicine.

Unfortunately, this seemingly rigorous, clear-cut approach has manifested more than a few problems (Westen & Bradley, 2005; Messer, 2004). Much like the testing movement in education, where teachers found themselves "teaching to the test," psychologists found their practices being shaped by the RCT "test." The critics of the RCT showed how professional practices were conforming, consciously or unconsciously, to the RCT worldview in order to make the EST list. In other words, the practices being studied tended to accommodate the particular RCT perspective on treatments, therapists, and patients.

With regard to treatments, this medical-model worldview of the RCT is biased toward "packaged" treatments for well-defined, compartmentalized disorders (e.g., Bohart, O'Hara, & Leitner, 1998). This model of treatment took its cues from the pharmaceutical industry, where "one must specify the treatment and make sure it is being applied correctly" (p. 143). According to this model, every patient would receive the same thing, and it is this thing, not the therapist or patient, that is considered the agent of change. Critics have argued that this view of treatment undermined many types of therapy, such as humanistic or psychodynamic therapies, in which "treatment" does not entail a manualized set of principles (e.g., Bohart et al.; Safran, 2001).

A related argument against this packaged view of treatment concerned the role of therapists. The assumptions or worldview of the RCT, these critics contended, turned the therapist into an interchangeable part, discounting the importance of the therapist's distinctive personality, practical wisdom, and unique relationship with the patient. Many researchers have worried, to use the words of Allen Bergin (1997), that the RCT manualization of treatments turned therapists into "cookie cutters" and researchers into "mechanotropes" (pp. 85–86). This worry has been validated by research suggesting that manualization often hinders important therapeutic factors, such as the therapeutic alliance and the therapist's genuineness, creativity, motivation, and emotional involvement (Duncan & Miller, 2006; Piper & Ogrodniczuk, 1999).

Third, critics have noted that the biases of RCTs shaped one's view of the patient, assuming that researchers and clinicians work with pure patient pathologies only. According to this argument, RCTs are limited to patients with textbook symptoms of a single DSM disorder; thus, their results "may apply only to a narrow and homogeneous group of patients" (Butcher, Mineka, & Hooley, 2004, p. 563). This limitation is no small problem, critics have warned, because the vast majority of U.S. patients are not pathologically "pure" in this narrow RCT sense. Rather, they are co- or "multi"-morbid in the sense that they are an amalgam of disorders (Morrison, Bradley, & Westen, 2003; Westen & Bradley, 2005). The prevalence of these "messy" patients is corroborated by the 35%–70% exclusion rates of RCTs for major disorders (Morrison et al., p. 110).

The common theme behind the above criticisms is that the biases of the EST movement stem from its narrow framework for validating evidence. Thus, it is not mere coincidence, critics have argued, that therapies that exemplify this type of treatment (e.g., behavioral or cognitive-behavioral treatments) are the most frequently listed as ESTs (Messer, 2004). The exclusion of other types of therapy (e.g., humanistic and psychodynamic therapies) has prompted critics to contend that the EST movement constitutes a methodological bias toward behavioral and cognitive-behavioral therapies (e.g., Slife, Wiggins, & Graham; Messer, 2004). If this first step has taught psychologists anything, it has taught that what the evidence seems to say has a great deal to do with what one considers evidence.

The Second Step: The Common Factors Movement

The second step—the common factors movement—was, in part, an attempt to learn from the shortcomings of the EST movement. Common factors advocates have argued that a focus on specific, "packaged" treatments for specific disorders is a narrow way of conceptualizing psychological research and practice (e.g., Westen & Bradley, 2005; Bohart et al., 1998). An alternative approach is to discover and validate factors of therapeutic change that are common across treatments. In this way, responsibility for change is not just attributed to the treatment, as in ESTs. Change is considered the result of a dynamic relationship among the "common factors" of therapy, which include the therapist, patient, and technique (APA, 2006, p. 275).

A common factors approach is especially appealing to the majority of practitioners, who consider themselves eclectics or integrationists. Its popularity has helped it to play a significant role in shaping APA's (2006) new policy statement on evidence-based practice. For this policy statement, evidence was liberalized not only to include studies of therapist and patient variables but also to include other methods than RCTs for conducting these studies (pp. 274–75). The main guideposts for selecting these methods, according to the underlying rationale of the APA policy, were their objectivity and their diversity. Methods should be *objective* to prevent the intrusion of human error and bias that would distort the findings (p. 276), and they should be *diverse* to prevent the shaping of practice that a focus on only one method might produce, such as the problems created by RCTs (pp. 272–74).

The problem, from our perspective, is that the APA culmination of this common factors approach is not objective and diverse enough. In other words, we applaud the goals but criticize the implementation. The APA policy is a clear step forward, in our view, but its conceptions of objectivity and diversity are inadequate. As we will attempt to show, this inadequacy means that the lessons of the EST movement have not been sufficiently learned. Recall that this first step restricted itself to a single ideal of evidence, the RCT, and thus disallowed any true diversity of methods. Recall also that several biases resulted from this restriction, obviating objectivity and shaping practice even before investigation. As we will argue, this same lack of diversity and objectivity has continued into the second approach to the evidence controversy.

Our basic criticism is this: Just as an EST framework uncritically restricts acceptable evidence to a *single method* ideal (the RCT), so does the APA policy uncritically restrict acceptable evidence to a *single epistemology.* By "epistemology" we mean the philosophy of knowing that provides the logic and guides the conduct of a group of methods (Slife & Williams, 1995). Although the EST framework is biased toward a certain *method*, the common factors framework is biased toward a certain *methodology*—a narrow brand of *empiricism.*

According to this empiricist epistemology, "we can only know, or know best, those aspects of our experience that are sensory" (Slife, Wiggins, & Graham, 2005, p. 84). This narrow conception of empiricism is fairly traditional in psychology. More liberal usages of empiricism differ substantially, such as William James' radical empiricism. James' empiricism encompasses "the whole of experience," including *non*-sensory experiences such as thoughts, emotions, and even spiritual experiences (James, 1902/1985; 1907/1975). Still, psychologists have interpreted the natural sciences to be grounded in the narrow empiricism. Historically, psychologists have wanted to be both rigorously scientific and comparable to medicine, leading them to embrace the narrower empiricism. As we will attempt to show, however, this restriction to a single epistemology is not based on evidence. Analogous to the EST restriction to a single method, the APA policy merely assumes and never justifies empiricism as the only appropriate epistemology for evidence-based practice, in spite of other promising epistemologies.

The reason for this lack of justification seems clear. Throughout much of the history of psychology, empiricism has been mistakenly understood not as a *particular* philosophy of science, but as a *non*-philosophy that makes reality transparent. Analogous to the way in which many EST proponents view RCTs, empiricism is not *a* way to understand evidence, but *the* way. Consequently, nowhere in the APA policy or its underlying report is a rationale provided for a commitment to empirical research, and nowhere is a consideration given for even the possibility of a "non-empirical" contribution to evidence-based practice.

This equation of evidence with empiricism is directly parallel to the EST movement's equation of evidence with RCT findings. Just as Westen and Bradley (2005) noted that "EBP > EST" (p. 271), we note that EBP > empirical. After all, there is no empirical evidence for empiricism, or for RCTs, for that matter. Both sets of methods spring from the human invention of philosophers and other humanists. Moses did not descend Mt. Sinai with the Ten Commandments in one hand and the principles of science in the other. Moreover, these principles could not have been scientifically derived, because one would need the principles (before their derivation) to conduct the scientific investigations to derive them.

Indeed, the irony of this epistemology's popularity is that many observers of psychology have long considered empiricism to be deeply problematic for psychological research. Again, the parallel to the dominance of RCTs is striking. Just as the majority of real-world patients, therapists, and treatments were perceived to defy RCT categories, so too the majority of real-world phenomena can be perceived to defy empirical categories. Indeed, many of the common factors for evidence-based practice are not, strictly speaking, empirical at all.

Rather, they are experiences and meanings that are not sensory, and thus not observable, in nature (Slife et al., 2005, p. 88).

Consider, for example, the efforts of APA Division 29 (Psychotherapy) to provide empirical support for therapy relationships, such as therapeutic alliance and group cohesion (Norcross, 2001; APA, 2006, p. 272). Although patients and therapists probably experience this alliance and cohesion, these relationships literally never fall on their retinas. The people involved in these relationships are observable in this sense, to be sure, but the "betweenness" of these relations— the actual alliance or cohesion themselves—never are. Their unobservability means, according to the method requirements of empiricism, that they must be operationalized, or made observable. Thus, it is not surprising, given its commitment to a narrow empiricism, that the APA policy report presumes that operationalization is a requirement of method (p. 274).

The problem with this requirement, however, is that any specified opera-tionalization, such as a patient's feelings about the relationship (e.g., Norcross, 2002), can occur without the therapeutic alliance, and any such alliance can occur without the specified operationalization. The upshot is that the construct (e.g., alliance) and the operationalization are two different things, yet the operationalization is the only thing studied in traditional research. Moreover, one can never know empirically the relation between the construct and its operationalization because pivotal aspects of this relation—the construct and relation itself—are never observable. Thus, APA's policy runs the risk of making psychotherapy research a compendium of operationalizations without any knowledge of how they relate to what psychologists want to study.

Problems such as these are the reason that alternative philosophies of science, such as qualitative methods, were formulated. Many qualitative methods were specifically formulated to investigate unobservable, but experi-enced, meanings of the world (Denzin & Lincoln, 2000; Patton, 1990; Slife & Gantt, 1999). The existence of this alternative philosophy of science implies another problem with the unjustified empiricist framework of the APA policy report—it runs roughshod over alternative frameworks, such as qualitative methods. Although the policy includes qualitative research on its list of acceptable methods (APA, p. 274), it fails to understand and value qualitative research as a different philosophy of science.

A clear indication of this failure is the use of the word "subjective" when the report describes the purpose of qualitative research (p. 274). In the midst of a report that extols "objective" inquiry, relegating only qualitative methods to the "subjective" is second-class citizenship, at best. More importantly, this relegation only makes sense within an empiricist framework. In non-empiricist philosophies, such as those underlying many qualitative methods, the notions of "objective" and "subjective" are largely irrelevant because most non-empiricist conceptions of science do not assume the dualism of a subjective and objective realm (Slife, 2005).

The bottom line is that a common factors approach to the evidence controversy is a clear advancement of the EBP project, but it is not an unqual-ified advance. Indeed, it recapitulates some of the same problems that it is attempting to correct. In both the EST and the common factors approaches, criteria for what is evidence shape not only the studies conducted but also the practices considered supported. Indeed, we would contend there is no method or methodology that is not ultimately biased in this regard. As philosophers of science have long taught, all methods of investigation must make assumptions about the world *before* it is investigated (Curd & Cover, 1998). The question remains, however, whether there can be a framework for understanding evidence that does not *automatically* shape practice before it is investigated.

Presaging the Next Step: The Ideas of William James

The answer, we believe, is "yes," and we do not have to reinvent the wheel to formulate this alternative. One of the intellectual parents of our discipline, William James, has already pointed the way. Consequently, we will first briefly describe three of James' pivotal ideas: his radical empiricism, his pluralism, and his pragmatism. Then, we will apply these ideas to the evidence-based practice issue, deriving our alternative to the current monopoly of empiricism— objective methodological pluralism.

James was actually quite critical of what psychologists consider empirical today. As mentioned above, his radical empiricism embraces the whole of experience, including non-sensory experiences such as thoughts, emotions, and spiritual experiences (James, 1902/1985; 1907/1975). His position implies, as he explicitly recognizes, that there are several epistemologies of investigation ("ways of knowing") rather than just one. As James (1909/1977) put it, "nothing includes everything" (p. 145). In other words, no philosophy of science is sufficient to understand everything.

Psychology needs, instead, *a pluralism* of such philosophies, which is the second of James's ideas and an intriguing way to actualize APA's desire for diversity. In other words, we not only need a diversity of methods, which the APA report (2006) clearly concedes (p. 274), we also need a diversity of meth*odologies* or philosophies underlying these methods. It is not coincidental, in this regard, that James (1902/1985) used qualitative methods to investigate spiritual meanings in his famous work, *Varieties of Religious Experiences.* His pluralism of methods dictated that he should not change or operationalize his phenomena of study to fit the method, but that he should change his method to best illuminate the phenomena—spiritual phenomena, in this case.

This approach to method implies the third of James's ideas—his pragmatism. According to James:

> Rationalism sticks to logic and . . . empiricism sticks to the external senses. Pragmatism is willing to take anything, to follow either logic or the senses and to count the humblest and most personal of experiences. [Pragmatism] will count mystical experiences if they have practical consequences. (James, 1907/1975, p. 61)

As James implies, the heart of pragmatism is the notion that one should never approach the study or understanding of anything with fixed schemes and methods. There is too much danger that the method will distort understanding of the phenomena being studied. This is not to say that one can or should approach such phenomena without some method or interpretive framework. Yet this framework does not have to be cast in stone; psychologists should allow the phenomenon itself to guide the methods we choose to study it.

This pragmatism may sound complicated, but it is not significantly different from what good carpenters do at every job—they let the task dictate the tools they use. They have a pluralism of tools or methods, rather than just one, because many tasks cannot be done with just one tool, such as a hammer. Moreover, not every carpentry job can be "operationalized" into a set of "nails." As Dupre' (1993) and others (e.g., Feyerabend, 1975; Viney, 2004) have noted, this pragmatism is the informal meta-method of physics, where the object of study is the primary consideration, and the method of studying it is a secondary consideration.

By contrast, APA's version of evidence-based practice is method-driven rather than object-driven. That is to say, psychologists have decided the logic of their investigation before they even consider what they are studying. If the object of study does not fit this logic, they have no choice but to modify it to fit this logic through operationalization. For example, an unobservable feeling, such as sadness, becomes operationalized as an observable behavior, such as crying.

The irony of this familiar research practice is that psychologists are driven more by an unrecognized and unexamined philosophy of science, as manifested through their methods, than by the objects they are studying. Indeed, they are changing their object of study—from sadness to crying—to accommodate this philosophy. We believe that this accommodation is contrary to good science, where everything including the philosophies that ground one's methods, should be subject to examination and comparison.

The Next Step: Objective Methodological Pluralism

This description of James' three pivotal ideas—his radical empiricism, pluralism, and pragmatism—sets the stage for our proposal on evidence-based practice: "objective methodological pluralism." First, this pluralism assumes a broader empiricism, in the spirit of James. To value only sensory experiences, as does the conventional empiricist, is to affirm a value that is itself unproven and non-empirical. There simply is no conceptual or empirical necessity to value only the sensory. We recognize that many would claim the success of this value in science, but we also recognize that no scientific comparison between such philosophical values has occurred. These claims of success, then, are merely opinion, uninformed by scientific findings.

In practical terms, this move from conventional empiricism to radical empiricism means that alternative methods, such as qualitative methods, are no longer second class citizens. They are no longer "subjective" and experimental methods considered "objective," because all methods ultimately depend on experiences of one sort or another. This creates more of a level playing field for methods—a pluralism—and allows for an even-handed assessment of each method's advantages and disadvantages.

Unlike the APA policy's conception, the criteria of this assessment are not already controlled by one, unexamined philosophy of science. They are guided, instead, by the object of one's study. This is the reason for the term "objective" in our alternative, *objective* methodological pluralism. Methods, we believe, should be driven not by some philosophy of method that is deemed to be correct *before* the object of study has even been considered. Methods should be driven by consideration of the objects themselves.

This consideration is itself evaluated pragmatically, in terms of the practical differences it makes in the lives of patients. As James realized, any evaluation of practical significance begs the question of "significant to what"? In other words, any methodological pluralism requires thoughtful disciplinary discussion of the moral issues of psychology, a discussion that has begun in a limited way in positive psychology (Seligman, 2002) What is the good life for a patient? When is a life truly flourishing? Such questions cannot be derived from the "is" of research; they must be discussed as the "ought" that guides this research and determines what practical significance really means.

Obviously, much remains to be worked out with a Jamesian pluralism. Still, we believe that this particular "working out" is not only possible but also necessary. The monopoly and problems of empiricism—the lessons of our first two steps in the evidence controversy—do not go away with a rejection of this pluralism. This is the reason we titled this article "the next step"—the difficulties with empiricism and APA's desire for diversity lead us logically, we believe, to this next general step. Admittedly, this kind of pluralism is a challenging prospect. Still, if carpenters can do it in a less complex enterprise, surely psychologists can. In any case, it is high time that psychologists face up to the challenge, because ignoring it will not make it go away.

References

APA Presidential Task Force on Evidence-Based Practice. (2006). Evidence-based practice in psychology. *American Psychologist, 61,* 271–285.

Bergin, A.E. (1997). Neglect of the therapist and the human dimensions of change: A Commentary. *Clinical Psychology: Science and Practice,* 4(1), 83–89.

Bohart, A. C., O'Hara, M, & Leitner, L. M. (1998). Empirically violated treatments: Disenfranchisement of humanistic and other psychotherapies. *Psychotherapy Research, 8,* 141–157.

Butcher, J. N., Mineka, S, & Hooley, J. M. (2004). *Abnormal psychology.* 12th ed. Boston: Pearson/Allyn & Bacon.

Curd, M., & Cover, J. A. (1998). *Philosophy of science: The central issues.* New York: W. W. Norton & Company.

Denzin, N. K., & Lincoln, Y. S. (Eds). (2000). *Handbook of qualitative methods.* Thousand Oaks, CA: Sage.

Duncan, B. L., & Miller, S. D. (2006). Treatment manuals do not improve outcomes. In J. C. Norcross, L. E. Beutler, & R. F. Levant (Eds.), *Evidence-based practices in mental health: Debate and dialogue on the fundamental questions* (pp. 140–149). Washington, D.C.: APA Books.

Dupre', J. (1993). *The disorder of things: Metaphysical foundations of the disunity of science.* Cambridge, MA: Harvard University Press.

Feyerabend, P. (1975). *Against method:* London: Verso.

James, W. (1975). *Pragmatism.* Cambridge, MA: Harvard University Press. (Original work published 1907)

James, W. (1977). *A pluralistic universe.* Cambridge, MA: Harvard University Press. (Original work published 1909)

James, W. (1985). *The varieties of religious experience.* Cambridge, MA: Harvard University Press. (Original work published 1902)

Kihlstrom, J. F. (2006). Scientific research. In J. C. Norcross, L. E. Beutler, & R. F. Levant (Eds.), *Evidence-based practices in mental health: Debate and dialogue on the fundamental questions* (pp. 23–31). Washington, D.C.: APA Books.

Messer, S. B. (2004). Evidence-based practice: Beyond empirically supported treatments. *Professional Psychology: Research and Practice, 35,* 580–588.

Messer, S. B. (2006). Patient values and preferences. In J. C. Norcross, L. E. Beutler, & R. F. Levant (Eds.), *Evidence-based practices in mental health: Debate and dialogue on the fundamental questions* (pp. 31–40). Washington, D.C.: APA Books.

Morrison, K. H., Bradley, R., & Westen, D. (2003). The external validity of controlled clinical trials of psychotherapy for depression and anxiety: A naturalistic study. *Psychology & Psychotherapy: Theory, Research, & Practice, 76:* 109–132.

Norcross, J. C. (2001). Purposes, processes, and products of the task force on empirically supported therapy relationships. *Psychotherapy: Theory, Research, Practice, Training, 38,* 345–356.

Norcross, J. C. (2002). Empirically supported therapy relationships. In J. C. Norcross (Ed.), *Psychotherapy relationships that work: Therapist contributions and responsiveness to patient needs* (pp. 3–32). Oxford, NY: Oxford University Press.

Norcross, J. C., Beutler, L. E., & Levant, R. F. (Eds.) (2006). *Evidence-based practices in mental health: Debate and dialogue on the fundamental questions.* Washington, D.C.: APA Books.

Patton, M. Q., (1990). *Qualitative evaluation and research methods.* (2nd Ed.). Newbury Park, CA: Sage.

Piper, W. E., & Ogrodniczuk, J. S. (1999). Therapy manuals and the dilemma of dynamically oriented therapists and researchers. *American Journal of Psychotherapy, 53,* 467–482.

Reed, G. M. (2006). Clinical expertise. In J. C. Norcross, L. E. Beutler, & R. F. Levant (Eds.), *Evidence-based practices in mental health: Debate and dialogue on the fundamental questions* (pp. 13–23). Washington, D.C.: APA Books.

Safran, J. D. (2001). When worlds collide: Psychoanalysts and the "empirically supported treatment" movement. *Psychoanalytic Dialogues, 11,* 659–681.

Seligman, M. E. P. (2002). *Authentic happiness/Using the new positive psychology to realize your potential for lasting fulfillment.* New York: Free Press.

Slife, B. D. (2005). Testing the limits of Henriques' proposal: Wittgensteinian lessons and hermeneutic dialogue. *Journal of Clinical Psychology, 61,* 1–14.

Slife, B. D., & Gantt, E. (1999). Methodological pluralism: A framework for psychotherapy research. *Journal of Clinical Psychology. 55* (12), 1–13.

Slife, B. D., Wiggins, B. J., & Graham, J. T. (2005). Avoiding an EST monopoly: Toward a pluralism of philosophies and methods. *Journal of Contemporary Psychotherapy, 35*(1), 83–97.

Slife, B. D., & Williams, R.N. (1995). *What's behind the research? Discovering hidden assumptions in the behavioral sciences.* Thousand Oaks, CA: Sage Publications.

Stirman, S. W., & DeRubeis, R. J. (2006). Research patients and clinical trials are frequently representative of clinical practice. In J. C. Norcross,

L. E. Beutler, & R. F. Levant (Eds.), *Evidence-based practices in mental health: Debate and dialogue on the fundamental questions* (pp. 171–179). Washington, D.C.: APA Books.

Viney, W. (2004). Pluralism in the sciences is not easily dismissed. *Journal of Clinical Psychology, 60,* 1275–1278.

Westen, D. (2006). Patients and treatments in clinical trials are not adequately representative of clinical practice. In J. C. Norcross, L. E. Beutler, & R. F. Levant (Eds.), *Evidence-based practices in mental health: Debate and dialogue on the fundamental questions* (pp. 161–171). Washington, D.C.: APA Books.

Westen, D., & Bradley, R. (2005). Empirically supported complexity: Rethinking evidence-based practice in psychotherapy. *Current Directions in Psychological Science, 14,* 266–271.

CHALLENGE QUESTIONS

Are Traditional Empirical Methods Sufficient to Provide Evidence for Psychological Practice?

1. The label "objective" is typically used only in reference to empirical evidence. Why is this typical, and what would Slife and Wendt say about this practice?
2. The APA Task Force bases its definition of evidence-based practice on a conception formulated by the Institute of Medicine. Find out what this definition is and form your own, informed opinion about its relevance or irrelevance to psychotherapy. Support your answer.
3. Many people think they would feel safer if their therapist used practices that have been validated by science. Explain what it is about science that leads people to feel this way.
4. William James is known as the father of American psychology. Why do you think the APA has largely neglected to take his pluralism into consideration?
5. Slife and Wendt believe that the methods of psychology (and any other science, for that matter) are based on and guided by philosophies, yet few psychology texts discuss these philosophies. Why do you feel that this is the case, and is the absence of this discussion justified?

ISSUE 3

Classic Dialogue:
Was Stanley Milgram's Study of
Obedience Unethical?

YES: Diana Baumrind, from "Some Thoughts on Ethics of Research: After Reading Milgram's 'Behavioral Study of Obedience,'" *American Psychologist* (vol. 19, 1964)

NO: Stanley Milgram, from "Issues in the Study of Obedience: A Reply to Baumrind," *American Psychologist* (vol. 19, 1964)

ISSUE SUMMARY

YES: Psychologist Diana Baumrind argues that Stanley Milgram's study of obedience did not meet ethical standards for research, because participants were subjected to a research design that caused undue psychological stress that was not resolved after the study.

NO: Social psychologist Stanley Milgram, in response to Baumrind's accusations, asserts that the study was well designed, the stress caused to participants could not have been anticipated, and the participants' anguish dissipated after a thorough debriefing.

$\mathbf{A}$re there psychological experiments that should not be conducted? Is the psychological distress that participants experience in some studies too extreme to justify the experimental outcomes and knowledge gained? Or is it sometimes necessary to allow participants to experience some anguish so that a researcher can better understand important psychological phenomena? These questions lie at the heart of ethical considerations in psychological research. They have traditionally been answered by the researcher, who attempts to weigh the costs and benefits of conducting a given study.

The problem is that a researcher's ability to accurately anticipate the costs and benefits of a study is severely limited. Researchers are likely to have an investment in their studies, which may lead them to overestimate the benefits and underestimate the costs. For these and other reasons, in 1974 the U.S. Department of Health, Education, and Welfare established regulations for the protection of human subjects. These regulations include the creation of institutional review boards, which are responsible for reviewing research proposals and ensuring that researchers adequately protect research participants.

The establishment of these regulations can be traced to past ethical controversies, such as the one raised in the following selection by Diana Baumrind regarding Stanley Milgram's famous 1963 study of obedience. Baumrind's primary concern is that the psychological welfare of the study's participants was compromised not only through the course of the study but also through the course of their lives. She contends that participants were prone to obey the experimenter because of the atmosphere of the study and the participants' trust in the experimenter. As a result, participants behaved in ways that disturbed them considerably. Baumrind maintains that these disturbances could not be resolved through an after-study debriefing but rather remained with the participants.

In response to these accusations, Milgram argues that the atmosphere of a laboratory generalizes to other contexts in which obedience is prevalent and is thus appropriate to a study of obedience. Furthermore, he and a number of other professionals never anticipated the results of the study; they were genuinely surprised by its outcome. Milgram also asserts that the psychological distress experienced by some participants was temporary, not dangerous, and that it dissipated after the true nature of the study was revealed.

POINT

- Milgram's indifference toward distressed participants reveals his lack of concern for their well-being.
- A study of obedience should not be conducted in the laboratory because subjects are particularly prone to behave obediently and to put trust in the researcher.
- The psychological distress experienced by participants exceeded appropriate limits.
- Participants experienced long-term, negative psychological consequences as a result of their participation in Milgram's experiment.
- In planning and designing the study, Milgram ignored issues regarding the extreme psychological distress that was experienced by some participants.

COUNTERPOINT

- Milgram made special efforts to assure participants that their behavior was normal.
- The laboratory setting is well suited to a study of obedience because it is similar to other contexts in which obedience is prevalent.
- The psychological distress was brief and not injurious.
- Participants spoke positively about the experiment, indicating that it was psychologically beneficial.
- The extreme psychological tension experienced by some participants was unanticipated by Milgram and many other professionals.

46

YES

Diana Baumrind

Some Thoughts on Ethics of Research

Certain problems in psychological research require the experimenter to balance his career and scientific interests against the interests of his prospective subjects. When such occasions arise the experimenter's stated objective frequently is to do the best possible job with the least possible harm to his subjects. The experimenter seldom perceives in more positive terms an indebtedness to the subject for his services, perhaps because the detachment which his functions require prevents appreciation of the subject as an individual.

Yet a debt does exist, even when the subject's reason for volunteering includes course credit or monetary gain. Often a subject participates unwillingly in order to satisfy a course requirement. These requirements are of questionable merit ethically, and do not alter the experimenter's responsibility to the subject.

Most experimental conditions do not cause the subjects pain or indignity, and are sufficiently interesting or challenging to present no problem of an ethical nature to the experimenter. But where the experimental conditions expose the subject to loss of dignity, or offer him nothing of value, then the experimenter is obliged to consider the reasons why the subject volunteered and to reward him accordingly.

The subject's public motives for volunteering include having an enjoyable or stimulating experience, acquiring knowledge, doing the experimenter a favor which may some day be reciprocated, and making a contribution to science. These motives can be taken into account rather easily by the experimenter who is willing to spend a few minutes with the subject afterwards to thank him for his participation, answer his questions, reassure him that he did well, and chat with him a bit. Most volunteers also have less manifest, but equally legitimate, motives. A subject may be seeking an opportunity to have contact with, be noticed by, and perhaps confide in a person with psychological training. The dependent attitude of most subjects toward the experimenter is an artifact of the experimental situation as well as an expression of some subjects' personal need systems at the time they volunteer.

The dependent, obedient attitude assumed by most subjects in the experimental setting is appropriate to that situation. The "game" is defined by the experimenter and he makes the rules. By volunteering, the subject agrees implicitly to assume a posture of trust and obedience. While the experimental

From *American Psychologist*, vol. 19, issue 6, 1964, pp. 421–423. Copyright © 1964 by American Psychological Association via the Copyright Clearance Center. Reprinted by permission.

conditions leave him exposed, the subject has the right to assume that his security and self-esteem will be protected.

There are other professional situations in which one member—the patient or client—expects help and protection from the other—the physician or psychologist. But the interpersonal relationship between experimenter and subject additionally has unique features which are likely to provoke initial anxiety in the subject. The laboratory is unfamiliar as a setting and the rules of behavior ambiguous compared to a clinician's office. Because of the anxiety and passivity generated by the setting, the subject is more prone to behave in an obedient, suggestible manner in the laboratory than elsewhere. Therefore, the laboratory is not the place to study degree of obedience or suggestibility, as a function of a particular experimental condition, since the base line for these phenomena as found in the laboratory is probably much higher than in most other settings. Thus experiments in which the relationship to the experimenter as an authority is used as an independent condition are imperfectly designed for the same reason that they are prone to injure the subjects involved. They disregard the special quality of trust and obedience with which the subject appropriately regards the experimenter.

Other phenomena which present ethical decisions, unlike those mentioned above, *can* be reproduced successfully in the laboratory. Failure experience, conformity to peer judgment, and isolation are among such phenomena. In these cases we can expect the experimenter to take whatever measures are necessary to prevent the subject from leaving the laboratory more humiliated, insecure, alienated, or hostile than when he arrived. To guarantee that an especially sensitive subject leaves a stressful experimental experience in the proper state sometimes requires special clinical training. But usually an attitude of compassion, respect, gratitude, and common sense will suffice, and no amount of clinical training will substitute. The subject has the right to expect that the psychologist with whom he is interacting has some concern for his welfare, and the personal attributes and professional skill to express his good will effectively.

Unfortunately, the subject is not always treated with the respect he deserves. It has become more commonplace in sociopsychological laboratory studies to manipulate, embarrass, and discomfort subjects. At times the insult to the subject's sensibilities extends to the journal reader when the results are reported. Milgram's (1963) study is a case in point. The following is Milgram's abstract of his experiment:

> This article describes a procedure for the study of destructive obedience in the laboratory. It consists of ordering a naive S to administer increasingly more severe punishment to a victim in the context of a learning experiment. Punishment is administered by means of a shock generator with 30 graded switches ranging from Slight Shock to Danger: Severe Shock. The victim is a confederate of E. The primary dependent variable is the maximum shock the S is willing to administer before he refuses to continue further. 26 Ss obeyed the experimental commands fully, and administered the highest shock on the generator. 14 Ss broke off the experiment at some point after

the victim protested and refused to provide further answers. The procedure created extreme levels of nervous tension in some Ss. Profuse sweating, trembling, and stuttering were typical expressions of this emotional disturbance. One unexpected sign of tension—yet to be explained—was the regular occurrence of nervous laughter, which in some Ss developed into uncontrollable seizures. The variety of interesting behavioral dynamics observed in the experiment, the reality of the situation for the S, and the possibility of parametric variation within the framework of the procedure, point to the fruitfulness of further study [p. 371].

The detached, objective manner in which Milgram reports the emotional disturbance suffered by his subject contrasts sharply with his graphic account of that disturbance. Following are two other quotes describing the effects on his subjects of the experimental conditions:

I observed a mature and initially poised businessman enter the laboratory smiling and confident. Within 20 minutes he was reduced to a twitching, stuttering wreck, who was rapidly approaching a point of nervous collapse. He constantly pulled on his earlobe, and twisted his hands. At one point he pushed his fist into his forehead and muttered: "Oh, God, let's stop it." And yet he continued to respond to every word of the experimenter, and obeyed to the end [p. 377].

In a large number of cases the degree of tension reached extremes that are rarely seen in sociopsychological laboratory studies. Subjects were observed to sweat, tremble, stutter, bite their lips, groan, and dig their fingernails into their flesh. These were characteristic rather than exceptional responses to the experiment.

One sign of tension was the regular occurrence of nervous laughing fits. Fourteen of the 40 subjects showed definite signs of nervous laughter and smiling. The laughter seemed entirely out of place, even bizarre. Full-blown, uncontrollable seizures were observed for 3 subjects. On one occasion we observed a seizure so violently convulsive that it was necessary to call a halt to the experiment . . . [p. 375].

Milgram does state that,

After the interview, procedures were undertaken to assure that the subject would leave the laboratory in a state of well being. A friendly reconciliation was arranged between the subject and the victim, and an effort was made to reduce any tensions that arose as a result of the experiment [p. 374].

It would be interesting to know what sort of procedures could dissipate the type of emotional disturbance just described. In view of the effects on subjects, traumatic to a degree which Milgram himself considers nearly unprecedented in sociopsychological experiments, his casual assurance that these tensions were dissipated before the subject left the laboratory is unconvincing.

What could be the rational basis for such a posture of indifference? Perhaps Milgram supplies the answer himself when he partially explains the subject's destructive obedience as follows, "Thus they assume that the discomfort caused the victim is momentary, while the scientific gains resulting from the experiment are enduring [p. 378]." Indeed such a rationale might suffice to justify the means used to achieve his end if that end were of inestimable value to humanity or were not itself transformed by the means by which it was attained.

The behavioral psychologist is not in as good a position to objectify his faith in the significance of his work as medical colleagues at points of breakthrough. His experimental situations are not sufficiently accurate models of real-life experience; his sampling techniques are seldom of a scope which would justify the meaning with which he would like to endow his results; and these results are hard to reproduce by colleagues with opposing theoretical views. . . . [T]he concrete benefit to humanity of his particular piece of work, no matter how competently handled, cannot justify the risk that real harm will be done to the subject. I am not speaking of physical discomfort, inconvenience, or experimental deception per se, but of permanent harm, however slight. I do regard the emotional disturbance described by Milgram as potentially harmful because it could easily effect an alteration in the subject's self-image or ability to trust adult authorities in the future. It is potentially harmful to a subject to commit, in the course of an experiment, acts which he himself considers unworthy, particularly when he has been entrapped into committing such acts by an individual he has reason to trust. The subject's personal responsibility for his actions is not erased because the experimenter reveals to him the means which he used to stimulate these actions. The subject realizes that he would have hurt the victim if the current were on. The realization that he also made a fool of himself by accepting the experimental set results in additional loss of self-esteem. Moreover, the subject finds it difficult to express his anger outwardly after the experimenter in a self-acceptant but friendly manner reveals the hoax.

A fairly intense corrective interpersonal experience is indicated wherein the subject admits and accepts his responsibility for his own actions, and at the same time gives vent to his hurt and anger at being fooled. Perhaps an experience as distressing as the one described by Milgram can be integrated by the subject, provided that careful thought is given to the matter. The propriety of such experimentation is still in question even if such a reparational experience were forthcoming. Without it I would expect a naive, sensitive subject to remain deeply hurt and anxious for some time, and a sophisticated, cynical subject to become even more alienated and distrustful.

In addition the experimental procedure used by Milgram does not appear suited to the objectives of the study because it does not take into account the special quality of the set which the subject has in the experimental situation. Milgram is concerned with a very important problem, namely, the social consequences of destructive obedience. He says,

> Gas chambers were built, death camps were guarded, daily quotas of corpses were produced with the same efficiency as a manufacture of appliances. These inhumane policies may have originated in the mind of a single person, but they could only be carried out on a massive scale if a very large number of persons obeyed orders [p. 371].

But the parallel between authority-subordinate relationships in Hitler's Germany and in Milgram's laboratory is unclear. In the former situation the SS man or member of the German Officer Corps, when obeying orders to slaughter, had no reason to think of his superior officer as benignly disposed towards himself or their victims. The victims were perceived as subhuman and not worthy of consideration. The subordinate officer was an agent in a great cause. He did not need to feel guilt or conflict because within his frame of reference he was acting rightly.

It is obvious from Milgram's own descriptions that most of his subjects were concerned about their victims and did trust the experimenter, and that their stressful conflict was generated in part by the consequences of these two disparate but appropriate attitudes. Their distress may have resulted from shock at what the experimenter was doing to them as well as from what they thought they were doing to their victims. In any case there is not a convincing parallel between the phenomena studied by Milgram and destructive obedience as that concept would apply to the subordinate-authority relationship demonstrated in Hitler Germany. If the experiments were conducted "outside of New Haven [Connecticut] and without any visible ties to [Yale University]," I would still question their validity on similar although not identical grounds. In addition, I would question the representativeness of a sample of subjects who would voluntarily participate within a noninstitutional setting.

In summary, the experimental objectives of the psychologist are seldom incompatible with the subject's ongoing state of well being, provided that the experimenter is willing to take the subject's motives and interests into consideration when planning his methods and correctives. Section 4b in *Ethical Standards of Psychologists* (APA, undated) reads in part:

> Only when a problem is significant and can be investigated in no other way, is the psychologist justified in exposing human subjects to emotional stress or other possible harm. In conducting such research, the psychologist must seriously consider the possibility of harmful aftereffects, and should be prepared to remove them as soon as permitted by the design of the experiment. Where the danger of serious aftereffects exists, research should be conducted only when the subjects or their responsible agents are fully informed of this possibility and volunteer nevertheless [p. 12].

From the subject's point of view procedures which involve loss of dignity, self-esteem, and trust in rational authority are probably most harmful in the long run and require the most thoughtfully planned reparations, if engaged in at all. The public image of psychology as a profession is highly related to our own actions, and some of these actions are changeworthy. It is important that as research psychologists we protect our ethical sensibilities rather than adapt our personal standards to include as appropriate the kind of indignities to which Milgram's subjects were exposed. I would not like to see experiments such as Milgram's proceed unless the subjects were fully informed of the dangers of serious aftereffects and his correctives were clearly shown to be effective in restoring their state of well being.

References

American Psychological Association. *Ethical Standards of Psychologists: A summary of ethical principles*. Washington, D.C.: APA, undated.

Milgram, S. Behavioral study of obedience. *J. Abnorm. Soc. Psychol.*, 1963, 67, 371–378.

Stanley Milgram

Issues in the Study of Obedience: A Reply to Baumrind

Obedience serves numerous productive functions in society. It may be ennobling and educative and entail acts of charity and kindness. Yet the problem of destructive obedience, because it is the most disturbing expression of obedience in our time, and because it is the most perplexing, merits intensive study.

In its most general terms, the problem of destructive obedience may be defined thus: If X tells Y to hurt Z, under what conditions will Y carry out the command of X, and under what conditions will he refuse? In the concrete setting of a laboratory, the question may assume this form: If an experimenter tells a subject to act against another person, under what conditions will the subject go along with the instruction, and under what conditions will he refuse to obey?

A simple procedure was devised for studying obedience (Milgram, 1963). A person comes to the laboratory, and in the context of a learning experiment, he is told to give increasingly severe electric shocks to another person. (The other person is an actor, who does not really receive any shocks.) The experimenter tells the subject to continue stepping up the shock level, even to the point of reaching the level marked "Danger: Severe Shock." The purpose of the experiment is to see how far the naive subject will proceed before he refuses to comply with the experimenter's instructions. Behavior prior to this rupture is considered "obedience" in that the subject does what the experimenter tells him to do. The point of rupture is the act of disobedience. Once the basic procedure is established, it becomes possible to vary conditions of the experiment, to learn under what circumstances obedience to authority is most probable, and under what conditions defiance is brought to the fore (Milgram, in press).

The results of the experiment (Milgram, 1963) showed, first, that it is more difficult for many people to defy the experimenter's authority than was generally supposed. A substantial number of subjects go through to the end of the shock board. The second finding is that the situation often places a person in considerable conflict. In the course of the experiment, subjects fidget, sweat, and sometimes break out into nervous fits of laughter. On the one hand, subjects want to aid the experimenter; and on the other hand, they do not want to shock the learner. The conflict is expressed in nervous reactions.

From *American Psychologist*, vol. 19, 1964, pp. 848–852. Copyright © 1964 by Alexandra Milgram. Reprinted by permission.

In a recent issue of *American Psychologist,* Diana Baumrind (1964) raised a number of questions concerning the obedience report. Baumrind expressed concern for the welfare of subjects who served in the experiment, and wondered whether adequate measures were taken to protect the participants. She also questioned the adequacy of the experimental design.

Patently, "Behavioral Study of Obedience" did not contain all the information needed for an assessment of the experiment. But . . . this was only one of a series of reports on the experimental program, and Baumrind's article was deficient in information that could have been obtained easily. . . .

At the outset, Baumrind confuses the unanticipated outcome of an experiment with its basic procedure. She writes, for example, as if the production of stress in our subjects was an intended and deliberate effect of the experimental manipulation. There are many laboratory procedures specifically designed to create stress (Lazarus, 1964), but the obedience paradigm was not one of them. The extreme tension induced in some subjects was unexpected. Before conducting the experiment, the procedures were discussed with many colleagues, and none anticipated the reactions that subsequently took place. Foreknowledge of results can never be the invariable accompaniment of an experimental probe. Understanding grows because we examine situations in which the end is unknown. An investigator unwilling to accept this degree of risk must give up the idea of scientific inquiry.

Moreover, there was every reason to expect, prior to actual experimentation, that subjects would refuse to follow the experimenter's instructions beyond the point where the victim protested; many colleagues and psychiatrists were questioned on this point, and they virtually all felt this would be the case. Indeed, to initiate an experiment in which the critical measure hangs on disobedience, one must start with a belief in certain spontaneous resources in men that enable them to overcome pressure from authority.

It is true that after a reasonable number of subjects had been exposed to the procedures, it became evident that some would go to the end of the shock board, and some would experience stress. That point, it seems to me, is the first legitimate juncture at which one could even start to wonder whether or not to abandon the study. But momentary excitement is not the same as harm. As the experiment progressed there was no indication of injurious effects in the subjects; and as the subjects themselves strongly endorsed the experiment, the judgment I made was to continue the investigation.

Is not Baumrind's criticism based as much on the unanticipated findings as on the method? The findings were that some subjects performed in what appeared to be a shockingly immoral way. If, instead, every one of the subjects had broken off at "slight shock," or at the first sign of the learner's discomfort, the results would have been pleasant, and reassuring, and who would protest?

Procedures and Benefits

A most important aspect of the procedure occurred at the end of the experimental session. A careful post-experimental treatment was administered to all subjects. The exact content of the dehoax varied from condition to condition and with increasing experience on our part. At the very least all subjects were told that the victim had not received dangerous electric shocks. Each subject had a friendly reconciliation with the unharmed victim, and an extended discussion with the experimenter. The experiment was explained to the defiant subjects in a way that supported their decision to disobey the experimenter. Obedient subjects were assured of the fact that their behavior was entirely normal and that their feelings of conflict or tension were shared by other participants. Subjects were told that they would receive a comprehensive report at the conclusion of the experimental series. In some instances, additional detailed and lengthy discussions of the experiments were also carried out with individual subjects.

When the experimental series was complete, subjects received a written report which presented details of the experimental procedure and results. Again their own part in the experiments was treated in a dignified way and their behavior in the experiment respected. All subjects received a follow-up questionnaire regarding their participation in the research, which again allowed expression of thoughts and feelings about their behavior.

The replies to the questionnaire confirmed my impression that participants felt positively toward the experiment. In its quantitative aspect (see Table 1), 84% of the subjects stated they were glad to have been in the experiment; 15% indicated neutral feelings, and 1.3% indicated negative feelings. To be sure, such findings are to be interpreted cautiously, but they cannot be disregarded.

Further, four-fifths of the subjects felt that more experiments of this sort should be carried out, and 74% indicated that they had learned something of personal importance as a result of being in the study. . . .

The debriefing and assessment procedures were carried out as a matter of course, and were not stimulated by any observation of special risk in the experimental procedure. In my judgment, at no point were subjects exposed to danger and at no point did they run the risk of injurious effects resulting from participation. If it had been otherwise, the experiment would have been terminated at once.

Table 1

Excerpt From Questionnaire Used in a Follow-up Study of the Obedience Research

Now that I have read the report and all things considered . . .	Defiant	Obedient	All
1. I am very glad to have been in the experiment	40.0%	47.8%	43.5%
2. I am glad to have been in the experiment	43.8%	35.7%	40.2%
3. I am neither sorry nor glad to have been in the experiment	15.3%	14.8%	15.1%
4. I am sorry to have been in the experiment	0.8%	0.7%	0.8%
5. I am very sorry to have been in the experiment	0.0%	1.0%	0.5%

Note: Ninety-two percent of the subjects returned the questionnaire. The characteristics of the nonrespondents were checked against the respondents. They differed from the respondents only with regard to age; younger people were overrepresented in the nonresponding group.

Baumrind states that, after he has performed in the experiment, the subject cannot justify his behavior and must bear the full brunt of his actions. By and large it does not work this way. The same mechanisms that allow the subject to perform the act, to obey rather than to defy the experimenter, transcend the moment of performance and continue to justify his behavior for him. The same viewpoint the subject takes while performing the actions is the viewpoint from which he later sees his behavior, that is, the perspective of "carrying out the task assigned by the person in authority."

Because the idea of shocking the victim is repugnant, there is a tendency among those who hear of the design to say "people will not do it." When the results are made known, this attitude is expressed as "if they do it they will not be able to live with themselves afterward." These two forms of denying the experimental findings are equally inappropriate misreadings of the facts of human social behavior. Many subjects do, indeed, obey to the end, and there is no indication of injurious effects.

The absence of injury is a minimal condition of experimentation; there can be, however, an important positive side to participation. Baumrind suggests that subjects derived no benefit from being in the obedience study, but this is false. By their statements and actions, subjects indicated that they had learned a good deal, and many felt gratified to have taken part in scientific research they considered to be of significance. A year after his participation one subject wrote:

> This experiment has strengthened my belief that man should avoid harm to his fellow man even at the risk of violating authority.

Another stated:

> To me, the experiment pointed up . . . the extent to which each individual should have or discover firm ground on which to base his decisions, no matter how trivial they appear to be. I think people should think more deeply about themselves and their relation to their world and to other people. If this experiment serves to jar people out of complacency, it will have served its end.

These statements are illustrative of a broad array of appreciative and insightful comments by those who participated.

The 5-page report sent to each subject on the completion of the experimental series was specifically designed to enhance the value of his experience. It laid out the broad conception of the experimental program as well as the logic of its design. It described the results of a dozen of the experiments, discussed the causes of tension, and attempted to indicate the possible significance of the experiment. Subjects responded enthusiastically; many indicated a desire to be in further experimental research. This report was sent to all subjects several years ago. The care with which it was prepared does not support Baumrind's assertion that the experimenter was indifferent to the value subjects derived from their participation.

Baumrind's fear is that participants will be alienated from psychological experiments because of the intensity of experience associated with laboratory procedures. My own observation is that subjects more commonly respond with distaste to the "empty" laboratory hour, in which cardboard procedures are employed, and the only possible feeling upon emerging from the laboratory is that one has wasted time in a patently trivial and useless exercise.

The subjects in the obedience experiment, on the whole, felt quite differently about their participation. They viewed the experience as an opportunity to learn something of importance about themselves, and more generally, about the conditions of human action.

A year after the experimental program was completed, I initiated an additional follow-up study. In this connection an impartial medical examiner, experienced in outpatient treatment, interviewed 40 experimental subjects. The examining psychiatrist focused on those subjects he felt would be most likely to have suffered consequences from participation. His aim was to identify possible injurious effects resulting from the experiment. He concluded that, although extreme stress had been experienced by several subjects,

> none was found by this interviewer to show signs of having been harmed by his experience. . . . Each subject seemed to handle his task [in the experiment] in a manner consistent with well established patterns of behavior. No evidence was found of any traumatic reactions.

Such evidence ought to be weighed before judging the experiment.

Other Issues

Baumrind's discussion is not limited to the treatment of subjects, but diffuses to a generalized rejection of the work.

Baumrind feels that obedience cannot be meaningfully studied in a laboratory setting: The reason she offers is that "The dependent, obedient attitude assumed by most subjects in the experimental setting is appropriate to that situation [p. 421]." Here, Baumrind has cited the very best reason for examining obedience in this setting, namely that it possesses "ecological validity." Here is one social context in which compliance occurs regularly. Military and job situations are also particularly meaningful settings for the study of obedience precisely because obedience is natural and appropriate to these contexts. I reject Baumrind's argument that the observed obedience does not count because it occurred where it is appropriate. That is precisely why it *does* count. A soldier's obedience is no less meaningful because it occurs in a pertinent military context. A subject's obedience is no less problematical because it occurs within a social institution called the psychological experiment.

Baumrind writes: "The game is defined by the experimenter and he makes the rules [p. 421]." It is true that for disobedience to occur the framework of the experiment must be shattered. That, indeed, is the point of the design. That is why obedience and disobedience are genuine issues for the subject. *He must really assert himself as a person against a legitimate authority.*

Further, Baumrind wants us to believe that outside the laboratory we could not find a comparably high expression of obedience. Yet, the fact that ordinary citizens are recruited to military service and, on command, perform far harsher acts against people is beyond dispute. Few of them know or are concerned with the complex policy issues underlying martial action; fewer still become conscientious objectors. Good soldiers do as they are told, and on both sides of the battle line. However, a debate on whether a higher level of obedience is represented by *(a)* killing men in the service of one's country, or *(b)* merely shocking them in the service of Yale science, is largely unprofitable. The real question is: What are the forces underlying obedient action?

Another question raised by Baumrind concerns the degree of parallel between obedience in the laboratory and in Nazi Germany. Obviously, there are enormous differences: Consider the disparity in time scale. The laboratory experiment takes an hour; the Nazi calamity unfolded in the space of a decade. There is a great deal that needs to be said on this issue, and only a few points can be touched on here.

1. In arguing this matter, Baumrind mistakes the background metaphor for the precise subject matter of investigation. The German event was cited to point up a serious problem in the human situation: the potentially destructive effect of obedience. But the best way to tackle the problem of obedience, from a scientific standpoint, is in no way restricted by "what happened exactly" in Germany. What happened exactly can *never* be duplicated in the laboratory or anywhere else. The real task is to learn more about the general problem of destructive obedience using a workable approach. Hopefully, such inquiry will stimulate insights and yield general propositions that can be applied to a wide variety of situations.
2. One may ask in a general way: How does a man behave when he is told by a legitimate authority to act against a third individual? In trying to find an answer to this question, the laboratory situation is one useful starting point—and for the very reason stated by Baumrind—namely, the experimenter does constitute a genuine authority for the subject. The fact that trust and dependence on the experimenter are maintained, despite the extraordinary harshness he displays toward the victim, is itself a remarkable phenomenon.
3. In the laboratory, through a set of rather simple manipulations, ordinary persons no longer perceived themselves as a responsible part of the causal chain leading to action against a person. The means through which responsibility is cast off, and individuals become thoughtless agents of action, is of general import. Other processes were revealed that indicate that the experiments will help us to understand why men obey. That understanding will come, of course, by examining the full account of experimental work and not alone the brief report in which the procedure and demonstrational results were exposed.

At root, Baumrind senses that it is not proper to test obedience in this situation, because she construes it as one in which there is no reasonable alternative to obedience. In adopting this view, she has lost sight of this fact: A substantial proportion of subjects do disobey. By their example, disobedience is shown to be a genuine possibility, one that is in no sense ruled out by the general structure of the experimental situation.

Baumrind is uncomfortable with the high level of obedience obtained in the first experiment. In the condition she focused on, 65% of the subjects obeyed to the end. However, her sentiment does not take into account that within the general framework of the psychological experiment obedience varied enormously from one condition to the next. In some variations, 90% of the subjects *dis*obeyed. It seems to be *not* only the fact of an experiment, but the particular structure of elements within the experimental situation that accounts for rates of obedience and disobedience. And these elements were varied systematically in the program of research.

A concern with human dignity is based on a respect for a man's potential to act morally. Baumrind feels that the experimenter *made* the subject shock the victim. This conception is alien to my view. The experimenter tells the subject to do something. But between the command and the outcome there is a paramount force, the acting person who may obey or disobey. I started with the belief that every person who came to the laboratory was free to accept or to reject the dictates of authority. This view sustains a conception of human dignity insofar as it sees in each man a capacity for *choosing* his own behavior. And as it turned out, many subjects did, indeed, choose to reject the experimenter's commands, providing a powerful affirmation of human ideals.

Baumrind also criticizes the experiment on the grounds that "it could easily effect an alteration in the subject's . . . ability to trust adult authorities in the future [p. 422]." But I do not think she can have it both ways. On the one hand, she argues the experimental situation is so special that it has no generality; on the other hand, she states it has such generalizing potential that it will cause subjects to distrust all authority. But the experimenter is not just any authority: He is an authority who tells the subject to act harshly and inhumanely against another man. I would consider it of the highest value if participation in the experiment could, indeed, inculcate a skepticism of this kind of authority. Here, perhaps, a difference in philosophy emerges most clearly. Baumrind sees the subject as a passive creature, completely controlled by the experimenter. I started from a different viewpoint. A person who comes to the laboratory is an active, choosing adult, capable of accepting or rejecting the prescriptions for action addressed to him. Baumrind sees the effect of the experiment as undermining the subject's trust of authority. I see it as a potentially valuable experience insofar as it makes people aware of the problem of indiscriminate submission to authority.

Conclusion

My feeling is that viewed in the total context of values served by the experiment, approximately the right course was followed. In review, the facts are these: *(a)* At the outset, there was the problem of studying obedience by means of a simple experimental procedure. The results could not be foreseen before the experiment was carried out. *(b)* Although the experiment generated momentary stress in some subjects, this stress dissipated quickly and was not injurious. *(c)* Dehoax and follow-up procedures were carried out to insure the subjects' well-being. *(d)* These procedures were assessed through questionnaire and psychiatric studies and were found to be effective. *(e)* Additional steps were taken to enhance the value of the laboratory experience for participants, for example, submitting to each subject a careful report on the experimental program. *(f)* The subjects themselves strongly endorse the experiment, and indicate satisfaction at having participated.

If there is a moral to be learned from the obedience study, it is that every man must be responsible for his own actions. This author accepts full responsibility for the design and execution of the study. Some people may feel it should not have been done. I disagree and accept the burden of their judgment.

Baumrind's judgment, someone has said, not only represents a personal conviction, but also reflects a cleavage in American psychology between those whose primary concern is with *helping* people and those who are interested mainly in *learning* about people. I see little value in perpetuating divisive forces in psychology when there is so much to learn from every side. A schism may exist, but it does not correspond to the true ideals of the discipline. The psychologist intent on healing knows that his power to help rests on knowledge; he is aware that a scientific grasp of all aspects of life is essential for his work, and is in itself a worthy human aspiration. At the same time, the laboratory psychologist senses his work will lead to human betterment, not only because enlightenment is more dignified than ignorance, but because new knowledge is pregnant with humane consequences.

References

Baumrind, D. Some thoughts on ethics of research: After reading Milgram's "Behavioral study of obedience." *Amer. Psychologist,* 1964, **19**, 421–423.

Lazarus, R. A laboratory approach to the dynamics of psychological stress. *Amer. Psychologist,* 1964, **19**, 400–411.

Milgram, S. Behavioral study of obedience. *J. Abnorm. Soc. Psychol.,* 1963, **67**, 371–378.

Milgram, S. Some conditions of obedience and disobedience to authority. *Hum. Relat.,* in press.

CHALLENGE QUESTIONS

Classic Dialogue:
Was Stanley Milgram's Study of
Obedience Unethical?

1. Investigate the role that your college's institutional review board (see the introduction to this issue) plays in protecting subjects from undue harm.
2. Sometimes people make the wrong decisions and end up hurting other people. Apart from utilizing institutional review boards, what can researchers do to avoid making wrong decisions regarding potentially harmful studies?
3. Imagine that you have just participated in Milgram's study. How would you feel about the deception that occurred? Is it ever appropriate to deceive participants in research studies? If so, when? If not, why not?
4. Both Baumrind and Milgram might agree that there are cases in which some low-level tension for research participants is allowable. Under what conditions might it be acceptable to allow participants to experience some distress? Under what conditions is it inappropriate to subject participants to any distress?
5. Baumrind raises the issue of trust. Do you think the participants in the Milgram study lost trust in psychological researchers or authority figures in general? Why, or why not?
6. If you were on an ethics review board and the Milgram study was brought before you, would you allow Milgram to run the study? Support your answer.

Internet References . . .

The Seville Statement on Violence

The United Nations Educational, Scientific and Cultural Organization (UNESCO) drafted a statement regarding violence in 1986 known as the Seville Statement on Violence. This link provides that statement.

```
http://portal.unesco.org/education/en/ev.php-
URL_ID=3247&URL_DO=DO_TOPIC&URL_SECTION=201.html
```

The Differences Between Men and Women

This site provides a statement prepared by the Relationship Institute regarding the differences between men and women.

```
http://www.relationship-institute.com/
freearticles_detail.cfm?article_ID=151
```

The National Center for Learning Disabilities

This site provides information, research, methods, and forums for parents and educators of children with learning disabilities.

```
www.ncld.org
```

Biological Issues

No behavioral or mental activity can occur without one's body. Many psychologists view our bodies and our biological processes as fundamental to all human activities, including emotion, perception, communication, and mental health. However, does this fundamental role of the body mean that it is the sole cause of our behaviors and our minds? Do biological differences such as gender determine behavioral differences like stereotypical male and female communication styles? Does the development of our bodies influence our most important emotions and behaviors such as love, hate, and the committing of violence? Do problems in social, emotional, or intellectual development necessarily arise from abnormal physical development? As evidenced by the growing field of neuroscience and its influence in the world of psychology, many experts believe that "matter is all that matters." That is, they believe that by studying the physical body we can learn everything there is to know about the mind, behaviors, thoughts, and emotions, because everything arises out of biology. After reading the following articles, what do you think?

- Are Humans Naturally Violent?
- Do Women and Men Communicate Differently?
- Do Brain Deficiencies Determine Learning Disabilities?

ISSUE 4

Are Humans Naturally Violent?

YES: Michael L. Wilson and Richard W. Wrangham, from "Intergroup Relations in Chimpanzees," *Annual Review of Anthropology* (2003)

NO: Robert W. Sussman, from "Are Humans Inherently Violent?" in Ruth Osterweis Selig, Marilyn R. London, P. Ann Kaupp, and eds., *Anthropology Explored: The Best of Smithsonian AnthroNotes, 2nd ed.* (Smithsonian Books, 2004)

ISSUE SUMMARY

YES: Field researcher Michael L. Wilson and biological anthropologist Richard Wrangham argue that humans are innately violent because their closest nonhuman relatives—chimpanzees—are themselves violent and aggressive.

NO: Biological anthropologist Robert W. Sussman asserts that neither humans nor chimpanzees are inherently violent, but culture and upbringing are significantly involved in the violence evident in both species.

Sometimes human history seems to be little more than the record of one violent event after another. Even ancient texts and religious scripture often describe heinous acts of violence. Where does such violence come from? How can it be so seemingly universal from era to era and culture to culture? One popular answer is that this violence is natural—that it is in our very nature to be violent. Such an answer is appealing because it accounts for so much of what we seem to know about violence. For instance, it seems to explain the apparent universality of violence across varied time periods and varied peoples. It also appears to account for the continuing violence in today's presumably more civil times.

This seemingly plausible theory about violence leads to many important questions. If it is true, as this theory seems to imply, that civilization and culture matter little, are we doomed to commit violence always? Is our own free will completely unable to prevent such violence, even in our personal relationships? Is there nothing that professionals can do to prevent or decrease senseless violence? Psychologists are especially interested in these questions because they are interested in the interventions, both individual and societal, that might be effective in curbing violence. Psychologists know that if we can answer the question of the ultimate origin of human violence, this might be helpful in solving the many problems related to violence today—in our high schools, our families, and our cities.

Michael Wilson and Richard Wrangham, the authors of the first selection, clearly believe that human beings are naturally violent. They argue that new descriptions of intergroup aggression among chimpanzees provide a stronger case for the theory that human violence is indeed a result of our evolutionary past. The authors note the many parallels between humans and our nearest evolutionary relatives—chimpanzees. One such parallel is that chimpanzees and hunter-gatherers share a tendency to respond aggressively in encounters with members of other social groups. Although many aspects of human intergroup aggression differ from that of chimpanzees, Wilson and Wrangham assert that their anthropological data suggest many common principles of evolved psychological tendencies.

In the second selection, Robert W. Sussman reviews many of these so-called universal principles of sociobiology and considers them to be weak. For example, most modern gatherer-hunters and apes are remarkably non-aggressive. Indeed, some were more often the hunted than the hunters. As another example, female pygmy chimpanzees typically choose peace, form alliances, and mate with less aggressive males. According to Sussman, a good look at the killing among chimpanzees shows how rarely this occurs, rather than showing how often. Sussman also points to the wise variations in the quantities and qualities of violence in different human cultures and individuals. He concludes that if we have the plasticity to change through learning and culture, then socialization practices and cultural histories determine our violence, not our nature. Finally, Sussman addresses some of Wilson and Wrangham's more recent work and provides responses to their arguments.

POINT	COUNTERPOINT
• Violence and war are defining marks of humanity.	• The evidence for this universal claim is weak.
• Chimpanzees generally form male-bonded communities and defend their territories with aggression and violence.	• In the communities monitored by ethologist Jane Goodall, only 10 percent were classified as violent, and many attacks resulted in no discernable injury.
• Humans were considered the only violent species until chimpanzees were observed killing chimpanzees.	• Looking carefully at the data reveals that there are many explanations for these killings other than natural violence.
• A behavioral biological approach provides more focused predictions for when aggression is likely to occur and how aggression can be reduced.	• If we have the capacity to change by learning from example, then our behavior is determined by socialization practices and not by our nature.

YES

**Michael L. Wilson and
Richard W. Wrangham**

Intergroup Relations
in Chimpanzees

Introduction

A widespread assumption in the 1960s and 1970s was that warfare resulted from features unique to the human lineage, such as weapons or the dense populations created by agriculture. The observation of lethal intergroup attacks in wild chimpanzees challenged this view. Numerous comparisons between chimpanzee aggression and human warfare followed these first observations. Shared traits, such as the cooperation of males to defend group resources and the occurrence of lethal intergroup attacks, suggested that key features of human warfare evolved either in the common ancestor of humans and chimpanzees or independently in the two lineages for similar reasons.

Until recently, however, these comparisons rested on a narrow foundation. Most of the detailed information on intergroup aggression came from two sites in Tanzania, Gombe and Mahale, raising the possibility that patterns of intergroup aggression observed there resulted from some unusual feature of those sites, such as artificial feeding by observers.

In recent years, however, a new generation of studies has advanced our understanding of intergroup relations. New descriptions of intergroup aggression are emerging from unprovisioned sites, including Taï National Park, Côte d'Ivoire, Kibale National Park, Uganda, and Budongo Forest Reserve, Uganda. New technologies and methods have enabled researchers to ask new questions and answer previously unanswerable old questions. Entry of data into increasingly powerful computer systems is enabling researchers to examine long-term ranging and grouping data in unprecedented detail. Genetic analysis has enabled researchers to test the proportion of infants born from intergroup mating. Field experiments have made possible controlled tests of hypotheses that are difficult to test using only observational data.

In this chapter we review the current information on chimpanzee intergroup relations and discuss how results from recent studies affect prior generalizations. First, we describe the emerging consensus regarding chimpanzee social structure, territory characteristics, and intergroup interactions. Then we examine how recent studies have clarified questions about

From *Annual Review of Anthropology*, vol. 32, 2003, pp. 363–365, 382–387. Copyright © 2003 by Annual Reviews, Inc. Reprinted by permission. References omitted.

the functional goals and proximate mechanisms underlying intergroup aggression. Finally, we discuss the relevance of these findings to intergroup aggression in humans.

The comparisons of chimpanzee and human intergroup aggression have attracted three main objections. First, critics claim that the data on intergroup aggression are too few to support claims that chimpanzees are inherently violent. Second, some argue that intergroup aggression results from human influence, especially provisioning chimpanzees with artificial food. Third, it has been suggested that chimpanzee violence is irrelevant to understanding human behavior. According to this view, we already know that humans can be violent and that humans can be peaceful as well; what matters for humans are environmental factors such as culture rather than biology.

As we discuss below, recent studies provide strong evidence against these criticisms. First, evidence from classic and more recent studies shows that intergroup aggression, including lethal attacks, is a pervasive feature of chimpanzee societies. Second, the occurrence of intergroup aggression at unprovisioned sites allows us to reject the hypothesis that intergroup aggression and other patterns of social behavior were the result of provisioning. Instead, chimpanzee intergroup aggression is best explained by principles of behavioral biology that apply to other species such as lions, wolves, and hyenas. Third, the argument that, because humans can be both warlike and peaceful, war is not the result of biology or instinct is aimed at an outdated view of biology. Animals, especially large-brained animals such as primates, are no longer viewed as response-stimulus robots but rather as strategic actors who make decisions based on assessments of costs and benefits. Recent studies have improved our understanding of the costs and benefits underlying intergroup aggression for chimpanzees. These studies illustrate the promise for obtaining a better understanding of human intergroup aggression using principles generated by behavioral biology. . . .

Relevance to Humans

The first four decades of research on wild chimpanzees have produced evidence of important similarities between aspects of chimpanzee and human intergroup aggression. Comparisons between the two species are made difficult, admittedly, by many factors. In chimpanzees, the description of intergroup aggression is still in an early phase. In humans, quantitative data from the most relevant groups (hunter gatherers) are so rare that different authors reach widely differing conclusions about the frequency of aggression.

Yet despite these problems, it is clear that intergroup aggression has occurred among many, possibly all, hunter-gatherer populations and follows a rather uniform pattern. From the most northern to the most southern latitudes, the most common pattern of intergroup aggression was for a party of men from one group to launch a surprise attack in circumstances in which the attackers were unlikely to be harmed. Attacks were sometimes unsuccessful but were, at other times, responsible for the deaths of one or many victims. Women and girls were sometimes captured.

One factor that complicates efforts to compare patterns of intergroup aggression in humans and chimpanzees is that in chimpanzees the only large social group is the community, whereas no precise equivalent of the chimpanzee community exists for humans. Instead, human group membership always exists on several levels: residential group, clan, tribe, nation, and so on. The existence of these multiple types of group complicates the comparison of aggressive patterns between chimpanzees and humans because it means that aggression between groups can occur at many more levels among humans than among chimpanzees. At one extreme, aggression can be found between residential groups that both belong to the same linguistic, cultural, and tribal unit, within which individuals can move and intermarry [internal warfare]. At the other extreme, it can occur between culturally distinct groups having different languages (or dialects) and little or no tendency for intermarriage or friendly contact (external warfare).

Despite this variation, a useful comparison can be made between chimpanzees and humans by identifying the level at which relations are essentially anarchic, i.e., characterized by the lack of any central or cultural authority. Human societies normally feature such a level. The Ache, for example, lived in bands of 10 to 70 individuals who, in turn, formed groups of up to 550. Within these regional groups, the only form of culturally sanctioned violence among men was the club fight. By contrast, "anyone not in the group, including other Ache, could be shot on sight."

Among foraging societies, such regional groups frequently included around 500 individuals. Both the size and internal structure of such groups varied extensively, however, in relation to ecological and cultural factors, as indicated by the wide variety of terms used to describe them (e.g., dialect group, maximum band, tribe).

Whatever the name used, this level of grouping suggests a similarity to the chimpanzee community because aggressive interactions at this level are not regulated by the predictable intervention of allies. This essential similarity suggests that shared principles may help explain the occasionally intense escalation of interactions between such groups. But of course the similarity gives way to major differences in scale and organization, given that humans can expand their regional groupings all the way to nation-states containing hundreds of millions of individuals living in complex networks.

Chimpanzees and hunter gatherers, we conclude, share a tendency to respond aggressively in encounters with members of other social groups; to avoid intensely aggressive confrontations in battle line (typically, by retreating); and to seek, or take advantage of, opportunities to use imbalances of power for males to kill members of neighboring groups.

These similarities have been explained in parallel ways in the two species, using concepts from evolutionary ecology. The essential notion is that natural selection has favored specific types of motivational systems. In particular, motivations have been favored that have tended, over evolutionary time, to give individuals access to the resources needed for reproduction.

The motivations that drive intergroup killing among chimpanzees and humans, by this logic, were selected in the context of territorial competition because reproduction is limited by resources, and resources are limited by territory size. Therefore, it pays for groups to achieve dominance over neighboring groups so that they can enlarge their territories. To achieve dominance, it is necessary to have greater fighting power than the neighbors. This means that whenever the costs are sufficiently low it pays to kill or damage individuals from neighboring groups. Thus, intergroup killing is viewed as derived from a tendency to strive for status. According to this view, these several aspects of human intergroup aggression do not appear exceptional compared to other animals.

Many other aspects of human intergroup aggression, however, differ extensively from chimpanzees, such as the ability of residential groups to form alliances, the possibilities for expressing formal peace relations, the capacity for symbolic domination [through cannibalism, for example], the ability to kill large numbers at a time, and the integration of intergroup relations with ideology. Such differences suggest to some critics that human warfare cannot usefully be compared to chimpanzee aggression. No ultimate explanation has yet been offered, however, as an alternative to the hypothesis that territorial competition for resources for reproduction favors a drive for intergroup dominance.

Finally, it is important not to confuse levels of explanation. The comparison of chimpanzees and humans is useful in suggesting common principles generating evolved psychological tendencies. But it is not useful in directly accounting for intraspecific variation, which is the central concern of the anthropology of war. As with chimpanzees and other species, however, models based on evolutionary principles (such as behavioral ecology) provide powerful tools for understanding intraspecific variation.

Lethal Raiding in *Pan* and *Homo:* Homology Or Homoplasy?

It is currently unclear whether the patterns of intergroup aggression seen in humans and chimpanzees result from homology (shared evolutionary history) or homoplasy (convergent evolution). Various lines of evidence suggest that our common ancestor with chimpanzees was very much like a chimpanzee. In the five to seven million years that followed the divergence of the lines leading to *Pan* and *Homo*, however, the human lineage developed into a bushy tree. A variety of woodland apes evolved, including *Ardipithecus, Australopithecus,* and *Paranthropus.* These creatures do not closely resemble any living species, and we can make only educated guesses about their feeding ecology and social structure. Considerable behavioral diversity exists among extant apes; woodland apes probably varied as well, with societies that evolved to meet different ecological challenges. We know that social behavior can change quickly over evolutionary time. The two extant species of *Pan*, chimpanzees and bonobos, differ considerably in their intergroup relations despite generally similar feeding ecology, morphology, and recent date of divergence. Fossils can provide only a limited amount of information about social behavior. For example, lions and tigers differ strikingly in their social behavior, despite being closely related enough to interbreed. If we had only fossils of lions and tigers, it is hard to imagine that we would be able to infer cooperative territory defense for the one and solitary seclusion for the other.

The relevance of chimpanzee violence to the evolution of human warfare does not depend on the possibility that both species inherited this trait from a common ancestor. Instead, chimpanzees provide a valuable referential model. Before observers reported accounts of chimpanzee intergroup aggression, anthropologists assumed that human warfare resulted from some factor unique to the human lineage, such as social stratification, horticulture, high population density, or the use of tools as weapons. The observation of warlike behavior in chimpanzees demonstrated that none of these factors was required. A similar lesson could be drawn from the warlike behavior of social carnivores, such as lions, wolves, and spotted hyenas. The relevance of carnivore behavior to human evolution might be discounted, however, given that carnivores possess many specialized traits; intergroup killing in carnivores could be a byproduct of morphological and behavioral evolution for cooperative hunting. The benefit of using chimpanzees as a referential model is that, as our evolutionary cousins, they give us a more realistic picture of traits our ancestors may have possessed.

The benefits and limitations of using chimpanzee data to understand the evolution of human warfare are similar to those presented by data on another trait shared by chimpanzees and humans: hunting. In both species, hunting is conducted mainly by males, who often hunt in groups. As Mitani & Watts point out, chimpanzee hunting differs in various ways from human hunting. For example, chimpanzees pursue prey through the trees and kill with their hands and teeth, whereas humans pursue prey on the ground and kill with weapons. Chimpanzees hunt opportunistically, and the degree of cooperation involved remains the subject of debate, whereas human hunting clearly involves planning and cooperation. We don't know if *"Pan prior"* hunted, and the extent to which the various early woodland apes hunted or scavenged continues to be debated. Nevertheless, much like the case with intergroup aggression, data from chimpanzees (and other primates, such as baboons) challenged previous views that humans were the only hunting primate, and ongoing studies continue to provide valuable insight for guiding our thinking about human evolution.

Conclusion

Recent studies have shown that the patterns of intergroup aggression reported from Gombe and Mahale in the 1970s are, in many ways, typical of chimpanzees. Chimpanzees at all long-term study sites defend group territories, and chimpanzees at four out of five sites have conducted lethal attacks on members of neighboring groups. Studies of unprovisioned communities demonstrate that these patterns of intergroup aggression are not the result of provisioning. Indeed, the Ngogo community, which Power considered a prime example of peaceful intergroup relations, turns out to have an exceptionally high rate of intergroup violence.

Instead of being a maladaptive aberration, chimpanzee intergroup aggression appears to be typical of aggression in other wild animals in that it tends to provide fitness benefits for the aggressors. Two sets of genetic paternity tests demonstrate that males successfully kept outside males from mating with females in their community, a result supported by consistent behavioral observations. Females reproduced more quickly when territories were larger, indicating that both females and males benefit from defense and acquisition of feeding territory.

The chimpanzee studies suggest that our understanding of human intergroup aggression, particularly small-scale non-state violence, would benefit from more extensive testing of hypotheses generated by behavioral biology. The few studies that have focused on testing evolutionary principles have provoked hostile critiques. The hostility apparent in such critiques reflects a widespread concern that "biological" is equivalent to "fixed" or "unchangeable." Contemporary behavioral biology, however, views primate aggression as a strategic response to appropriate environmental conditions. Rather than viewing human aggression as inevitable, an approach rooted in behavioral biology would provide more focused predictions for when aggression is likely to occur and how aggression can be reduced.

Even among chimpanzees, rates of intergroup aggression vary considerably among sites and over time within sites. Understanding the factors responsible for that variation constitutes the next frontier in studies of chimpanzee intergroup relations. The range of variation may well prove greater than so far observed. For example, under appropriate conditions, captive chimpanzees can be induced to accept new adult males into their group, something not yet observed in the wild. Newly introduced males are predictably aggressive to one another, but appropriated management can lead to eventual acceptance.

Such observations indicate both that biology provides chimpanzees with clear dispositions (e.g., hostility toward stranger males) but also that even chimpanzees, under the right conditions, can learn to overcome such hostility. A fully developed behavioral biology of human intergroup aggression offers similar hope for understanding—and addressing—the roots of violence in our own species.

Robert W. Sussman

 **NO**

Are Humans Inherently Violent?

By challenging the authors of the book Demonic Males, *primatologist Robert Sussman asks us to look at our basic human nature and ask what we can learn about ourselves from other primates. The chapter poses other questions, such as how genetics and learning help explain human behavior, what role aggression plays in chimpanzee and human society, and whether humans and chimpanzees share certain biologically fixed behaviors.*

Are human beings forever doomed to be violent? Is aggression fixed within our genetic code, an inborn action pattern that threatens to destroy us? Or, as asked by Richard Wrangham and Dale Peterson in their recent book, *Demonic Males: Apes and the Origins of Human Violence*, can we get beyond our genes, beyond our essential "human nature"?

Wrangham and Peterson's belief in the importance of violence in the evolution and nature of humans is based on new primate research that they assert demonstrates the continuity of aggression from our great ape ancestors. The authors argue that twenty to twenty-five years ago most scholars believed human aggression was unique. Research at that time had shown great apes to be basically nonaggressive, gentle creatures. Furthermore, the separation of humans from our ape ancestors was thought to have occurred 15–20 million years ago (mya). Although Raymond Dart, Sherwood Washburn, Robert Ardrey, E. O. Wilson, and others had argued through much of the twentieth century that hunting, killing, and extreme aggressive behaviors were biological traits inherited from our earliest hominid hunting ancestors, many anthropologists still believed that patterns of aggression were environmentally determined and culturally learned behaviors, not inherited characteristics.

Demonic Males discusses new evidence that killer instincts are not unique to humans but rather are shared with our nearest relative, the common chimpanzee. The authors argue that it is this inherited propensity for killing that allows hominids and chimps to be such good hunters.

According to Wrangham and Peterson, the split between humans and the common chimpanzee was only 6–8 mya. Furthermore, humans may have split from the chimpanzee-bonobo line after gorillas, with bonobos (pygmy chimps) separating from chimps only 2.5 mya. Because chimpanzees may be the modern ancestor of all these forms, and because the earliest australopithecines were quite chimpanzee-like, Wrangham speculates (in a separate article) that "chimpanzees are a conservative species and an amazingly good model

From *Anthropology Explored: The Best of Smithsonian AnthroNotes, Second Edition,* April 2004, pp. 30–45. Copyright © 2004 by Robert W. Sussman. Reprinted by permission.

for the ancestor of hominids." If modern chimpanzees and modern humans share certain behavioral traits, these traits have "long evolutionary roots" and are likely to be fixed, biologically inherited parts of our basic human nature and not culturally determined.

Wrangham argues that chimpanzees are almost on the brink of humanness:

> Nut-smashing, root-eating, savannah-using chimpanzees, resembling our ancestors, and capable by the way of extensive bipedalism. Using ant-wands, and sandals, and bowls, meat-sharing, hunting cooperatively. Strange paradox . . . a species trembling on the verge of hominization, but so conservative that it has stayed on that edge. . . .

Since humans and chimpanzees share these violent urges, the implication is that human violence has long evolutionary roots. "We are apes of nature, cursed over six million years or more with a rare inheritance, a Dostoyevskyan demon. . . . The coincidence of demonic aggression in ourselves and our closest kin bespeaks its antiquity."

Intellectual Antecedents

From the beginning of Western thought, the theme of human depravity runs deep, related to the idea of humankind's fall from grace and the emergence of original sin. This view continues to pervade modern "scientific" interpretations of the evolution of human behavior. Recognition of the close evolutionary relationship between humans and apes, from the time of Darwin's *Descent of Man* on, has encouraged theories that look to modern apes for evidence of parallel behaviors reflecting this relationship.

By the early 1950s large numbers of australopithecine fossils and the discovery that the large-brained "fossil" ancestor from Piltdown, in England, was a fraud led to the realization that our earliest ancestors were more like apes than like modern humans. Accordingly, our earliest ancestors must have behaved much like other nonhuman primates. This, in turn, led to a great interest in using primate behavior to understand human evolution and the evolutionary basis of human nature. The subdiscipline of primatology was born.

Raymond Dart, discoverer of the first australopithecine fossil some thirty years earlier, was also developing a different view of our earliest ancestors. At first Dart believed that australopithecines were scavengers barely eking out an existence in the harsh savanna environment. But from the fragmented and damaged bones found with the australopithecines, together with dents and holes in these early hominid skulls, Dart eventually concluded that this species had used bone, tooth, and antler tools to kill, butcher, and eat their prey, as well as to kill one another. This hunting hypothesis "was linked from the beginning with a bleak, pessimistic view of human beings and their ancestors as instinctively bloodthirsty and savage." To Dart, the australopithecines were

> confirmed killers: carnivorous creatures that seized living quarries by violence, battered them to death, tore apart their broken bodies,

dismembered them limb from limb, slaking their ravenous thirst with the hot blood of victims and greedily devouring livid writhing flesh.

Cartmill, in a 1993 book, shows that this interpretation of early human morality is reminiscent of earlier Greek and Christian views. Dart's own 1953 treatise begins with a seventeenth-century quote from the Calvinist writer R. Baxter: "of all the beasts, the man-beast is the worst/to others and himself the cruellest foe."

Between 1961 and 1976 Dart's view was picked up and extensively popularized by the playwright Robert Ardrey (*The Territorial Imperative, African Genesis*). Ardrey believed it was the human competitive and killer instinct, acted out in warfare, that made humans what they are today: "It is war and the instinct for territory that has led to the great accomplishments of Western Man. Dreams may have inspired our love of freedom, but only war and weapons have made it ours."

Man the Hunter

In the 1968 volume *Man the Hunter*, Sherwood Washburn and Chet Lancaster presented a theory of the evolution of hunting, emphasizing that it is this behavior that shaped human nature and separated early humans from their primate relatives.

> To assert the biological unity of mankind is to affirm the importance of the hunting way of life. . . . However much conditions and customs may have varied locally, the main selection pressures that forged the species were the same. The biology, psychology and customs that separate us from the apes . . . we owe to the hunters of time past . . . for those who would understand the origins and nature of human behavior there is no choice but to try to understand "Man the Hunter."

Rather than amassing evidence from modern hunters and gatherers to prove their theory, Washburn and Lancaster use the nineteenth-century concept of cultural "survivals": behaviors that persist as evidence of an earlier time but are no longer useful in society.

> Men enjoy hunting and killing, and these activities are continued in sports even when they are no longer economically necessary. If a behavior is important to the survival of a species . . . then it must be both easily learned and pleasurable.

Man the Dancer

Using a similar logic for the survival of ancient "learned and pleasurable" behaviors, perhaps it could easily have been our propensity for dancing rather than our desire to hunt that can explain much of human behavior. After all, men and women love to dance; it is a behavior found in all cultures but has even less obvious function today than hunting. Our love of movement and dance might explain, for example, our propensity for face-to-face sex, and even the evolution of bipedalism and the movement of humans out of trees and onto the ground.

Could the first tool have been a stick to beat a dance drum, and the ancient Laetoli footprints evidence of two individuals going out to dance the "Afarensis shuffle"? Although it takes only two to tango, a variety of social interactions and systems might have been encouraged by the complex social dances known in human societies around the globe. I am joking, of course, but the evidence for man the dancer is just as good (or lacking) as is that for man the hunter or man the killer. . . .

Beyond Our Genes

Wrangham and Peterson's book *Demonic Males* goes beyond the assertion of human inborn aggression and propensity toward violence. The authors ask a critical question: Are we doomed to be violent forever because this pattern is fixed within our genetic code, or can we go beyond our past—get out of our genes, so to speak? The authors believe that we can look to the bonobo or pygmy chimpanzee as one potential savior, metaphorically speaking.

Bonobos, although even more closely related to the common chimpanzee than humans, have become a peace-loving, lovemaking alternative to chimpanzee-human violence. How did this happen? In chimpanzees and humans, females of the species select partners that are violent: "[W]hile men have evolved to be demonic males, it seems likely that women have evolved to prefer demonic males . . . as long as demonic males are the most successful reproducers, any female who mates with them is provided with sons who themselves will likely be good reproducers." However, among pygmy chimpanzees females form alliances and have chosen to mate with less aggressive males. So, after all, it is not violent males that have caused humans and chimpanzees to be their inborn, immoral, dehumanized selves; it is, rather, poor choices by human and chimpanzee females.

Like Dart, Washburn, and Wilson before them, Wrangham and Peterson believe that tendencies to killing and violence are inherited from our ancient relatives of the past. However, unlike these earlier theorists, Wrangham and Peterson argue this is not a trait unique to hominids, nor is it a by-product of hunting. In fact, it is just this violent nature and a natural "blood lust" that makes both humans and chimpanzees such good hunters. It is the bonobos that help the authors come to this conclusion. Because bonobos have lost the desire to kill, they also have lost the desire to hunt.

> [B]onobos tell us that the suppression of personal violence carried with it the suppression of predatory aggression. The strongest hypothesis at the moment is that bonobos came from a chimpanzee-like ancestor that hunted monkeys and hunted one another. As they evolved into bonobos, males lost their demonism, becoming less aggressive to each other. In doing so, they lost their lust for hunting monkeys too . . . Murder and hunting may be more closely tied together than we are used to thinking . . .

The Selfish Gene Theory

Like Ardrey, Wrangham and Peterson believe that blood lust ties killing and hunting tightly together, but in the latter's argument it is killing that drives hunting. This lust to kill is based upon the sociobiological tenet of the selfish gene. "The general principle that behavior evolves to serve selfish ends has been widely accepted; and the idea that humans might have been favored by natural selection to hate and to kill their enemies has become entirely, if tragically, reasonable."

The authors make two arguments that humans and chimpanzees share biologically fixed behaviors: (1) they are more closely related to each other than chimpanzees are to gorillas, and (2) chimpanzees are a good model for our earliest ancestor and retain conservative traits that should be shared by both.

The first of these statements is still hotly debated and, using various genetic evidence, the chimp-gorilla-human triage is so close that it is difficult to tell exact divergence time or pattern among the three. The second statement is just not true. Chimpanzees have been evolving for as long as humans and gorillas, and there is no reason to believe ancestral chimps were similar to present-day chimps. The fossil evidence for the last 5–8 million years is extremely sparse, and it is likely that many forms of apes have become extinct, just as have many hominids.

Furthermore, even if the chimpanzee were a good model for the ancestral hominid, this would not mean that humans would necessarily share specific behavioral traits. As even Wrangham and Peterson emphasize, chimps, gorillas, and bonobos all behave very differently in their social behavior and in their willingness to kill conspecifics.

Evidence Against "Demonic Males"

The proof of the "demonic male" theory must rest solely on the evidence that violence and killing in chimpanzees and in humans are behaviors that are similar in pattern; have ancient, shared evolutionary roots; and are inherited. Besides killing of conspecifics, Wrangham "includes infanticide, rape, and regular battering of females by males" as a part of this inherited legacy of violent behaviors shared by humans and chimpanzees.

Wrangham and Peterson state: "That chimpanzees and humans kill members of neighboring groups of their own species is . . . a startling exception to the normal rule for animals." "Fighting adults of almost all species normally stop at winning: They don't go on to kill." However, as Wrangham points out, there are exceptions, such as lions, wolves, and spotted hyenas, and I would add a number of other predators. In fact, most species do not have the weapons to kill one another as adults.

Just how common is conspecific killing in chimpanzees? This is where the real controversy may lie. Jane Goodall described the chimpanzee as a peaceful, nonaggressive species during the first twenty-four years of study at Gombe (1950–1974). During one year of concentrated study, Goodall observed 284 agonistic encounters; of these, 66 percent were due to competition for introduced bananas, and only 34 percent "could be regarded as attacks occurring in 'normal' aggressive contexts." Only 10 percent of the 284 attacks were classified as "violent," and "even attacks that appeared punishing to me often resulted in no discernable injury. . . . Other attacks consisted merely of brief pounding, hitting or rolling of the individual, after which the aggressor often touched or embraced the other immediately."

Chimpanzee aggression before 1974 was considered no different from patterns of aggression seen in many other primate species. In fact, Goodall explains in her 1986 monograph *The Chimpanzees of Gombe* that she uses data mainly from after 1975 because the earlier years present a "very different picture of the Gombe chimpanzees" as being "far more peaceable than humans." Other early naturalists' descriptions of chimpanzee behavior were consistent with those of Goodall and confirmed her observations. Even different communities were observed to come together with peaceful, ritualized displays of greeting.

Then, between 1974 and 1977, five adult males from one subgroup were attacked and disappeared from the area, presumably dead. Why after twenty-four years did the patterns of aggression change? Was it because the stronger group saw the weakness of the other and decided to improve their genetic fitness? But surely there were stronger and weaker animals and subgroups before this time. Perhaps we can look to Goodall's own perturbations for an answer. In 1965 Goodall began to provide "restrictive human-controlled" feeding. A few years later she realized that

> the constant feeding was having a marked effect on the behavior of the chimps. They were beginning to move about in large groups more often than they had ever done in the old days. Worst of all, the adult males were becoming increasingly aggressive. When we first offered the chimps bananas the males seldom fought over their food; . . . now . . . there was a great deal more fighting than ever before.

The possibility that human interference was a main cause of the unusual behavior of the Gombe chimps was the subject of an excellent but generally ignored book by Margaret Power. Wrangham and Peterson cite this book in a footnote, but as with many other controversies, they essentially ignore its findings, stating that chimpanzee violence might have been considered unnatural behavior if it weren't for the evidence of similar behavior occurring since 1977 and "elsewhere in Africa."

Further Evidence

What is this evidence from elsewhere in Africa? Wrangham and Peterson provide only four brief examples, none of which is very convincing:

1. Between 1979 and 1982, the Gombe group extended its range to the south, and conflict with a southern group, Kalande, was suspected. In 1982 a "raiding" party of males reached Goodall's camp. The authors state: "Some of these raids may have been lethal." However,

Goodall describes this "raid" as follows: One female "was chased by a Kalande male and mildly attacked. . . . Her four-year-old son . . . encountered a second male—but was only sniffed." Although Wrangham and Peterson imply that these encounters were similar to those between 1974 and 1977, no violence was actually witnessed. The authors also refer to the discovery of the dead body of Humphrey; what they do not mention is Humphrey's age, thirty-five, and that wild chimps rarely live past thirty-three years.

2. Six adult males from one community in the Japanese study site of Mahale disappeared one by one over the twelve-year period from 1970 to 1982. None of the animals was observed being attacked or killed, and one was sighted later roaming as a solitary male.

3. In another site in West Africa, Wrangham and Peterson report that Boesch and Boesch believe "that violent aggression among the chimpanzees is as important as it is in Gombe." However, in the paper referred to, the Boesches simply state that encounters by neighboring chimpanzee communities are more common in their site than in Gombe (one per month versus one every four months). There is no mention of violence during these encounters.

4. At a site that Wrangham began studying in 1984, an adult male was found dead in 1991. Wrangham states: "In the second week of August, Ruizoni was killed. No human saw the big fight." Wrangham gives us no indication of what has occurred at this site since 1991.

In fact, this is the total amount of evidence of warfare and male-male killing among chimpanzees after thirty-seven years of research. The data for infanticide and rape among chimpanzees are even less impressive. In fact, data are so sparse for these behaviors among chimps that Wrangham and Peterson are forced to use examples from the other great apes, gorillas and orangutans. However, just as for killing among chimpanzees, both the evidence and the interpretations are suspect and controversial.

Can We Escape Our Genes?

What if Wrangham and Peterson are correct and we and our chimp cousins are inherently sinners? Are we doomed to be violent forever because this pattern is fixed within our genetic code? After 5 million years of human evolution and 120,000 or so years of *Homo sapiens* existence, is there a way to rid ourselves of our inborn evils?

What does it do for us, then, to know the behavior of our closest relatives. Chimpanzees and bonobos are an extraordinary pair. One, I suggest shows us some of the worst aspects of our past and our present; the other shows an escape from it. . . . Denial of our demons won't make them go away. But even if we're driven to accepting the evidence of a grisly past, we're not forced into thinking it condemns us to an unchanged future.

In other words, we can learn how to behave by watching bonobos. But if we can change our inherited behavior so simply, why haven't we been able to do this before *Demonic Males* enlightened us? Surely there are variations in the amounts of violence in different human cultures and individuals. If we have the capacity and plasticity to change by learning from example, then our behavior is determined by socialization practices and by our cultural histories and not by our nature. This is true whether the examples come from benevolent bonobos or conscientious objectors.

Conclusion

The theory presented by Wrangham and Peterson, although it also includes chimpanzees as our murdering cousins, is very similar to "man the hunter" theories proposed in the past. It also does not differ greatly from earlier European and Christian beliefs about human ethics and morality. We are forced to ask: Are these theories generated by good scientific fact, or are they just "good to think" because they reflect, reinforce, and reiterate our traditional cultural beliefs, our morality, and our ethics? Is the theory generated by the data, or are the data manipulated to fit preconceived notions of human morality and ethics?

Since the data in support of these theories have been weak, and yet the stories created have been extremely similar, I am forced to believe that "man the hunter" is a myth, that humans are not necessarily prone to violence and aggression, but that this belief will continue to reappear in future writings on human nature. Meanwhile, primatologists must continue their field research, marshaling the actual evidence needed to answer many of the questions raised in Wrangham and Peterson's volume.

Update

Since I wrote my original article in 1998, Richard Wrangham has attempted to address some of the questions about and criticisms of the theories concerning innate aggression in humans and chimpanzees that he proposed in his earlier publication, *Demonic Males*. He now cites ten chimpanzee kills recorded on the basis of direct observations or fresh bodies and up to ten more suspicious disappearances. These occur at four different research sites that have been studied for a total of ninety years. He also reports that in four other sites, where chimpanzees have been studied for an additional eighty years, lethal violence has not been observed. More importantly, Wrangham further develops his theoretical argument, in particular using three major concepts to support his hypothesis that violent behavior is basic to both humans and chimpanzees. These three concepts are coalitionary killing, the imbalance-of-power hypothesis, and a dominance drive.

Wrangham believes that warfare in humans and violent, deadly attacks in chimpanzees are examples of a phenomenon he labels "coalitionary killing." Adult males in these species collaborate to kill or brutally wound other adults. Coalitionary killing generally is rare among animal species but is found in social insects and some social carnivores. Among primates it occurs only in chimpanzees and humans. "The ancient origin of warfare is supported by the rarity of coalitionary lethal violence toward adult conspecifics in other primates, and by evidence that . . . chimpanzees and humans share a common ancestor around 5–6 mya."

Second, Wrangham believes that the principal adaptive explanation linking coalitionary killing in chimpanzees and humans is what he refers to as the "imbalance-of-power hypothesis." This "states that coalitionary kills occur because of two factors: intergroup hostility, and large power asymmetries between rival parties." Thus, chimpanzee males will attack other conspecifics if they outnumber them and have a low risk of injury to themselves. "By wounding or killing members of the neighboring community, males from one community increase their relative dominance over the neighbors . . . this tends to lead to increased fitness of the killers." Because of the complexity of modern warfare, these types of lethal raids can be seen more readily in humans in "primitive" warfare among "pre-state" societies. Wrangham believes that the imbalance-of-power hypothesis is also relevant to dominance interactions among members of the same community, and some of the coalitionary kills he cites occurred within chimpanzee communities.

Third and finally, Wrangham believes that the long-term evolutionary explanation of coalitionary killing is attributed to a "dominance drive" that favors unprovoked aggression. Such aggression is brought about by the opportunity to attack at times of low personal risk, thus substantially reducing competition from neighboring communities. The dominance drive is related to increased fitness, allowing the killers to leave more of their dominant-killer genes to the next generation.

Although there are a number of problems with each of these points, I will concentrate only on what I consider to be the most serious flaw of each argument . . .

Regarding coalitionary killing, Wrangham assumes that certain behaviors resulting in conspecific killing among ants, wolves, chimpanzees, and humans (especially those in primitive, pre-state societies) are similar phenomena. Presumably they have the same biological bases and motivations and therefore are driven by the same underlying natural causes. Thus he gives these behaviors a label, "coalitionary killing," and in creating a name, he creates a phenomenon. Yet the extremely vague similarities between the behaviors observed do not necessarily indicate that the behaviors have any biological similarity whatsoever.

When comparisons are made between human and animal behavior and it is assumed that behaviors that are similar in appearance have similar functions and evolutionary histories, a basic principle of biology is violated. Form alone does not provide information about function or shared genetic or evolutionary history. Referring to "rape" in dragonflies, "slavery" in ants, or "coalitionary killing" in chimpanzees and humans may sound like science but is, as Marks states, "a science of metaphorical, not of biological, connections."

With regard to the imbalance-of-power argument, are we to believe that whenever a group of chimpanzees or humans perceives weakness in another individual or group, that group will attack and kill? Does this depend upon a genetic relationship? If not, why not? In what precise circumstances do we actually see coalitionary killing, and when does it not occur? One would expect that if violence occurred every time there was a potential imbalance of power in chimpanzee group meetings and in within-group dominance interactions, surely coalitionary killing would be much more common than the ten to twenty incidents recorded in 170 years of observation. In fact, killing is exceedingly rare given the potential for these conditions. Furthermore, do all humans or human groups attempt, or at least wish, to kill individuals in weaker, nonrelated groups? Given the drive for dominance and the imbalance-of-power hypothesis, why not? Do humans normally desire to do so but are restrained by laws and regulations and the fear of punishment? Is this why it is easier to compare primitive, pre-state human societies with chimpanzees, since such societies are less constrained by laws and regulations because they are closer to "nature"? As Wrangham states, "[M]ales are expected by this hypothesis to take advantage of power over neighbors, especially when unfettered by social or cultural constraints."

In fact, neither chimpanzees nor humans attack in all circumstances of imbalance of power, and coalitionary killing is extremely rare in both species. Wrangham agrees that it is the context that is critical for understanding violent behavior, and it is the context that is not explained by (or relevant to) the proposed hypotheses. "Whether or not an individual employs violence is expected to depend on the proximate stimuli, about which we still know little. . . . Such questions are critical for understanding who becomes violent, and when." It seems necessary to have a good understanding of the circumstances and proximate causes of a behavior before developing evolutionary explanations for that behavior.

Finally, with regard to the dominance drive argument, Robert Hinde, one of the most respected animal behaviorists of our time, has considered the concept of psychological and behavioral "drives" at length. He emphasizes that the word *drive* is problematic because it has been used in so many different ways. The term may refer to hypothesized entities that are believed to exist but that have not yet been identified, or to stimuli or responses, or to physiological or psychological states, or to neurological or non-neurological states. The term can also refer to biogenic states, in which changes in behavior are related directly to changes in the internal state of the organism, or psychogenic states, in which they are not. Hinde warns:

> Even within one usage, however, there is a tendency to use drive as a blanket variable—drive concepts are used to provide unitary explanations of a variety of characteristics of behavior which may depend, in fact, on diverse mechanisms. . . . A unitary concept of drive can be taken to imply that these diverse characteristics of behavior depend on the same features of the underlying mechanism. There is no a priori reason why this should be so, and some reasons for thinking to the contrary.

Where measures of behavior can be directly correlated, such as drinking leading to a cessation of thirst, the proposition of an intervening drive variable may be a valuable tool for research. However, when correlation between behaviors is not perfect, "such a concept is misleading and can be a positive hindrance." The use of the concept of drive in relation to the extremely complex set of behavioral and contextual phenomena related to dominance seems to me to be entirely inappropriate.

Wrangham argues that those who criticize his theory do not appreciate the relevance of biological arguments for understanding warfare or the importance of the comparative method in biology. I disagree. Rather, I believe his critics are simply not convinced that the concepts of "coalitionary killing," the "imbalance-of-power hypothesis," and a "dominance drive" are sufficient to explain violent behavior in chimpanzees or humans.

CHALLENGE QUESTIONS

Are Humans Naturally Violent?

1. What might Wilson and Wrangham's position about our violent nature mean for psychology, especially in the therapy setting?
2. Sussman attributes the popularity of Wilson and Wrangham's position to our Western cultural tradition, not to scientifically demonstrated facts. Describe how you think this is possible with scientists. (Hint: Consider the work of the philosopher of science Thomas Kuhn.)
3. Why is the selfish-gene theory so important to the arguments of each of these authors? How does it help Wilson and Wrangham and hurt the arguments of Sussman?
4. On what issues do these authors agree?
5. There are important disagreements between these authors on the interpretations of the same sets of data. Find the original publication of one such set and provide your own informed opinion about whose interpretation is the more correct and discuss why you think so.

ISSUE 5

Do Women and Men Communicate Differently?

YES: Julia T. Wood, from *Gendered Lives: Communication, Gender, and Culture* (Wadsworth, 2001)

NO: Laura L. Winn and Donald L. Rubin, from "Enacting Gender Identity in Written Discourse: Responding to Gender Role Bidding in Personal Ads," *Journal of Language and Social Psychology* (December 2001)

ISSUE SUMMARY

YES: University professor and communication researcher Julia T. Wood explains how communication styles differ in men and women by examining gender roles in typical childhood games, men's and women's communication practices, and common misunderstandings between the sexes.

NO: Professors and researchers Laura L. Winn and Donald L. Rubin describe an empirical study aimed at understanding social roles and argue that these contextual factors, not biological sex, play the defining role in communication styles.

T he importance of communication for any sort of human interaction has led to considerable psychological research and treatment conceptions. For instance, many marital counseling techniques are based on the idea that good, effective communication is the foundation of a successful marriage or relationship. The problem is that not everyone seems to communicate the same way.

Some of the most popular ideas of communication differences center on stereotypes of gender. For example, men and women are often portrayed in the media or popular psychology as using completely different communication styles and techniques, speaking different languages, or even being from different "planets." Women are stereotypically seen as more expressive, "feelings-oriented," and tentative or hedging, and their communication is intended to create and maintain relationships. Men, on the other hand, are generally considered more competitive and assertive, and their communication is calculated more to convey information.

Are these communication stereotypes valid? This is another way of putting the dispute under consideration by these authors. These gender stereotypes sometimes hold up under scientific scrutiny, but often they seem to be incorrect, or at least insufficient to explain apparent gender differences. What conclusion can we draw from the psychological research on these communication issues? The question is important because it has so many implications for marriage, community, and counseling.

Dr. Wood is adamant in her assertion that the different genders do communicate differently. She begins her article by examining childhood and the way that boys and girls are socialized into gender roles. Specifically, she looks at the ways in which groups of boys and girls typically play together and how these styles of play and interaction contribute to future communication differences. Dr. Wood then outlines the most basic differences between male and female communication styles, which correspond in large measure to the predominant stereotype. She believes that "language reflects and sustains cultural views of masculinity and femininity." She concludes, "Women and men constitute their gender identities through their styles of communication."

In the "No" article, Drs. Winn and Rubin conduct a study using personal ads to test the theory that "individuals vary their language choices within interactions, depending on their social goals." The idea is that because social goals determine language choices, differences in communication will be due not to gender, but to an individual's specific context and desired outcomes. In this sense, communication styles should not differ when males and females have similar contexts and the same social goals, and Winn and Rubin interpret the study's results as supportive. Contextual factors were more potent than the writers' gender in affecting participants' writing. When individuals communicate differently, the source of the differences lies in context, not gender.

POINT	COUNTERPOINT
• Differences in male and female communication are the result of gender roles imposed by society.	• Individual communication differences are based on the social goals of the communicator.
• Men and women generally fit stereotypic communication styles.	• A person can change his/her communication style based on the situation.
• Children are socialized into gender roles at a very young age, and they conform to those roles fairly strictly thereafter.	• Gender roles are conformed to when such conformity will bring about a desired result.
• Research often confirms stereotypic gender differences in communication.	• Some studies show that gender plays a minimal role (or none at all) in determining communication differences.

YES

Julia T. Wood

Gendered Lives: Communication, Gender, and Culture

Gendered Interaction: Masculine and Feminine Styles of Verbal Communication

Language not only expresses cultural views of gender but also constitutes individuals' gender identities. The communication practices we use define us as masculine or feminine; in large measure, we create our own gender through talk. Because language constitutes masculinity and femininity, we should find generalizable differences in how women and men communicate. Research bears out this expectation by documenting rather systematic differences in the ways men and women typically use language. . . .

Studies of gender and communication convincingly show that in many ways women and men operate from dissimilar assumptions about the goals and strategies of communication. [M]en and women live in two different worlds and that this is evident in the disparate forms of communication they use. Given this, it seems appropriate to consider masculine and feminine styles of communicating as embodying two distinct speech communities. To understand these different communities and the validity of each, we will first consider how we are socialized into feminine and masculine speech communities. After this, we will explore divergencies in how women and men typically communicate. Please note the importance of the word *typically* and others that indicate we are discussing generalizable differences, not absolute ones. Some women are not socialized into feminine speech, or they are and later reject it; likewise, some men do not learn or choose not to adopt a masculine style of communication. What follows describes gendered speech communities into which *most* women and men are socialized.

The Lessons of Childplay

. . . One way to gain insight into how boys and girls learn norms of communication is to observe young children at play. In interactions with peers, boys and girls learn how to talk and how to interpret what each other says; they discover how to signal their intentions with words and how to respond appropriately to others' communication; and they learn codes to demonstrate involvement and interest. In short, interacting with peers teaches children rules of communication. . . .

Boys' games.   Boys' games usually involve fairly large groups—nine individuals for each baseball team, for instance. Most boys' games are competitive, have clear goals, and are organized by rules and roles that specify who does what and how to play. Because these games are structured by goals, rules, and roles, there is little need to discuss how to play, although there may be talk about strategies to reach goals. [In] boys' games, an individual's status depends on standing out, being better, and often dominating other players. In their games, boys engage in more heckling, storytelling, interrupting, and commanding than girls typically do. From these games, boys learn how to interact in their communities. Specifically, boys' games cultivate three communication rules:

1. Use communication to assert yourself and your ideas; use talk to achieve something.
2. Use communication to attract and maintain an audience.
3. Use communication to compete with others for the "talk stage," so that they don't gain more attention than you; learn to wrest the focus from others and onto yourself.

These communication rules are consistent with other aspects of masculine socialization. . . . For instance, notice the emphasis on individuality and competition. Also, we see that these rules accent achievement—doing something, accomplishing a goal. Boys learn they must *do things* to be valued members of the team. It's also the case that intensely close, personal relationships are unlikely to be formed in large groups. Finally, we see the undercurrent of masculinity's emphasis on being invulnerable and guarded: If others are the competition from whom you must seize center stage, then you cannot let them know too much about yourself and your weaknesses.

Girls' games.   Turning now to girls' games, we find that quite different patterns exist, and they lead to distinctive understandings of communication. Girls tend to play in pairs or in very small groups rather than large ones. Also, games like house and school do not have preset, clear-cut goals, rules, and roles. There is no analogy for the touchdown in playing house. Because girls' games are not structured externally, players have to talk among themselves to decide what they're doing and what roles they have. Playing house, for instance, typically begins with a discussion about who is going to be the daddy and who the mommy. This is typical of the patterns girls use to generate rules and roles for their games. The lack of stipulated goals for the games is also important, because it tends to cultivate in girls an interest in the process of interaction more than its products. For their games to work, girls have to cooperate and work out problems by talking: No external rules exist to settle disputes. From these games, . . . girls learn normative communication patterns of their speech communities. Specifically, girls' games teach three basic rules for communication:

1. Use collaborative, cooperative talk to create and maintain relationships. The *process* of communication, not its content, is the heart of relationships.
2. Avoid criticizing, outdoing, or putting others down; if criticism is necessary, make it gentle; never exclude others.
3. Pay attention to others and to relationships; interpret and respond to others' feelings sensitively.

[T]he typically smaller size of girls' play groups fosters cooperative discussion and an open-ended process of talking to organize activity, whereas the larger groups in which boys usually play encourage competition and external rules to structure activity. [B]oys used talk to exert control and give orders, whereas girls were more likely to make requests. . . . Girls in the groups typically used inclusive and nondirective language, whereas boys tended to issue commands, used talk to compete, and worked to establish status hierarchies in their groups.

These basic patterns in communication echo and reinforce other aspects of gender socialization. Girls' games stress cooperation, collaboration, and sensitivity to others' feelings. Also notice the focus on process encouraged in girls' games. Rather than interacting to achieve some outcome, girls learn that communication itself is the goal. Whereas boys learn they have to do something to be valuable, the lesson for girls is *to be*. Their worth depends on being good people, which is defined by being cooperative, inclusive, and sensitive. The lessons of child's play are carried forward. In fact, the basic rules of communication that adult women and men employ turn out to be only refined and elaborated versions of the very same ones evident in girls' and boys' childhood games.

Gendered Communication Practices

In her popular book *You Just Don't Understand: Women and Men in Communication,* linguist Deborah Tannen declares that "communication between men and women can be like cross cultural communication, prey to a clash of conversational styles." Her study of men's and women's talk led her to identify distinctions between the speech communities typical of women and men. Not surprisingly, Tannen traces gendered communication patterns to differences in boys' and girls' communication with parents and peers. Like other scholars, Tannen believes that women and men typically engage in distinctive styles of communication with different purposes, rules, and understandings of how to interpret talk. . . .

Women's speech.   For most women, communication is a primary way to establish and maintain relationships with others. They engage in conversation to share themselves and to learn about others. This is an important point: For women, talk *is* the essence of relationships. Consistent with this primary goal, women's speech tends to display identifiable features that foster connections, support, closeness, and understanding.

Equality between people is generally important in women's communication. To achieve symmetry, women often match experiences to indicate "You're not alone in how you feel." Typical ways to communicate equality would be saying, "I've done the same thing many times," "I've felt the same way," or "Something like that happened to me too and I felt like you do." Growing out of the quest for equality is a participatory mode of interaction in which communicators respond to and build on each other's ideas in the process of conversing. Rather than a rigid "You tell your ideas then I'll tell mine" sequence, women's speech more characteristically follows an interactive pattern in which different voices weave together to create conversations.

Also important in women's speech is showing support for others. To demonstrate support, women often express understanding and sympathy with a friend's situation or feelings. "Oh, you must feel terrible," "I really hear what you are saying," or "I think you did the right thing" are communicative clues that we understand and support how another feels. Related to these first two features is women's typical attention to the relationship level of communication. You will recall that the relationship level of talk focuses on feelings and the relationship between communicators rather than on the content of messages. . . .

A fourth feature of women's speech style is conversational "maintenance work." This involves efforts to sustain conversation by inviting others to speak and by prompting them to elaborate their experiences. Women, for instance, ask a number of questions that initiate topics for others: . . . Communication of this sort opens the conversational door to others and maintains interaction.

Inclusivity also surfaces in a fifth quality of women's talk, which is responsiveness. Women usually respond in some fashion to what others say. A women might say "Tell me more" or "That's interesting"; perhaps she will nod and use eye contact to signal she is engaged; perhaps she will ask a question such as "Can you explain what you mean?" Responsiveness reflects learned tendencies to care about others and to make them feel valued and included. It affirms another person and encourages elaboration by showing interest in what was said.

A sixth quality of women's talk is personal, concrete style. Typical of women's conversation are details, personal disclosures, anecdotes, and concrete reasoning. These features cultivate a personal tone in women's communication, and they facilitate feelings of closeness by connecting communicators' lives. . . .

A final feature of women's speech is tentativeness. This may be expressed in a number of forms. Sometimes women use verbal hedges such as "I kind of feel you may be overreacting." In other situations they qualify statements by saying "I'm probably not the best judge of this, but . . . " Another way to keep talk provisional is to tag a question onto a statement in a way that invites another to respond: "That was a pretty good movie, wasn't it?" "We should get out this weekend, don't you think?" Tentative communication leaves open the door for others to respond and express their opinions. . . .

Men's speech.   Masculine speech communities tend to regard talk as a way to exert control, preserve independence, entertain, and enhance status. Conversation is often seen as an arena for proving oneself and negotiating prestige. This leads to two general tendencies in men's communication. First, men often use talk to establish and defend their personal status and their ideas, by asserting themselves, telling jokes and stories, or by challenging others. Second, when they wish to comfort or support another, they typically do so by respecting the other's independence and avoiding communication they regard as condescending.

To establish their status and value, men often speak to exhibit knowledge, skill, or ability. Equally typical is the tendency to avoid disclosing personal information that might make a man appear weak or vulnerable. For instance, if someone expresses a problem, a man might say "The way you should handle that is . . . ," "Don't let him get to you," or "You ought to just tell him . . . " On the relationship level of communication, giving advice does two things. First, it focuses on instrumental activity—what another should do or be—and does not acknowledge feelings. Second, it expresses superiority and maintains control. It says "I know what you should do" or "I would know how to handle that." The message may be perceived as implying the speaker is superior to the other person. Between men, advice giving seems understood as a give-and-take, but it may be interpreted as unfeeling and condescending by women whose rules for communicating differ.

A second prominent feature of men's talk is instrumentality—the use of speech to accomplish instrumental objectives. In conversation, this is often expressed through problem-solving efforts to get information, discover facts, and suggest solution. Again, between men this is usually a comfortable orientation, because both speakers have typically been socialized to value instrumentality. However, conversations between women and men are often derailed by the lack of agreement on what this informational, instrumental focus means. To many women it feels as if men don't care about their feelings. When a man focuses on the content level of meaning after a woman has disclosed a problem, she may feel he is disregarding her emotions and concerns. He, on the other hand, may well be trying to support her in the way that he has learned to show support—suggesting ways to solve the problem.

A third feature of men's communication is conversational command. Despite jokes about women's talkativeness, research indicates that in most contexts, men talk more than women. This tendency, although not present in infancy, is evident in preschoolers. Compared with girls and women, boys and men talk more frequently and for longer periods of time. Further, men engage in other verbal behaviors that sustain prominence in interaction. They may reroute conversations by using what another said as a jump-off point for their own topic, or they may interrupt. Although both sexes engage in interruptions, most research suggests that men do it more frequently. Not only do men seem to interrupt more than women, but they may do so for different reasons. [M]en use interruptions to control conversation by challenging other speakers or wresting the talk stage from them, whereas women interrupt to indicate interest and to respond. . . . A different explanation is that men generally interrupt more than women because interruptions are considered normal and good-natured within the norms of masculine speech communities. Whereas interruptions that reroute conversation might be viewed as impolite and intrusive within feminine speech communities, the outgoing, give-and-take character of masculine speech may render interruptions just part of normal conversation.

Fourth, men tend to express themselves in fairly direct, assertive ways. Compared with women, their language is typically more forceful and authoritative. Tentative speech such as hedges and disclaimers is used less frequently by men than by women. This is consistent with gender socialization in which men learn to use talk to assert themselves and to take and hold positions. When another person does not share that understanding of communication, however, speech that is absolute and directive may seem to close off conversation and leave no room for others to speak.

Fifth, compared with women, men communicate more abstractly. They frequently speak in general terms that are removed from concrete experiences and distanced from personal feelings. The abstract style typical of men's speech reflects the public and impersonal contexts in which they often operate and the less personal emphasis in their speech communities. Within public environments, norms for speaking call for theoretical, conceptual, and general thought and communication. Yet, within more personal relationships, abstract talk sometimes creates barriers to knowing another intimately.

Finally, men's speech tends not to be highly responsive, especially not on the relationship level of communication. Men, more than women, give what are called "minimal response cues," which are verbalizations such as "yeah" or "umhmm." In interaction with women, who have learned to demonstrate interest more vigorously, minimal response cues generally inhibit conversation because they are perceived as indicating lack of involvement. Men's conversation also often lacks expressed sympathy, understanding, and self-disclosures. Within the rules of men's speech communities, sympathy is a sign of condescension, and revealing personal problems is seen as making one vulnerable. Yet women's speech rules count sympathy and disclosure as demonstrations of equality and support. This creates potential for misunderstanding between women and men.

Misinterpretations Between Women and Men

Showing support. The scene is a private conversation between Martha and George. She tells him she is worried about her friend. George gives a minimum response cue, saying only "Oh." To Martha this suggests he isn't interested, because women make and expect more . . . "listening noises" to signal interest. . . . George is probably thinking if she wants to tell him something she will, because his rules of speech emphasize using talk to assert oneself. Even without much encouragement, Martha continues by describing the tension in her friend's marriage and her own concern about how she can help. She says, "I feel so bad for Barbara, and I want to help her, but I don't know what to do." George then says, "It's their problem, not yours. Just butt out and let them settle their own relationship." At this, Martha explodes: "Who asked for your advice?" George is now completely frustrated and confused. He thought Martha wanted advice, so he gave it. She is hurt that George didn't tune into her feelings and comfort her about her worries. Each is annoyed and unhappy.

The problem here is not so much what George and Martha say and don't say. Rather, it's how they interpret each other's communication—actually, how they *misinterpret* it, because each relies on rules that are not familiar to the other. They fail to understand that each is operating by different rules of talk. George is respecting Martha's independence by not pushing her to talk. When he thinks she directly requests advice, he offers it in an effort to help. Martha, on the other hand, wants comfort and a connection with George—that is her purpose in talking with him. She finds his advice unwelcome and dismissive of her feelings. He doesn't offer sympathy, because his rules for communication define this as condescending. Yet within Martha's speech community, not to show sympathy is to be unfeeling and unresponsive.

"Troubles talk."   [T]alk about troubles, or personal problems, [is] a kind of interaction in which hurt feelings may result from the contrast between most men's and women's rules of communication. A woman might tell her partner that she is feeling down because she did not get a job she wanted. In an effort to be supportive, he might respond by saying, "You shouldn't feel bad. Lots of people don't get jobs they want." To her this seems to dismiss her feelings—to be-little them by saying lots of people experience her situation. Yet within masculine speech communities, this is a way of showing respect for another by not assuming that she or he needs sympathy.

Now let's turn the tables and see what happens when a man feels troubled. When he meets Nancy, Craig is unusually quiet because he feels down about not getting a job offer. Sensing that something is wrong, Nancy tries to show interest by asking, "Are you okay? What's bothering you?" Craig feels she is imposing and trying to get him to show a vulnerability he prefers to keep to himself. Nancy probes further to show she cares. As a result, he feels intruded on and withdraws further. Then Nancy feels shut out.

But perhaps Craig does decide to tell Nancy why he feels down. After hearing about his rejection letter, Nancy says, "I know how you feel. I felt so low when I didn't get that position at Datanet." She is matching experiences to show Craig that she understands his feelings and that he's not alone. Within his communication rules, however, this is demeaning his situation by focusing on her, not him. When Nancy mentions her own experience, Craig thinks she is trying to steal the center stage for herself. Within his speech community, that is one way men vie for dominance and attention. Yet Nancy has learned to share similar experiences as a way to build connections with others.

The point of the story.   Another instance in which feminine and masculine communication rules often clash and cause problems is in relating experiences. Typically, men have learned to speak in a linear manner in which they move sequentially through major points in a story to get to the climax. Their talk tends to be straight-forward without a great many details. The rules of feminine speech, however, call for more detailed and less linear storytelling. Whereas a man is likely to provide rather bare information about what happened, a woman is more likely to embed the information within a larger context of the people involved and other things going on. Women include details not because all of the specifics are important in themselves but because recounting them shows involvement and allows a conversational partner to be more fully part of the situation being described.

Because feminine and masculine rules about details differ, men often find women's way of telling stories wandering and unfocused. Conversely, men's style of storytelling may strike women as leaving out all of the interesting details. Many a discussion between women and men has ended either with his exasperated demand, "Can't you get to the point?" or with her frustrated question, "Why don't you tell me how you were feeling and what else was going on?" She wants more details than his rules call for; he is interested in fewer details than she has learned to supply.

Relationship talk.   "Can we talk about us?" is the opening of innumerable conversations that end in misunderstanding and hurt. . . . [M]en and women tend to have very different ideas about what it means to talk about relationships. In general, men are inclined to think a relationship is going fine as long as there is no need to talk about it. They are interested in discussing the relationship only if there are particular problems to be addressed. In contrast, women generally think a relationship is working well as long as they can talk about it with partners. The difference here grows out of the fact that men tend to use communication to do things and solve problems, whereas women generally regard the *process* of communicating as a primary way to create and sustain relationships with others. For many women, conversation is a way to be with another person—to affirm and enhance closeness. Men's different rules stipulate that communication is to achieve some goal or fix some problem. No wonder men often duck when their partners want to "discuss the relationship," and women often feel a relationship is in trouble when their partners are unwilling to talk about it. . . .

Public speaking.   Differences in women's and men's communication patterns also surface in public contexts. In Western society, the public sphere traditionally has been considered men's domain. . . . [O]ne of the constraints on women's efforts to gain legal rights in the 1800s was the proscription against women speaking in public. Although many women are now active and vocal in public life, feminine forms of communication are still devalued. The assertive, dominant, confident masculine style is the standard for public speaking, whereas the more collaborative, inclusive feminine style of communicating is considered less effective. This male generic standard for public speaking places feminine speakers at a disadvantage in public life. Their style of speaking is judged by a standard that neither reflects nor respects their communication goals and values. Women such as former Texas governor Ann Richards who are considered effective public speakers manage to combine the traditionally feminine communication style (which includes personal compassion and use of anecdotal information) with more masculine qualities such as assertiveness and instrumentality. Even today, a conventionally feminine communication style is usually devalued, because masculine standards of public speaking still prevail.

Summary

. . . [L]anguage reflects and sustains cultural views of masculinity and femininity. By defining, classifying, and evaluating gender, language reinforces social views of men as the standard and women as marginal and men and masculinity as more valuable than women and femininity. From generic male terms to language that demeans and diminishes women, verbal communication is a powerful agent of cultural expression. . . .

. . . [W]omen and men constitute their gender identities through their styles of communication. Because males and females tend to be socialized into distinct speech communities, they learn different rules about the purposes of communication and ways to indicate support, interest, and involvement. Because women and men have some dissimilar rules for talk, they often misread each other's meanings and misunderstand each other's motives. This frequently leads to frustration, hurt, and tension between people who care about each other and misjudgments of people speaking in public settings. Appreciating and respecting the distinctive validity of each style of communication is a foundation for better understanding between people. Further, learning to use different styles of communication allows women and men to be more flexible and effective in their interactions with each other. . . .

Laura L. Winn and
Donald L. Rubin

 **NO**

Enacting Gender Identity in Written Discourse: Responding to Gender Role Bidding in Personal Ads

Recent theories depict social identity as enacted or constructed within interactions. Individuals may choose to either emphasize or de-emphasize aspects of their identities in response to the characteristics of a situation. Communication adaptation theory (CAT) holds that individuals vary their language choices within interactions, depending on their social goals. Thus, speakers may choose to emphasize (or de-emphasize) particular aspects of their identities as a way of aligning with (or distancing from) interaction partners. In this manner, situational influences may have a profound effect on discourse. In fact, as Meyerhoff noted, the primary value of CAT is that it is designed to address the interactive nature of identity construction. . . .

Gender schematic information is a particularly influential aspect of social identity formation. Of particular interest to the current study was the way participants might use language to frame gendered identities within their writing. In her review of linguistic studies that have investigated CAT with respect to gender, Yaeger-Dror noted that message senders will often converge with, or match, the speech patterns of their interlocutors. However, Yaeger-Dror also noted that the social goal of the message sender is equally influential. Sometimes, these social goals can lead to linguistic divergence rather than convergence. In some cases, divergence may emerge because the social goal is to complement rather than match the language strategies of the other interactant. The act of matching the discourse of one's interlocutor would seem to indicate a bid for solidarity; however, if one wished to express dominance, then elements of divergence might emerge. Studies on gender-related linguistic markers demonstrate that such goals (e.g., solidarity) often override the sex of the message sender as potential influences on language style. In fact, both types of influences need to be considered.

For instance, Hogg suggested that at least for oral forms of discourse, the use of gender-linked linguistic markers may be subject to considerable situational influence. In fact, although gender differences in speech often occur, these are just as likely to be indicators of gender-related role behaviors as markers of biological sex. On the basis of speech accommodation theory, Hogg predicted that there would be both biological gender-related and gender

From *Journal of Language and Social Psychology*, vol. 20, no. 4, December 2001, pp. 393–418. Copyright © 2001 by Sage Publications via the Copyright Clearance Center. Reprinted by permission.

role-related differences in speakers' behavior, related to the speakers' convergence with the gender of their interlocutors. Speakers were recorded interacting in both a same-sex dyad and mixed-sex larger groups. It was expected that the dyadic situation would elicit more solidarity goals for speakers and that the group situation, being more formal, would elicit more control-oriented strategies.

Results of this study showed that female speakers used more "masculine" (i.e., instrumental) terms and fewer "feminine" (i.e., expressive) terms in heterogeneous group situations than when they spoke in all-female dyads. In dyads, both men and women adapted their speech to the more affiliative context of the situation, whereas in groups, both men and women used more instrumental speech, indicating an awareness of the different needs of this context. Overall, men exhibited less overall speech adaptation than women, despite the context. . . .

The current study was conducted as a means of further investigating gender-linked use of linguistic markers in managing written identity presentation. We chose the heterosexual personal ad context as a way of obtaining cross-sex targeted discourse. . . .

Construction of Social Identity

Conceptualizations of social identity in the context of oral as well as written discourse have evolved considerably in recent times. Contemporary identity theory regards social identity as nonessentialist, socially constructed, and enacted. Asserting that social identities are nonessentialist implies that social categories can encompass substantial variation, so that one's communication traits cannot be reliably determined on the basis of membership in a particular identity category. Bipolar categorization of gender itself has undergone considerable challenge. Likewise, many scholars within language and gender research hold that the dichotomous distinction between male and female no longer seems appropriate for describing communication behavior. . . .

To assert that social identities are enacted is to recognize that one creates identification through verbal performance and in negotiation with one's interactants. Thus, one may emphasize one aspect of identity (e.g., gender) in one context and emphasize another aspect (e.g., ethnicity) in another context. In fact, as much of the literature on language code shifting reveals, one may emphasize or de-emphasize various aspects of identity even within the course of one conversation.

Written language serves as a vehicle for expressing and constructing many facets of social identity, no less than does speech. Although oral discourse is accompanied by a rich array of prosody, kinesics, and other nonverbal signals, writing is more constrained by its medium and also less transactional than oral speech forms. Still, the distinctions between oral and written linguistic codes are more a matter of degree than kind. For example, the use of punctuation in written discourse may function similarly to the use of intonation patterns in oral communication. By the same token, written discourse may contain linguistic markers by which writers convey ethnic, role, and gender identity. . . .

Patterns of planned convergence and divergence may arise when gender identity is negotiated within discourse.

Gender and Language

Early studies of gender and language associate female speakers with features that hedge or blunt assertions (e.g., "maybe," "sort of," "I guess") and avoid conflict with listeners by the use of politeness formulas (e.g., "if you don't mind" or the use of question forms rather than bald requests). Other "markers" commonly associated with female language include the use of double-sided arguments (e.g., "It was probably Shakespeare's sister, but then again, some people believe it was Marlowe"), expressions of uncertainty (e.g., "I don't know, but . . ."), and the use of certain vocabulary likely to be judged as trivial (e.g., fine-grained color terms such as *fuchsia*).

Curiously, research on language and gender remains vulnerable to criticism for failing to take into account more dynamic models of identity. For instance, both Crawford and Aries specifically targeted studies aimed at establishing catalogues of discrete language features that discriminate between male and female speakers. They argued that across the literature, men's and women's language is more similar than different and that apparent differences are quite context specific. Rather than enumerating superficial sex differences, it would be more productive for researchers to examine features of interaction contexts that lead speakers to enact gender roles in particular ways.

Similarly, both Freimuth and Hornstein and Kramarae challenged the tradition of dichotomizing gender differences within empirical studies. They argued, like Bem, for the expansion of gendered identity to a more continuum-based perspective. In fact, in a recent study, Grob, Meyers, and Schuh challenged the "dual cultures" model of gender. They found that male and female speakers were more similar than different in their use of previously gender-linked linguistic markers of tag questions, hedges, and interruptions. Grob et al. discussed the implications of a gender similarity model for language-related study, concluding that a more continuous or more complex view of gender is warranted. Because language use is socioculturally conditioned, where gender differences do exist, they are more likely due to differences in gender role schemata than to biological sex.

Within oral discourse, if women are found to use more standard dialect features than men, the reason may be that women are more often compelled by the terms of their employment to function in contexts demanding linguistic propriety, whereas men may be less subject to those particular workplace demands on language. On the other hand, if women use "you know" more often than men, the reason may be that they are failing to receive the back-channel cues from their listeners, affirming that they still have their listeners' attention. This view receives support from studies on men's language as well. Men who by happenstance find themselves occupying interaction roles more typically occupied by women (e.g., a powerless witness in a trial) are likely to enact those roles using language that is stereotypically associated with women's speech. Consequently, there is considerable support for a view of gender identity as dynamically constructed through language choice rather than as a static label. . . .

Personal Ads

Most studies of personal ads consider only the writers' and readers' biological sex, failing to consider more theory-driven issues of gender role identity. However, the findings of a few studies suggest that gender identity (as opposed to biological sex alone) can be an important factor for the process of identity bargaining within the context of mate selection. For instance, Willis and Carlson considered over 800 personal ads placed in newspapers. They asked college students to rate (a) which ads they would prefer if they were interested in selecting dating partners and (b) which ad was most likely to be "successful." Those ads preferred mainly by men (i.e., rated lowest by women) and those preferred mainly by women (i.e., rated lowest by men) were labeled "sexually dimorphic," meaning that the content of the ads was likely to appeal to only one gender. Those that were preferred by both men and women were considered to be more androgynous by the authors. The ads that appeared to "target" opposite-gender readers (by emphasizing the writers' own gender traits) were more likely to be successful. Thus, it appears that within this context, individuals privilege more stereotypical gender identity bids. . . .

Koestner and Wheeler employed Bem's gender role schema theory directly and examined the instrumental and expressive content within personal ads collected from local newspapers. Instrumental traits tend to be more "male valued" (e.g., assertive, independent, and goal oriented), whereas expressive traits tend to be more "female valued" (e.g., warm, caring, and family oriented). Ads that referenced educational and professional status were coded as instrumental. The authors found that both women and men were likely to write ads that offered what they apparently believed the other preferred. Women shaped their social identities in more instrumental terms, whereas men emphasized more expressive traits. At the same time, women were more likely to describe their desired partners in expressive terms, whereas men listed more instrumental qualities in describing their ideal mates.

Consequently, the findings of Koestner and Wheeler suggest that within the discourse of personal ads, individuals are likely to base their descriptions of both themselves and their ideal partners on their beliefs about what their readers may prefer. This is consistent with CAT, in which individuals are seen to adapt their language in one of two ways. Language users may adapt by converging with their interlocutors' language styles, or they may adapt by using styles that diverge in a manner that complements rather than mimics their interlocutors' styles. Koestner and Wheeler's findings suggest that personal ad writers tend to adapt by complementing rather than converging with the role identities of their intended audiences.

However, because contextual comparisons were not available in this study, that conclusion is tentative at best. . . .

The present study was designed to examine adaptation in the gender identity of individuals as portrayed in their written discourse. As suggested by CAT, we predicted that characteristics of the hypothetical audience would influence writers' self-presentations. Therefore, we manipulated the gender role orientation (instrumentality or expressivity) of the hypothetical target audience. To maximize the chance that writers would indeed attempt to attract readers, writers were given instructions to this effect for both letter-writing tasks. Much of the research conducted within the frame of CAT indicates that attraction, or solidarity, in interpersonal relationships is often accomplished via converging language styles. Alternatively, a complementary language style may occur when there is reason to believe that attraction or solidarity may best be expressed by adopting a slightly divergent language style. . . .

Method

Participants

A total of 84 undergraduate college students attending a large, southeastern U.S. University participated in the study. Participants were recruited from introductory communication courses and received course credit for their involvement. Participants' ages ranged between 18 and 34, with a mean age of 21.4 years.

Stimulus Materials

Two personal ads were constructed for each of the two study conditions. The first ad was intended as a bid for an expressive gender role schema companion (enjoys walking in the woods, attending art shows, and seeking a meaningful relationship). The other ad bid for a prototypical instrumental gender role schema companion (enjoys fitness training and NASCAR races and seeks a mate to "walk on the wild side"). The ad texts were otherwise comparable (equal length, physical layout, etc.). The ad texts were constructed from portions of personal ads appearing in the local newspaper. They were presented to participants in a format designed to simulate an actual newspaper ad.

Participants also completed a 20-item adaptation of the Bem Sex Role Inventory (BSRI). This scale asks participants to rate themselves according to whether they tend to exhibit 10 expressive traits (e.g., caring) and 10 instrumental traits (e.g., assertiveness). Responses were rated on a Likert-type scale ranging from 1 (*never true*) to 7 (*always true*). Finally, participants completed a brief questionnaire inquiring about their familiarity with personal ads and also about the stability and types of intimate relationships in which they were currently involved.

Procedure

Participants engaged in two writing tasks. For the first, they wrote self-descriptions that could hypothetically be submitted to a dating service. Participants were instructed to represent themselves as honestly as possible so that the dating service could match them with companions who would be truly compatible. This first writing sample was intended to assess each participant's "baseline" gender self-presentation before exposure to the stimulus ads. Participants were instructed to write letters that described themselves realistically and yet that would be most likely to attract someone to whom they would be compatible.

Following this first writing episode, participants read one of the two simulated personal ads (either instrumental or expressive). Participants were instructed to produce a second writing sample, intended to be a letter of response to the personal ad. For this second writing task, participants were asked to assume that they had chosen the particular ad and were interested in meeting this person. They were also told to "try to present yourself in a way that this person would find appealing" to maximize the chance that they would write letters designed to attract (rather than repel) the hypothetical other. . . .

Discussion

Our goal was to consider the joint effects of two contextual factors, (a) audience-related gender role bidding and (b) type of writing task, on the written language of men and women in light of communication adaptation and communication accommodation theories. In addition to considering the biological gender of the language users, we also took into account their instrumental and expressive gender role schemata. For some language features associated with gendered language (e.g., nonessentials, hedges, connectives), either biological gender or psychological gender schemata exerted independent effects. In general, however, the results support previous notions that the writing context plays at least as much of a role in shaping gender-typed language use as the gender of the writer. For a number of such features (markers of excitability, use of first-person pronouns), writers appeared to be adopting a complementary or interpersonal compensation strategy rather than converging with the perceived gender role orientation of their audience.

Gender Effects

Our first research question focused on effects of the biological gender of the writer, in contrast with psychological gender role orientation, on the production of gender-typed written language. Given that linguistic style is socioculturally rather than biologically conditioned, and given previous findings that biological sex is not the dominant determinant of female-typed language, we surmised that we would find few effects of biological sex after covarying for gender role schemata. The results, however, were mixed on this score. Two language features, syntactic complexity and first-person pronouns, showed no effects for either the writer's own biological gender or gender role orientation.

Simple main effects for biological sex, but no covariate effects for gender role schema, did emerge for two variables. Replicating previous findings, women as compared with men in this study did produce a higher relative frequency of nonessentials (e.g., parenthetical expressions), postulated as indices of digression and nonlinearity in women's discourse. Women also expressed more markers of excitability (e.g., exclamations), postulated as tokens of emotionality. Consequently, for these two language features at least, the results show some support for the prevalent idea that women tend to use more female-typed language features in their writing. These findings contradict our supposition in the present study that gender role schemata are more predictive of gender-typed language than is biological sex.

Connectives (e.g., "because," "unless," "then," "and") were associated not only with biological sex but also with psychological gender roles. For connectives, women and low instrumentals tended to produce more connectives than men and high instrumentals. This finding runs contrary to previous suppositions, which attribute more hierarchically organized discourse rich in explicit connections to men. However, these results do again replicate those found in Rubin and Green's study.

A number of gender-related effects also emerged for the category of hedges (e.g., "kinda," "I think," "probably," "might have"). People who reported high levels of expressive gender role orientation used hedges infrequently. Although hedges have been stereotypically associated with women's speech, empirical research has generally not borne out any such association. In the present study, the negative slope for expressive gender role schemata on this variable suggests that personality traits such as nurturing and cooperativeness can actually depress expressions of tentativeness.

Nor was there any main effect of biological sex on use of hedges once the effects of psychological gender had been partialed out. On the other hand, the analysis of interaction effects suggested that women did use hedges more adaptively than men, for example, deploying a higher frequency of hedges when responding to an expressive gender role bid compared with an instrumental gender role bid. Indeed, a similar result emerged for connectives. For these two language features, then, it appears that women were more responsive to the perceived nature of the audience than men. Similarly, Hogg found that women engaged in more adaptive use of gender-typed features than men. . . .

Audience Effects

The . . . most central research question concerned the effects of the gender role bid (instrumental or expressive) issued by the hypothetical target audience's personal ads. No main effects for this factor emerged, but we were especially interested in any interactions that may have emerged between writing task and gender role bid of the advertisement. It is within those interactions that one would find the most direct evidence of communication adaptation.

Consider, for example a writer whose "baseline" style as evinced in the description written to an indeterminate audience is gender typed as feminine (e.g., many markers of excitability and nonessentials). If this individual is asked to respond to an instrumental gender role personal ad, he or she may adapt by reducing the frequency of these language features, in which case we would conclude that adaptation by convergence had taken place. Alternatively, this writer might have actually increased his or her level of excitability and nonessential markers; this would constitute a form of divergence.

Linguistic divergence, according to CAT, often serves as a strategy for conveying a hostile or alienated posture vis-à-vis one's interlocutor, in other words, for increasing psychosocial distance. On the other hand, CAT also acknowledges that divergent linguistic style can also be a means of expressing affiliative affect, as when one member of a dyad complements the seemingly opposite language pattern of his or her partner. Thus, for example, when one partner responds to his or her mate's dominance display by expressing submissiveness, that divergence is surely a form of complementary communication adaptation. By the same token, when men and women enacting heterosexual courtship interactions, as in the elicitation procedure for this study, diverge in their use of gender-typed language features, it seems most reasonable to interpret such patterns as instances of complementary language use.

Two language variables in these data did evince just such a complementary pattern. First, there was indeed a statistically significant interaction between writing task and gender role bid of the personal ad for markers of excitability. In responding to the instrumental gender role bid (traditional masculine values), participants increased their use of this female-typed feature. The instrumental ad thus appeared to elicit a complementary adaptation from writers (an increase in excitability markers relative to baseline self-descriptions). In a parallel fashion, the interaction for first-person pronouns showed similar evidence of complementary adaptation. In the face of an expressive gender role bid (traditionally feminine), writers reduced their output of these female-typed markers from their baseline output.

Thus, this study provides at least some evidence of a complementary type of communication adaptation in the context of responding to personal ads. If the person who places the ad expresses an instrumental gender role identity himself or herself, the linguistic response is to emphasize the responder's expressive gender role identity by increasing the output of subjectivity markers. Conversely, if the ad appears to express an instrumental gender role identity, the responder may use excitability markers to emphasize his or her expressive traits. It must be noted, of course, that this linguistic complementary pattern emerged for only two of the six gender-typed language features. Furthermore, it must be acknowledged that this interaction between writing task and gender bid from which we infer this complementary type of adaptation is only one of several significant sources of variation for these language variables.

Limitations and Directions for Future Research

Several methodological limitations to the current study must also be noted. First, although the stimulus personal ads were fabricated by using real models, they expressed very uniformly expressive and instrumental traits. This arrangement was necessary for the potency of the experimental manipulation. In most naturalistic personal ads, however, gender role traits of one type are mitigated by at least some traits from the alternative gender role position. Thus, the resulting gender role bids may have been more caricatured and possibly less attractive than those appearing in natural texts. Second, the extent to which participants were invested in the experimental task remains uncertain. No doubt, the intensity of their language adaptations differs in genuine interpersonal contexts compared with a laboratory writing context. Nonetheless, there is no reason to expect that the direction of these language shifts would differ were we to sample from a corpus of actual responses to personal ads. . . .

In sum, we conclude that contextual influences need to be accounted for when analyzing gender and language use in written discourse. The findings of the present study, though modest, do offer some concrete illustration of ways in which people enact varying gender identities in the face of an interlocutor's bid for one or another gender role. These identities are enacted by modulating the use of socially meaningful language features, for example, in a manner that complements the interlocutor's apparent gender identity.

CHALLENGE QUESTIONS

Do Women and Men Communicate Differently?

1. What are the stereotypical communication styles of men and women? Provide examples from your own experience.
2. Why is communication considered so important to psychology?
3. Describe Communication Adaptation Theory. How does this theory explain communication differences?
4. How do the two sets of authors agree? Is there a sense in which they could both answer the title question affirmatively?
5. If men and women do communicate differently, what implication would this have for marriage and marital therapy?

ISSUE 6

Do Brain Deficiencies Determine Learning Disabilities?

YES: Sally E. Shaywitz and Bennett A. Shaywitz, from "Reading Disability and the Brain," *Educational Leadership* (March 2004)

NO: Gerald Coles, from "Danger in the Classroom: 'Brain Glitch' Research and Learning to Read," *Phi Delta Kappan* (January 2004)

ISSUE SUMMARY

YES: Sally and Bennett Shaywitz, codirectors of the National Institute of Child Health and Human Development, suggest that reading disabilities stem from "brain glitches".

NO: Educational psychologist Gerald Coles believes that learning "disabilities" come from myriad sources, and each source needs to be considered when diagnosing and treating disabilities.

The prominent federal program No Child Left Behind includes the educational objective that *all* children will learn to read by the end of third grade. It also assumes that this goal can be accomplished through the use of "effective, research-based reading programs." While the motives of this program are surely laudable, is this lofty ideal possible? Many scholars are skeptical because there seems to be such a wide range of abilities and situations among children. Some situations include economic, emotional, and cultural impediments that prevent children from reaching this goal. Perhaps more importantly, many children have learning disabilities, a broad group of diagnoses generally referring to difficulty in one or more areas related to learning, such as reading or math.

The issue in question here is whether this latter problem, the issue of learning disabilities, is the result of a malfunctioning brain. Many neuroscientists, psychologists, and others believe that the solutions to reading and other learning disabilities can be found in the brain itself. They conduct various studies to examine brain functions, look for which specific areas of the brain are used in reading and learning, and attempt to understand the neurological differences between good readers and poor readers. In another camp are experts who believe that, while brain functioning is important, and indeed malfunctioning physiology may impede normal learning ability in some cases, there are other influential factors. From this position, each case of "learning disability" should be carefully examined to discover its true origins, and each child should receive the help appropriate to his/her particular problem.

Sally and Bennett Shaywitz are prolific researchers and writers in the area of learning and development. They have also been instrumental in establishing the No Child Left Behind reading program. Their fundamental assertion in the first article is, "Spoken language is instinctive—built into our genes and hardwired in our brains." According to these researchers, reading and language actually *originate* in our neural networks. Therefore, reading disabilities occur when the "wiring" malfunctions in the particular area of the brain responsible for reading. Their research, which uses functional MRI (fMRI) scans to examine different regions of the brain, found what they call brain "glitches"; places where the brains of people with learning disabilities seem to function differently than those of people without disabilities.

In stark contrast to the Shaywitzes, Dr. Coles is highly critical of brain-based explanations. He holds that reading problems can come from social, cultural, economic, and other factors, and there is no way to distinguish those who have abnormal brains from those who are simply poor readers. As a consequence, many disadvantaged children are incorrectly classified as learning disabled. "Never have these 'brain glitch' explanations been more pervasively intrusive for all beginning readers and their teachers across the nation . . . This work is a danger . . . both because it applies unproven labels to an ever-larger number of children and because it promotes a single kind of instruction that . . . contains no promise for leaving no beginning reader behind." He concludes that little the Shaywitzes say has been proven and that care should be taken not to adopt a one-size-fits-all program to improve reading when there are so many different reasons for poor reading.

POINT	COUNTERPOINT
• fMRI scans can identify areas in the brain that malfunction during reading.	• fMRI scans track blood flow and active engagement of the brain, not malfunction.
• To learn to read, beginners must learn the phonetic code and develop phonetic awareness.	• There are many different styles of readers, some phonetic and some not.
• Dyslexia and other reading disabilities have their origin in the brain.	• Many other sources of stress can hinder early reading development.
• Different areas of the brain have specialized functions, and specific operations happen in those areas.	• All neurological functions work through a network involving many different parts of the brain.

YES

Sally E. Shaywitz and
Bennett A. Shaywitz

Reading Disability and the Brain

The past decade has witnessed extraordinary progress in our understanding of the nature of reading and reading difficulties. Never before have rigorous science (including neuroscience) and classroom instruction in reading been so closely linked. For the first time, educators can turn to well-designed, scientific studies to determine the most effective ways to teach reading to beginning readers, including those with reading disability (National Reading Panel, 2000).

What does the evidence tell us? Several lines of investigation have found that reading originates in and relies on the brain systems used for spoken language. In addition, accumulating evidence sheds light on the nature of reading disability, including its definition, prevalence, longitudinal course, and probable causes. Although the work is relatively new, we have already made great progress in identifying the neural systems used for reading, identifying a disruption in these systems in struggling readers, and understanding the neural mechanisms associated with the development of fluent reading.

Reading and Spoken Language

Spoken language is instinctive—built into our genes and hardwired in our brains. Learning to read requires us to take advantage of what nature has provided: a biological module for language.

For the object of the reader's attention (print) to gain entry into the language module, a truly extraordinary transformation must occur. The reader must convert the print on the page into a linguistic code: the phonetic code, the only code recognized and accepted by the language system. Unless the reader-to-be can convert the printed characters on the page into the phonetic code, these letters remain just a bunch of lines and circles, totally devoid of meaning. The written symbols have no inherent meaning of their own but stand, rather, as surrogates for the sounds of speech.

To break the code, the first step beginning readers must take involves spoken language. Readers must develop *phonemic awareness*. They must discover that the words they hear come apart into smaller pieces of sound.

On the basis of highly reliable scientific evidence, investigators in the field have now reached a strong consensus: Reading reflects language, and

From *Educational Leadership*, March 1, 2004. Copyright © 2004 by ASCD. Reprinted by permission. The Association for Supervision and Curriculum Development is a worldwide community of educators advocating sound policies and sharing best practices to achieve the success of each learner. To learn more, visit ASCD at www.ascd.org

reading disability reflects a deficit within the language system. Results from large and well-studied populations with reading disability confirm that in young school-age children and in adolescents, a weakness in accessing the sounds of spoken language represents the most robust and specific correlate of reading disability. Such findings form the foundation for the most successful, evidence-based interventions designed to improve reading (National Reading Panel, 2000).

Understanding Reading Disability

Reading disability, or *developmental dyslexia*, is characterized by an unexpected difficulty in reading in children and adults who otherwise possess the intelligence, motivation, and education necessary for developing accurate and fluent reading. Dyslexia is the most common and most carefully studied of the learning disabilities, affecting 80 percent of all individuals identified as learning disabled and an estimated 5–17 percent of all children and adults in the United States.

Incidence and Distribution of Dyslexia

Recent epidemiological data indicate that like hypertension and obesity, reading ability occurs along a continuum. Reading disability falls on the left side of the bell-shaped curve representing the normal distribution of reading ability.

Dyslexia runs in families: One-fourth to one-half of all children who have a parent with dyslexia also have the disorder, and if dyslexia affects one child in the family, it is likely to affect half of his or her siblings. Recent studies have identified a number of genes involved in dyslexia.

Good evidence, based on surveys of randomly selected populations of children, now indicates that dyslexia affects boys and girls equally. Apparently, the long-held belief that only boys suffer from dyslexia reflected bias in school-identified samples: The more disruptive behavior of boys results in their being referred for evaluation more often, whereas girls who struggle to read are more likely to sit quietly in their seats and thus be overlooked.

Longitudinal studies indicate that dyslexia is a persistent, chronic condition rather than a transient "developmental lag." Children do not outgrow reading difficulties. The evidence-based interventions now available, however, can result in improved reading in virtually all children.

Neurobiological Origins of Dyslexia

For more than a century, physicians and scientists have suspected that dyslexia has neurobiological origins. Until recently, however, they had no way to examine the brain systems that we use while reading. Within the last decade, the dream of scientists, educators, and struggling readers has come true: New advances in technology enable us to view the working brain as it attempts to read.

Perhaps the most convincing evidence for a neurobiological basis of dyslexia comes from the rapidly accumulating and converging data from functional brain imaging investigations. The process of functional brain imaging is quite simple. When we ask an individual to perform a discrete cognitive task, that task places processing demands on specific neural systems in the brain. Through such techniques as functional magnetic resonance imaging (fMRI), we can measure the changes that take place in neural activity in particular brain regions as the brain meets those demands. Because fMRI uses no ionizing radiation and requires no injections, it is noninvasive and safe. We can use it to examine children or adults on multiple occasions.

Using functional brain imaging, scientists around the world have discovered not only the brain basis of reading but also a glitch in the neural circuitry for reading in children and adults who struggle to read. Our studies and those of other investigators have identified three regions involved in reading, all located on the left side of the brain. In the front of the brain, Broca's area (technically the inferior frontal gyrus) is involved in articulation and word analysis. Two areas located in the back of the brain are involved in word analysis (the parieto-temporal region) and in fluent reading (the occipito-temporal region, also referred to as the word form area).

Studies of dyslexic readers document an underactivation of the two systems in the back of the brain together with an overactivation of Broca's area in the front of the brain. The struggling readers appear to be turning to the frontal region, which is responsible for articulating spoken words, to compensate for the fault in the systems in the back of the brain.

Researchers have observed this neurobiological signature of dyslexic readers across cultures and across different languages. The observation of this same pattern in both children and adults supports the view that reading difficulties, including the neural disruption, do not go away with maturity. To prevent failure for students with a reading disability, we must identify the disability early and provide effective reading programs to address the students' needs.

The Importance of Fluency

In addition to identifying the neural systems used for reading, research has now revealed which systems the brain uses in two important phases in the acquisition of literacy.

Beginning reading—breaking the code by slowly, analytically sounding out words—calls on areas in the front of the brain (Broca's area) and in the back of the brain (the parieto-temporal region).

But an equally important phase in reading is fluency—rapid, automatic reading that does not require attention or effort. A fluent reader looks at a printed word and instantly knows all the important information about that word. Fluent reading develops as the reader builds brain connections that eventually represent an exact replica of the word—a replica that has integrated the word's pronunciation, spelling, and meaning.

Fluency occurs step-by-step. After systematically learning letters and their sounds, children go on to apply this knowledge to sound out words slowly and analytically. For example, for the word "back," a child may initially represent the word by its initial and final consonants: "b—k." As the child progresses, he begins to fill in the interior vowels, first making some errors—reading "back" as "bock" or "beak," for example—and eventually sounding out the word correctly. Part of the process of becoming a skilled reader is forming successively more detailed and complete representations of familiar words.

After the child has read the word "back" correctly over and over again, his brain has built and reinforced an exact model of the word. He now reads that word fluently—accurately, rapidly, and effortlessly. Fluency pulls us into reading. A student who reads fluently reads for pleasure and for information; a student who is not fluent will probably avoid reading.

In a study involving 144 children, we identified the brain region that makes it possible for skilled readers to read automatically. We found that the more proficiently a child read, the more he or she activated the occipito-temporal region (or word form area) in the back of the brain. Other investigators have observed that this brain region responds to words that are presented rapidly. Once a word is represented in the word form area, the reader recognizes that word instantly and effortlessly. This word form system appears to predominate when a reader has become fluent. As a result of this finding, we now know that development of the word form area in the left side of the brain is a key component in becoming a skilled, fluent reader.

Helping Struggling Readers Become More Fluent

Our study of 144 children also revealed that struggling readers compensate as they get older, developing alternate reading systems in the front of the brain and in the *right* side of the brain—a functioning system, but, alas, not an automatic one. These readers do not develop the critical left-side word form region necessary for rapid, automatic reading. Instead, they call on the alternate secondary pathways. This strategy enables them to read, but much more slowly and with greater effort than their classmates.

This research evidence of a disruption in the normal reading pathways provides a neurobiological target for reading interventions. In a new study, we hypothesized that an evidence-based, phonologically mediated reading intervention would help dyslexic readers develop the fast-paced word form systems serving skilled reading, thus improving their reading accuracy and fluency. Under the supervision of Syracuse University professor Benita Blachman, we provided 2nd and 3rd grade struggling readers daily with 50 minutes of individual tutoring that was systematic and explicit, focusing on helping the students understand the *alphabetic principle*, or how letters and combinations of letters represent the sounds of speech.

Students received eight months (105 hours) of intervention during the school year in addition to their regular classroom reading instruction. The experimental intervention replaced any additional reading help that the students might have received in school. Certified teachers who had taken part in an intensive training program provided the tutoring.

Immediately after the yearlong intervention, students in the experiment made significant gains in reading fluency and demonstrated increased activation in left hemisphere regions, including the inferior frontal gyrus and the parieto-temporal region. One year after the experimental intervention ended, these students were reading accurately and fluently and were activating all three left-side brain regions used by good readers. A control group of struggling readers receiving school-based, primarily nonphonological reading instruction had not activated these reading systems.

These data demonstrate that an intensive, evidence-based reading intervention brings about significant and durable changes in brain organization so that struggling readers' brain activation patterns come to resemble those of typical readers. If we provide intervention at an early age, then we can improve reading fluency and facilitate the development of the neural systems that underlie skilled reading.

Evidence-Based Effective Reading Instruction

In addition to new neurological research on the nature of reading, educators can draw on a body of rigorous, well-designed, scientific studies to guide reading instruction. In 1998, the U.S. Congress mandated the National Reading Panel to develop rigorous scientific criteria for evaluating reading research, apply these criteria to existing reading research, identify the most effective teaching methods, and then make findings accessible for parents and teachers. As a member of the Panel, I can attest to its diligence. After two years of work, the Panel issued its report (2000).

The major findings of the report indicate that in order to read, all children must be taught alphabetics, comprising phonemic awareness and phonics; reading fluency; vocabulary; and strategies for reading comprehension. These elements must be taught systematically, comprehensively, and explicitly; it is inadequate to present the foundational skills of phonemic awareness and phonics incidentally, casually, or fragmentally. Children do not learn how letters represent sounds by osmosis; we must teach them this skill explicitly. Once a child has mastered these foundational skills, he or she must be taught how to read words fluently.

Good evidence now indicates that we can teach reading fluency by means of repeated oral reading with feedback and guidance. Using these methods, we can teach almost every child to read. It is crucial to align all components of a program with one another—for example, to provide so-called decodable booklets that give the student practice in the specific letter-sound linkages we are teaching. The use of decodable booklets enables the repeated practice necessary to build the automatic systems in the word form region that lead to fluent reading.

Neuroscience and Reading Research Agree

We are now in an era of evidence-based education. Objective scientific evidence—provided by brain imaging studies and by the National Reading Panel's rigorous scientific review of the literature—has replaced reliance on philosophy or opinion.

In considering a reading program, educators should ask several key questions:

- Is there scientific evidence that the program is effective?
- Was the program or its methodology reviewed by the National Reading Panel?
- In reading instruction, are phonemic awareness and phonics taught systematically and explicitly?
- How are students taught to approach an unfamiliar word? Do they feel empowered to try to analyze and sound out an unknown word first rather than guess the word from the pictures or context?
- Does the program also include plenty of opportunities for students to practice reading, develop fluency, build vocabulary, develop reading comprehension strategies, write, and listen to and discuss stories?

Children are only 7 or 8 years old once in their lifetime. We cannot risk teaching students with unproven programs. We now have the scientific knowledge to ensure that almost every child can become a successful reader. Awareness of the new scientific knowledge about reading should encourage educators to insist that reading programs used in their schools reflect what we know about the science of reading and about effective reading instruction.

Gerald Coles  **NO**

Danger in the Classroom: 'Brain Glitch' Research and Learning to Read

Did you know that recent studies of the brain and reading support the reading instruction mandated in George W. Bush's No Child Left Behind (NCLB) legislation? And did you know that this research also supports the legislation he has proposed to dismantle Head Start's comprehensive approach to preschool education? And were you aware that, thanks to this brain research, we now know how children learn to read and which areas of the brain must first be stocked to promote skilled reading? Did you realize that we now have strong brain-based evidence that the best reading instruction is heavily prescriptive, skills-emphasis, building-blocks teaching that starts with small pieces of written language and proceeds to larger ones—and teachers are fortunate because these features are contained in reading programs like Open Court?

You didn't know all that? Good, because none of it is true, although you would never know that if you just listened to the President, the educators and assorted researchers who support his educational agenda, and the media who repeat their assertions.

Over 25 years ago, when I began appraising theories about faulty brain wiring in beginning readers, my criticism of the research then being conducted was limited to ersatz explanations of so-called brain dysfunctions in children called "learning disabled," "reading disabled," or "dyslexic." Contrary to the assertions made then, the research had never shown that the overwhelming number of these children did not have normal brains. Certainly a portion of poor readers had problems that were the result of exposure to such toxins as lead and cadmium, to food additives, and to other environmental influences. But, I argued, there was no evidence that they accounted for more than a small portion of the large numbers of children given these labels and shunted into special education programs.

At some point, thanks to increased, widespread criticism of these "brain-based" explanations, I had thought a change had started toward more informed, measured interpretations. However, my naive thinking has long been gone. Not only are explanations about "brain glitches," to use the term employed by reading researcher Sally Shaywitz, now being applied more

From *Phi Delta Kappa* by Gerald Coles, pp. 344–351. Copyright © 2004 by Phi Delta Kappan. Reprinted by permission.

forcefully to "dyslexics," but they have also been reworked to explain how all children learn to read, what single method of instruction must be used to teach them, and why the single method mandated in Bush's Reading First, part of the NCLB legislation, is a wise, scientifically based choice. Thus never have these "brain glitch" explanations been more pervasively intrusive for all beginning readers and their teachers in classrooms across the nation. . . .

A new best seller, *Overcoming Dyslexia*, by Sally Shaywitz, who has received considerable NICHD [National Institutes of Child Health and Human Development] funding for her research, claims to present "the advances in brain science" that inform what "at last we know," which are "the specific steps a child or adult must take to build and then reinforce the neural pathways deep within the brain for skilled reading." Shaywitz served on the panel whose findings, she proudly explains to readers, "are now part of the groundbreaking No Child Left Behind Legislation," . . .

In this article I will argue that, despite all the unbridled assertions about the wonder of it all, this new "brain glitch" research is theoretically, empirically, and conceptually deficient, as was the deficit-driven work that preceded it by decades. . . . More than ever, claims about the research constitute an ideological barrier to a sounder understanding of the connections between brain activity and learning to read. More than ever, this work is a danger in the classroom both because it applies unproven labels to an ever-larger number of children and because it promotes a single kind of instruction that, based on the actual empirical evidence mustered for it, contains no promise for leaving no beginning reader behind. To all of this, add the false and cruel expectations that these claims generate in parents.

To help illustrate my critique, I will use as an example a recent, highly publicized study on reading and brain activity whose co-authors include Reid Lyon, Sally Shaywitz, and several other researchers whose work argues for building-blocks teaching and has been used as evidence for Reading First instruction. (For convenience I call it the Shaywitz/Lyon study).

Is the Brain "Reading"?

Functional magnetic resonance imagery (fMRI) is a valuable diagnostic and investigative technology that can measure blood flow in the brain and thereby provide information about certain kinds of brain activity when someone is performing a task. However, like every technology used in research, its value and the information it produces are never better than the initial theory and concepts that steer its application. Perhaps the biggest misrepresentation in the "brain glitch" research is that the color scans produced by fMRI provide information about "reading." In fact, they provide no such thing, because the "reading" tasks under study are largely a person's performance on simple sound and sound/symbol (phonics) tasks with words and parts of words, rather than performance in reading as conventionally defined, that is, reading and comprehending sentences and paragraphs. (The same misrepresentation appears in claims about "reading" contained in the report of the National Reading Panel, the chief research document cited in the Reading First legislation.)

The puny definition of reading used in this research appears not to concern the investigators, though, because they design their studies on the assumption that these simple tasks involving words and parts of words embrace the core requirements for beginning readers: that is, mastery of phonological awareness (distinguishing and manipulating sounds in words) and sound/symbol relationships. As the Shaywitz/Lyon study explains, there is now "a strong consensus" (that is, a broad unanimity of professional opinion) that phonological awareness is the first building block within the sequence and that reading disability reflects a deficit in this "lower level component" of "the language system." Only after mastering this component can beginning readers effectively continue to master other reading skills.

That's the claim. The reality is that the so-called strong consensus does not exist. I and others have published thorough research reviews that critique—and dismiss—the "lower level component" model and the supposed empirical evidence showing the superior effect of early, direct, and intensive instruction in word sounds on later reading. As I have also argued, this narrow, do-as-you're-told instruction not only pushes aside numerous issues that bear on beginning literacy—such as children's backgrounds, interests, problem-solving approaches, and definitions of "reading"—it also masquerades as a bootstrap policy solution for poor children that takes off the table all other policies required to address the many needs that influence learning success or failure. However, for the advocates of this "strong consensus," especially those linked to the political power pushing these claims, conflicting views are never allowed to ruffle their harmony.

Hence, an experiment, such as those reported in the Shaywitz/Lyon study, can be designed in which subjects do "lower level component" tasks, such as deciding if nonwords rhyme ("Do leat and bete rhyme?") or making judgments requiring both phonological and semantic knowledge ("Are corn and rice in the same category?"), and the researchers can claim that the data generated tell us a great deal about "reading," the reading process, and the best kinds of instruction. The conclusions in this work display no awareness of the self-fulfilling prophecy at play when the research focuses solely on "lower level components" decontextualized from a full appraisal of reading, uses no other model of reading and instruction, and then concludes that these components are the initial and key ones in learning to read.

A Real "Brain Glitch"?

Looking more deeply into the research design of the "brain glitch" studies, we find a problem that dyslexia researchers have long encountered but not overcome when organizing an experiment so that data on brain activity can be meaningfully interpreted: the experiment must start by grouping dyslexics separately from other kinds of poor readers. This distinction is required because even in studies using the fMRI, the data are about brain activity associated with the word-level tasks, not about micro brain damage. Therefore, fMRI differences in brain activity among a group of unsorted poor readers would not provide information about the cause and meaning of the various differences in activity.

To solve the problem, these studies and previous ones employing simpler technologies try first to separate from a group of poor readers those whose problems are assumed to have non-neurological causes, such as emotional, familial, social class, and similar "exclusionary" influences, as they have been called. If these poor readers are excluded, researchers have reasoned, the probability is high that the reading problems of those who remain are caused by a "brain glitch." While this might make sense in theory, in practice it has not worked, because researchers have not created evaluation methods and criteria for separating the two groups of poor readers.

Even worse, for decades, researchers have frequently stated that they have used a thorough process of distinguishing between the two groups, but the assertion has rarely been accompanied by evidence. In the Shaywitz/Lyon study, for example, dyslexics were supposedly identified after the researchers had determined that the subjects' reading problems were not caused by emotional problems or "social, cultural, or economic disadvantage." Yet the researchers, so dedicated to obtaining and reporting a surfeit of brain data, offered not a whit of information on this process of elimination. Presumably, readers of the published study were expected to accept without question the assertion that genuine dyslexics had been identified and that these children could then be compared to "nonimpaired" readers (an odd term, since it refers to normal or average readers but is used in the study to underline a priori the assumption that the dyslexics' brains were impaired).

The need to provide evidence of thorough appraisals of the roots of subjects' reading problems is usually obvious to anyone who has actually taught poor readers and, therefore, knows that there can be numerous contextual causes of poor reading in middle-class children that will not be readily apparent. In my extensive work with children, young adults, and adults with severe reading problems, I have found that causes can be uncovered only after spending considerable time *both* evaluating and teaching a student, with the latter especially necessary. Poor teaching—such as using a one-size-fits-all reading program, insufficient individualized instruction, too much phonics, too little phonics—is just one of the many influences that can produce reading problems in a variety of ways, but those problems will not be apparent without thorough analysis of a person's instructional history and current active reading.

Many unusual family circumstances and stresses can impair a child's early reading progress. A parent losing a job, a family moving to another city in the middle of the first grade, overworked parents, grandparents dying around the time a child began school are all examples of problems I have identified. These experiences hinder reading development by distracting and stressing a child, but they are not overt "emotional" problems. Even when a poor reader comes from a family that appears "normal," only an extensive exploration of the family dynamics can determine whether this appearance might cloak problems that have affected a child's beginning reading.

By not providing criteria and evidence that the "dyslexics" are different from other poor readers, the brain research studies use another self-serving, self-fulfilling prophecy: because the fMRI shows differences in brain activity between "dyslexic" and "nonimpaired" readers, the differences in brain activity must be visual demonstrations of impairment and nonimpairment. How do we know the fMRI data reveal impairment? Because one of the groups was initially identified as impaired. How do we know the group was impaired? Because the group was first identified as impaired and the fMRI data corroborated the impairment. No other explanations can explain the dyslexics' different brain activity. Impaired, for sure! No question about it. . . .

Fixing the "Brain Glitch"

Beyond finding "brain glitches," researchers have reported other good news: building-block skills instruction can remedy the glitch. "An effective reading program" can produce "brain repair," Shaywitz reports. "The brain can be rewired." . . .

Nearly 20 years ago, Leonide Goldstein and I published a study on differences in brain hemisphere activation in adult beginning readers as they were learning to read. We found that these adults, when they were poor readers or nonreaders, did, indeed, demonstrate brain activation that was different from that found among good readers. However, as their reading improved, through the use of a holistic, comprehensive teaching approach over many months, their brain activation changed toward that commonly found in good readers. We interpreted these data as evidence that new knowledge and competencies were linked to concomitant changes in brain structure and functioning, as one would expect for *all kinds of learning*. There was nothing in the data to suggest that these beginning readers started learning to read with anything other than normal brains that were configured as they were at the beginning of the study because the students had not learned to read; no data suggested that the educational intervention we provided somehow repaired or circumvented dysfunctional brain areas.

To restate a central point for appraising these glitch-fixing interventions: although researchers insist that the training programs they use repair or ameliorate brain hardware or glitches, there is no evidence in any of their studies that this rewiring was different from that which is concomitant with the learning that continues throughout our learning lives. Nor does this so-called repair demonstrate that phonological processing is the *initial* key component in learning to read. The subjects apparently lacked this ability and then learned this ability, and their brain processing changed accordingly. Using modern technology to identify and track brain changes related to changes in reading ability is an extraordinary achievement. Using the achievement for ideological ends is not.

Emotionless "Cognition"

Like the assumed "consensus" on building-blocks instruction, "brain glitch" research assumes that cognition—that is, the process that creates images, concepts, and mental operations—is not a construct but an independent reality that actually describes the brain processes associated with reading. Ignored in this assumption is the ever-growing evidence suggesting that thinking is an inseparable interaction of both cognition and emotion (feelings, desires, enthusiasms, antipathies, etc.) . . .

Unfortunately, none of this new perspective on the "continuous and interwoven cognitive-emotional fugue," . . . has entered the "brain glitch" research. As a result, the question of whether diminished activity in a portion of the brain of someone doing a reading task might be a consequence of an emotional response, in that emotional memories can exert a powerful influence on "thought processes," remains unaddressed. By purging emotions and focusing only on cognition, the "brain glitch" research also purges the alternative: a holistic instructional approach based on the assumption that classrooms are filled with whole children for whom learning is always grounded in the fugue of cognition and affect.

How the Brain Works: Modules?

The interrelationships and interactions missing from the narrow cognitive model of "brain glitch" research lead us to a final concern. A chief premise of this research holds that the brain has specific modules for specialized operations that work in sequence with other modules in learning written language and that foremost of these is at least one module that can process basic sound and sound/symbol skills. This kind of modular model has a certain palpable, visual appeal (not unlike "building-blocks instruction"), but the actual existence of such modules is a theory, not a fact, that has increasingly been questioned. Most likely, the modular model is not one that explains how the brain actually works.

For instance, Merlin Donald, a psychologist who has written extensively on human consciousness, rejects the explanation that modules perform "specialized operations," such as deciphering portions of language. While language areas of the brain, such as those related to aspects of reading, are important in processing particular functions, all are intertwined in extensive networks (a polyphony) of brain areas that are simultaneously and interactively communicating and constructing and reconstructing particular areas within the whole. Yes, the brain has fundamental mechanisms for beginning to learn written language, but it does not begin with a "fixed pattern of connectivity." Instead, the "connectivity pattern is set by experience" with "countless interconnection points, or synapses, which connect neurons to one another in various patterns." In other words, learning and experience create and shape the brain's circuits and how they are used in learning to read; the circuits are not predetermined.

Linguist Philip Lieberman has also criticized modular explanations, calling them "neophrenological theories," that is, theories that "map complex behaviors to localized regions of the brain, on the assumption that a particular part of the brain regulates an aspect of behavior." In these theories, he remarks, the functional organization of the brain is run by "a set of petty bureaucrats each of which controls a behavior." Like Donald, Lieberman proposes that converging behavioral and neurobiological data indicate that human language is composed not of a hierarchical system but of neural networks, including the traditional cortical "language" areas (Broca's and Wernicke's areas), formed through circuits that link populations of neurons in neuroanatomical structures that are distributed throughout the brain. Lieberman stresses, "Although specific operations may be performed in particular parts of the brain, these operations must be integrated into a *network* that regulates an observable aspect of behavior. And so, a particular aspect of behavior usually involves activity in neuroanatomical structures distributed throughout the brain" (emphasis in original). . . .

The view of a "connectivity pattern" that emerges and is activated as children learn to read contrasts with the model of step-by-step progression from module to module. If the former is an accurate model of brain organization and functioning, it suggests that the connectivity pattern should be the focus of research because only by looking at the overall pattern can researchers begin to determine the functioning and interrelationships of any part and the causal, consequential, or interactive function of that part within the entire pattern.

From the perspective of a connectivity pattern model, not only do the brain areas involved in grasping the sound/symbol correspondence *not* have to be primed first before other areas of the pattern can become effectively operable, the creation and functioning of these areas depends on connections within the entire pattern. And because the pattern is not innately fixed, if instruction were to stimulate certain areas more than others, a particular connectivity pattern would emerge. That specific pattern, however, might not necessarily be the sole one required for reading success and might not be superior to other connectivity patterns. Moreover, a more complex connectivity pattern could be created through richer written language learning. None of this is addressed in the "brain glitch" research.

Conclusion

Philip Lieberman offers a caveat worth emphasizing when appraising "brain glitch" research, learning to read, and the Bush agenda for education: "We must remember that we stand on the threshold of an understanding of how brains really work. The greatest danger perhaps rests in making claims that are not supported by data." Unfortunately, not only have "brain glitch" researchers seldom been guided by such a caveat, they have tended to misconstrue the data and have drawn conclusions that serve to justify unwarranted beliefs, instructional policy, and the politics that have driven the research in the first place. . . .

For research on the brain and reading to become productive, what is needed most is the discarding of fundamental assumptions that have not been validated. Building-blocks instruction has not been proved to be the best way to teach reading. Phonological awareness has not been proved to be the initial, essential component that determines reading success. Thinking does not involve "cognition" alone. The modular organization of the brain is, at best, a disputed theory. Brain activation differences do not necessarily reflect "brain glitches." Dyslexia remains no more a proven malady among a substantial percentage of beginning readers than when Glasgow ophthalmologist James Hinshelwood first discussed it as "congenital word-blindness" at the end of the 19th century.

To make research on the brain and reading work, it must be informed by the complexity of reading acquisition, and it must begin to address such questions as: Will alternative teaching approaches configure brain activity in alternative ways? Will children's differing assumptions about what it means to "read" correspond to differing brain activity and organization? How do different aspects of reading, such as comprehension, syntax, and word analysis, interact in certain reading tasks and what kinds of brain activity do the interactions produce? How does the knowledge children bring to literacy learning affect brain activity?

These and similar questions can begin to contribute to a better understanding of the relationship between brain function and reading acquisition, which in turn can help promote ecological approaches that are grounded in an understanding of the unified interrelationships of brain, active child, and learning environment. They can also begin to help identify genuine brain-related reading impairments. Developing this kind of understanding of integrated interrelationships will require that we eschew views that are either "brain based" or conceive of the brain as an extraneous "black box."

By adding to the current pretensions about the superiority of one brand of "scientifically based" reading instruction, "brain glitch" research remains a danger in the classroom. Unfortunately, because of the political power connected to this sham science and brainless instruction, a mighty effort is required to end that danger.

CHALLENGE QUESTIONS

Do Brain Deficiencies Determine Learning Disabilities?

1. What is a learning disability? Where do they come from? How are they identified?
2. Can fMRI scans help neuroscientists and psychologists understand and treat learning disabilities? How? Cite some evidence.
3. How might a generalized reading program, such as that proposed by the Shayitzes, be beneficial? Could it be harmful? How?
4. Explain Dr. Coles's concern about distinguishing between poor readers with brain malfunction and those with non-neurological problems. What are the self-fulfilling prophecies he describes?
5. According to the Shaywitzes, what are the glitches in the brains of poor readers? Do you agree that all poor readers have brain glitches? Why or why not?

Internet References . . .

Developmental Psychology

This website provides academic resources and links related to developmental psychology.

http://www.psy.pdx.edu/PsiCafe/Areas/
Developmental/

Nature vs. Nurture

An overview of the debate on whether nature or nurture (genes or environment) is more influential in human development.

http://en.wikipedia.org/wiki/Nature_versus_
nurture

Divorcerate.org

This site gives up-to-date information on the divorce rates of the United States, Great Britain, Canada, and other countries. It also provides information on whether or not divorced couples have children, have been previously married, and what age those couples were when they decided to get married.

http://www.divorcerate.org/

Children of Divorce: All Kinds of Problems

This Americans for Divorce Reform page offers links to studies of problems experienced by children of divorce.

http://www.divorcereform.org/all.html

Family Research Institute

The Family Research Institute is a nonprofit organization that conducts research on issues pertaining to families. This site has links to many publications of studies and papers on different topics, including divorce and homosexuality.

http://www.familyresearchinst.org/index.html

Human Development

*T*he objective of most developmental psychologists is to document the course of our physical, social, and intellectual changes over the entire span of our lives. Childhood has probably received the most attention because it is often thought to set the stage for the rest of human development. But what has the greatest influence on human development during these early years? One of the oldest controversies in psychology is known as the nature/nurture debate. This is the question of the relative influence of genes (or nature) and environment (or nurture) on development. If the environment is considered important, most psychologists assume that a child's family is the primary context of development. Hence, they study family dynamics and composition in order to better understand these influences. Two family issues have been hotly debated in this regard. Do children whose parents divorce suffer negative consequences, and are children raised by homosexual parents at a higher risk for unhealthy development?

- Does the Environment Influence Human Development More than Genes?

- Does the Divorce of Parents Harm Their Children?

- Does Research Show that Homosexual Parenting Has No Negative Effects?

ISSUE 7

Does the Environment Influence Human Development More than Genes?

YES: Paul Ehrlich and Marcus Feldman, from "Genes and Cultures: What Creates Our Behavioral Phenome?" *Current Anthropology* (February 2003)

NO: Gary Marcus, from "Making the Mind: Why We've Misunderstood the Nature-Nurture Debate," *Boston Review* (December 2003/ January 2004)

ISSUE SUMMARY

YES: Stanford University professors of biology Paul Ehrlich and Marcus Feldman argue that a complete account of human behavior must place a great deal more emphasis on culture than biology.

NO: Psychologist Gary Marcus states that genes are more influential than experience because they limit behavioral possibilities and create virtually unlimited developmental differences.

One of the oldest and most important questions in all psychology, and one of the first ideas presented to students in introductory psychology classes, is known as the nature-nurture debate. This debate concerns the contributions of biology (nature) and learning (nurture) to our personal traits, behaviors, and personalities: are we born with these aspects of our identity or do we acquire them through experience? Many psychologists would say that this debate has been resolved: nurture works on what nature gives us. Nature and nurture are interactive. Still, the matter is not settled as to how much each of these two factors works on us. Does the environment shape behavior more than genes, or does biology trump experience?

In the first article, biologists Paul Ehrlich and Marcus Feldman argue that we have a "gene shortage." In other words, we do not have enough genes, and our DNA is not complex enough, to account for all the differences in human behavior. We have no choice but to consider the overwhelming influence of culture and environment. According to these authors, evolutionary psychologists "overestimate how much of human behavior is primarily traceable to biological universals that are reflected in our genes." Ehrlich and Feldman use examples of the "universal" fear of snakes and some theories of mate selection to illustrate how culture, rather than genes, is more influential in determining behavior. They conclude that "an evolutionary approach to changing behavior must primarily focus on *cultural* evolution" because only then can we begin to understand behavior differences.

Psychologist Gary Marcus takes issue with Ehrlich and Feldman and their idea of a "gene shortage," among other ideas. He focuses specifically on brain development, explaining how genes play a dominant role in brain formation. Genes are not blueprints or dictators, but providers of opportunity; and environment can only take advantage of the opportunities provided by genes. Marcus provides several illustrations to show how altering genes in animals drastically alters behavior, even given the same environments. He also discusses the notion of "cascading," which involves the myriad ways that genes influence each other as part of elaborate networks. As he puts it, "a single . . . gene at the top of a complex network can . . . launch a cascade of hundreds or thousands of other genes." Marcus argues that cascading makes the relatively small number of genes—the "gene shortage"—irrelevant because of the intricacy of genes cascading through enormously complex networks. He concludes by recognizing the importance, but most importantly the limitations, of the environment within our biologogy.

POINT	COUNTERPOINT
• There are not enough genes to account for all behavioral differences.	• The relationship between genes and behavior doesn't have to be one-to-one.
• Cultural evolution is more important than biological evolution in determining behavior.	• Biological evolution has produced the gene combinations necessary to allow cultural influences on behavior.
• There are cultural norms which regulate the behavior of members of a particular society.	• There are biological universals of behavior among all members of a species, governed by genetic commonalities.
• There are too many variations among humans for biological determinism to make sense.	• The 30,000 genes we have interact with each other to account for all differences.

YES

**Paul Ehrlich and
Marcus Feldman**

Genes and Cultures: What Creates Our Behavioral Phenome?

The recent publication of the first draft of the human genome has brought to public attention the relationship between two concepts, genotype and phenotype—a relationship that had previously been discussed largely by academics. The genotype of an organism is encoded in the DNA that is held in chromosomes and other structures inside its cells. The phenotype is what we are able to observe about that organism's biochemistry, physiology, morphology, and behaviors. We will use the term "phenome" to circumscribe a set of phenotypes whose properties and variability we wish to study. Our focus will be on that part of the human phenome that is defined by behaviors and especially on the behavioral phenome's connection with the human genome.

Our understanding of human behavioral traits has evolved; explanations of the control of those traits offered 50 years ago differ from those most common today. In prewar decades genetic determinism—the idea that genes are destiny—had enormous influence on public policy in many countries: on American immigration and racial policies, Swedish sterilization programs, and, of course, Nazi laws on racial purity. Much of this public policy was built on support from biological, medical, and social scientists, but after Hitler's genocidal policies it was no longer politically correct to focus on putative hereditary differences. The fading of genetic determinism was an understandable reaction to Nazism and related racial, sexual, and religious prejudices which had long been prevalent in the United States and elsewhere. Thus, after World War II, it became the norm in American academia to consider all of human behavior as originating in the environment—in the way people were raised and the social contexts in which they lived.

Gradually, though, beginning in the 1960s, books like Robert Ardrey's *Territorial Imperative* and Desmond Morris's *The Naked Ape* began proposing explanations for human behaviors that were biologically reductionist and essentially genetic. Their extreme hereditarian bias may have been stimulated by the rapid progress at that time in understanding the role of DNA, which spurred interest in genetics in both scientists and the public. But perhaps no publication had broader effect in reestablishing genetic credibility in the behavioral sciences than Arthur Jensen's article "How Much Can We Boost IQ?" Although roundly criticized by quantitative geneticists and shown to be based

From *Current Anthropology*, vol. 44, no. 1, February 2003, pp. 87–89, 92–95. Copyright © 2003 by University of Chicago Press via the Copyright Clearance Center. Reprinted by permission.

on the fraudulent data of Sir Cyril Burt, Jensen's work established a tradition that attempts to allocate to genetics a considerable portion of the variation in such human behaviors as for whom we vote, how religious we are, how likely we are to take risks, and, of course, measured IQ and school performance. This tradition is alive and well today.

Within the normal range of human phenotypic variation, including commonly occurring diseases, the role of genetics remains a matter of controversy even as more is revealed about variation at the level of DNA. Here we would like to reexamine the issue of genetics and human behavior in light of the enormous interest in the Human Genome Project, the expansion of behavioral genetics as described above, and the recent proliferation of books emphasizing the genetic programming of every behavior from rape to the learning of grammar. The philosopher Helena Cronin and her coeditor, Oliver Curry, tell us in the introduction to Yale University Press's "Darwinism Today" series that "Darwinian ideas . . . are setting today's intellectual agenda." In the *New York Times*, Nicholas Wade has written that human genes contain the "behavioral instructions" for "instincts to slaughter or show mercy, the contexts for love and hatred, the taste for obedience or rebellion—they are the determinants of human nature."

Genes, Cultures, and Behavior

It is incontrovertible that human beings are a product of evolution, but with respect to behavior that evolutionary process involves chance, natural selection, and, especially in the case of human beings, transmission and alteration of a body of extragenetic information called "culture." Cultural evolution, a process very different from genetic evolution by natural selection, has played a central role in producing our behaviors.

This is not to say that genes are uninvolved in human behavior. *Every* aspect of a person's phenome is a product of interaction between genome and environment. An obvious example of genetic involvement in the behavioral phenome is the degree to which most people use vision to orient themselves—in doing everything from hitting a baseball to selecting new clothes for their children. This is because we have evolved genetically to be "sight animals"—our dominant perceptual system is vision, with hearing coming in second. Had we, like dogs, evolved more sophisticated chemical detection, we might behave very differently in response to the toxic chemicals in our environment. The information in our DNA required to produce the basic morphology and physiology that make sight so important to us has clearly been molded by natural selection. And the physical increase in human brain size, which certainly involved a response to natural selection (although the precise environmental factors causing this selection remain something of a mystery), has allowed us to evolve language, a high level of tool use, the ability to plan for the future, and a wide range of other behaviors not seen in other animals.

Thus at the very least, genetic evolution both biased our ability to perceive the world and gave us the capacity to develop a vast culture. But the long-running nature-versus-nurture debate is not about sight versus smell.

It is about the degree to which differences in today's human behavioral patterns from person to person, group to group, and society to society are influenced by genetic differences, that is, are traceable to differences in human genetic endowments. Do men "naturally" want to mate with as many women as possible while women "naturally" want to be more cautious in choosing their copulatory partners? Is there a "gay gene"? Are human beings "innately" aggressive? Are differences in educational achievement or income "caused" by differences in genes? And are people of all groups genetically programmed to be selfish? A critical social issue to keep in mind throughout our discussion is what the response of our society would be if we knew the answer to these questions. Two related schools of thought take the view that genetic evolution explains much of the human behavioral phenome; they are known as evolutionary psychology and behavioral genetics.

Evolutionary Psychology

Evolutionary psychology claims that many human behaviors became universally fixed as a result of natural selection acting during the environment of evolutionary adaptation, essentially the Pleistocene. A shortcoming of this argument, as emphasized by the anthropologist Robert Foley (1995–96), lies in the nonexistence of such an environment. Our ancestors lived in a wide diversity of habitats, and the impacts of the many environmental changes (e.g., glaciations) over the past million years differed geographically among their varied surroundings. Evolutionary psychologists also postulate that natural selection produced modules ("complex structures that are functionally organized for processing information") in the brain that "tell" us such things as which individuals are likely to cheat, which mates are likely to give us the best or most offspring, and how to form the best coalitions. These brain "modules," which are assumed to be biological entities fixed in humans by evolution, also have other names often bestowed on them by the same writers, such as "computational machines," "decision-making algorithms," "specialized systems," "inference engines," and "reasoning mechanisms." The research claims of evolutionary psychology have been heavily criticized by, among others, colleagues in psychology.

   Those critics are correct. There is a general tendency for evolutionary psychologists vastly to overestimate how much of human behavior is primarily traceable to biological universals that are reflected in our genes. One reason for this overestimation is the ease with which a little evolutionary story can be invented to explain almost any observed pattern of behavior. For example, it seems logical that natural selection would result in the coding of a fear of snakes and spiders into our DNA, as the evolutionary psychologist Steven Pinker thinks. But while Pinker may have genes that make him fear snakes, as the evolutionist Jared Diamond points out, such genes are clearly lacking in New Guinea natives. As Diamond says, "If there is any single place in the world where we might expect an innate fear of snakes among native peoples, it would be in New Guinea, where one-third or more of the snake species are poisonous, and certain non-poisonous constrictor snakes are sufficiently big to be dangerous." Yet there is no sign of innate fear of snakes or spiders among the indigenous people, and children regularly "capture large spiders, singe off the legs and hairs, and eat the bodies. The people there laugh at the idea of an inborn phobia about snakes, and account for the fear in Europeans as a result of their stupidity in being unable to distinguish which snakes might be dangerous." Furthermore, there is reason to believe that fear of snakes in other primates is largely learned as well.

Another example is the set of predictions advanced by Bruce Ellis about the mating behavior that would be found in a previously unknown culture. The first five characteristics that "the average woman in this culture will seek . . . in her ideal mate," he predicts, are:

1. He will be dependable, emotionally stable and mature, and kind/considerate toward her.
2. He will be generous. He may communicate a spirit of caring through a willingness to share time and whatever commodities are valued in this culture with the woman in question.
3. He will be ambitious and perceived by the woman in question as clever or intelligent.
4. He will be genuinely interested in the woman in question, and she in him. He may express his interest through displays of concern for her well-being.
5. He will have a strong social presence and be well liked and respected by others. He will possess a strong sense of efficacy, confidence, and self-respect.

Evolutionary theory does not support such predictions, even if an "average woman" could be defined. First of all, it would be no small developmental trick genetically to program detailed, different, and *independent* reproductive strategies into modules in male and female brains. Those brains, after all are minor variants of the same incredibly complex structures, and, furthermore, the degree to which they are organized into modules is far from clear. If the women in the unknown culture actually chose mates meeting Ellis's criteria, a quite sufficient alternative evolutionary explanation would be that women (simultaneously with men) have evolved big brains, are not stupid, and respond to the norms of their cultures. Scientifically, the notion that the detailed attributes of desirable mates must be engraved in our genetic makeup is without basis, especially in light of the enormous cultural differences in sexual preferences.

For any culture, Ellis's evolutionary arguments would require that in past populations of women there were DNA-based differences that made some more likely to choose in those ways and others more likely to seek mates with other characteristics. And those that chose as Ellis predicts would have to have borne and raised more children that survived to reproduce than those with other preferences. Might, for example, a woman who married a stingy male who kept her barefoot and pregnant out-reproduce the wife of a generous and considerate mate? That is the way genetic evolution changes the characteristics of populations over time: by some genetic variants' out-reproducing others.

When that happens, we say that natural selection has occurred. But, unfortunately, there are no data that speak to whether there is (or was) genetic variation in human mate preferences—variation in, say, ability to evaluate specifically whether a potential mate is "ambitious"—upon which selection could be based. And there are no data for any population showing that women who seek those characteristics in their sexual partners are more successful reproductively—are represented by more children in the subsequent generation—than women who seek husbands with other characteristics. Ellis is simply confusing the preferences of women he knows in his society with evolutionary fitness. . . .

What Does Determine the Behavioral Phenome?

Geneticists know that a large portion of the behavioral phenome must be programmed into the brain by factors in the environment, including the internal environment in which the fetus develops and, most important, the cultural environment in which human beings spend their entire lives. Behavioral scientists know, for instance, that many dramatic personality differences *must* be traced to environmental influences. Perhaps the most important reason to doubt that genetic variation accounts for a substantial portion of observed differences in human behavior is simply that we lack an extensive enough hereditary apparatus to do the job—that we have a "gene shortage." To what extent could genes control the production of these differences?

It is important to remember that behaviors are the results of charge changes that occur in our network of neurons, the specialized cells that make up our nervous system. Behaviors are ultimately under some degree of control in the brain. Neuron networks are the locus of the memories that are also important to our behavior. That genes can control some general patterns is unquestioned; they are obviously involved in the construction of our brains. They might therefore also build in the potential for experience to affect a large part of the details involved in the neural circuitry. But they cannot be controlling our individual behavioral choices.

Human beings have only three times as many genes as have fruit flies (many of those genes appear to be duplicates of those in the flies, and the biochemistry of fly nerve cells seems quite close to ours). But in addition to having sex and eating (what flies mostly do) we get married, establish charities, build hydrogen bombs, commit genocide, compose sonatas, and publish books on evolution. It is a little hard to credit all this to the determining action of those few additional genes. Those genes are, however, likely to have contributed to the increased brain size and complexity that support the vast cultural superstructure created by the interaction of our neurons and their environments. They may also contribute to the wonderful flexibility and plasticity of human behavior—the very attributes that make our behavior less rather than more genetically determined. But to understand the development of and variation in specific human behaviors such as creating charities and cheesecakes, we must invoke culture, its evolution, and its potential interaction with biology.

It might be argued that since a relative handful of genes can control our basic body plan—one's height depends on millions of the body's cells' being stacked precisely—a handful could also determine our behavioral phenome. Genes initiate a process of development that might be analogized with the way a mountain stream entering a floodplain can initiate the development of a complex delta. Why, then, couldn't just a few genes have evolved to program millions of our behaviors? In theory they might have, but in that case human behavior would be very stereotyped. Consider the problem of evolving human behavioral flexibility under such circumstances of genetic determination. Changing just one behavioral pattern—say, making women more desirous of mating with affluent men—would be somewhat analogous to changing the course of one distributary (branch in the delta) without altering the braided pattern of the rest of the delta. It would be difficult to do by just changing the flow of the mountain stream (equivalent to changing the genes) but easily accomplished by throwing big rocks in the distributary (changing the environment).

This partial analogy seems particularly apt in that it is apparently difficult for evolution to accomplish just one thing at a time. There are two principal reasons for this. The first is the complexity of interactions among alleles and phenotypic traits, especially pleiotropy and epistasis. Because there are relatively so few of them, most genes must be involved in more than one process (pleiotropy). Then if a mutation leads to better functioning of one process, it may not be selected for because the change might degrade the functioning of another process. And changes in one gene can modify the influence of another in very complex ways (epistasis). Second, because they are physically coupled to other genes on the same chromosome, the fates of genes are not independent. Selection that increases the frequency of one allele in a population will often, because of linkage, necessarily increase the frequency of another. Selection favoring a gene that made one prefer tall mates might also result in the increase of a nearby gene that produced greater susceptibility to a childhood cancer.

The Mysteries of Environmental Control

Behavioral scientists are still, unhappily, generally unable to determine the key environmental factors that influence the behavioral phenome. For instance, in the case of the Dionne quintuplets, quite subtle environmental differences—perhaps initiated by different positions in the womb or chance interactions among young quints, their parents, and their observers—clearly led to substantially different behavioral and health outcomes in five children with identical genomes. As their story shows, we really know very little about what environmental factors can modify behavior. For example, some virtually undetectable differences in environments may be greatly amplified as developing individuals change their own environments and those of their siblings. Equally, subtle and undetected environmental factors may put individuals with the same genetic endowments on similar life courses even if they are reared apart, perhaps explaining anecdotes about the similarities of some reunited identical twins.

We also know too little about the routes through which genes may influence behavior, where again changes may be behaviorally amplified. Suppose that a study shows that identical twins, separated at birth, nonetheless show a high correlation of personality type—both members of twin pairs tend to be either introverted or extraverted. This is interpreted as a high heritability of introversion and extraversion. What really is heavily influenced by genetics, however, could be height, and tall people in that society (as in many societies) may be better treated by their peers and thus more likely to become extraverted. Genes in this case will clearly be involved in personality type but by such an indirect route as to make talk of "genes for introversion or extraversion" essentially meaningless.

And, of course, scientists *do* know that what appears to be "genetic" is often simply a function of the environment. An example suggested by the philosopher Elliott Sober illustrates this. In England before the 18th century, evolutionary psychologists (had there been any) would have assumed that males had a genetic proclivity for knitting. The knitting gene would have been assumed to reside on the Y chromosome. But by the 19th century, evolutionary psychologists would have claimed that women had that genetic proclivity, with the knitting gene on the X chromosome. With historical perspective, we can see that the change was purely culture-driven, not due to a genetic change. As it did with knitting, the environment, especially the cultural environment, seems to do a good job of fine-tuning our behavior. A major challenge for science today is to elucidate how that fine-tuning occurs.

Would Selection Generally Favor Genetic Control of Behavior?

Would we be better off if we had more than enough genes to play a controlling role in every one of our choices and actions and those genes could operate independently? Probably not. One could imagine a Hobbesian battle in which genes would compete with each other to improve the performance of the reproducing individuals that possessed them—genes for caution being favored in one environment one day and genes for impulsiveness in another environment the next ("Look before you leap," "He who hesitates is lost"). It is difficult to imagine how *any* organism could make the grade evolutionarily if its behavior were completely genetically determined and interactions between its genes and its environments did not exist. Even single-celled organisms respond to changes in their surroundings. Without substantial environmental inputs, evolution would not occur and life could not exist.

Biological evolution has avoided that problem by allowing our behavior to be deeply influenced by the environments in which genes operate. In normal human environments, genes are heavily involved in creating a basic brain with an enormous capacity for learning—taking in information from the environment and incorporating that information into the brain's structure. It is learning that proceeds after birth as an infant's brain uses inputs such as patterns of light from the eyes to wire up the brain so that it can see, patterns of sound that wire up the brain so that it can speak one or more languages, and so on. As the brain scientist John Allman put it, "the brain is unique among the organs of the body in requiring a great deal of feedback from experience to develop its full capacities." And the situation is not so different for height. There aren't enough genes to control a child's growth rate from day to day—adding cells rapidly in favorable (e.g., food-rich) situations and slowly or not at all under starvation. And there aren't enough genes to govern the growth of each column of cells, some to regulate those in each column on the right side of the spine, some for each in the left. Instead, all growth patterns depend on environmental feedback. . . .

Conclusions

What the recent evidence from the Human Genome Project tells us is that the interaction between genes, between the separate components of genes, and between controlling elements of these separate components must be much more complex than we ever realized. Simple additive models of gene action or of the relationship between genes and environments must be revised. They have formed the basis for our interpretation of phenotype-genotype relationships for 84 years, ever since R. A. Fisher's famous paper that for the first time related Mendelian genes to measurable phenotypes. New models and paradigms are needed to go from the genome to the phenome in any quantitative way. The simplistic approach of behavioral genetics cannot do the job. We must dig deeper into the environmental and especially cultural factors that contribute to the phenome. The ascendancy of molecular biology has, unintentionally, militated against progress in studies of cultural evolution.

Theories of culture and its evolution in the 20th century, from Boas's insistence on the particularity of cultural identities to the debates between material and cultural determinism described by Sahlins, were proudly nonquantitative. Recent discussions on the ideational or symbolic nature of the subjects of cultural evolution, while critical of attempts to construct dynamical models of cultural evolution based on individual-to-individual cultural transmission, nevertheless acknowledge the centrality of cultural evolution to human behavioral analysis. Thus, although the quantitative paradigms used in behavioral genetics do not inform evolutionary analysis, this does not mean that we cannot or should not take an evolutionary approach to the understanding and modification of human behavior. Genetically evolved features such as the dominance of our visual sense should always be kept in mind, but an evolutionary approach to changing behavior in our species must primarily focus on *cultural* evolution. In the last 40,000 years or so, the scale of that cultural evolution has produced a volume of information that dwarfs what is coded into our genes. Just consider what is now stored in human memories, libraries, photographs, films, video tapes, the Worldwide Web, blueprints, and computer data banks—in addition to what is inherent in other artifacts and human-made structures. Although there have been preliminary investigations by Cavalli-Sforza and Feldman and Boyd and Richerson, scientists have barely begun to investigate the basic processes by which that body of information changes (or remains constant for long periods)—a task that social scientists have been taking up piecemeal and largely qualitatively for a very long time. Developing a unified quantitative theory of cultural change is one of the great challenges for evolutionary and social science in the 21st century.

Identifying the basic mechanisms by which our culture evolves will be difficult; the most recent attempts using a "meme" approach appear to be a dead end. Learning how to influence that evolution is likely to be more difficult still and fraught with pitfalls. No sensible geneticist envisions a eugenic future in which people are selected to show certain behavioral traits, and most thinking people are aware of the ethical (if not technical and social) problems of trying to change our behavior by altering our genetic endowments. Society has long been mucking around in cultural evolution, despite warnings of the potential abuses of doing so. Nazi eugenic policies and Soviet, Cambodian, Chinese, and other social engineering experiments stand as monuments to the ethical dangers that must be guarded against when trying systematically to alter either genetic or cultural evolution.

Nevertheless, we are today all involved in carrying out or (with our taxes) supporting experiments designed to change behavior. This is attested to by the advertising business, Head Start programs, and the existence of institutions such as Sing Sing Prison and Stanford University. The data used by evolutionary psychologists to infer the biological antecedents of human behavior, while not telling us anything about genetic evolution, may actually be helpful in improving our grasp of cultural evolution. What seems clear today, however, is that evolutionary psychology and behavioral genetics are promoting a vast overemphasis on the part played by genetic factors (and a serious underestimation of the role of cultural evolution) in shaping our behavioral phenomes.

Gary Marcus  **NO**

Making the Mind: Why We've Misunderstood the Nature-Nurture Debate

What do our minds owe to our nature, and what to our nurture? The question has long been vexed, in no small part because until recently we knew relatively little about the nature of nature—how genes work and what they bring to the biological structures that underlie the mind. But now, 50 years after the discovery of the molecular structure of DNA, we are for the first time in a position to understand directly DNA's contribution to the mind. And the story is vastly different from—and vastly more interesting than—anything we had anticipated.

The emerging picture of nature's role in the formation of the mind is at odds with a conventional view, recently summarized by Louis Menand. According to Menand, "every aspect of life has a biological foundation in exactly the same sense, which is that unless it was biologically possible it wouldn't exist. After that, it's up for grabs." More particularly, some scholars have taken recent research on genes and on the brain as suggesting a profoundly limited role for nature in the formation of the mind.

Their position rests on two arguments, what Stanford anthropologist Paul Ehrlich dubbed a "gene shortage" and widespread, well-documented findings of "brain plasticity." According to the gene shortage argument, genes can't be very important to the birth of the mind because the genome contains only about 30,000 genes, simply too few to account even for the brain's complexity—with its billions of cells and tens of billions of connections between neurons—much less the mind's. "Given that ratio," Ehrlich suggested, "it would be quite a trick for genes typically to control more than the most general aspects of human behavior."

According to the brain plasticity argument, genes can't be terribly important because the developing brain is so flexible. For instance, whereas adults who lose their left hemisphere are likely to lose permanently much of their ability to talk, a child who loses a left hemisphere may very well recover the ability to speak, even in the absence of a left hemisphere. Such flexibility is pervasive, down to the level of individual cells. Rather than being fixed in their fates the instant they are born, newly formed brain cells—neurons—can sometimes shift their function, depending on their context. A cell that would ordinarily help to give us a sense of touch can (in the right circumstances) be recruited into the visual system and accept signals from the eye. With that high level of brain plasticity, some imagine that genes are left on the sidelines, as scarcely relevant onlookers.

All of this is, I think, a mistake. It is certainly true that the number of genes is tiny in comparison to the number of neurons, and that the developing brain is highly plastic. Nevertheless, nature—in the form of genes—has an enormous impact on the developing brain and mind. The general outlines of how genes build the brain are finally becoming clear, and we are also starting to see how, in forming the brain, genes make room for the environment's essential role. While vast amounts of work remain to be done, it is becoming equally clear that understanding the coordination of nature and nurture will require letting go of some long-held beliefs.

How to Build a Brain

In the nine-month dash from conception to birth—the flurry of dividing, specializing, and migrating cells that scientists call embryogenesis—organs such as the heart and kidney unfold in a series of ever more mature stages. In contrast to a 17th century theory known as preformationism, the organs of the body cannot be found preformed in miniature in a fertilized egg; at the moment of conception there is neither a tiny heart nor a tiny brain. Instead, the fertilized egg contains information: the three billion nucleotides of DNA that make up the human genome. That information, copied into the nucleus of every newly formed cell, guides the gradual but powerful process of successive approximation that shapes each of the body's organs. The heart, for example, begins as a simple sheet of cell that gradually folds over to form a tube; the tube sprouts bulges, the bulges sprout further bulges, and every day the growing heart looks a bit more like an adult heart.

Even before the dawn of the modern genetic era, biologists understood that something similar was happening in the development of the brain—that the organ of thought and language was formed in much the same way as the rest of the body. The brain, too, develops in the first instance from a simple sheet of cells that gradually curls up into a tube that sprouts bulges, which over time differentiate into ever more complex shapes. Yet 2,000 years of thinking of the mind as independent from the body kept people from appreciating the significance of this seemingly obvious point.

The notion that the brain is drastically different from other physical systems has a long tradition; it can be seen as a modernized version of the ancient belief that the mind and body are wholly separate—but it is untenable. The brain is a physical system. Although the brain's function is different from that of other organs, the brain's capabilities, like those of other organs, emerge from its physical properties. We now know that strokes and gunshot wounds can interfere with language by destroying parts of the brain, and that Prozac and Ritalin can influence mood by altering the flow of neurotransmitters. The fundamental components of the brain—the neurons and the synapses that connect them—can be understood as physical systems, with chemical and electrical properties that follow from their composition.

Yet even as late as the 1990s, latter-day dualists might have thought that the brain developed by different principles. There were, of course, many hints that genes must be important for the brain: identical twins resemble each other more than nonidentical twins in personality as well as in physique; mental disorders such as schizophrenia and depression run in families and are shared even by twins reared apart; and animal breeders know that shaping the bodies of animals often leads to correlated changes in behavior. All of these observations provided clues of genetic effects on the brain.

But such clues are achingly indirect, and it was easy enough to pay them little heed. Even in the mid-1990s, despite all the discoveries that had been made in molecular biology, hardly anything specific was known about how the brain formed. By the end of that decade, however, revolutions in the methodology of molecular biology—techniques for studying and manipulating genes—were beginning to enter the study of the brain. Now, just a few years later, it has become clear that to an enormous extent the brain really is sculpted by the same processes as the rest of the body, not just at the macroscopic level (i.e., as a product of successive approximation) but also at the microscopic level, in terms of the mechanics of how genes are switched on and off, and even in terms of which genes are involved; a huge number of the genes that participate in the development of the brain play important (and often closely related) roles in the rest of the body. . . .

The . . . power of genes holds even for the most unusual yet most characteristic parts of neurons: the long axons that carry signals away from the cell, the tree-like dendrites that allow neurons to receive signals from other nerve cells, and the trillions of synapses that serve as connections between them. What your brain does is largely a function of how those synaptic connections are set up—alter those connections, and you alter the mind—and how they are set up is no small part a function of the genome. In the laboratory, mutant flies and mice with aberrant brain wiring have trouble with everything from motor control (one mutant mouse is named "reeler" for its almost drunken gait) to vision. And in humans, faulty brain wiring contributes to disorders such as schizophrenia and autism.

Proper neural wiring depends on the behavior of individual axons and dendrites. And this behavior once again depends on the content of the genome. For example, much of what axons do is governed by special wiggly, almost hand-like protuberances at the end of each axon known as growth cones. Growth cones (and the axonal wiring they trail behind them) are like little animals that swerve back and forth, maneuvering around obstacles, extending and retracting feelers known as filopodia (the "fingers" of a growth cone) as the cone hunts around in search of its destination—say in the auditory cortex. Rather than simply being launched like projectiles that blindly and helplessly follow whatever route they first set out on, growth cones constantly compensate and adjust, taking in new information as they find their way to their targets.

Growth cones don't just head in a particular direction and hope for the best. They "know" what they are looking for and can make new plans even if experimentally induced obstacles get in their way. In their efforts to find their destinations, growth cones use every trick they can, from "short-range" cues emanating from the surface of nearby cells to long-distance cues that broadcast their signals from millimeters away—miles and miles in the geography of an axon. For example, some proteins appear to serve as "radio beacons" that can diffuse across great distances and serve as guides to distant growth cones—provided that they are tuned to the right station. Which stations a growth cone picks up—and whether it finds a particular signal attractive or repellent—depends on the protein receptors it has on its surface, in turn a function of which genes are expressed within.

Researchers are now in a position where they can begin to understand and even manipulate those genes. In 2000, a team of researchers at the Salk Institute in San Diego took a group of thoracic (chest) motor neurons that normally extend their axons into several different places, such as axial muscles (midline muscles that play a role in posture), intercostal muscles (the muscles between the ribs), and sympathetic neurons (which, among other things, participate in the fast energy mobilization for fight-or-flight responses), and by changing their genetic labels persuaded virtually the entire group of thoracic neurons to abandon their usual targets in favor of the axial muscles. (The few exceptions were a tiny number that apparently couldn't fit into the newly crowded axial destinations and had to find other targets.)

What this all boils down to, from the perspective of psychology, is an astonishingly powerful system for wiring the mind. Instead of vaguely telling axons and dendrites to send and accept signals from their neighbors, thereby leaving all of the burden of mind development to experience, nature in effect lays down the cable: it supplies the brain's wires—axons and dendrites—with elaborate tools for finding their way on their own. Rather than waiting for experience, brains can use the complex menagerie of genes and proteins to create a rich, intricate starting point for the brain and mind.

The sheer overlap between the cellular and molecular processes by which the brain is built and the processes by which the rest of the body is built has meant that new techniques designed for the study of the one can often be readily imported into the study of the other. New techniques in staining, for instance, by which biologists trace the movements and fates of individual cells, can often be brought to bear on the study of the brain as soon as they are developed; even more important, new techniques for altering the genomes of experimental animals can often be almost immediately applied to studies of brain development. Our collective understanding of biology is growing by leaps and bounds because sauce for the goose is so often sauce for the gander.

Nature and Nurture Redux

This seemingly simple idea—that what's good enough for the body is good enough for the brain—has important implications for how we understand the roles of nature and nurture in the development of the mind and brain.

Beyond the Blueprint

Since the early 1960s biologists have realized that genes are neither blueprints nor dictators; instead, as I will explain in a moment, genes are better seen as *providers of opportunity*. Yet because the brain has for so long been treated as separate from the body, the notion of genes as sources of options rather than purveyors of commands has yet to really enter into our understanding of the origins of human psychology.

Biologists have long understood that all genes have two functions. First, they serve as templates for building particular proteins. The insulin gene provides a template for insulin, the hemoglobin genes give templates for building hemoglobin, and so forth. Second, each gene contains what is called a regulatory sequence, a set of conditions that guide whether or not that gene's template gets converted into protein. Although every cell contains a complete copy of the genome, most of the genes in any given cell are silent. Your lung cells, for example, contain the recipe for insulin but they don't produce any, because in those cells the insulin gene is switched off (or "repressed"); each protein is produced only in the cells in which the relevant gene is switched on. So individual genes are like lines in a computer program. Each gene has an IF and a THEN, a precondition (IF) and an action (THEN). And here is one of the most important places where the environment can enter: the IFs of genes are responsive to the environment of the cells in which they are contained. Rather than being static entities that decide the fate of each cell in advance, genes—because of the regulatory sequence—are dynamic and can guide a cell in different ways at different times, depending on the balance of molecules in their environment.

This basic logic—which was worked out in the early 1960s by two French biologists, François Jacob and Jacques Monod, in a series of painstaking studies of the diet of a simple bacterium—applies as much to humans as to bacteria, and as much for the brain as for any other part of the body. Monod and Jacob aimed to understand how *E. coli* bacteria could switch almost instantaneously from a diet of glucose (its favorite) to a diet of lactose (an emergency backup food). What they found was that this abrupt change in diet was accomplished by a process that switched genes on and off. To metabolize lactose, the bacterium needed to build a certain set of protein-based enzymes that for simplicity I'll refer to collectively as lactase, the product of a cluster of lactase genes. Every *E. coli* had those lactase genes lying in wait, but they were only expressed—switched on—when a bit of lactose could bind (attach to) a certain spot of DNA that lay near them, and this in turn could happen only if there was no glucose around to get in the way. In essence, the simple bacterium had an IF-THEN—if lactose and not glucose, then build lactase—that is very much of a piece with the billions of IF-THENs that run the world's computer software.

The essential point is that genes are IFs rather than MUSTs. So even a single environmental cue can radically reshape the course of development. In the African butterfly *Bicyclus anynana*, for example, high temperature during development (associated with the rainy season in its native tropical climate) leads the butterfly to become brightly colored; low temperature (associated with a dry fall) leads the butterfly to become a dull brown. The growing butterfly doesn't learn (in the course of its development) how to blend in better—it will do the same thing in a lab where the temperature varies and the foliage is constant; instead it is genetically programmed to develop in two different ways in two different environments.

The lesson of the last five years of research in developmental neuroscience is that IF-THENs are as crucial and omnipresent in brain development as they are elsewhere. To take one recently worked out example: rats, mice, and other rodents devote a particular region of the cerebral cortex known as barrel fields to the problem of analyzing the stimulation of their whiskers. The exact placement of those barrel fields appears to be driven by a gene or set of genes whose IF region is responsive to the quantity of a particular molecule, Fibroblast Growth Factor 8 (FGF8). By altering the distribution of that molecule, researchers were able to alter barrel development: increasing the concentration of FGF8 led to mice with barrel fields that were unusually far forward, while decreasing the concentration led to mice with barrel fields that were unusually far back. In essence, the quantity of FGF8 serves as a beacon, guiding growing cells to their fate by driving the regulatory IFs of the many genes that are presumably involved in barrel-field formation.

Other IF-THENs contribute to the function of the brain throughout life, e.g., supervising the control of neurotransmitters and participating . . . in the process of laying down memory traces. Because each gene has an IF, every aspect of the brain's development is in principle linked to some aspect of the environment; chemicals such as alcohol that are ingested during pregnancy have such enormous effects because they fool the IFs that regulate genes that guide cells into dividing too much or too little, into moving too far or not far enough, and so forth. The brain is the product of the actions of its component cells, and those actions are the products of the genes they contain within, each cell guided by 30,000 IFs paired with 30,000 THENs—as many possibilities as there are genes. (More, really, because many genes have multiple IFs, and genes can and often do work in combination.)

From Genes to Behavior

Whether we speak of the brain or other parts of the body, changes in even a single gene—leading to either a new IF or a new THEN—can have great consequences. Just as a single alteration to the hemoglobin gene can lead to a predisposition for sickle-cell anemia, a single change to the genes involved in the brain can lead to a language impairment or mental retardation.

And at least in animals, small differences within genomes can lead to significant differences in behavior. A Toronto team, for example, recently used genetic techniques to investigate—and ultimately modify—the foraging habits of *C. elegans* worms. Some *elegans* prefer to forage in groups, others are loners, and the Toronto group was able to tie these behavioral differences to differences in a single amino acid in the protein template (THEN) region of a particular gene known as npr-1; worms with the amino acid valine in the critical spot are "social" whereas worms with phenylalanine are loners. Armed with that knowledge and modern genetic engineering techniques, the team was able to switch a strain of loner *C. elegans* worms into social worms by altering that one gene.

Another team of researchers, at Emory University, has shown that changing the regulatory IF region of a single gene can also have a significant effect on social behavior. Building on an observation that differences in sociability in different species of voles correlated with how many vasopressin receptors they had, they transferred the regulatory IF region of sociable prairie voles' vasopressin receptor genes into the genome of a less sociable species, the mouse—and in so doing created mutant mice, more social than normal, with more vasopressin receptors. With other small genetic modifications, researchers have created strains of anxious, fearful mice, mice that progressively increase alcohol consumption under stress, mice that lack the nurturing instinct, and even mice that groom themselves constantly, pulling and tugging on their own hair to the point of baldness. Each of those studies demonstrates how behavior can be significantly changed when even a single gene is altered.

Still, complex biological structures—whether we speak of hearts or kidneys or brains—are the product of the concerted actions and interactions of many genes, not just one. A mutation in a single gene known as FOXP2 can interfere with the ability of a child to learn language; an alteration in the vasopressin gene can alter a rodent's sociability—but this doesn't mean that FOXP2 is solely responsible for language or that vasopressin is the only gene a rat needs in order to be sociable. Although individual genes can have powerful effects, no trait is the consequence of any single gene. There can no more be a single gene for language, or for the propensity for talking about the weather, than there can be for the left ventricle of a human heart. Even a single brain cell—or a single heart cell—is the product of many genes working together.

The mapping between genes and behavior is made even more complex by the fact that few if any neural circuits operate entirely autonomously. Except perhaps in the case of reflexes, most behaviors are the product of multiple interacting systems. In a complex animal like a mammal or a bird, virtually every action depends on a coming together of systems for perception, attention, motivation, and so forth. Whether or not a pigeon pecks a lever to get a pellet depends on whether it is hungry, whether it is tired, whether there is anything else more interesting around, and so forth. Furthermore, even within a single system, genes rarely participate directly "on-line," in part because they are just too slow. Genes do seem to play an active, major role in "off-line" processing, such as consolidation of long-term memory—which can even happen during sleep—but when it comes to rapid on-line decision-making, genes, which work on a time scale of seconds or minutes, turn over the reins to neurons, which act on a scale of hundredths of a second. The chief contribution of genes comes in advance, in laying down and adjusting neural circuitry, not in the moment-by-moment running of the nervous system. Genes build neural structures—not behavior.

In the assembly of the brain, as in the assembly of other organs, one of the most important ideas is that of a cascade, one gene influencing another, which influences another, which influences another, and so on. Rather than acting in absolute isolation, most genes act as parts of elaborate networks in which the expression of one gene is a precondition for the expression of the next. The THEN of one gene can satisfy the IF of another and thus induce it to turn on. Regulatory proteins are proteins (themselves the product of genes) that control the expression of other genes and thus tie the whole genetic system together. A single regulatory gene at the top of a complex network can indirectly launch a cascade of hundreds or thousands of other genes leading to, for example, the development of an eye or a limb.

In the words of Swiss biologist Walter Gehring, such genes can serve as "master control genes" and exert enormous power on a growing system. PAX6, for example, is a regulatory protein that plays a role in eye development, and Gehring has shown that artificially activating it in the right spot on a fruit fly's antenna can lead to an extra eye, right there on the antenna—thus, a simple regulatory gene leads directly and indirectly to the expression of approximately 2,500 other genes. What is true for the fly's eye is also true for its brain—and also for the human brain: by compounding and coordinating their effects, genes can exert enormous influence on biological structure.

From a Tiny Number of Genes to a Complex Brain

The cascades in turn help us to make sense of the alleged gene shortage, the idea that the discrepancy between the number of genes and the number of neurons might somehow minimize the importance of genes when it comes to constructing brain or behavior.

Reflection on the relation between brain and body immediately vitiates the gene shortage argument: if 30,000 genes weren't enough to have significant influence on the 20 billion cells in the brain, they surely wouldn't have much impact on the trillions that are found in the body as a whole. The confusion, once again, can be traced to the mistaken idea of genome as blueprint, to the misguided expectation of a one-to-one mapping from individual genes to individual neurons; in reality, genomes describe processes for building things rather than pictures of finished products: better to think of the genome as a compression scheme than a blueprint.

Computer scientists use compression schemes when they want to store and transmit information efficiently. All compression schemes rely in one way or another on ferreting out redundancy. For instance, programs that use the GIF format look for patterns of repeated pixels (the colored dots of which digital images are made). If a whole series of pixels are of exactly the same color, the software that creates GIF files will assign a code that represents the color of those pixels, followed by a number to indicate how many pixels in a row are of the same color. Instead of having to list every blue pixel individually, the GIF format saves space by storing only two numbers: the code for blue and the number of repeated blue pixels. When you "open" a GIF file, the computer converts those codes back into the appropriate strings of identical bits; in the meantime, the computer has saved a considerable amount of memory. Computer scientists have devised dozens of different compression schemes, from JPEGs for photographs to MP3s for music, each designed to exploit a different kind of redundancy. The general procedure is always the same: some end product is converted into a compact description of how to reconstruct that end product; a "decompressor" reconstructs the desired end product from that compact description.

Biology doesn't know in advance what the end product will be; there's no StuffIt Compressor to convert a human being into a genome. But the genome is very much akin to a compression scheme, a terrifically efficient description of how to build something of great complexity—perhaps more efficient than anything yet developed in the labs of computer scientists (never mind the complexities of the brain—there are trillions of cells in the rest of the body, and they are all supervised by the same 30,000-gene genome). And although nature has no counterpart to a program that stuffs a picture into a compressed encoding, it does offer a counterpart to the program that performs decompression: the cell. Genome in, organism out. Through the logic of gene expression, cells are self-regulating factories that translate genomes into biological structure.

Cascades are at the heart of this process of decompression, because the regulatory proteins that are at the top of genetic cascades serve as shorthand that can be used over and over again, like the subroutine of a software engineer. For example, the genome of a centipede probably doesn't specify separate sets of hundreds or thousands of genes for each of the centipede's legs; instead, it appears that the leg-building "subroutine"—a cascade of perhaps hundreds or thousands of genes—gets invoked many times, once for each new pair of legs. Something similar lies behind the construction of a vertebrate's ribs. And within the last few years it has become clear that the embryonic brain relies on the same sort of genetic recycling, using the same repeated motifs—such as sets of parallel connections known as topographic maps—over and over again, to supervise the development of thousands or even millions of neurons with each use of a given genetic subroutine. There's no gene shortage, because every cascade represents the shorthand for a different reuseable subroutine, a different way of creating more from less.

From Prewiring to Rewiring

In the final analysis, I think the most important question about the biological roots of the mind may not be the question that has preoccupied my colleagues and myself for a number of years—the extent to which genes prewire the brain—but a different question that until recently had never been seriously raised: the extent to which (and ways in which) genes make it possible for experience to *rewire* the brain. Efforts to address the nature-nurture question typically falter because of the false assumption that the two—prewiring and rewiring—are competing ideas. "Anti-nativists"—critics of the view that we might be born with significant mental structure prior to experience—often attempt to downplay the significance of genes by making what I earlier called "the argument from plasticity": they point to the brain's resilience to damage and its ability to modify itself in response to experience. Nativists sometimes seem to think that their position rests on downplaying (or demonstrating limits on) plasticity.

In reality, plasticity and innateness are almost logically separate. Innateness is about the extent to which the brain is prewired, plasticity about the extent to which it can be rewired. Some organisms may be good at one but not the other: chimpanzees, for example, may have intricate innate wiring yet, in comparison to humans, relatively few mechanisms for rewiring their brains. Other organisms may be lousy at both: *C. elegans* worms have limited initial structure, and relatively little in the way of techniques for rewiring their nervous system on the basis of experience. And some organisms, such as humans, are well-endowed in both respects, with enormously intricate initial architecture and fantastically powerful and flexible means for rewiring in the face of experience. . . .

CHALLENGE QUESTIONS

Does the Environment Influence Human Development More than Genes?

1. Describe the "gene shortage" argument. Why are genes, according to this argument, not responsible for the wide variations among human behaviors?
2. Describe Marcus's rebuttal to the gene shortage argument. How does he explain how only 30,000 genes can determine not only the complexities of the brain and the body, but also of behavior?
3. Why do Ehrlich and Feldman place so much emphasis on culture?
4. How do you experience your own life? Do you feel that your genes are the major determinant of your behavior, or are you primarily shaped through your experiences? Explain.
5. Are there any alternatives to the nature-nurture dichotomy? Could there be other influences on our behavior besides our bodies and the environment? What about the question of human agency (see Issue 9)? Can we choose some of our own behavior in such a way that it is not solely determined by some nature-nurture interaction?

ISSUE 8

Does the Divorce of Parents Harm Their Children?

YES: Judith S. Wallerstein, from "Growing Up in the Divorced Family," *Clinical Social Work Journal* (Winter 2005)

NO: E. Mavis Hetherington and John Kelly, from *For Better or For Worse: Divorce Reconsidered* (W.W. Norton, 2002)

ISSUE SUMMARY

YES: Clinical psychologist Judith S. Wallerstein argues not only that children are harmed when their parents divorce but also that these negative side effects continue into their adult lives.

NO: Developmental psychologist E. Mavis Hetherington and writer John Kelly do not deny that divorce can have harmful immediate effects on children, but they contend that most of these children eventually become well adjusted.

One of the unfortunate facts of modern life is that first marriages stand a 50 percent chance of breaking up and second marriages stand a 67 percent chance of doing the same. Since these percentages have been fairly constant for two generations, some researchers have estimated that almost a quarter of all people living today between the ages of 18 and 44 have parents who are divorced. What effect, if any, does the divorce of parents have on their children? Does divorce have a lasting influence, or is it eventually overcome by other life events?

Answering these questions is one of the many interests of two subdisciplines of psychology—clinical and developmental. Clinical psychologists are concerned with influences that would hinder a person from living a fulfilling life. They might wonder if divorce contributes to the problems that prevent such a life and lead to the need for psychotherapy and counseling. Developmental psychologists have similar interests. Their emphasis, however, is often on how events in childhood and adolescence, such as parental divorce, affect successful aging and development. As it happens, the senior authors of the following selections represent these very subdisciplines. Although they are two of the leading researchers on the effects of divorce, they come to dramatically different conclusions about these effects.

Judith S. Wallerstein contends in her article that divorce substantially harms children. She argues that children of divorce not only suffer while living with either their father or mother but suffer well into their adult lives. Wallerstein clams that adolescents of divorced families often become involved with drugs, alchohol, and sexual activity earlier than adolescents of intact families. And once they are adults, she claims that these children suffer from acute anxiety when attempting to love and form permanent relationships. Support for these claims comes in the form of specific cases as well as data from longitudinal research (investigations that study the same people across their life spans) conducted by Wallerstein and others over a 25-year period.

In the second selection, E. Mavis Hetherington and John Kelly draw on three major longitudinal studies to assert a more positive view of the effects of divorce. The most prominent of these studies is the Virginia Longitudinal Study of Divorce (VLS). Contrary to Wallerstein's belief that children suffer well into their adult lives, the VLS leads Hetherington and Kelly to conclude that 80 percent of the children from divorced homes become reasonably well adjusted. Although this conclusion might seem counterintuitive, given the obvious trauma of divorce, Hetherington and Kelly insist that divorce is not a form of "developmental predestination." They realize that the effects of divorce may echo as these children marry and form families of their own, but they contend that the vast majority of young people from divorced families cope well in relationships of all types.

POINT	COUNTERPOINT
• Divorce is a scar with many and varied long-term negative consequences.	• Divorce carries no inevitable long-term effects because people have and do overcome this event.
• Longitudinal studies show that children of divorced parents are less well adjusted as adults than children of intact homes.	• Other longitudinal studies show that the legacy of divorce is largely overcome by adulthood.
• Many children of divorced parents have difficulties establishing relationships of lasting commitment.	• Children of divorce may have more problems, but many are caring spouses and parents.
• Children of divorce are more likely to adopt "at risk" lifestyles.	• Although divorce can have some negative side effects, children of divorce eventually overcome those side effects.

YES

Judith S. Wallerstein

Growing Up in the Divorced Family

Growing Up in the Divorced Family

I begin with a favorite quote from a distinguished family judge. Rosemary Pfeiffer of the San Mateo Court in Northern California, in an address to the Family Court Services Regional Conference in 1985, told us, "If one were to use situation comedies as an analogy for our work with families, then the long running show M.A.S.H. would be my choice. Like the legendary M.A.S.H. unit, our lives in both a professional and a personal sense are marked by drama, comedy, and tragedy. We live our lives within a frontline emergency situation, in which we are called upon without adequate preparation or sufficient notice to diagnosis injuries and to treat traumas. We bandage the wounded, we give them all the support and rehabilitation that we can call up, based on our own resources, and we send them on their way. The difference of course is that the injuries and trauma which we deal with are those injuries and traumas to the heart."

The judge's poignant words converge with the moving testimony of Joanne, a child of divorce. Like so many other communications, mostly via e-mail, that I have received since the publication of *The Unexpected Legacy of Divorce*, Joanne's message to me was welcomed but entirely unexpected. She explained that she was 20-years-old and still struggling very hard with her parents' divorce, which jolted her seemingly tranquil world when she was 15. "I read your books," she wrote, "and all that you said struck home. It's like you had met me and reported my story and my feelings. You validated what I experienced. And I felt comforted. As if you had been there with me."

She went on to say, "I remember the day my mom and dad told us that they had decided to divorce, as if it was yesterday. The sky was overcast. The house looked gray. It was surreal. I retreated into my own mind as it spun out of control, imagining all the milestones that we would encounter as a broken family. Tears were streaming down my face, but I felt that I needed to take charge and correct the situation. There is no way, I told myself, that this is not going to happen. "It's already happening," my dad said, as if he were reading my thoughts, "so accept the reality." So there we were, three crying children with no say, and one very sad and one uncomfortable parent.

"Today, I still find myself thinking a lot about my folks' divorce even though my folks are 3000 miles away and it's 5 years ago. I enjoy college, but I

From *Clinical Social Work Journal*, vol. 33, iss. 4, Winter 2005, pp. 401–413,415. Copyright © 2005 by Springer Science and Business Media via Copyright Clearance Center. Reprinted by permission.

never can escape that part of my past, as it shapes so many of my beliefs and reactions to the world today. It baffles me that my sentiments are still so tender almost 5 years later. It's a door I can't close. But I felt it was only me, and something was wrong with me, until I read your books."

Joanne's statement that she cannot close the door on her parents' divorce and that it continues to shape many of her beliefs and reactions to the world converges with the concern of the judge and the concerns of many clinicians who work with divorced and remarried families. Both the legal and the clinical disciplines have at long last recognized that we are in new territory and how much we need to work together to improve our understanding and our psychological and legal interventions. The books of mine that Joanne found so congenial to her own experience, as have so many thousands of adult children of divorce, portrayed the inner lives and experiences of a group of 131 children and their parents from the time of the family's marital breakup until the children reached full adulthood. These books comprise the first and only such report that tells the story of "growing up divorced" in American society through the eyes of those who lived it. When we first met the young participants of our study, they were between the ages of 3 and 18. Initially, they were seen at the separation and well before the legal divorce, then again at 18 months, 5, 10, 15, and 25 years afterwards.

Today, these adult children of divorce are 28–43-years-old. Their parents divorced during the first wave of the divorce revolution of the early 1970s, when the national divorce rate began its steep rise. These children are the vanguard of an army of adults from divorced families, who currently make up one quarter of the American population now in their twenties, thirties, and forties. This high number is not surprising, as the divorce rate has been hovering at close to one half of all first marriages and 60% of second marriages, for the past several decades. What is less well known is that the majority of couples divorcing in the 1990s had a child age 6 or under at the time of the breakup. These youngsters spend the bulk of their growing-up years in post-divorce families, trying to cope with a range of changing relationships of one or both parents including cohabitations and remarriages. Their losses will be compounded by their parents' broken love affairs, second or even third divorces, and by the several years of diminished parenting that are inevitable as both parents struggle to rebuild their lives and recapture their hope of achieving a rewarding and lasting life partnership. These children are the invisible clients in our divorce proceedings, and their lives are the ones most influenced by a proceeding in which they have no standing and only feeble voices usually ignored.

As children and as young adults they, as well as their parents, make up a large segment of our patients. Although we have no figures representing their presence in private clinical practice, children of divorce, including those in their parents' second marriages, are three times as likely as children from intact families to be referred for psychological help by teachers. Drug, alcohol abuse, and sexual activity start significantly earlier for them than for adolescents from intact families. As adults they marry less and divorce significantly more than adults raised in intact families. Additionally, they show a range of psychological difficulties in adulthood that have been reported in several long-term studies.

The child who is raised in the divorced or remarried family grows to adulthood in a different culture from the child raised in an intact family. The divorced family is a new *kind* of family with an inherently unstable structure and by no means just a truncated version of the traditional family that we know. Both the courts and the clinical professions, including psychoanalysts, have been slow to recognize the distinctiveness of this population. We and they have relied on blueprints borrowed from our knowledge of the relatively stable intact family for our understanding and for our legal and psychological efforts to help. Thus we have located our major interventions at the time of the breakup in full denial of the long-term process of divorce and its continuing challenges for the child. We have clung as well to the equally unrealistic notion that if we can establish conditions such as cooperation between the divorced parents and contact with both parents, which approximate those of the intact well-functioning two-parent family, then the children will be protected during the long years that follow. . . .

The Child's Experience in the Divorced Family

Today the very notion of an average expectable family seems ironic, even absurd. Relationships that include the visiting parent, or joint custody, or live-in lovers, or stepparents and stepsiblings, or second divorces and their effects on attachment and development, have no counterpart in the intact family. Moreover, it is not only the family structure that changes with divorce or remarriage. What is striking is that the entire patterning of conscious and unconscious psychological needs, wishes, and expectations that parents and children bring to each other is profoundly altered under the impact of divorce and its multiple ripple effects.

It is important to understand at the outset that the agenda of the divorced parent who seeks to rebuild his or her social, sexual, and economic life is out of sync with the needs of the child, especially the young child, for the kind of supportive parenting that requires time, constant attention, and sacrifice. Indeed, the loss of the ex-spouse's presence often gives rise to an intense dependence by the adult on the child, which is at odds with our expectation of the child's dependence on the parent. This reversal of roles can readily translate into the adult's temporary or lasting inability to distinguish his or her own needs and wishes from those that are attributed to the child. Following the divorce, parents often find they need the child to fill their own emptiness, to ward off depression, to give purpose to their lives, to give them the courage to go on. "All weekend when my daughter is with her dad, I pace restlessly from lonely room to lonely room trying to ward off a depression that threatens to engulf me," I was told by a 35-year-old divorced mother. Consciously or unconsciously, parents in crisis turn to the child as surrogate spouse, confidante, advisor, sibling, parent, caretaker, ally within the marital wars, or as extended conscience and ego control. The child at divorce has an extraordinary capacity to restore the parent's shaken self-image. Even very young children are pressed into this role: "He understands everything I say," declared the successful businessman of his 3-year-old son. "Sometimes I talk to him for hours." In our playroom, this same child, during the course of a conversation about his father, repeatedly pretended that he was a little car being run over by a Mack truck—a strikingly different take on this relationship. . . .

Parent–child relationships not only change at the breakup but continue to change during the years that follow. In all families, the parent–child relationships are dynamically embedded in the parents' union. A stable marital bond has a powerful capacity to support and stabilize each parent's relationship with the child. When this bond is broken by divorce, a wide range of passions spill over into all domains of the family. These emotions, as noted, have the power to derail parent–child relationships that were in place during the intact family. But, beyond the immediate changes, the relationship with the child will change during subsequent years, with a love affair, with a new marriage, with a second or third divorce, and of course with career and work demands and changed financial pressures. Several fathers told me of years when they did not visit their children because they were not feeling well physically or emotionally, or even financially. "I had nothing to offer them," they reported. It is also true that a passionate love affair or exciting sexual relationship can trump a parent–child relationship and push it to the periphery of attention. And of course the influence of a stepparent on the parent's relationships with the children of the first marriage is powerful and unpredictable. Many a stepmother has told me, "I'm ashamed to say this, but I wanted the man, not the kids."

One immediate consequence of these chronic uncertainties in the postdivorce family is the eruption of persistent anxiety in the child, setting into motion a hypervigilant tracking of each parent. Simply stated, despite the passionate fights for custody and tussles over visiting arrangements at the breakup, children who grow up in divorced homes typically feel insecure. They worry about another loss or sudden change in their family or household. They worry for many years about their parents' well-being. "Will my mom jump over the Golden Gate Bridge?" asked one 10-year-old. "Will my dad die if he doesn't quit smoking?" asked another. Unfortunately, children's feelings of insecurity and powerlessness have often been compounded in recent years by courts, which, heedless of a child's special need for a secure, stable home, and unresponsive to the child's bonding with the custodial parent, or her preferences and concerns, have not hesitated to remove the child from the home of one parent and place her with the other, on the rising tide of accusations of enmeshment or alienation, or following a custodial parent's need to relocate to be with her new husband, or following a child's reluctance to visit a parent who is overbearing, needy, or inattentive, or whose demands violate the child's sense of morality. . . .

Children grow up more quickly in divorced and remarried families. They have to. Having been forced to stand between their two worlds and to examine each carefully in their lifelong efforts to understand the events that changed their lives, they are often more independent in their thinking than children in intact homes. Often, they have had to take responsibility for themselves and for their siblings as well. Moreover, the distance between the child's role and the parent's role is diminished as both share in running the household, including concerns about money.

Typically, children have their own point of view about their family and about what went wrong. They reject the pale, often platitudinous "Bambi-like" explanations that parents and many clinicians advise for the breakup. They fill in the gaps with their own explanations: "My parents lied and cheated on each other," an 11-year-old told me. "I have decided to tell the truth." Sometimes they sound wise beyond their years. "My father is a smart man, he knows a lot, and he has a great sense of humor. But he has never made sacrifices for anyone in his life," one adolescent boy told me. Commenting on the reasons for her parents' divorce, a 15-year-old said, with simple eloquence, "They each gave too little and asked too much." Although children were sometimes drawn to side with one parent against the other, these alliances were short-lived and did not last through the adolescent years. The notion that children are puppets who mindlessly join the assault of one parent against the other does not hold up in our work.

Through all their growing-up years, children can be intensely and painfully aware, sometimes haunted, by disparities in the post-divorce well-being of their parents. They are moved by love and compassion to want to take care of the more suffering parent. It is especially difficult for adult daughters to leave their lonely mothers, and many are consumed with guilt when they do so. Often they blame the more successful parent for the troubled parent's unhappy state. The passionate loyalty of children to a needy parent is deeply touching. "How many volts are in that wire?" asked a 9-year-old, suddenly, while out riding with his alcoholic father, who had enlisted his help to restore the marriage. "I would hold that wire for you," said the child. "Dad, I would die for you."

Many adolescents are very angry at the court order and the parents that lock them into a custody or visiting schedule that intrudes on their social lives. As I have reported in an earlier publication, the children who were ordered against their wishes to visit a parent at frequent intervals and were required to do so over their strong objections during adolescence, rejected that parent as soon as they reached their majority. If the purpose of court-ordered visiting is to enable child and parent to get to know each other and enjoy a friendly, even loving relationship, that strategy has boomeranged badly. Parents cannot rely on the power of the courts to create a loving or enduring relationship with a child. It might be very helpful if parents were informed by their attorneys that rejection by the young person when he reaches the age of 18 might well be the harvest of a rigid enforcement of an unwelcome schedule with the adolescent youngster. For parents who look forward, as they age, to the love and support of their children, this would be a very important message for them to hear.

On the encouraging side, parents who reappeared after several years of absence or neglect and were financially helpful and emotionally available to their young adult children were welcomed. One young woman told me, "He was a terrible father. We were starving and he had plenty. But he is a wonderful grandfather. I told him, 'I cannot forgive you for the past but I love you now.' "

Overall, the children of divorce in our study reported significantly less playtime and far less participation in extracurricular activities such as sports or music or other enrichment programs than those in intact families. This was usually due to interruptions in team sports schedules and other activities because of visiting and custody arrangements, as well as less money to pay for such activities, and less availability of parents to routinely transport the child or to attend events. When custody and visiting plans are drawn up, the lack of consideration for the child's interests, and preferences as to how she wishes to spend her time separate from her parents, can be quite striking. The child's time is divided between Mom and Dad as if the child herself has disappeared from the equation and become mere property. The result is often heartbreaking for the child. As one sad little 7-year-old in joint custody explained to me, "My coach said, 'Son, you're a really good pitcher, but you have to be here if you want to pitch!' "

We found that although children in joint custody gained more contact with both parents, they suffered greater losses in peer activities and friendships than those in sole custody. As one boy put it, "Kids don't keep 'pointment books. They [his friends] forget that I am coming and I don't get invited to lots of stuff." Many children have expressed what one child poignantly said to me, "The day they divorced was the day my childhood ended." These are important issues because, over the years, children who were able to draw support from school, sport teams, grandparents, teachers, and coaches, or from their own hobbies and talents, had happier childhoods and brought greater social maturity and a richer background of interests to adulthood.

The Long-Term Effects of Divorce

I turn now to our findings on the long-term effects of divorce. Our findings are in accord with the very few other studies that have followed the course of children of divorce from childhood to adulthood, although our methods have differed significantly. In a full-scale review of a longitudinal survey over the 1990s, Amato noted that adults and children score lower than their counterparts in married-couple families on a variety of indicators of well-being. He found that adults raised in divorced families suffered from a deficit in social skills and had special problems in handling conflicts within their own marriages. Cherlin and his colleagues drew their divorce population from a public health study in the United Kingdom begun in 1958. Although they found that many of the children's difficulties were evident prior to the divorce, their most recent work showed that subjects from divorced families were experiencing serious psychological difficulties after they reached adulthood which had not been foreseen. Both Amato and Cherlin relied on structured questionnaires directed to one parent and teachers, and to symptom lists to establish psychopathology in lieu of clinical assessment and personal contact with the child who was being evaluated. Their data collection did not include any interviews with children. Hetherington studied 900 youths from intact, divorced, and remarried families using a wide range of research methods including videos, psychological tests and structured interviews with children, parents, and teachers. She reported that 20–25% of the children were psychiatrically troubled adults as compared with 10% of those raised in intact families. Although the media hailed this as good news, Hetherington herself noted that this percentage is greater than the association between smoking and cancer. . . .

The central finding of our study is that, at adulthood, the experience of having been through parental divorce as a child impacts detrimentally on the capacity to love and be loved within a lasting, committed relationship. At young adulthood when love, sexual intimacy, commitment and marriage take center stage, children of divorce are haunted by the ghosts of their parents' divorce and terrified that the same fate awaits them. These fears, which crescendo at young adulthood, impede their developmental progress into full adulthood. Many eventually overcome their fears, but the struggle to do so is painful and can consume a decade or more of their lives. In addition to overcoming their fear of failure, they have a great deal to learn about the give and take of intimate living with another person, about how to deal with differences, and how to resolve conflicts. This is knowledge that other children acquire from growing up with both parents and learning from them how to negotiate the inevitable ebb and flow of marital life. As our study ended, 60% of the women and 40% of the men had been able to establish reasonably gratifying and enduring relationships that included a satisfying sexual relationship. Close to 40% had opted for parenthood. But the remainder were still in limbo. A good number enjoyed successful careers but suffered with severe loneliness. Since most of these people were still in their mid thirties, the book is not closed on their lives.

One third of the men and women were openly pessimistic about marriage and divorce, and sought to avoid both. "If you don't marry, then you don't divorce," was their mantra. But the majority were eager, even desperate for a lasting relationship and fearful that they would never achieve it. They did not want the lives their parents led. Their message was clear: "My parents' divorce is still incomprehensible to me. They met in college. They fell in love. They were compatible in their tastes and values. So, what is to keep the same fate from happening to me?" Over and over, they told us, "I'd love to get married, but I'm sure that I'd jinx it." Or, "Any relationship I'm in will dissolve." . . .

They complained that they were unprepared for marriage. "I've never seen a man and a woman on the same beam." "Sometimes I feel that I have been raised on a desert island. Combining love with sexual intimacy is a strange idea to me." Most regarded their parents' divorce as representing the failure to achieve one of the most important of life's tasks, even though many acknowledged that their parents had little in common and wondered why they had ever married. They complained about their parents' ineptness in personal relationships. "My mom never taught me about men. She didn't know anything." Asked whether they would consult their fathers, they answered, yes, about business, but never about a personal problem. "I learned from my dad how not to parent," said one man, expecting his first child. "Is that enough?" I asked. "That's all I have. It will have to do," was the grim reply.

Their despair led them to search for love in strange places, to make impulsive destructive choices, to hang on for years to exploitative partners, to hide their search for love behind promiscuity, to accept whoever volunteered to move in; or to avoid intimate contact altogether and to refer to themselves well into their forties as "a child of divorce," as if this were a fixed identity that defined them forevermore. . . .

One finding that has special clinical implications was that over half of our subjects reported memory fragments and flashbacks which captured key moments of the family breakup or incidents from the years that followed. These images reflected the suffering of the parent which the child had perceived and internalized when she was very young. The rawness of the parental suffering following the breakup left an indelible emotional mark. One young woman explained why she remained for 5 years with a college boyfriend who was very attached to her but with whom she felt she had nothing in common. She said, "I could never do to another human being what my mother did to my father." . . .

Conclusions

The findings from this study call for a shift in our dominant paradigm of understanding the impact of divorce on children and in the interventions that have been developed to mitigate its effects. The widely accepted premise has been that divorce represents an acute crisis from which resilient children recover, typically within a 2-year period, and then resume their normal developmental progress, if three conditions obtain: (1) the parents are able to settle their differences without fighting; (2) the financial arrangements are fair; and (3) the child has continued contact with both parents over the years that follow. Implicit in this model is the notion that, after the turmoil of the divorce, the parent–child relationships return to the *status quo ante*; parenting resumes much as it was before the split, and the child continues to do well, or even better, minus the pre-divorce marital conflict.

A parallel paradigm has placed loss at the center of the divorce for the child. With loss in mind, it has been proposed that the hazard to the child is primarily the loss of one parent, usually the father. It is held in this view that the child will be protected against long-term problems if continued contact with both parents is assured.

Our findings are that where parents got along and both maintained caring relationships with their children of the first marriage, undiminished by their post-divorce relationships, and where both parents were doing reasonably well in their personal lives, the childhood and adolescence of the children were better protected. But we report that a civil or even cooperative relationship between the parents did not shield the children from suffering intense anxiety and fear of failure in love and marriage when they reached late adolescence and young adulthood.

Similarly, remaining in frequent contact with both parents may have eased childhood years if their playtime and peer relationships were protected. But it did not reduce their suffering in adulthood, especially if the condition of the parents was discrepant and one parent was lonely and unhappy. On a happier note, those children who were raised in second marriages that were gratifying to both parents and who felt fully integrated within these second marriages, came to adulthood with far greater confidence in themselves and their future family. . . .

E. Mavis Hetherington
and John Kelly

 **NO**

For Better or For Worse

My interest in divorce grew out of my work in another area of family life. I think I have always had a special interest in the role fathers play in girls' lives because I had the good fortune to have a father who promoted female achievement and independence at a time when fathers rarely encouraged either.

In the late 1960s, my interest in fathers and daughters led to a startling research finding. At the time, informed opinion held that a mother shaped a daughter's gender identity, a father a son's. But a series of studies I did in the 1960s showed that fathers play the more important role in the gender identity of both boys and girls. The finding raised an interesting and important question: What happens to a girl when a father is absent due to death or divorce?

In my first study of families without fathers, I found that peers and especially mothers step in and assume the gender-shaping role men play in two-parent families. But the new study also raised a new question. Why did girls from divorced families have more social and psychological problems than girls from widowed families? Was there a unique developmental dynamic—perhaps even a uniquely harmful dynamic—in divorced families?

The Virginia Longitudinal Study (VLS), the most comprehensive study of divorce ever conducted, was intended to answer this question.

Most earlier research had relied only on the report of a single family member, usually a mother, to study the effects of divorce. The VLS expanded the study base to include not only the mother, father, and one focal child and a sibling in the family, but also people around the family. I also used a vast array of study tools, including interviews, questionnaires, standardized tests, and observations. Some of these instruments had never been used before, though they are now common in family studies. For example, I devised detailed methods of observing family interactions and activities; I and my team of investigators studied families in the home as they solved problems, as they chatted over dinner, and in the hours between the child's arrival at home and bedtime. We had a very personal look at how our families behaved when they disagreed, fought, relaxed, played, and soothed each other.

The VLS also was the first study to employ a structured diary in studying divorce. In order to assess each adult's mood fluctuations and activities, I had them keep diaries. Three days a week at half-hour intervals, parents had to note where they were, who they were with, what they were doing, and how they were feeling. If a person was having sex, she had to note that in the diary; the same was true if she were out on a date, having a fight at work, sitting in a singles bar, arguing with her mother, or trying to soothe an upset child.

The diaries yielded a great deal of unique and very fine-grained detail. For example, I found that a woman's feelings of anger and helplessness usually lasted longer after a fight with a son than a daughter. I also found that casual sex produced extreme depression and feelings of being unloved in many women and sent a few to the edge. Though suicide attempts were rare in the VLS, the seven that did occur were all attempts by women, and all were triggered by casual sex.

The children in the study—who were age four at the start of the VLS—received even more intense scrutiny. They were observed alone and with parents, peers, and siblings. We observed them at home, in school, on the playground, and also at the Hetherington Laboratory at the University of Virginia. Parents, teachers, and study observers were asked to assess each "target child." As the child grew older, the list of assessors grew to include peers, brothers and sisters, and the child himself, who was periodically asked to make self-assessments.

One of the most important aspects of the VLS was the use of a non-divorced comparison group. With its help, we were able to distinguish between the normal changes all families and family members undergo and changes that were linked directly to the impact of divorce and remarriage.

Initially, the Virginia Longitudinal Study of Divorce, which was launched in 1972, was intended to study how seventy-two preschool children and their families adapted to divorce at two months, one year, and two years. To provide a yardstick of comparison, seventy-two non-divorced families were also included in the study. The study's two-year time limit reflected then current thinking that most families had restabilized by two years after divorce.

But then something unexpected happened. The seventy-two men and women in my divorced group began to remarry and form stepfamilies, and the seventy-two couples in my married comparison group began to divorce. I seemed to be studying a moving target!

At first, I was frustrated. Didn't these folks have any respect for science? But then I realized I had been given a golden opportunity. Women's liberation and employment, no-fault divorce, the sexual revolution, self-actualization, the movements of the sixties and seventies, all were dramatically changing American mating habits. In the blink of an eye, the entire country seemed to jump from the paternal certainties of *Father Knows Best* to the postmodern chaos of *The Brady Bunch*.

Politicians, religious leaders, newspapers, magazines, and television documentaries decried the "breakdown of the nuclear family"; my fellow academics hailed the "emergence of the non-traditional family." But whatever phrase people chose, everyone agreed: America was in the midst of an unprecedented social change—one that would be played out for decades to come in the nation's living rooms, bedrooms, courtrooms, and legislatures.

But was the change positive or negative or a little bit of both? . . .

Mostly Happy: Children of Divorce as Young Adults

David Coleman has his father's imposing height and muscularity, but whereas on Richard, size added to his air of menace, making him look explosive even at rest, the son's six-foot-three frame has the opposite effect. It underscores his gentleness, makes you notice it in a way you wouldn't if he were a smaller, more delicate-looking man.

At a time when genetic theories threatened to reduce human development to a branch of biology, the difference between gentle David and violent Richard reminds us of the powerful role nurture plays in development. Genes are important, yes, certainly, but life experiences—especially with those closest to us—can take a given set of genes and make them add up in many different ways.

Much of the credit for the way David and his older sister, Leah, have ended up goes to Janet. Both benefited immensely from her ability to maintain a stable, loving, emotionally safe environment through Richard's stalking, through the family's sojourn on welfare, and through [stepfather] Nick and Leah's fights. When the VLS ended, David had taken over much of the responsibility for running "Janet's Garden," and Leah was a happily married mother, with a young daughter.

In the 1970s, a fierce debate broke out about the future of children like David and Leah. Critics of the divorce revolution believed that as the generation of children from divorced families matured, American society would descend into disorder and chaos. The collapse of the two-parent family, the traditional engine of socialization, critics argued, would lead to a *Clockwork Orange* generation of unstable, reckless, indulgent young adults, who would overrun the nation's prisons, substance abuse centers, and divorce courts.

"Nonsense," declared supporters of the divorce revolution, who saw divorce as a kind of cleansing agent. At last, the dark gloomy oppressive Victorian house that was the nuclear family would get a long-overdue spring cleaning, one that would produce a new and more egalitarian, tolerant, and fulfilled generation of men and women.

While I found evidence to support both views, the big headline in my data is that *80 percent of children from divorced homes eventually are able to adapt to their new life and become reasonably well adjusted.* A subgroup of girls even become exceptionally competent as a result of dealing with the challenges of divorce, enjoy a normal development, and grow into truly outstanding young adults. The 20 percent who continue to bear the scars of divorce fall into a troubled group, who display impulsive, irresponsible, antisocial behavior or are depressed. At the end of the VLS, troubled youths were having difficulty at work, in romantic relationships, and in gaining a toehold in adult life. They had the highest academic dropout rate and the highest divorce rate in the study, and were more likely to be faring poorly economically. In addition, being troubled and a girl made a young woman more likely to have left home early and to have experienced at least one out-of-wedlock pregnancy, birth, or abortion.

However, coming from a non-divorced family did not always protect against growing into a troubled young adult. Ten percent of youths in non-divorced families, compared to 20 percent in divorced and remarried families, were troubled. Most of our troubled young men and women came from families where conflict was frequent and authoritative parenting rare. In adulthood, as was found in childhood and adolescence, those who had moved from a highly contentious intact home situation to a more harmonious divorced family situation, with a caring, competent parent, benefited from the divorce and had fewer problems. But the legacy of the stresses and inept parenting associated with divorce and remarriage, and especially with living in a complex stepfamily, are still seen in the psychological, emotional, and social problems in 20 percent of young people from these families.

A piece of good news about our youths was that their antisocial behavior declined as they matured. Much of the adolescent exploration, experimentation, and sense of invulnerability had abated. Although excessive use of alcohol remained a problem for one quarter, drug abuse and lawbreaking had declined in all of our groups; but the decrease had been most marked in those who married.

What about the other 80 percent of young people from divorced and remarried families?

While most were not exactly the New Man or New Woman that the divorce revolution's supporters had predicted, they were behaving the way young adults were supposed to behave. They were choosing careers, developing permanent relationships, ably going about the central tasks of young adulthood, and establishing a grown-up life.

They ranged from those who were remarkably well adjusted to Good Enoughs and competent-at-a-costs, who were having a few problems but coping reasonably well to very well.

Finally, it should be a reassuring finding for divorced and remarried parents, and their children, that for every young man or woman who emerged from postnuclear family life with problems, four others were functioning reasonably or exceptionally well.

I think our findings ultimately contain two bottom-line messages about the long-term effects of divorce on children. The first is about parents, especially mothers. If someone creates a Nobel Prize for Unsung Hero, my nominee will be the divorced mother. Even when the world was collapsing round them, many divorced mothers found the courage and resiliency to do what had to be done. Such maternal tenacity and courage paid off. Despite all the emotional and financial pressures imposed by marital failure, most of our divorced women managed to provide the support, sensitivity, and engagement their children needed for normal development. And while divorce creates developmental risks, except in cases of extraordinary stress, children can be protected by vigorous, involved, competent parenting.

The second bottom line is about flexibility and diversity. Divorce is not a form of developmental predestination. Children, like adults, take many different routes out of divorce; some lead to unhappiness, others to a rewarding and fulfilling life. And since over the course of life, new experiences are being encountered and new relationships formed, protective and risk factors alter, and the door to positive change always remains open. . . .

Twenty Years Later

The adverse effects of divorce and remarriage are still echoing in some divorced families and their offspring twenty years after divorce, but they are in the minority. The vast majority of young people from these families are reasonably well adjusted and are coping reasonably well in relationships with their families, friends, and intimate partners. Most are moving toward establishing careers, economic independence, and satisfying social and intimate relationships. Some are caring spouses and parents. Although the divorce may resonate more in the memories of these children, most parents and children see the divorce as having been for the best, and have moved forward with their lives.

Points to Remember

- Parent, child, and sibling relationships that have been close in childhood seldom deteriorate in adulthood.
- Even if absence doesn't make the heart grow fonder, conflict usually diminishes once the protagonists are apart and contact becomes optional. Disengagement often replaces conflict in stepparent-stepchild and sibling relationships in divorced and remarried families in young adulthood.
- Biologically related siblings, whether in divorced, non-divorced, or remarried families, tend to have both more attached and more rivalrous relationships than those found in stepsiblings.
- Men remain reluctant to do their fair share. In most first- and second-generation VLS homes, the burden of household labor continued to fall predominantly on female shoulders. After a demanding eight- or ten-hour day at the office, many of our women would come home to cope with unmade beds, unwashed laundry, unfed children, and the morning's unwashed breakfast dishes in the sink.
- A family history of divorce does leave children of divorce relationship- and marriage-challenged. Children of divorce are often reluctant to commit wholeheartedly to a marriage, have fewer relationship skills, and in some cases show a genetic predisposition to destabilizing behaviors like antisocial behavior, impulsivity, and depression.
- Gender affects a person's divorce risk more than the kind of family the person was brought up in. In divorced, remarried, and non-divorced families alike, male belligerence, withdrawal, and lack of affection often produce thoughts of divorce in a woman; female contempt, nagging, or reciprocated aggression, thoughts of divorce in a man.
- Although marital instability is higher in offspring from divorced families, marriage to a stable, supportive spouse from a non-divorced family eliminates the intergenerational transmission of divorce. A caring, mature spouse can teach their partner from a divorced family skills they never learned at home.

- Young adults from complex stepfamilies continue to have more adjustment and family problems than young adults in other kinds of stepfamilies.
- For most youths, the legacy of divorce is largely overcome. Twenty years after divorce, most men and women who had grown up in divorced families and stepfamilies are functioning reasonably well. Only a minority still exhibited emotional and social problems, and had difficulties with intimate relationships and achievement.

CHALLENGE QUESTIONS

Does the Divorce of Parents Harm Their Children?

1. How is it that two top researchers can differ so much in their conclusions? Does this necessarily mean their conclusions are flawed?
2. Interview a student whose parents are divorced. Make sense of their experiences from one or the other of these authors' perspectives.
3. What policy decisions might be made if those in power were only to become aware of one of the authors' findings?
4. If you and your spouse were faced with the possibility of divorce, what would you do with the information obtained from one or both of these selections?
5. What impact, if any, would the information contained in both selections make on a couple considering marriage?

ISSUE 9

Does Research Show that Homosexual Parenting Has No Negative Effects?

YES: **Ellen C. Perrin and Committee on Psychosocial Aspects of Child and Family Health**, from "Technical Report: Coparent or Second-Parent Adoption by Same-Sex Parents," *Pediatrics* (April 2002)

NO: **Richard N. Williams**, from "The Effect on Children of the Sexual Orientation of Parents: How Should the Issue Be Decided," Invited Address to the National Association for Research and Therapy of Homosexuality (2000)

ISSUE SUMMARY

YES: Professor of pediatric medicine Ellen C. Perrin and her colleauges review four areas of research to show that parental sexual orientation creates no unusual or additional risk to children.

NO: Social psychologist Richard Williams reviews the research literature and finds both that a political agenda pervades these studies and that potentially meaningful differences were not mentioned or pursued.

There is no question that politicians rely heavily on psychological research for making important decisions. Legislators want to make sure that their policies ensure justice, are nondiscriminatory, and avoid any hidden dangers for their constituents. In this sense, psychological information helps drive political policy. But can the reverse also be true—where politics sometimes drive psychological research? Many psychological researchers would say "no" to this question, because social science investigations are viewed as objective and thus value- and politics-free. However, some feminists have long contended that certain forms of research are "male" in nature, and some philosophers of science have argued that all methods are underlain with important philosophies of knowing that bias them in significant ways (see Issue 2).

An important case of the possibility of such research bias concerns the controversial issue of homosexual parenting. The central question is whether gay men and lesbians are effective and appropriate parents. If there is a higher risk of unhealthy development in children raised by homosexual parents, then legislation giving gays and lesbians full parental rights may be dangerous to both the children and society. If, on the other hand, the children of homosexuals can develop normally, then legislation restricting their parental rights is discriminatory and unfair.

For the author of the first article, Ellen Perrin, psychological information on this issue is both abundant and fairly clear. She briefly reviews this research in four main categories: the attitudes and behaviors of gay and lesbian parents, the psychosexual development of their children, these children's social experience, and the emotional status of these children. While acknowledging that the samples studied are "small and nonrepresentative" and the children involved are relatively young, Perrin and her colleagues conclude that "there is no systematic difference between gay and nongay parents." In fact, "no data have pointed to any risk to children as a result of growing up in a family with 1 or more gay parents." Stigma and discrimination can accompany such families, but Perrin argues that these are the fault of a heterosexist society, not the fault of homosexual parents.

Richard Williams, on the other hand, notes the multiple shortcomings of the current research—some of which Perrin mentions. He asserts that "the literature in this area is of uniformly poor quality" and proceeds to describe the most common problems, including small and nonrepresentative samples and ages of children. Perhaps even more problematic is that several of the studies he reviewed "actually found potentially meaningful differences, but failed to mention them, or pursue them." He then describes, in some detail, nine of these differences and shows how they undermine the current conclusion that there are no differences. His conclusion is that higher quality research is needed before we can state that homosexual parenting has no negative effects on children.

POINT

- There is no systematic difference between hetero- and homosexual parents.

- Methodological and conceptual rigor in research design is important, but we should focus on results.

- Children raised by homosexual parents are at no greater risk for unhealthy development.

- A greater quantity of research is needed to conclusively settle the issue.

COUNTERPOINT

- Research in this area has been poorly conducted and thus not able to fully substantiate any claim regarding these differences.

- Correcting methodological and conceptual problems in research design is critical for accurate and valid results.

- Potentially meaningful differences in parents were not acknowledged or pursued.

- New studies must be of a much higher *quality* or they will be of little use.

YES

Ellen C. Perrin

Technical Report: Coparent or Second-Parent Adoption by Same-Sex Parents

Current Situation

Accurate statistics regarding the number of parents who are gay or lesbian are impossible to obtain. The secrecy resulting from the stigma still associated with homosexuality has hampered even basic epidemiologic research. A broad estimate is that between 1 and 9 million children in the United States have at least 1 parent who is lesbian or gay.

Most individuals who have a lesbian and/or gay parent were conceived in the context of a heterosexual relationship. When a parent (or both parents) in a heterosexual couple "comes out" as lesbian or gay, some parents divorce and others continue to live as a couple. If they do decide to live separately, either parent may be the residential parent or children may live part-time in each home. Gay or lesbian parents may remain single or they may have same-sex partners who may or may not develop stepparenting relationships with the children. These families closely resemble stepfamilies formed after heterosexual couples divorce, and many of their parenting concerns and adjustments are similar. An additional concern for these parents is that pervasively heterosexist legal precedents have resulted in denial of custody and restriction of visitation rights to many gay and lesbian parents.

Increasing social acceptance of diversity in sexual orientation has allowed more gay men and lesbians to come out before forming intimate relationships or becoming parents. Lesbian and gay adults choose to become parents for many of the same reasons heterosexual adults do. The desire for children is a basic human instinct and satisfies many people's wish to leave a mark on history or perpetuate their family's story. In addition, children may satisfy people's desire to provide and accept love and nurturing from others and may provide some assurance of care and support during their older years.

Many of the same concerns that exist for heterosexual couples when they consider having children also face lesbians and gay men. All parents have concerns about time, finances, and the responsibilities of parenthood. They worry about how children will affect their relationship as a couple, their own and their children's health, and their ability to manage their new parenting role in addition to their other adult roles. Lesbians and gay men undertaking parenthood face additional challenges, including deciding whether to conceive or adopt a child, obtaining donor sperm or arranging for a surrogate mother (if conceiving), finding an accepting adoption agency (if adopting), making legally binding arrangements regarding parental relationships, creating a substantive role for the nonbiologic or nonadoptive parent, and confronting emotional pain and restrictions imposed by heterosexism and discriminatory regulations.

Despite these challenges, lesbians and gay men increasingly are becoming parents on their own or in the context of an established same-sex relationship. Most lesbians who conceive a child do so using alternative insemination techniques with a donor's sperm. The woman or women may choose to become pregnant using sperm from a completely anonymous donor, from a donor who has agreed to be identifiable when the child becomes an adult, or from a fully known donor (eg, a friend or a relative of the nonconceiving partner). Lesbians also can become parents by fostering or adopting children, as can gay men. These opportunities are increasingly available in most states and in many other countries, although they are still limited by legal statutes in some places.

A growing number of gay men have chosen to become fathers through the assistance of a surrogate mother who bears their child. Others have made agreements to be coparents with a single woman (lesbian or heterosexual) or a lesbian couple. Still other men make arrangements to participate as sperm donors in the conception of a child (commonly with a lesbian couple), agreeing to have variable levels of involvement with the child but without taking on the responsibilities of parenting.

When a lesbian or a gay man becomes a parent through alternative insemination, surrogacy, or adoption, the biologic or adoptive parent is recognized within the legal system as having full and more or less absolute parental rights. Although the biologic or adoptive parent's partner may function as a coparent, he or she has no formal legal rights with respect to the child. Most state laws do not allow for adoption or guardianship by an unmarried partner unless the parental rights of the first parent are terminated. An attorney can prepare medical consent forms and nomination-of-guardian forms for the care of the child in the event of the legal parent's death or incapacity. These documents, however, do not have the force of an adoption or legal guardianship, and there is no guarantee that a court will uphold them. Some states recently have passed legislation that allows coparents to adopt their partner's children. Other states have allowed their judicial systems to determine eligibility for formal adoption by the coparent on a case-by-case basis. Coparent (or second-parent) adoption has important psychologic and legal benefits.

Historically, gay men and lesbians have been prevented from becoming foster parents or adopting children and have been denied custody and rights of visitation of their children in the event of divorce on the grounds that they would not be effective parents. Legal justifications and social beliefs have presumed that their children would experience stigmatization, poor peer relationships, subsequent behavioral and emotional problems, and abnormal psychosexual development. During the past 20 years, many investigators have tried to determine whether there is any empiric support for these assumptions.

Research Evidence

The focus of research has been on 4 main topic areas. Investigators have concentrated on describing the attitudes and behaviors of gay and lesbian parents and the psychosexual development, social experience, and emotional status of their children.

Parenting Attitudes and Behavior, Personality, and Adjustment of Parents

Stereotypes and laws that maintain discriminatory practices are based on the assumption that lesbian mothers and gay fathers are different from heterosexual parents in ways that are important to their children's well-being. Empirical evidence reveals in contrast that gay fathers have substantial evidence of nurturance and investment in their paternal role and no differences from heterosexual fathers in providing appropriate recreation, encouraging autonomy, or dealing with general problems of parenting. Compared with heterosexual fathers, gay fathers have been described to adhere to stricter disciplinary guidelines, to place greater emphasis on guidance and the development of cognitive skills, and to be more involved in their children's activities. Overall, there are more similarities than differences in the parenting styles and attitudes of gay and nongay fathers.

Similarly, few differences have been found in the research from the last 2 decades comparing lesbian and heterosexual mothers' self-esteem, psychologic adjustment, and attitudes toward child rearing. Lesbian mothers fall within the range of normal psychologic functioning on interviews and psychologic assessments and report scores on standardized measures of self-esteem, anxiety, depression, and parenting stress indistinguishable from those reported by heterosexual mothers.

Lesbian mothers strongly endorse child-centered attitudes and commitment to their maternal roles and have been shown to be more concerned with providing male role models for their children than are divorced heterosexual mothers. Lesbian and heterosexual mothers describe themselves similarly in marital and maternal interests, current lifestyles, and child-rearing practices. They report similar role conflicts, social support networks, and coping strategies.

Children's Gender Identity and Sexual Orientation

The gender identity of preadolescent children raised by lesbian mothers has been found consistently to be in line with their biologic sex. None of the more than 300 children studied to date have shown evidence of gender identity confusion, wished to be the other sex, or consistently engaged in cross-gender behavior. No differences have been found in the toy, game, activity, dress, or friendship preferences of boys or girls who had lesbian mothers, compared with those who had heterosexual mothers.

No differences have been found in the gender identity, social roles, or sexual orientation of adults who had a divorced homosexual parent (or parents), compared with those who had divorced heterosexual parents. Similar proportions of young adults who had homosexual parents and those who had heterosexual parents have reported feelings of attraction toward someone of the same sex. Compared with young adults who had heterosexual mothers, men and women who had lesbian mothers were slightly more likely to consider the possibility of having a same-sex partner, and more of them had been involved in at least a brief relationship with someone of the same sex, but in each group similar proportions of adult men and women identified themselves as homosexual.

Children's Emotional and Social Development

Because most children whose parents are gay or lesbian have experienced the divorce of their biologic parents, their subsequent psychologic development has to be understood in that context. Whether they are subsequently raised by 1 or 2 separated parents and whether a stepparent has joined either of the biologic parents are important factors for children but are rarely addressed in research assessing outcomes for children who have a lesbian or gay parent.

The considerable research literature that has accumulated addressing this issue has generally revealed that children of divorced lesbian mothers grow up in ways that are very similar to children of divorced heterosexual mothers. Several studies comparing children who have a lesbian mother with children who have a heterosexual mother have failed to document any differences between such groups on personality measures, measures of peer group relationships, self-esteem, behavioral difficulties, academic success, or warmth and quality of family relationships. Children's self-esteem has been shown to be higher among adolescents whose mothers (of any sexual orientation) were in a new partnered relationship after divorce, compared with those whose mothers remained single, and among those who found out at a younger age that their parent was homosexual, compared with those who found out when they were older.

Prevalent heterosexism and stigmatization might lead to teasing and embarrassment for children about their parent's sexual orientation or their family constellation and restrict their ability to form and maintain friendships. Adult children of divorced lesbian mothers have recalled more teasing by peers during childhood than have adult children of divorced heterosexual parents. Nevertheless, children seem to cope rather well with the challenge of understanding and describing their families to peers and teachers.

Children born to and raised by lesbian couples also seem to develop normally in every way. Ratings by their mothers and teachers have demonstrated children's social competence and the prevalence of behavioral difficulties to be comparable with population norms. In fact, growing up with parents who are lesbian or gay may confer some advantages to children. They have been described as more tolerant of diversity and more nurturing toward younger children than children whose parents are heterosexual.

In 1 study, children of heterosexual parents saw themselves as being somewhat more aggressive than did children of lesbians, and they were seen by parents and teachers as more bossy, negative, and domineering. Children of lesbian parents saw themselves as more lovable and were seen by parents and teachers as more affectionate, responsive, and protective of younger children, compared with children of heterosexual parents. In a more recent investigation, children of lesbian parents reported their self-esteem to be similar to that of children of heterosexual parents and saw themselves as similar in aggressiveness and sociability.

Recent investigations have attempted to discern factors that promote optimal well-being of children who have lesbian parents. The adjustment of children who have 2 mothers seems to be related to their parents' satisfaction with their relationship and specifically with the division of responsibility they have worked out with regard to child care and household chores. Children with lesbian parents who reported greater relationship satisfaction, more egalitarian division of household and paid labor, and more regular contact with grandparents and other relatives were rated by parents and teachers to be better adjusted and to have fewer behavioral problems.

Children in all family constellations have been described by parents and teachers to have more behavioral problems when parents report more personal distress and more dysfunctional parent-child interactions. In contrast, children are rated as better adjusted when their parents report greater relationship satisfaction, higher levels of love, and lower interparental conflict regardless of their parents' sexual orientation. Children apparently are more powerfully influenced by family processes and relationships than by family structure.

Summary

The small and nonrepresentative samples studied and the relatively young age of most of the children suggest some reserve. However, the weight of evidence gathered during several decades using diverse samples and methodologies is persuasive in demonstrating that there is no systematic difference between gay and nongay parents in emotional health, parenting skills, and attitudes toward parenting. No data have pointed to any risk to children as a result of growing up in a family with 1 or more gay parents. Some among the vast variety of family forms, histories, and relationships may prove more conducive to healthy psychosexual and emotional development than others.

Research exploring the diversity of parental relationships among gay and lesbian parents is just beginning. Children whose parents divorce (regardless of sexual orientation) are better adjusted when their parents have high self-esteem, maintain a responsible and amicable relationship, and are currently living with a partner. Children living with divorced lesbian mothers have better outcomes when they learn about their mother's homosexuality at a younger age, when their fathers and other important adults accept their mother's lesbian identity, and perhaps when they have contact with other children of lesbians and gay men. Parents and children have better outcomes when the daunting tasks of parenting are shared, and children seem to benefit from arrangements in which lesbian parents divide child care and other household tasks in an egalitarian manner as well as when conflict between partners is low. Although gay and lesbian parents may not, despite their best efforts, be able to protect their children fully from the effects of stigmatization and discrimination, parents' sexual orientation is not a variable that, in itself, predicts their ability to provide a home environment that supports children's development.

Richard N. Williams  **NO**

Effects of Parents' Sexual Orientation on Children: How Should the Issue Be Decided

I spent the mid and late 1970's in graduate study in Social Psychology. This was during what I call the "Cute Phase" of the discipline. Social Psychologists were studying all sorts of relevant social issues, such as aggression, prejudice, persuasion, and even human sexuality in "cute" ways. The studies had clever titles and aimed at social relevance as justification. After a few lab studies and a few in a more realistic setting, researchers were eager to draw far-reaching conclusions about social issues of the day. Some of you will remember Senator William Proxmire from Wisconsin who periodically bestowed his "Golden Fleece Award" to honor the greatest misuses of federal funds for trivial and frivolous projects. Social psychological research studies won more than its fair share. I studied with a winner of a Golden Fleece—for whom it was a mark of distinction. From this experience I developed an enduring skepticism about the project of allowing psychological research to be invoked as a justification for social policy or practice. Nothing in contemporary psychological research has been able to assuage my concern. I have become more convinced that psychological research cannot bear so great a burden as to be the foundation or the reason for social and legal policies and practices that impact the lives of real people. As social institutions of all sorts have weakened, fractured, given way, or fallen out of favor, the social sciences have been thrust into the breach. Today, psychology and religion and other cultural traditions compete for legitimacy in the same arena. However, I do not believe, and have argued elsewhere, that the social sciences are currently (or perhaps permanently) not up to the task, either conceptually or epistemologically, of providing a foundation for law, policy, or practice.

In 1996, I was asked to be a witness for the state of Hawaii in the *Baehr v. Miike* court case. It involved a challenge to state laws governing marriage which would not allow same-gender marriage on the basis of the equal rights amendment to the Hawaii state constitution. It was decided early in the case that both sides would make their case based on social scientific research on the topic—focused loosely on the "best interests of the child." This meant that the arguments for and against same-sex marriage would not be made on the bases of values, morality, or arguments about the nature and effects of homosexuality itself. This case, that had the potential to revolutionize the institution of marriage in an entire state, was to be decided on the basis of social scientific research data and opinion. This was and continues to be for me a frightening proposition. The fundamental question must be whether the social sciences—including psychology—really are capable of producing data, and from those data, knowledge of a type and quality that justifies serious decisions affecting in profound ways not only the individual lives of real persons, but institutions and cultures for years and generations to come. Unfortunately, I do not believe they are capable of doing so. This suspicion was reinforced by my experience in the Hawaii case.

My role in the legal case was to evaluate the quality and the findings of research on the topic of the effects on children of the sexual orientation of their parents. I read the research and prepared well. The research was conceptually and methodologically flawed—and fatally so. However, it was soon apparent that the merits of the research would not really be weighed. Rather political considerations, including value judgments and concerns about philosophical orthodoxy trumped considerations of scientific merit. I found it somewhat ironic that after being certified as an expert in research methodology, my testimony was dismissed by the judge for reasons stated in two simple sentences in the official decision. First, by my own admission I did not believe that evolution was a science in the way it took itself to be, and second, I was out of the mainstream. Apparently experts are only really experts if they are in the mainstream and agree with the majority. Although this attitude can be found in the legal system, I am sure, by experience that psychologists are not immune from it. I presented my testimony for about an hour and a half, but not a word of it found its way into the judge's decision. So much for the use of social scientific research in matters of law and public policy.

Research Literature on Sexual Orientation

The social scientific research literature on homosexuality, although significant in quantity, reflects the immaturity, the uncertainty, and the problematic philosophical commitments that characterize the state of the social sciences at the beginning of the twenty-first century. Psychology seems to be a perpetually immature science fraught with genuine problems, both methodological and philosophical (see, e.g., Slife & Williams, 1995). When the social sciences in their intellectually troubled state, and lacking methodological rigor sufficient to permit them to actually answer significant theoretical or practical questions, or to speak authoritatively on social issues, are allowed to speak authoritatively on the issue of homosexuality we really should be careful, critical, and sophisticated in evaluating the research literature they produce.

In the capacity of an expert witness for the State I reviewed the research that dealt specifically with potential effects on children of the sexual orientation of their parents. The research explored more particularly whether there are negative effects suffered by children when reared by homosexual parents. Since 1996, I have returned to the literature from time to time, but have found nothing that would alter my evaluations and findings which are presented here. It is not uncommon to see references in the literature to the fact that as many as a hundred or more studies have been conducted investigating the effects on children of the sexual orientation of their parents. The usual conclusion is that no negative effects have been found, and that, thus, it is reasonable to conclude that there are no negative effects.

The literature in this area is of uniformly poor quality, a conclusion clearly supported by other scholars. Notwithstanding this lack of rigor, the conclusion most commonly reached in the literature is that there are no effects on children of the sexual orientation of parents. This conclusion is both unwarranted due to the lack of rigor in the studies, and wrong, because of the existence of findings of some significant differences present in the studies but either ignored or left unexplored. As a first step in my own evaluation of the literature, I applied three standards of rigor in selecting studies for review. First, I included only studies where some quantitative data were reported. Although I am acquainted with qualitative research methods and am convinced of their value, qualitative studies in this area of research are not yet very influential, and they also lack rigor. Second I confined my review to studies in which data were actually collected from children themselves rather than relying on parents' reports of their children's behavior. Third, I imposed a criterion that to be included in the review a study must include data from the children of both heterosexual and homosexual parents. These last two criteria are based on elementary standards of rigor to be expected of any credible social scientific study. However, when these criteria were applied, the body of over a hundred studies shrank to nine. In evaluating these nine studies, the following conceptual and empirical problems became evident.

General Problem with the Research Literature

Predicting and finding "No Effect." Granting that the body of literature on the topic of same-sex parenting generally fails to find significant negative effects, it is still a violation of the most elementary scientific logic to conclude, therefore, that there really *are* no effects. In other words, science cannot "prove a negative." The reason for this is simple. Failure to find significant effects in a study may mean that there really are none; however just such a failure would also be predicted by poor measures, bad experimental designs, poor controls, and high levels of experimental error, among other things. In other words failure to find an effect is uninterpretable because it is not known whether the researchers failed to find it because it really isn't there or whether they just designed their study poorly or used a measure that was not sensitive to the effect in the first place. It is for this reasons that absent findings cannot accrue, growing eventually into significance. Nonsignificant findings do not grow into statistical significance. Put slightly differently, one cannot affirm positive results from insignificant findings because no scientific study, nor any body of scientific studies ever constitutes a crucial test of an hypothesis if the studies rely on empirical observation, i.e., induction. This is so simply because in principle any future observation may yield the effect in question, and induction cannot rule out such a possibility.

Bad studies are not better than no studies at all. Some have argued, while acknowledging the poor quality of the studies in this area, that it is still important to base conclusions and understandings on poor data rather than rely on no data at all. The logic of this position does not hold up to scrutiny. It is, essentially, to argue that it is better to trust data, and, thus, conclusions we *know to be wrong*, rather to rely on reasoning, evidence, and conclusions which *may be wrong*. Approached from a slightly different angle we might look for a counter example. Near the turn of the century the decision was made to screen immigrants to the United States by administering an IQ test. Note that it was the best data available for screening out the "mentally deficient." However, subsequent investigation has shown that what was really tested was some species of English proficiency, not mental deficiency at all. To conclude that it was better to use bad data rather than no data at all is to ignore the impact of the decisions produced from the bad data in the lives of the individuals who were affected by them. We should not risk a similar mistake in the area of sexual orientation and its effects on children.

Statistical significance is too conservative a criterion. The concept of statistical significance has developed in the social sciences as a hedge against the too-liberal claiming of effects by enthusiastic social scientists. One is not allowed to recognize, or claim, an effect unless the chances of its occurring in the data are small, fewer than five in one hundred. Thus, an effect in the data large enough to have occurred by chance at a level of six in one hundred would not be "found." The report of such an occurrence should rightly be that "there was no effect." If our concern is genuinely to look at the possibility that parents' sexual orientation might affect their children we should not employ a statistical filter so fine that it has the potential to exclude, or leave undiscovered, potentially very many subtle and nonrobust effects. Simply put, traditional statistical significance is the wrong criterion for a research enterprise designed to search for potential harm and alert us to possibilities. Thus the conclusion that there is no effect as defined by statistical significance is simply not justifiable.

Small sample size. The sample size in all nine studies was small, never having more than 30 parents or 50 children in the study. While samples of this size may be sufficient to meet statistical requirements for testing specific and limited statistical hypotheses, they do not permit generalization to larger populations of persons—homosexual or heterosexual. To draw conclusions about the meaning of findings from such small samples in terms of larger populations or real persons, as people are inclined to do with the data we are discussing, is illegitimate. It is also the case that sample size interacts with statistical significance. There is a mathematical relationship which dictates that the larger the sample the more likely it is that a significant effect will be found. Conversely, the smaller the sample the less likely it is that an effect will be detected. Thus to claim that there is some general significance to the fact that no effect was found when sample sizes were so small is twice illegitimate. On the other hand, when significant effects are found with such a small sample, a researcher should be alert to the effect, because it accrued when the mathematical probabilities were "stacked against it." I shall return to this point below.

Nonrepresentative samples. In research studies designed to reach general conclusions about populations, such as the effect on children of the sexual orientation of parents, it is crucial that the samples chosen for study be representative of the populations about whom generalizations will be made. The studies in the area of research we are discussing fail to meet this criterion. It is obviously easier to claim that a large sample is more likely to represent the population than a small sample, since the larger the sample the more likely it will include the full spectrum of members of the population. Thus, small sample size contributes to making the samples nonrepresentative. The standard means of achieving representative samples for study is to randomly select from the population. This is seldom done in practice because it is extremely difficult; however, the farther one deviates from random sampling, the less generalizable the findings of any study become. In the studies I reviewed, the samples were not random samples. The samples were most often recruited by advertizing in gay and lesbian publications, or through personal acquaintances. These are not selection criteria that permit reliable generalizations. In addition, all the studies included children of lesbian mothers. There are no credible studies of gay fathers that meet the criteria outlined here. This also affects generalizability. Finally, it is interesting to note that people on both sides of the spectrum of opinion regarding homosexuality are agreed that generalizability is a real problem in drawing conclusions about research on the gay community.

Inappropriate and problematic criterion measures. A research study is no better than the measures that constitute the data. Several of the studies I reviewed used measures that seem inappropriate for investigating the hypothesis in question. For example, Flaks, Ficher, Masterpasqua, & Joseph compared children of heterosexual and homosexual mothers on the variable of "cognitive development," and found no differences. However, the measure they employed was the Wechsler intelligence scale for children. It is unclear whether the construct measured by intelligence scales is congruent with what is commonly meant by cognitive development. Ignoring the conflation of these two constructs, one familiar with the area of intelligence testing knows that this measure of intelligence (as is the case with other established intelligence tests) has been refined over the years to be resistant to any effects of culture, gender, or other psychological or cultural variables. Thus to use a measure specially crafted to be resistant to effects of culturally important things, and then to conclude, based on lack of any effects in the data, that there are no culturally important effects is, at best, circular reasoning. Other studies employed measures designed to discriminate clinical (pathological) from nonclinical (nonpathological) populations. Such measures might not be expected to distinguish between essentially normal groups if the differences were sub-pathological. The instruments would not be expected to be sensitive to many potentially important variables not included in the clinical syndrome to which the instrument is sensitive. This issue further erodes the value of these studies in reaching conclusions about the effects of parents' sexual orientation on children.

Lack of adequate control of potentially influential variables. Studies with sufficient rigor to allow for valid conclusions to be drawn, what might be called limited "crucial tests," achieve their persuasive power by being able to isolate the variable of interest—in this case, the sexual orientation of parents—from all other variables that might reasonably be expected to have an influence on the data. None of the studies was able to achieve an acceptable level of control over such extraneous variables. For example, in all studies but one, the children of lesbian mothers had spent at least some time in a heterosexual home. Groups of parents were not always equated in terms of education or socio-economic status. Heterosexual and homosexual households were not identical in the presence of other adults, children's access to fathers, and other family variables. In other words, these studies could not isolate sexual orientation of parents as a potentially influential variable from the joint effects of a number of other variables which might mediate or mask differences. This lack of adequate control simply means that the studies did not really test what they purport to test. To draw conclusions from studies with no adequate controls is not justified by any scientific criteria.

Age of children studied. All of the studies reviewed but one studied children at a relatively early age. Only Golombok and Tasker followed the children into young adulthood (early twenties). Many of the effects on children related to the sexual orientation of their parents might not be expected to manifest themselves in very young children, but rather in older children as they develop their own identity and begin to come to grips more directly with issues of sexuality. At best it is premature to conclude that there is no effect on children until research has followed the children into adulthood.

Significant Effects Found in the Research on Homosexual Parenting

Care should be exercised in talking about differences found in research studies that have the design and analysis problems just outlined. However, when such difference are found, they should be examined because, if our concern is to be sure there are not detrimental effects on children, we should be sensitive to any that might be present—not as a final test of the hypothesis under examination, but as a clue as to where further (and better) research might be directed. It is interesting to note that several of the studies reviewed actually found potentially meaningful differences, but failed to mention them, or pursue them. This fact speaks, perhaps, to the motivations of the researchers, as well as to the quality of the work. The following differences were found in the literature reviewed.

Golombok, Spencer, & Rutter found, but did not pursue differences between heterosexual and homosexual mothers in their sample in the reasons for the breakdown of their prior marriages. They also found that lesbian mothers were more likely than heterosexual mothers to have received psychiatric care. Lesbian children had more contact with their fathers than did children of heterosexual mothers. If contact with fathers is a potentially positive influence this difference could mask other differences related to parents' sexual orientation between groups of children where fathers are not so present. Lesbian mothers had significantly more female than male children living with them. While 70 percent of lesbian mothers reported no clear preference for the sexual orientation of their children, a similar finding was not reported for heterosexual mothers. Any of these findings could have an influence on the data and a potentially important effect in our understanding of the issue. These findings are seldom mentioned in the literature.

Javaid reported that seven of 13 lesbian mothers reported acceptance of homosexual behavior in their children. None of the heterosexual mothers reported such acceptance. While this is hardly counterintuitive nor unexpected, it is interesting to note that the author never bothered to test the significance of the difference in this proportion. After performing the test, I found it to be significant. Kirkpatrick, et al. reported a reliable difference in reasons given by lesbian versus heterosexual mothers for their prior divorce. For lesbian mothers the dominant reason was lack of psychological intimacy. For heterosexual mothers the dominant reason was their husbands' drug and alcohol abuse. This variable might not only effect the findings (or lack thereof) reported by the authors, but might also be a source of hypotheses for future work on this topic.

One finding that appeared, but was not pursued in two separate studies came from self-esteem scores of children reared by lesbian versus heterosexual mothers. Huggins found no difference between the mean self-esteem scores of children in these two groups. However, a closer examination of the data presented—which Huggins did not carry out—revealed a marked difference in the variance (the range) of self-esteem scores between the two groups. Children of lesbian mothers had a much broader range of self-esteem scores—very high to very low. Scores of children of heterosexual mothers tended to cluster much closer together. In order to be sure that the test of the difference between the two means was indeed valid, the author should have tested the difference between the variances. It was not possible to tell whether such a test was done. When I performed the test, I found the difference in the variance of the self-esteem scores to be significant. This finding, with potential implications for psychological adjustment was not noted, tested, nor mentioned in the study. What makes the findings even more potentially important is Patterson's report of what may be a similar finding. She reports that children of lesbian mothers are significantly higher on measures of both "stress reaction," and "well being." These findings are not developed by Patterson, but are consistent with Huggins' findings indicating possible polarization of affect in children of lesbian parents compared to children of heterosexual mothers. This finding calls into question any sweeping conclusion that no differences have been found between groups of children related to the sexual orientation of their parents.

Perhaps the most important and interesting of the nine studies in this review is the longitudinal study by Golombok and Tasker. This is the only study that followed children reared by heterosexual and lesbian mothers into adulthood and took measures of the adult children. While the authors conclude that their data demonstrate no important effects of mothers' sexual orientation on adult children there are just such findings reported. On two of five measures of sexual orientation administered to the adult children, there were significant differences between children of homosexual versus heterosexual mothers. Children of lesbian mothers were significantly more likely to have considered having a homosexual relationship, and significantly more likely to have had actual involvement in a same-sex relationship. On a third measure, of "sexual orientation," nine of 25 children of lesbian mothers compared to four of 20 children of heterosexual mothers reported such attraction. The statistical significance level of this difference is .19. The probability is roughly one in five that this difference could have occurred by chance alone. While this fails to rise to the level of "statistical significance," it might be socially or culturally significant, or common enough in these populations to be clinically or even personally significant both in the children's personal lives and in their relationships. Golombok and Tasker also reported that the increased level of same-gender sexual interest in children of lesbian mothers was significantly correlated with a) the number of the lesbian mothers' partners, b) lesbian mothers' openness in physical affection with their female partners, and c) lesbian mothers' preference for their children's own sexual orientation. We should be careful not to make too much of findings from a study that has some methodological problems; however, this study is, in my opinion, the best of those sufficiently rigorous to have been included in my review. So, while scholars may disagree about the theoretical impact of these findings on our understanding of homosexuality and its effects, and about their psychological impact on children, what can be unequivocally stated is that the conclusion that there is no evidence of effects on children of being reared in a homosexual versus a heterosexual household is simply false.

Following my extensive review of the literature in 1996, I have revisited the literature on possible effects on children of the sexual orientation of their parents. In 2003 I reviewed the literature to see whether things had changed substantially and found 5 more studies that met the criteria of rigor (bringing the total by my count to 14), but all partook of one or more the problems extant in the literature as a whole. One other study of older children of Lesbian mothers reported differences in children's acceptance of homosexuality and greater "ability" to act on same-sex attractions. Such findings are not surprising, but potentially significant, and at a minimum, refute claims of "no difference." An important recent article by Stacey and Biblarz, who are clear and aggressive advocates of homosexual rights, reviews essentially the same body of literature as I did in 1996, and reports effects related to the sexual orientation of parents, and calls for courage and serious theorizing and research that take on the real issues. I concur with this call, albeit from an alternative theoretical position. Another review of the literature in 2007 turned up a handful of articles still building on an absence of findings, and one or two that find some differences but make nothing of them. . . .

CHALLENGE QUESTIONS

Does Research Show that Homosexual Parenting Has No Negative Effects?

1. How does social science research inform public policy? Why is it important that influential research be carried out professionally and with a high level of scientific rigor?
2. Why does the author of the first selection believe that the sexual orientation of parents has no effect on children?
3. Find and examine a study similar to the ones discussed in these articles. Does it have some of the problems common to other research in this area? What are its strong points?
4. Correcting for the problems Williams mentions, attempt to design your own research study to examine the effects of parental sexual orientation on children.
5. What difference would it make in the world if research were able to definitively show that homosexual parenting has no negative effect on children? What if it definitively showed that there are negative effects?

Internet References . . .

The Dilemma of Determinism

This is a link to the classic paper written by William James, one of psychology's founding fathers, in which he discusses the doctrine of determinism versus the idea of human agency.

http://www.rci.rutgers.edu/~stich/104_Master_File/
104_Readings/James/James_DILEMMA_
OF_DETERMINISM.pdf

Informal Education

This website is dedicated to expanding knowledge in many areas. The following link provides a brief history of Howard Gardner and his theory of multiple intelligences, as well as links to other helpful sites.

http://www.infed.org/thinkers/gardner.htm

Cognitive Processes

*P*sychology *is often defined as the study of behavior and cognition. Consequently, cognitive processes are a pivotal arena for psychological research. Perhaps most intriguing is the nature and limits of our mental processes. For example, how much control do we truly have over our actions? Some psychologists contend that we do not have any real choices and that we are ultimately determined by our environment and an unchangeable past, such as our memories. In this sense, whatever control we think we have is illusory. How would society change if this were true? Another important arena of cognitive research concerns the nature of human intelligence. Traditional intelligence tests typically provide one overall score, as if it is valid to speak of intelligence as one entity, cutting across all activities and skills. Is this true? Much recent research has placed this notion of overall intelligence in jeopardy. Is it better to think of many different intelligences corresponding to different aspects of thought and behavior?*

- Are Human Activities Determined?
- Is the Theory of Multiple Intelligences Valid?

ISSUE 10

Are Human Activities Determined?

YES: John A. Bargh and Tanya L. Chartrand, from "The Unbearable Automaticity of Being," *American Psychologist* (July 1999)

NO: Amy Fisher Smith, from "Automaticity: The Free Will Determinism–Debate Continued," An Original Article Written for This Text (2006)

ISSUE SUMMARY

YES: Psychologists John A. Bargh and Tanya L. Chartrand assert that people are controlled not by their purposeful choices and intentions but by the environment through automatic cognitive processes.

NO: In response, psychologist Amy Fisher Smith agrees that people do, in fact, have automatic behaviors but she believes these behaviors can be explained by mental processes akin to a free will.

Imagine yourself as a juror with an accused rapist standing in front of you. The rapist explains to you that his behavior is the product of a history of child abuse and that he had no control over his violent actions toward the victim. In other words, he presents himself as having been ultimately determined by his environment. Would you believe this rapist's explanation? Or, would you tend to assume that he could have acted otherwise than his tragic history—that he has something like a free will?

Many people do not realize there are many psychological theories that ultimately assume we do not have any choices and that we are the product of an unchangeable past. One such theory, radical behaviorism, states that we are mere products of our environment, implying that the accused rapist is not personally responsible for his crime. His past experiences with the environment (e.g., reinforcement history) are responsible. Contrast these implications with the theory of Carl Jung, a noted psychoanalyst. Although he believes in many unconscious and, thus, automatic behaviors, Jung views the person as the free agent of all of them. From this perspective, the rapist would be ultimately responsible for his actions, despite his unfavorable childhood.

In the first selection, psychological researchers John A. Bargh and Tanya L. Chartrand would seem to disagree with this view. They contend that most of a person's everyday life is determined not by his or her conscious intentions and purposeful choices but by mental processes that are determined by the environment. Bargh and Chartrand explain that perceiving an action increases a person's likelihood of performing that action. For example, if a man sees a movie that depicts violence against another, he is more likely to become violent because he has witnessed this action. Since perceptual activity is primarily involuntary, Bargh and Chartrand conclude that the environment controls our mental activity and, hence, our actions. Because goals are also considered to be mental activity, Bargh and Chartrand suggest that goals are automatically activated by the environment as well.

Theoretical psychologist, Amy Fisher Smith, responds to Bargh and Chartrand's arguments by agreeing with their data on automatic behaviors but rejecting their interpretation of that data. Specifically, she questions whether their findings have to be interpreted within a deterministic framework. She contends that this framework is contrary to many of the assumptions that society needs for people's behaviors. For example, Smith believes that people are rightly viewed as responsible agents, both personally and culturally. She then offers an alternative way of understanding automatic thoughts and behaviors in which people are not determined by environmental stimuli, but are actively interpreting what they perceive in the environment. Finally, Smith argues that the activation of goals is ultimately directed by the person and not by the environment, even though we might not have an immediate awareness of our guiding beliefs and assumptions.

POINT

- Our environment determines the way we think and behave.

- Individuals are more likely to repeat an action they see.

- The environment automatically activates both conscious and unconscious goals.

- We are ultimately not responsible for our actions.

- Data on automatic behaviors prove that we are determined by forces beyond our control.

COUNTERPOINT

- It is possible to understand automatic behaviors in a nondeterministic way.

- We are not passively shaped by stimuli from the environment.

- Individuals ultimately direct their own goals by actively bestowing meaning upon experiences.

- The legal system generally views people as agentic beings.

- The automaticity data do not objectively reveal that the environment determines our thoughts and behaviors.

YES

John A. Bargh and
Tanya L. Chartrand

The Unbearable Automaticity of Being

> The strongest knowledge—that of the total unfreedom of the human will—
> is nonetheless the poorest in successes, for it always has the strongest
> opponent: human vanity.
>
> —Nietzsche, *Human, All Too Human*

Imagine for a moment that you are a psychology professor who does experiments on conscious awareness. You keep finding that your subtle manipulations of people's judgments and even behavior are successful—causing your experimental participants to like someone or to dislike that same person, to feel happy or sad, to behave rudely or with infinite patience. However, none of your participants have a clue as to what caused them to feel or behave in these ways. In fact, they don't believe you, and sometimes even argue with you, when you try to explain your experiment to them and how they were caused to feel or behave.

Now, let's say you are home with your family for the holidays or on vacation. Your aunt or brother-in-law asks politely what your job is like. You attempt to explain your research and even some of your more interesting findings. Once again you are met with incredulity. "This can't be so," says your brother-in-law. "I can't remember this ever happening to me, even once."

Our thesis here—that most of a person's everyday life is determined not by their conscious intentions and deliberate choices but by mental processes that are put into motion by features of the environment and that operate outside of conscious awareness and guidance—is a difficult one for people to accept. One cannot have any experiences or memories of being nonconsciously influenced, of course, almost by definition. But let us move from the layperson to the experts (namely, psychological researchers) and see what they have to say about the relative roles played by conscious versus nonconscious causes of daily experience.

The major historical perspectives of 20th-century psychology can be distinguished from one another based on their positions on this question: Do people consciously and actively choose and control (by acts of will) these various experiences and behaviors, or are those experiences and behaviors instead

From *American Psychologist*, vol. 54, no. 7, July 1999, pp. 462–466, 468–469, 476. Copyright © 1999 by American Psychological Association via Copyright Clearance Center. Reprinted by permission of the author. References omitted.

determined directly by other factors, such as external stimuli or internal, unconscious forces?

Freud, for example, considered human behavior to be determined mainly by biological impulses and the unconscious interplay of the psychic forces those impulses put into motion. The individual was described as usually unaware of these intrapsychic struggles and of their causal effect on his or her behavior, although it was possible to become aware of them (usually on Freud's couch) and then change one's patterns of behavior.

Early behaviorist theory similarly proposed that behavior was outside of conscious control, but placed the source of the control not in the psyche but in external stimulus conditions and events. Environmental events directed all behavior in combination with the person's reinforcement history.

A third major perspective emerged in midcentury with Rogers's self theory and the humanist movement. In what was a reaction to the then-dominant Freudian and behavioristic perspectives, in which "people were thought to be either pushed by their inner drives or pulled by external events," the "causal self" was placed as a mediator between the environment and one's responses to it. In these self-theories, behavior was adapted to the current environment, but it was determined by an act of conscious choice. Fifty years later, this perspective remains dominant among theories of motivation and self-regulation.

Finally, the contemporary cognitive perspective, in spirit as well as in practice, seeks to account for psychological phenomena in terms of deterministic mechanisms. Although there exist models that acknowledge the role played by higher-order choice or "executive" processes, the authors of these models generally acknowledge that the lack of specification of how these choices are made is an inadequacy of the model. Neisser's seminal book *Cognitive Psychology*, for example, describes the "problem of the executive," in which the flexible choice and selection processes are described as a homunculus or "little person in the head" that does not constitute a scientific explanation. This position is echoed in Barsalou's text, in which he too calls free will a homunculus, noting that "most cognitive psychologists believe that the fundamental laws of the physical world determine human behavior completely."

Fortunately, contemporary psychology for the most part has moved away from doctrinaire either-or positions concerning the locus of control of psychological phenomena, to an acknowledgment that they are determined jointly by processes set into motion directly by one's environment and by processes instigated by acts of conscious choice and will. Such dual-process models, in which the phenomenon in question is said to be influenced simultaneously by conscious (control) and nonconscious (automatic) processes, are now the norm in the study of attention and encoding, memory, emotional appraisal, emotional disorders, attitudes and persuasion, and social perception and judgment. Thus, the mainstream of psychology accepts both the fact of conscious or willed causation of mental and behavioral processes and the fact of automatic or environmentally triggered processes. The debate has shifted from the existence (or not) of these different causal forces to the circumstances under which one versus the other controls the mind. Is everyday life mainly comprised of consciously or of nonconsciously caused evaluations, judgments, emotions, motivations, and behavior?

As Posner and Snyder noted a quarter century ago, this question of how much conscious control we have over our judgments, decisions, and behavior is one of the most basic and important questions of human existence. The title of the present article makes our position on this question a matter of little suspense, but to make the reasons for that position clear and hopefully compelling, we must start by defining what we mean by a conscious mental process and an automatic mental process. The defining features of what we are referring to as a *conscious* process have remained consistent and stable for over 100 years: These are mental acts of which we are aware, that we intend (i.e., that we start by an act of will), that require effort, and that we can control (i.e., we can stop them and go on to something else if we choose). In contrast, there has been no consensus on the features of a single form of *automatic* process; instead two major strains have been identified and studied over the past century, similar only in that they do not possess all of the defining features of a conscious process.

First, research on skill acquisition focused on intentional, goal-directed processes that became more efficient over time and practice until they could operate without conscious guidance. These were intentional but effortless mental processes. Second, research on the initial perceptual analysis or encoding of environmental events (called "preattentive" or "preconscious" processing) showed that much of this analysis takes place not only effortlessly, but without any intention or often awareness that it was taking place. The "new look" in perception of the 1940s and 1950s, in which threatening or emotion-laden words or symbols were purportedly shown to be "defended against" through having higher perceptual thresholds than more neutral stimuli, is a prototypic example of this line of research. These are the two classic forms of "not-conscious" mental processes; both forms operate effortlessly and without need for conscious guidance, but one (mental skills) requires an act of will to start operation, and the other (preconscious) does not.

So much for how the field of psychology has historically thought about automatic processes; let's return to our aunts and in-laws. What does the concept mean to them? The popular meaning of "automatic" is something that happens, no matter what, as long as certain conditions are met. An automatic answering machine clicks into operation after a specified number of phone rings and then records whatever the caller wants to say. No one has to be at home to turn it on to record whenever the phone happens to ring. Automatic piloting systems on airplanes now perform many sophisticated and complex functions to keep the plane on course and to land it under poor visibility and weather conditions, actually making air travel safer than when such functions were handled entirely by the human pilots.

In modern technological societies one encounters many such automatic devices and systems in the course of daily life. They are all devised and intended to free us from tasks that don't really require our vigilance and intervention, so that our time and energy can be directed toward those that do. And these systems also perform their tasks with a greater degree or reliability, as they are not prone to sources of human error, such as fatigue, distraction, and boredom.

Just as automatic mechanical devices free us from having to attend to and intervene in order for the desired effect to occur, automatic mental processes free one's limited conscious attentional capacity from tasks in which they are no longer needed. Many writers have pointed out how impossible it would be to function effectively if conscious, controlled, and aware mental processing had to deal with every aspect of life, from perceptual comprehension of the environment (both physical and social) to choosing and guiding every action and response to the environment. But none put it so vividly as the philosopher A. N. Whitehead:

> It is a profoundly erroneous truism, repeated by all copy-books and by eminent people making speeches, that we should cultivate the habit of thinking of what we are doing. The precise opposite is the case. Civilization advances by extending the number of operations which we can perform without thinking about them. Operations of thought are like cavalry charges in a battle—they are strictly limited in number, they require fresh horses, and must only be made at decisive moments.

Whitehead presaged what psychological research would discover 86 years later. Baumeister, Tice, and their colleagues recently demonstrated just how limited conscious self-regulatory capacities are in a series of studies on what they called "ego depletion." In their experiments, an act of self-control in one domain (being told not to eat any of the chocolate chip cookies sitting in front of you) seriously depletes a person's ability to engage in self-control in a subsequent, entirely unrelated domain (persistence on a verbal task), which was presented to participants as being a separate experiment. . . .

Tice and Baumeister concluded after their series of eight such experiments that because even minor acts of self-control, such as making a simple choice, use up this limited self-regulatory resource, such conscious acts of self-regulation can occur only rarely in the course of one's day. Even as they were defending the importance of the conscious self for guiding behavior, Baumeister et al. concluded it plays a causal role only 5% or so of the time.

Given one's understandable desire to believe in free will and self-determination, it may be hard to bear that most of daily life is driven by automatic, nonconscious mental processes—but it appears impossible, from these findings, that conscious control could be up to the job. As Sherlock Holmes was fond of telling Dr. Watson, when one eliminates the impossible, whatever remains—however improbable—must be the truth.

It follows, as Lord Whitehead argued, that most of our day-to-day actions, motivations, judgments, and emotions are not the products of conscious choice and guidance, but must be driven instead by mental processes put into operation directly by environmental features and events. Is this the case? The logical and empirical limits on conscious self-regulation tell us where to look for automatic phenomena—not only in perceptual activity and crude, simple processes (to which cognitive psychologists originally believed they were limited, but everywhere. We and other researchers have been looking, and here is what we have found.

Perceiving Is for Doing

Humans and other primates have an innate capacity for imitative behavior and vicarious learning. This has led many theorists over many years to argue that there must be a strong associative connection between representations used in perceiving the behavior of others and those used to behave in the same way oneself. Some have even argued that the same representation is used both in perceiving others' behavior and to behave that way oneself. William James, following the ideas of the physiologist William Carpenter, popularized the principle of "ideo-motor action" to account for how merely thinking about an action increases its likelihood of occurring. For Carpenter as well as James, the important feature of ideomotor action was that mere ideation about the behavior was sufficient to cause one to act—no separate act of volition was necessary. Although James argued that "thinking is for doing," we sought to extend the source of ideation from inside the head to out in the world—specifically, by considering whether merely perceiving an action increases the person's likelihood of performing the same act.

Automatic Perception Induces the Ideas

Of course, one's own thinking is more or less under one's own conscious control, so the principle of ideomotor action by itself does not mean the resultant behavior is caused by nonconscious, external environmental events. But because perceptual activity is largely automatic and not under conscious or intentional control (the orange on the desk cannot be perceived as purple through an act of will), perception is the route by which the environment directly causes mental activity—specifically, the activation of internal representations of the outside world. The activated contents of the mind are not only those in the stream of consciousness but also include representations of currently present objects, events, behavior of others, and so on. In short, the "ideo" in ideomotor effects could just as well come from outside the head as within it.

When one considers that this automatic perception of another person's behavior introduces the idea of action—but from the outside environment instead of from internal, intentionally directed thought—a direct and automatic route is provided from the external environment to action tendencies, via perception. The idea that social perception is a largely automated psychological phenomenon is now widely accepted. Many years of research have demonstrated the variety of ways in which behaviors are encoded spontaneously and without intention in terms of relevant trait concepts, how contextual priming of trait concepts changes the perceiver's interpretation of an identical behavior (through temporarily increasing their accessibility or readiness to be used), and how stereotypes of social groups become activated automatically on the mere perception of the distinguishing features of a group member.

Perceptual interpretations of behavior, as well as assumptions about an individual's behavior based on identified group membership, become automated like any other representation if they are frequently and consistently made in the presence of the behavioral or group membership features.

The Perception–Behavior Link

Thus, the external environment can direct behavior non-consciously through a two-stage process: automatic perceptual activity that then automatically creates behavioral tendencies through the perception–behavior link. That is, the entire environment–perception–behavior sequence is automatic, with no role played by conscious choice in producing the behavior. Berkowitz posited that such a mechanism underlies media effects on behavior and modeling effects more generally. In his account, perceiving the aggressiveness (for example) of an actor in a movie or television show activated, in an unintentional and nonconscious manner, the perceiver's own behavioral representation of aggressiveness, thereby increasing the likelihood of aggressive behavior. Carver et al. experimentally tested this hypothesis by first exposing some participants (and not others) to hostility-related words in a first "language experiment," and then—in what was believed to be a separate experiment—putting the participants in the role of a "teacher" who was to give shocks to a "learner" participant. Those who had been "primed" with hostile-related stimuli subsequently gave longer shocks to the learner than did control participants.

Carver et al. had explicitly told their participants to give the shocks, however, and so the question remained whether external events could induce the idea of the behavior itself. Bargh, Chen, and Burrows found that it indeed could. When trait constructs or stereotypes were nonconsciously activated during an unrelated task (i.e., "primed"), participants were subsequently more likely to act in line with the content of the primed trait construct or stereotype. In one experiment, participants were first exposed to words related to either rudeness (e.g., rude, impolite, obnoxious), politeness (e.g., respect, considerate, polite) or neither (in the control condition) in an initial "language experiment." They were then given a chance to interrupt an ongoing conversation (in order to ask for the promised next experimental task). Significantly more participants in the "rude" priming condition interrupted (67%) than did those in the control condition (38%), whereas only 16% of those primed with "polite" interrupted the conversation.

Experiment 2 extended these findings to the case of stereotype activation. In a first task, participants were primed (in the course of an ostensible language test) either with words related to the stereotype of the elderly (e.g., Florida, sentimental, wrinkle) or with words unrelated to the stereotype. As predicted, participants primed with the elderly-related material subsequently behaved in line with the stereotype—specifically, they walked more slowly down the hallway after leaving the experiment. Dijksterhuis, Bargh, and Miedema have shown that these effects also hold for another central feature of the elderly stereotype—forgetfulness. Those participants whose stereotype for the elderly had been unobtrusively activated in the "first experiment" subsequently could not remember as many features of the room in which that experiment was conducted as could control participants. (For similar findings of behavioral consequences of automatic stereotype activation with different stereotypes, including those for professors and for soccer hooligans, see Dijksterhuis & van Knippenberg. . . .

Goals and Motivations

Although the effect of perception on behavior occurs passively, without the need for a conscious choice or intention to behave in the suggested manner, this does not mean that people do not have goals and purposes and are merely passive experiencers of events. People are active participants in the world with purposes and goals they want to attain. Much, if not most, of our responses to the environment in the form of judgments, decisions, and behavior are determined not solely by the information available in that environment but rather by how it relates to whatever goal we are currently pursuing.

For example, when we are trying to get a new acquaintance to like us and perhaps be our friend, the things about that person to which we pay attention and later best remember are quite different than if we meet the same person in a different context, such as if they are a person to whom we are considering subletting our apartment or someone sitting across from us late at night on the subway. And as for behavioral responses to one's environment, the idea that behavior is largely purposive and determined by one's current goals has long had broad support within psychology—not only among those with a humanistic orientation but among cognitive psychologists and neobehaviorists as well.

But if the currently-held goal largely determines whether judgments are made (and the quality of those judgments) and how one behaves, this would seem to rule out much of a role for automatic, environmentally driven influences. How can the environment directly control much of anything if goals play such a mediational role?

The answer is as follows: if (and perhaps only if) the environment itself activates and puts the goal into motion. To entertain this possibility, one must assume that goals are represented mentally and like any other mental representation are capable of becoming automatically activated by environmental features. There is no reason, a priori, to assume that goal representations cannot become automated in the same way that stereotypes and other perceptual structures do, as long as the same conditions for development of automatic activation occur.

The Acquisition of Automaticity

What are those conditions? As discussed above, the development of most acquired forms of automaticity (i.e., skill acquisition) depends on the frequent and consistent pairing of internal responses with external events. Initially, conscious choice and guidance are needed to perform the desired behavior or to generate what one hopes are accurate and useful expectations about what is going to happen next in the situation. But to the extent the same expectations are generated, or the same behavior is enacted, or the same goal and plan are chosen in that situation, conscious choice drops out as it is not needed—it has become a superfluous step in the process. According to James,

> It is a general principle in Psychology that consciousness deserts all processes where it can no longer be of use . . . We grow unconscious of every feeling which is useless as a sign to lead us to our ends, and where one sign will suffice others drop out, and that one remains, to work alone.

Intentional Acquisition of Automaticity

At some level, people are aware of this phenomenon by which conscious choice-points drop out of mental sequences to the extent they are no longer needed (because the same choice is made frequently and consistently at a given point). This is shown by the fact that we often use it in a strategic fashion in order to develop a desired skill, such as driving a car or playing the violin. We purposefully engage in the considerable practice (frequent and consistent performances) required to sublimate many of the components of the skill. In this way, the conscious capacity that is freed up from not having to direct and coordinate the lower level components of the skill can be used instead to plot and direct higher-level strategy during the game or performance. And so, one sees the teenager go from being an overwhelmed tangle of nerves at the first attempts to drive a car to soon being able to do so while conversing, tuning the radio, and getting nervous instead over that evening's date.

Unintentional Acquisition of Automaticity

But what we find most intriguing, in considering how mental processes recede from consciousness over time with repeated use, is that the process of automation itself is automatic. The necessary and sufficient ingredients for automation are frequency and consistency of use of the same set of component mental processes under the same circumstances—regardless of whether the frequency and consistency occur because of a desire to attain a skill, or whether they occur just because we have tended in the past to make the same choices or to do the same thing or to react emotionally or evaluatively in the same way each time. These processes also become automated, but because we did not start out intending to make them that way, we are not aware that they have been and so, when that process operates automatically in that situation, we aren't aware of it.

This is how goals and motives can eventually become automatically activated by situations. For a given individual, his or her motivations (e.g., to gain the love and respect of one's parents) are represented in memory at the most abstract level of an organized hierarchy, followed by the various goals one can pursue to satisfy those motivations (e.g., to be a success, to become a lawyer, to have a family). Each of these motivations is associated with goals that will fulfill it, and these goals in turn have associated with them the various plans and strategies that can be used to attain the goals (e.g., study hard). These plans are in turn linked to specific behaviors by which the plan is carried out.

However, an individual's motivations are chronic and enduring over time. And thus, because of the stability over time of one's motivations, in many situations a given individual will frequently and consistently pursue the same goal. If the same goal is pursued within the same situation, then conscious choice eventually drops out of the selection of what goal to pursue—the situational features themselves directly put the goal into operation. . . .

Conclusions

The heavier the burden, the closer our lives come to the earth, the more real and truthful they become. Conversely, the absolute absence of a burden causes man to be lighter than air, to soar into the heights, take leave of the earth and his earthly being, and become only half real, his movements free as they are insignificant. What then shall we choose? Weight or lightness?

For many years now, researchers have studied two main types of mental processes, both in isolation and in interaction with each other. The two types are known by a variety of names—conscious–nonconscious, controlled–automatic, explicit–implicit, systematic–heuristic—but it is clear which one is "heavy" and which one is "light." To consciously and willfully regulate one's own behavior, evaluations, decisions, and emotional states requires considerable effort and is relatively slow. Moreover, it appears to require a limited resource that is quickly used up, so conscious self-regulatory acts can only occur sparingly and for a short time. On the other hand, the nonconscious or automatic processes we've described here are unintended, effortless, very fast, and many of them can operate at any given time. Most important, they are effortless, continually in gear guiding the individual safely through the day. Automatic self-regulation is, if you will, thought lite—"one third less effort than regular thinking." The individual is free, in Kundera's sense, of the burden of their operation.

Some of the automatic guidance systems we've outlined are "natural" and don't require experience to develop. These are the fraternization of perceptual and behavioral representations and the connection between automatic evaluation processes on the one hand and mood and behavior on the other. Other forms of automatic self-regulation develop out of repeated and consistent experience; they map onto the regularities of one's experience and take tasks over from conscious choice and guidance when that choice is not really being exercised. This is how goals and motives can come to operate nonconsciously in given situations, how stereotypes can become chronically associated with the perceptual features of social groups, and how evaluations can become integrated with the perceptual representation of the person, object, or event so that they become active immediately and unintentionally in the course of perception.

To produce the empirical evidence on which these claims rest, we and others have conducted a variety of experiments in which goals, evaluations, and perceptual constructs (traits, stereotypes) were primed in an unobtrusive manner. Through use of these priming manipulations, the mental representations were made active to later exert their influence without an act of will and without the participants' awareness of the influence. Yet in all of these studies, the effect was the same as when people are aware of and intend to engage in that process. Thus it is no coincidence that goals, evaluations, and perceptual constructs have the same essential structure, because the underlying principle is the same in all three: Mental representations designed to perform a certain function will perform that function once activated, regardless of where the activation comes from. The representation does not "care" about the source of the activation; it is blind to it and has no "memory" about it that might cause it to behave differently depending on the particular source. The activated mental representation is like a button being pushed; it can be pushed by one's finger intentionally (e.g., turning on the electric coffeemaker) or accidentally (e.g., by the cat on the countertop) or by a decision made in the past (e.g., by setting the automatic turn-on mechanism the night before). In whatever way the start button is pushed, the mechanism subsequently behaves in the same way.

And so, the evaluations we've made in the past are now made for us and predispose us to behave in consistent ways; the goals we have pursued in the past now become active and guide our behavior in pursuit of the goal in relevant situations; and our perceptions of the emotional and behavioral reactions of others make us tend to respond in the same way, establishing bonds of rapport and liking in a natural and effortless way. Thus "the automaticity of being" is far from the negative and maladaptive caricature drawn by humanistically oriented writers; rather, these processes are in our service and best interests—and in an intimate, knowing way at that. They are, if anything, "mental butlers" who know our tendencies and preferences so well that they anticipate and take care of them for us, without having to be asked.

Amy Fisher Smith

 **NO**

The Dangers of Automatically Interpreting "Automaticity": The New Face of Determinism

> Joe is a regular guy who is driving in fairly heavy traffic, when suddenly, another driver cuts in front of Joe, causing him to slam on the brakes to avoid a near collision. Joe's heart is racing; his knuckles are white from gripping the steering wheel; and his breathing is short and fast. Joe finds himself enraged at the other driver. He begins to honk at the other driver, screaming obscenities and threats—possibly even attempting to follow the other driver to demand an apology or to exact some sort of revenge.

Joe represents a classic example of road rage—people who fly off the handle in inappropriate ways when confronted with offensive or dangerous driving in other drivers. How are behaviors such as Joe's road rage to be explained? Many psychologists are currently puzzling over such phenomena, especially since the anger of someone like Joe seems so automatic and non-conscious. In other words, Joe's rage seems to be an involuntary reaction—his rage does not seem to be something that he necessarily "chooses." Does this mean that Joe is determined—or forced—by his environment to become enraged? Would this mean that Joe is not responsible for his rage? Where does Joe's free will and choice enter in as a factor, if at all?

Answers to these questions are vital to psychologists. What is at stake is whether we are determined by environmental stimuli or whether we have some degree of freedom from such stimuli. If we are determined, it means that we can never really be responsible for our behaviors, because our behaviors are always caused by some other factor, stimulus, or situation outside of us. Alternatively, if we have agency or free will, it means that we can choose courses of behavior—we can act otherwise than the environmental stimuli might suggest. The ability to choose also means that we can be held accountable for our behaviors, because we are the initiating agents of our action—not some outside source.

A Deterministic Interpretation

One recently proposed theory (Bargh & Chartrand, 1999) attempts to explain our emotional responses (like Joe's road rage) as being caused and determined by environmental triggers (like the dangerous driver mentioned above). Bargh and Chartrand (1999), the proponents of this "automaticity" theory, argue that not only our emotional responses, but our thoughts and behaviors, are initiated and determined by environmental stimuli. If we consider Joe's road rage from this perspective, Joe does not consciously and willfully decide to become angry or enraged when the other driver cuts him off. Rather, Joe seems to be involuntarily responding to a specific environmental trigger—namely, the other bad driver. From Bargh and Chartrand's (1999) perspective, we automatically respond to external "features of the environment" (p. 462) in an "environment–perception– behavior sequence" with "no role played by conscious choice in producing the behavior" (p. 466). In other words, Joe perceives a "feature" or stimulus in the environment (i.e., the other driver), and then he automatically responds to this threatening stimulus in an unthinking way with a defensive emotion—anger or rage.

This means that Joe could not help but become enraged by the other driver. Indeed, Joe was determined to become so enraged. This determinism means that Joe is not responsible for his actions—the other driver is—and thus we cannot really hold Joe accountable for his rage, because his emotional response and subsequent behaviors are viewed as an involuntary and uncontrollable reaction to a specific trigger in the environment. What if exposure to the dangerous driver leads Joe to physically assault the other driver, or worse, what if Joe harms or kills the other driver? From the perspective of Bargh and Chartrand's (1999) determinism, the harmed or killed driver is to blame—not Joe.

Bargh and Chartrand's (1999) determinism is not limited to an understanding of emotional responses and behaviors like Joe's road rage (p. 473). Rather, Joe's road rage is a model for understanding *all* thoughts, emotions, and behaviors, whether conscious or non-conscious, voluntary or involuntary. When the authors discuss consciously chosen goals, for instance, they state that the "environment itself activates and puts the goal into motion" (Bargh & Chartrand, 1999, p. 468). This means that even when we think that we are consciously and willfully choosing our actions, we are actually engaged in a self-deception, because the environment has unwittingly set "the goal into motion" (p. 468). In other words, we do not really choose goals—ever. Rather, exposure to a particular kind of stimulus automatically activates both conscious and non-conscious goals, in which case, the goals themselves are never freely chosen.

A Free Will-ist Possibility

Interestingly, this deterministic view runs counter to many of the assumptions that we naturally make about our behaviors, both personally and culturally. For instance, we generally view ourselves as agents of our own actions, and this agentic view is embedded in our culture's legal system. From most judicial perspectives, Joe would be held accountable if he harmed the other driver in the road rage incident, because our legal system often presumes that people have a choice about their thoughts and actions. There are exceptions to the general rule (e.g., insanity defense), but for the most part, people are viewed as responsible agents. Hence, an age-old question is implicitly raised in Bargh and Chartrand's (1999) thesis—are we determined or are we free?

This article has two purposes. First, I critically examine Bargh and Chartrand's (1999) explanation of "automaticity"—the non-conscious and involuntary thoughts, behaviors, and emotions that they describe as being determined by the environment. Second, I offer a different way of understanding these non-conscious thoughts and behaviors that explains all the "data" like Joe's experiences and yet does not result in us losing our free will. Let us begin by noting how often people seem to act in ways that are automatic and non-conscious. Once we have mastered certain skills like driving, for instance, most of us can drive automatically without consciously choosing or intending the behavioral skills that are required (Bargh & Chartrand, 1999, p. 468). For instance, we commonly say that we drive on "auto-pilot," meaning that we coordinate the steering with the acceleration and breaking without consciously intending to do so.

Hence, the question is not whether automatic and non-conscious behaviors exist—they do. The question is whether automatic behaviors have to be explained as determined by environmental triggers as Bargh and Chartrand (1999) argue. Consider Joe again. Do we have to explain Joe's automatic rage as determined by environmental cues? Are there other equally plausible explanations or interpretations of Joe's automatic behavior that avoid such deterministic outcomes? Such alternative interpretations *are* possible.

The Relationship Between Interpretation and Data

The issue of interpretation is an important one—not only for the case of Joe's automatic road rage—but to scientific inquiry in general. As philosophers of science and many researchers have long noted, empirical findings (i.e., data) that emerge from scientific experiments are not immutable facts (Kuhn, 1962/ 1996; Popper, 1963). Rather, the data or brute "facts" that emerge in experiments must be meaningfully organized and interpreted in terms of the researcher's pre-existing theoretical frame of reference. The data themselves cannot tell us the facts of the matter, because the data themselves are not completely organized. What is needed is the organizing and meaning-making properties of the researcher's theory to make sense of the data. As Slife and Williams (1995) argue, "the experimental data are not experimental *findings* without the organization imposed on them by the scientist" (p. 75).

Data, then, are always interpreted, and this interpretation arises from the researchers' pre-existing philosophical and theoretical commitments as well as the history, traditions, expectations, and values of the researcher (Slife & Williams, 1995). The empirical findings or "data" about automaticity that Bargh and Chartrand (1999) report are equally interpreted. The automaticity data themselves do not objectively reveal that automatic thoughts and behaviors are determined by environmental triggers. Rather, Bargh and Chartrand

(1999) bring their deterministic theory to the automaticity data as an organizing framework, and therefore they *interpret* the data in light of their deterministic assumptions.

Because data are not inherently meaningful or organized in themselves, there are multiple interpretations of data possible at any given time. Another way to say this is that our theories are underdetermined by the empirical data (Curd & Cover, 1998; Duhem, 1982). As much as we might like to access the brute facts of the matter through scientific experimentation, there are always multiple theories available to us to make sense of the data. Of course, there are limitations to the number of applicable theories given the configuration of the data, but there is more than one theory-contender at play. The question is which theory or interpretation seems to fit or explain the data the best. Hence, scientists and researchers are often concerned with competing explanations or interpretations of the *same* data rather than with the data themselves.

Bargh and Chartrand (1999) either fail to recognize that they have a particular interpretation of the data, or they refuse to recognize an alternative theory that might make equally good sense of the data. They seem to presume that their deterministic interpretation of the automaticity data is the fact of the matter, when, in principle, there are multiple interpretations of the automaticity data, some of which might not lead to deterministic outcomes. Paradoxically, Bargh and Chartrand (1999) automatically bring their pre-investigatory theoretical assumptions to the automaticity data without either telling the reader or consciously realizing that they are doing so. In other words, they are non-consciously and automatically interpreting the automaticity data according to their deterministic assumptions. Before considering how other kinds of theories and assumptions might help us to *re*-interpret the automaticity data, we will examine the philosophical and theoretical assumptions made by Bargh and Chartrand (1999), which led them to view non-conscious and automatic behavior as determined.

Empiricistic Interpretations of Automaticity

When Bargh and Chartrand (1999) state that the environment initiates behavior, they seem to be tacitly assuming that there are triggering events that begin in the environment, cross space, and enter our minds through our senses. Whether or not they know it, the authors subscribe to a particular philosophical or theoretical position—that of empiricism. Empiricism posits the environment as the originator of cognitive representations (Robinson, 1995; Slife & Williams, 1995). Environmental stimuli, as experienced through our senses, take precedence in the empiricistic model, because such stimuli are thought to initiate and incrementally build-up the contents of the mind over time. From this perspective, Joe can only know what he has been exposed to in the environment via his senses, because his mind is the result of an accumulation of past sensory experiences. Perception itself is thought to be a relatively transparent vehicle for this building-up or accumulation process. In other words, empiricists assume that what we perceive is an accurate representation of what exists in the environment. Perception is not thought to add or subtract anything from the objects of experience. Joe's perception of the other driver is thought to be relatively transparent. That is, Joe simply takes into his mind an objective representation of the other driver, and then responds automatically with road rage.

Bargh and Chartrand (1999) make these empiricistic assumptions when they explain that "perception is the route by which the environment directly causes mental activity—specifically, the activation of internal representations of the outside world" (p. 465). Consistent with their empiricistic bias, Bargh and Chartrand (1999) presume that environmental objects or stimuli "directly cause" cognitions and emotions (p. 465). Another way to say this is that environmental objects determine cognitions and emotions. Of course, the authors do not see this direct causation or determinism in their data; this presumption is "read in" to the data from their empiricistic framework. Nevertheless, given their interpretation of direct causation, the authors contend that environmental stimuli—rather than conscious choice or independent will—"introduce(s) the idea of action" or behavior (p. 465).

What initiates thought and action, then, is not us. Rather, what initiates thought and action are objects and events that we are exposed to in the environment. This means that Joe is like a captain-less and rudderless boat at sea, passively moving where the wind and waves take him. He is completely vulnerable to the active stimulus forces impinging upon him from the outside. In this view, Joe will never be the initiating center of his own action. Joe might think that he chooses behaviors and goals, but he is really automatically responding in a passive and non-thinking way to environmental cues. Bargh and Chartrand (1999) elaborate, ". . . a direct and automatic route is provided from the external environment to [behavioral] action tendencies, via perception" (p. 465).

In their defense, Bargh and Chartrand (1999) might claim that the "automaticity" theory is itself born out of the facts of empirical research. That is, they only view the environment as the initiator of thought and behavior, because previous scientific research has suggested that this is the case. The problem with this claim has to do with the relationship between interpretation and scientific "data" that was discussed previously. Recall that data are always interpreted. When Bargh and Chartrand (1999) argue that the "environment directly causes mental activity" (p. 465), they are making an *inference* or an interpretation of causation. They infer or presume that a causal relationship exists between the environmental stimuli and the cognition/behavior when such a relationship cannot be observed directly.

The philosopher David Hume showed us this problem of causation long ago, and much of what he argued is still considered relevant today (Jones, 1969; Slife & Williams, 1995). For Hume, the presumed causal connection between events is something that we attribute to events, rather than something that exists independently of us in nature. Hume argued that what we call causation is nothing more than the repeated occurrence of a pairing of events (Jones, 1969). That is, when we see one event follow another event (e.g., when we see Joe become enraged when exposed to a dangerous driver), we presume that the first event causes or produces the second event.

However, there is no empirical evidence for this presumed causal connection. In other words, Bargh and Chartrand (1999) cannot directly see or observe the causal force that they presume exists between the environmental stimulus and the cognition/behavior. The causal force itself does not fall upon the retina of the researcher to be observed. The only empirical evidence is the observation of two seemingly related events—two events that occur in temporal sequence—the environmental stimulus (e.g., the driver who cuts in front of Joe) and the emotional/behavioral response (e.g., Joe's road rage). Do Bargh and Chartrand (1999) "see" the cause (e.g., image of the driver) *produce* the emotional response? Or do they see merely the driver, and then the response? Correlation does not imply causation, as Hume has taught us.

Just as they read causation into the automaticity data, Bargh and Chartrand (1999) read determinism into the data, all in accordance with their pre-held empiricistic causal framework. In other words, because they have already decided (from the outset) that the environment is the source or originator of cognition, it logically follows that cognition and behaviors (automatic or otherwise) are caused and determined by the environment. Their already deciding and accepting these empiricistic assumptions as fact also means that they are not really attempting to test these assumptions. They are, rather, looking for *how* cognition/behavior are determined by the environment, instead of *whether* they are determined by the environment.

Alternative Interpretations of Automaticity

If Bargh and Chartrand (1999) have, in fact, brought their own philosophic bias (i.e., empiricism) to the automaticity data, resulting in a deterministic view, are there non-deterministic philosophies or theories available that fit the automaticity data equally well, or perhaps better? Recall that the data of scientific experiments are always underdetermined, meaning that there are multiple interpretations of data possible (Duhem, 1982). Why shouldn't we consider some of these alternatives? Why are we tied to one philosophical perspective (empiricism) in our interpretation of the automaticity data? At a minimum, we ought to consider other theories and their applicability to the automaticity data like Joe's road rage. The question, as it is for many scientists, is one of competing theoretical explanations. Which theory fits the automaticity data the best?

As just such an alternative to empiricism, there is an entire tradition of thought beginning with the philosophies of Continental Rationalism and moving through to Continental Hermeneutics that emphasize the active role of the mind rather than the passive role suggested by empiricism (Bernstein, 1983; Gadamer, 1960/1995; Heidegger, 1926/1962; Wood, 2001). These philosophies are complex, but for our purposes they can be boiled down to some basic points. Perhaps foremost, we are not thought to simply take in environmental stimuli via the "environment–perception–behavior" sequence that Bargh and Chartrand (1999) discuss (p. 466). Rather, the mind is given at least an equal priority, because the mind is assumed to extend order and structure to what it encounters in the environment, even as perception occurs. Another way to say this is that we actively interpret what we encounter in the environment, rather than passively taking in stimuli to be shaped by it.

Consider Joe again. The emphasis of these Continental philosophies on interpretation would imply that Joe is not passively and automatically responding in an unthinking way to the stimulus of the dangerous driver. Rather, Joe actively brings an entire interpretive world-view to his driving experience that tacitly affects how he understands driving, driving etiquette, and other drivers. Whether or not Joe becomes enraged has to do with the nature of the interpretive worldview, which he actively creates. What if Joe implicitly believes that his goals and progress should not be impeded—particularly his driving goals and progress. If Joe maintains this belief, he is more likely to become angered and enraged when other drivers cut him off (thereby impeding his driving progress).

Consider an alternative interpretation of belief system, to emphasize the mind's activity, and perhaps even "free will." What if Joe implicitly believes that people who are in a hurry *should* cut other people off? If Joe brings this interpretive framework to his driving situation, then he is probably less likely to become angry or enraged when he is cut-off by another driver. Indeed, he might even expect to be cut-off by other drivers given his appreciation of their being in a hurry. In this case, Joe automatically interprets drivers who cut people off as drivers with important things to do, and therefore, he does not become enraged when such drivers cut him off.

In this situation, when Joe is confronted with the stimulus of a bad driver, the stimulus itself is not objectively imprinted on a passive mind to ultimately direct behavior as the empiricists might claim. Rather, the stimulus is actively made meaningful within the interpretive framework that Joe brings with him to the driving experience. In this case, what empiricists like to call a "stimulus" is really not a stimulus at all, because whatever is stimulating to us has to do with what our minds consider meaningful rather than any intrinsic, objective property of the "stimulus" itself. The point, from the Continental perspective, is that a stimulus is not a stimulus without a mind that actively bestows meaning upon it.

This emphasis on interpretation implies that perception is not as transparent as empiricism might suggest. Recall that in the empiricistic view, we are thought to take in stimuli as they exist in the environment. From the Continental perspective, this transparency contention is problematic, because different persons can be exposed to the same stimulus, but respond in very divergent ways given their propensity to interpret stimuli differently. When confronted with the stimulus of another driver, Joe may interpret the driver as "bad" (e.g., taking my space in line) and become enraged, whereas a different driver might interpret the same driver as "good" (e.g, helping his wife get to the hospital) and not become enraged. This emphasis on active interpretation means that the mind affects environmental stimuli as much as environmental stimuli affect the mind, and therefore, cognitions and behavior cannot be completely determined by environmental triggers.

The Nature of Interpretive Frameworks

One question that arises with respect to the Continental tradition and its emphasis on an active mind has to do with the nature of the interpretive frameworks themselves. How is it that we come to create such interpretive frameworks? How is it that Joe's interpretive framework constitutes the particular meanings that it does rather than other meanings?

The empiricist response to this question is "Joe's previous sensory experience!" Empiricists like Bargh and Chartrand (1999) might argue that Joe's "interpretive driving framework" is the result of being exposed over time to certain kinds of driving stimuli that have accumulated in mind and shaped the interpretive framework that Joe is currently using. Maybe Joe was exposed to a road-raging father when he was a child. In this case, Joe passively takes in the stimulus of a raging father, which imprints upon his mind, initiating and shaping Joe's beliefs and expectations for driving. Consistent with an empiricistic view, Joe's mind is like a sponge, passively absorbing objective stimulus events. Being exposed to a road-raging father means that Joe is determined to be a road-rager himself.

However, for rationalists and hermeneuticists, interpretive frameworks are not the result of accumulated past sensory experiences. Rather, our interpretive frameworks (and the mind itself) are not thought to be solely or exclusively dependent on environmental stimuli. This means that we come into the world with an intelligent, structuring and organizing mind that actively interprets stimuli that it encounters *from birth* (Rychlak, 1981)! Even from birth, then, we can view Joe as actively organizing and structuring his experience rather than being wholly shaped by the environment. Joe can extend meanings to "stimuli" or situations that are completely of his own making.

Hence, when Joe is exposed as a child to a road-raging father, what matters is how Joe actively interprets and understands his father's behavior—and these interpretations and meanings are not necessarily contingent on previous sensory inputs. Joe, then, has the capacity to think and reason to other courses of thought and behavioral action than those modeled by his father. This means that Joe has a *choice* about his thoughts, emotions, and behaviors. *Joe* is the originator of his interpretive frameworks. *Joe* is at least partially responsible for the meanings that he extends to his driving and other experiences, which means that Joe is accountable for his actions.

Because the Continental tradition allows for this kind of freedom and choice, people like Joe and everyone else are thought to have possibility. We are not determined by environmental triggers—this means that we are without possibility. Rather, we have the possibility to interpret and understand events in multiple ways. We have the possibility to change our interpretations and understandings, and thereby change ourselves, and therefore we are viewed as active agents with the capacity for free will and choice.

Non-Consciousness and Free Will

But how can our automatic and non-conscious thoughts, emotions, and behaviors be "chosen" or actively created by us? As we noted early on, Joe did not seem to "choose" to become enraged. Is it really possible to view Joe's automatic road rage as chosen by him and ultimately within his control? Hermeneutic philosophies are particularly helpful here, because they emphasize the often tacit, implicit, and unthematized nature of the mind's active interpreting process (Heidegger, 1926/1962). In other words, much of the mind's active extension of meanings through interpretive frameworks occurs outside of our conscious awareness. We still respond to stimuli automatically in the way that Bargh and Chartrand (1999) describe, but this automaticity is not automatically involuntary—it is *automatically voluntary*.

Consider Joe again. Recall from the rationalistic and hermeneutic perspective that Joe's road rage is dependent upon his pre-existing interpretive framework—his worldview of meanings surrounding driving, driving etiquette, and other drivers. From this perspective, Joe only becomes enraged when his interpretive framework is filled with meanings that lead to rage—for instance, Joe's belief that his goals and progress should not be impeded. Joe does not necessarily have an immediate, conscious awareness of his guiding beliefs and assumptions. On the contrary, these guiding beliefs and assumptions—the nexus of the interpretive framework—are mostly non-conscious. They recede into the background. Indeed, Joe probably takes these beliefs and assumptions for granted—they are the givens of his experience and are not immediately and consciously known.

Nevertheless, as was discussed earlier, the interpretations and understandings that Joe extends to experience—however conscious or non-conscious—are of his own making. In other words, he continues to be an active shaper of the interpretations and meanings that constitute his interpretive frameworks. He may simply lack an awareness of his active shaping. As Merleau-Ponty (1983/1942), a famous Continental philosopher argues, consciousness is "a network of significative intentions which are sometimes clear to themselves and sometimes, on the contrary, lived rather than known" (p. 173).

This alternative agentic or free-willist account of automaticity not only fits the experience of Joe, but fits all of the automaticity data that Bargh and Chartrand (1999) cite. Whatever it is that we do automatically—respond with road rage, socially interact with others, activate goals, form evaluations and judgments—we can view all of these thoughts, emotions, and behaviors as ultimately being directed by the person rather than by the environment. This is good news, because it means that we are not doomed to the determinism that accompanies Bargh and Chartrand's empiricistic theoretical framework. We do not have to view people as passive responders to environmental stimuli who are ultimately shaped by their environments.

On the contrary, we can view persons as actively shaping and interpreting what they encounter such that they can never be reduced to the environment alone. However, much of this active shaping and interpretation escapes our notice, because it occurs non-consciously and automatically. Despite the non-consciousness and automaticity, we are still willing complicated patterns of behavior. The test of agency is whether we can act otherwise—whether we can change the pattern of thought and behavior and act differently.

If Joe decides to see a professor about a course grade, he does not consciously *will* each literal, physical step along the way to the professor's office. Rather, he has automatically willed a whole pattern of behavior (e.g., going to see a professor), the parts of which (e.g., the literal steps) remain outside of his awareness. Was Joe's automatic walking the result of exposure to a stimulus in the environment? The test, again, is whether Joe can behave otherwise. If a friend calls out to Joe along the walk, he may non-consciously choose to alter the pattern of his behavior. He may not visit the professor after all, opting instead to visit with his friend. The point is that Joe always has the possibility of changing the pattern of non-conscious behavior. Joe may continue toward the professor, or he may stop and visit with his friend. In either case, Joe is non-consciously willing his behavior—and therefore he is agentic and free.

Because the automaticity data are as easily subsumed by a free willist account as by a deterministic account, why not consider the free willist view? The question may now be which of these competing theories fits the data the best—and if our experience of ourselves is grounded in free will rather than determinism—then the free willist view ought to be taken under serious consideration.

References

Bargh, J. A., & Chartrand, T. L. (1999). The unbearable automaticity of being. *American Psychologist, 54* (7), 462–479.

Bernstein, R. J. (1983). *Beyond objectivism and relativism: Science, hermeneutics, and praxis.* Philadelphia: University of Pennsylvania Press.

Curd, M., & Cover, J. A. (1998). *Philosophy of science: The central issues.* New York: W. W. Norton & Co.

Duhem, P. (1982). *The aim and structure of physical theory.* Princeton, NJ: Princeton University Press.

Gadamer, H. G. (1995). *Truth and method* (2nd rev.ed.). (J. Weinsheimer & D. G. Marshall, Trans.). New York: Continuum. (Original work published 1960).

Heidegger, M. (1962). *Being and time.* (J. Macquarrie & E. Robinson, Trans.). San Francisco: Harper Collins. (Original work published 1926).

Kuhn, T. S. (1996). *The structure of scientific revolutions* (3rd ed.). Chicago, IL: University of Chicago Press. (Original work published 1962).

Jones, W. T. (1969). *Hobbes to Hume: A history of western philosophy* (2nd ed.). New York: Harcourt Brace Jovanovich.

Merleau-Ponty, M. (1983). *The structure of behavior.* (Trans. A. L. Fisher). Pittsburgh, PA: Duquesne University Press. (Original work published 1942).

Popper, K. (1963). *Conjectures and refutations: The growth of scientific knowledge.* London: Routledge & Kegan Paul.

Robinson, D. N. (1995). *An intellectual history of psychology* (3rd ed.). Madison, WI: University of Wisconsin Press.

Rychlak, J. F. (1981). *Introduction to personality and psychotherapy: A theory-construction approach.* Dallas, TX: Houghton Mifflin.

Slife, B. D., & Williams, R. N. (1995). *What's behind the research? Discovering hidden assumptions in the behavioral sciences.* Thousand Oaks, CA: Sage.

Wood, A. W. (2001). *Basic writings of Kant.* New York: Random House.

CHALLENGE QUESTIONS

Are Human Activities Determined?

1. Bargh/Chartrand and Smith interpret the same sets of data in completely different ways. How can this be possible? (Hint: Read the Smith article carefully.)
2. On what issues do Bargh/Chartrand and Smith agree? How does this help the effectiveness of Smith's argument?
3. As Smith notes, Bargh/Chartrand do not tell their readers that other interpretations of their data are possible. Do you believe they should? Why or why not?
4. Consider the implications of both Bargh/Chartrand and Smith's theories. If your life were determined or free, how would it be different than how you currently understand it?
5. Do you agree with Smith that free will is our everyday experience of ourselves? Why or why not? How much confidence should we put in that type of experience?

ISSUE 11

Is the Theory of Multiple Intelligences Valid?

YES: Howard Gardner, from *Multiple Intelligences: New Horizons* (Basic Books, 2006)

NO: John White, from "Howard Gardner: The Myth of Multiple Intelligences," Lecture at Institute of Education, University of London (November 2004)

ISSUE SUMMARY

YES: Psychologist Howard Gardner argues for the validity of his theory of multiple intelligences because it both reflects the data collected about intelligent human behavior and explains why people excel in some areas but fail in others.

NO: Educational philosopher John White believes that Gardner cannot prove the existence of multiple types of intelligence and argues that people who are generally able to adapt well will excel in whatever field they choose.

People who saw Michael Jordan play professional basketball were amazed by his grace and poise. Even when ill, he could outscore most other players. What was the source of his abilities? Did his proficiency at playing basketball necessarily imply that he was good at other activities? After all, Jordan was also generally acknowledged as being bright, articulate, and socially skilled. On the other hand, his attempt to play major league baseball was less than successful. Can people only be really good at one thing and not any others, or is some general ability—some general intelligence—involved?

The traditional view of intelligence is that there is a single factor, often called *g*, that underlies most other abilities. The other abilities may require some unique pieces of information to perform successfully, such as playing a musical instrument, but those persons with a high *g* are thought to be quicker in acquiring this information or more easily adaptable to these new circumstances. Most tests of intelligence assume and reinforce this more traditional view of intelligence because they seem to imply that a person's intelligence can be represented as a single, measurable quantity or score.

Howard Gardner, however, has recently challenged this popular tradition. In the first article of this issue, this renowned psychologist has argued that intelligence is best understood not as a single general capacity, but as a number of distinct and relatively independent abilities. Michael Jordan may have bodily-kinesthetic intelligence, but that does not mean he has musical intelligence. Gardner argues that the single-factor theory of intelligence is outdated and should be replaced by a theory of multiple intelligences. He believes that individuals have profiles reflecting both strengths and weaknesses in different areas of intelligence. According to Gardner a good test-taker—the usual recipient of a high "IQ" score—is not necessarily any "smarter" than a good presenter; they both happen to be more intelligent in different areas.

In the second selection, John White examines Gardner's position in some detail, calling it the "myth of multiple intelligences." White begins his critique of Gardner's theory by describing Gardner's original attempt (1983) to define intelligence. According to White, Gardner's original definition was itself too narrow. Instead of defining different types of intelligence as Gardner does, White believes that intelligence has a lot to do with the general flexibility or adaptability of a person in achieving their goals. The more intelligent a person is, the more capable that person is of achieving their goals, no matter how divergent these goals may be. In this sense, then, White's proposal is a recent update of the more traditional general approach to intelligence that Gardner is attempting to replace.

POINT

- Humans are best understood as having a number of relatively independent intellectual faculties.
- Multiple intelligence theory gives a framework for why people succeed in some areas but fail in others.
- Evidence from brain research, human development, evolution, and cross-cultural comparisons support the theory of multiple intelligences.
- Multiple intelligence theory has important educational implications.

COUNTERPOINT

- The existence of multiple types of intellectual faculties has not been proven.
- People who are generally "intelligent" will be able to succeed because they understand how to adapt to the differing performance areas.
- The research cited by Gardner could just as well be used to support general intelligence theory.
- The acceptance of multiple intelligence theory in educational settings could give students a false picture of themselves.

YES

Howard Gardner

In a Nutshell

The original scene: Paris, 1900—La Belle Epoque. The city fathers approached a talented psychologist named Alfred Binet with an unusual request. Families were flocking to the capital city from the provinces, and a good many of their children were having trouble with their schoolwork. Could Binet devise some kind of a measure that would predict which youngsters would succeed and which would fail in the primary grades of Paris schools?

As almost everybody knows, Binet succeeded. In short order, his discovery came to be called the "intelligence test"; his measure, the IQ, for "intelligence quotient" (mental age divided by chronological age and multiplied by 100). Like other Parisian fashions, the IQ soon made its way to the United States, where it enjoyed a modest success until World War I, when it was used to test over one million American military recruits. With its use by the U.S. armed forces, and with America's victory in the conflict, Binet's invention had truly arrived. Ever since, the IQ test has looked like psychology's biggest success— a genuinely useful scientific tool.

What is the vision that led to the excitement about IQ? At least in the West, people had always relied on intuitive assessments of how smart other people were. Now intelligence seemed to be quantifiable. Just as you could measure someone's actual or potential height, now, it seemed, you could measure someone's actual or potential intelligence. We had one dimension of mental ability along which we could array everyone.

The search for the perfect measure of intelligence has proceeded apace. Here, for example, are some quotations from an advertisement for one such test:

> Need an individual test which quickly provides a stable and reliable esti-
> mate of intelligence in four or five minutes per form? Has three forms?
> Does not depend on verbal production or subjective scoring? Can be used
> with the severely physically handicapped (even paralyzed) if they can sig-
> nal yes or no? Handles two-year-olds and superior adults with the same
> short series of items and the same format? Only $16.00 complete.

Now, a single test that can do all that is quite a claim. American psycho-
logist Arthur Jensen suggests that we could look at reaction time to assess intelligence: a set of lights go on; how quickly can the subject react? British psychologist Hans Eysenck recommends that investigators of intelligence look

From *Multiple Intelligences: New Horizons*, Basic Books, 2006, pp. 3–24. Copyright © 2006 by Howard Gardner. Reprinted by permission.

directly at brain waves. And with the advent of the gene chip, many look forward to the day when we can glance at the proper gene locus on the proper chromosome, read off someone's IQ, and confidently predict his or her life chances. . . .

I would like to present an alternative vision—one based on a radically different view of the mind, and one that yields a very different view of school. It is a pluralistic view of mind, recognizing many different and discrete facets of cognition, acknowledging that people have different cognitive strengths and contrasting cognitive styles. I introduce the concept of an individual-centered school that takes this multifaceted view of intelligence seriously. This model for a school is based in part on findings from sciences that did not even exist in Binet's time: cognitive science (the study of the mind) and neuroscience (the study of the brain). One such approach I have called the theory of multiple intelligences. Let me tell you something about its sources and claims to lay the groundwork for the discussions on education in the chapters that follow.

I introduce this new point of view by asking you to suspend for a moment the usual judgment of what constitutes intelligence, and let your thoughts run freely over the capabilities of human beings—perhaps those that would be picked out by the proverbial visitor from Mars. Your mind may turn to the brilliant chess player, the world-class violinist, and the champion athlete; certainly, such outstanding performers deserve special consideration. Are the chess player, violinist, and athlete "intelligent" in these pursuits? If they are, then why do our tests of "intelligence" fail to identify them? If they are not intelligent, what allows them to achieve such astounding feats? In general, why does the contemporary construct of intelligence fail to take into account large areas of human endeavor?

To approach these questions I introduced the theory of multiple intelligences (MI) in the early 1980s. As the name indicates, I believe that human cognitive competence is better described in terms of a set of abilities, talents, or mental skills, which I call *intelligences*. All normal individuals possess each of these skills to some extent; individuals differ in the degree of skill and in the nature of their combination. I believe this theory of intelligence may be more humane and more veridical than alternative views of intelligence and that it more adequately reflects the data of human "intelligent" behavior. Such a theory has important educational implications.

What Constitutes an Intelligence?

The question of the optimal definition of intelligence looms large in my inquiry. And it is here that the theory of multiple intelligences begins to diverge from traditional points of view. In the classic psychometric view, intelligence is defined operationally as the ability to answer items on tests of intelligence. The inference from the test scores to some underlying ability is supported by statistical techniques. These techniques compare responses of subjects at different ages; the apparent correlation of these test scores across ages and across different tests corroborates the notion that the general faculty of intelligence, called *g* in short, does not change much with age, training, or experience. It is an inborn attribute or faculty of the individual.

Multiple intelligences theory, on the other hand, pluralizes the traditional concept. An intelligence is a computational capacity—a capacity to process a certain kind of information—that originates in human biology and human psychology. Humans have certain kinds of intelligences, whereas rats, birds, and computers foreground other kinds of computational capacities. An intelligence entails the ability to solve problems or fashion products that are of consequence in a particular cultural setting or community. The problem-solving skill allows one to approach a situation in which a goal is to be obtained and to locate the appropriate route to that goal. The creation of a cultural product allows one to capture and transmit knowledge or to express one's conclusions, beliefs, or feelings. The problems to be solved range from creating an end for a story to anticipating a mating move in chess to repairing a quilt. Products range from scientific theories to musical compositions to successful political campaigns.

MI theory is framed in light of the biological origins of each problem-solving skill. Only those skills that are universal to the human species are considered (again, we differ from rats, birds, or computers). Even so, the biological proclivity to participate in a particular form of problem solving must also be coupled with the cultural nurturing of that domain. For example, language, a universal skill, may manifest itself particularly as writing in one culture, as oratory in another culture, and as the secret language composed of anagrams or tongue twisters in a third.

Given the desideratum of selecting intelligences that are rooted in biology and that are valued in one or more cultural settings, how does one actually identify an intelligence? In coming up with the list, I reviewed evidence from various sources: knowledge about normal development and development in gifted individuals; information about the breakdown of cognitive skills under conditions of brain damage; studies of exceptional populations, including prodigies, savants, and autistic children; data about the evolution of cognition over the millennia; cross-cultural accounts of cognition; psychometric studies, including examinations of correlations among tests; and psychological training studies, particularly measures of transfer and generalization across tasks. Only those candidate intelligences that satisfied all or a healthy majority of the criteria were selected as bona fide intelligences. A more complete discussion of each of these criteria and of the intelligences that were initially identified may be found in *Frames of Mind*, especially chapter 4. In that foundational book I also consider how the theory might be disproved and compare it with competing theories of intelligence. An update of some of these discussions is presented in *Intelligence Reframed*, and in the chapters that follow.

In addition to satisfying the aforementioned criteria, each intelligence must have an identifiable core operation or set of operations. As a neurally based computational system, each intelligence is activated or triggered by certain kinds of internal or external information. For example, one core of musical intelligence is the sensitivity to pitch relations, and one core of linguistic intelligence is the sensitivity to the phonological features of a language.

An intelligence must also be susceptible to encoding in a symbol system—a culturally contrived system of meaning that captures and conveys important forms of information. Language, picturing, and mathematics are but three nearly worldwide symbol systems that are necessary for human survival and productivity. The relationship of an intelligence to a human symbol system is no accident. In fact, the existence of a core computational capacity anticipates the actual or potential creation of a symbol system that exploits that capacity. While it may be possible for an intelligence to develop without an accompanying symbol system, a primary characteristic of human intelligence may well be its gravitation toward such an embodiment.

The Original Set of Intelligences

Having sketched the characteristics and criteria for an intelligence, I turn now to a brief consideration of each of the intelligences that were proposed in the early 1980s. I begin each sketch with a thumbnail biography of a person who demonstrates an unusual facility with that intelligence. (These biographies were developed chiefly by my longtime colleague Joseph Walters.) The biographies illustrate some of the abilities that are central to the fluent operation of a given intelligence. Although each biography illustrates a particular intelligence, I do not wish to imply that in adulthood intelligences operate in isolation. Indeed, except in abnormal individuals, intelligences always work in concert, and any sophisticated adult role will involve a melding of several of them. Following each biography is a survey of the various sources of data that support each candidate as an intelligence.

Musical Intelligence

When Yehudi Menuhin was three years old, his parents smuggled him into San Francisco Orchestra concerts. The sound of Louis Persinger's violin so entranced the young child that he insisted on a violin for his birthday and Louis Persinger as his teacher. He got both. By the time he was ten years old, Menuhin was an international performer.

Violinist Yehudi Menuhin's musical intelligence manifested itself even before he had touched a violin or received any musical training. His powerful reaction to that particular sound and his rapid progress on the instrument suggest that he was biologically prepared in some way for a life in music. Menuhin is one example of evidence from child prodigies that support the claim that there is a biological link to a particular intelligence. Other special populations, such as autistic children who can play a musical instrument beautifully but who cannot otherwise communicate, underscore the independence of musical intelligence.

A brief consideration of the evidence suggests that musical skill passes the other tests for an intelligence. For example, certain parts of the brain play important roles in the perception and production of music. These areas are characteristically located in the right hemisphere, although musical skill is not as clearly localized in the brain as natural language. Although the particular susceptibility of musical ability to brain damage depends on the degree of training and other individual characteristics, there is clear evidence that amusia, or a selective loss of musical ability, occurs. . . .

Bodily-Kinesthetic Intelligence

Fifteen-year-old Babe Ruth was playing catcher one game when his team was taking a "terrific beating." Ruth "burst out laughing" and criticized the pitcher loudly. Brother Mathias, the coach, called out, "All right, George, YOU pitch!" Ruth was stunned and nervous: "I never pitched in my life . . . I can't pitch." The moment was transformative, as Ruth recalls in his autobiography: "Yet, as I took the position, I felt a strange relationship between myself and that pitcher's mound. I felt, somehow, as if I had been born out there and that this was a kind of home for me." As sports history shows, he went on to become a great major league pitcher (and, of course, attained legendary status as a hitter).

Like Menuhin, Babe Ruth was a prodigy who recognized his "instrument" immediately on his first exposure to it, before receiving any formal training.

Control of bodily movement is localized in the motor cortex, with each hemisphere dominant or controlling bodily movements on the contralateral side. In right-handers, the dominance for bodily movement is ordinarily found in the left hemisphere. The ability to perform movements when directed to do so can be impaired even in individuals who can perform the same movements reflexively or on a nonvoluntary basis. The existence of apraxia constitutes one line of evidence for a bodily-kinesthetic intelligence.

The evolution of specialized body movements is of obvious advantage to the species, and in human beings this adaptation is extended through the use of tools. Body movement undergoes a clearly defined developmental schedule in children; there is little question of its universality across cultures. Thus, it appears that bodily-kinesthetic "knowledge" satisfies many of the criteria for an intelligence.

The consideration of bodily-kinesthetic knowledge as "problem solving" may be less intuitive. Certainly carrying out a mime sequence or hitting a tennis ball is not solving a mathematical equation. And yet, the ability to use one's body to express an emotion (as in a dance), to play a game (as in a sport), or to create a new product (as in devising an invention) is evidence of the cognitive features of body usage. . . .

Logical-Mathematical Intelligence

Along with the companion skill of language, logical-mathematical reasoning provides the principal basis for IQ tests. This form of intelligence has been thoroughly investigated by traditional psychologists, and it is the archetype of "raw intelligence" or the problem-solving faculty that purportedly cuts across domains. It is perhaps ironic, then, that the actual mechanism by which one arrives at a solution to a logical-mathematical problem is not as yet completely understood—and the processes involved in leaps like those described by McClintock remain mysterious.

Logical-mathematical intelligence is supported as well by empirical criteria. Certain areas of the brain are more prominent in mathematical calculation than others; indeed, recent evidence suggests that the linguistic areas in the frontotemporal lobes are more important for logical deduction, and the visuospatial areas in the parietofrontal lobes for numerical calculation. There are savants who perform great feats of calculation even though they are tragically deficient in most other areas. Child prodigies in mathematics abound. The development of this intelligence in children has been carefully documented by Jean Piaget and other psychologists.

Linguistic Intelligence

. . . As with the logical intelligence, calling linguistic skill an intelligence is consistent with the stance of traditional psychology. Linguistic intelligence also passes our empirical tests. For instance, a specific area of the brain, called Broca's area, is responsible for the production of grammatical sentences. A person with damage to this area can understand words and sentences quite well but has difficulty putting words together in anything other than the simplest of sentences. Other thought processes may be entirely unaffected.

The gift of language is universal, and its rapid and unproblematic development in most children is strikingly constant across cultures. Even in deaf populations where a manual sign language is not explicitly taught, children will often invent their own manual language and use it surreptitiously. We thus see how an intelligence may operate independently of a specific input modality or output channel.

Spatial Intelligence

Navigation around the Caroline Islands in the South Seas is accomplished by native sailors without instruments. The position of the stars, as viewed from various islands, the weather patterns, and water color are the principal signposts. Each journey is broken into a series of segments, and the navigator learns the position of the stars within each of these segments. During the actual trip the navigator must mentally picture a reference island as it passes under a particular star. From that envisioning exercise, he computes the number of segments completed, the proportion of the trip remaining, and any corrections in heading that are required. The navigator cannot see the islands as he sails along; instead he maps their locations in his mental picture of the journey.

Spatial problem solving is required for navigation and for the use of the notational system of maps. Other kinds of spatial problem solving are brought to bear in visualizing an object from different angles and in playing chess. The visual arts also employ this intelligence in the use of space.

Evidence from brain research is clear and persuasive. Just as the middle regions of the left cerebral cortex have, over the course of evolution, been selected as the site of linguistic processing in right-handed persons, the posterior regions of the right cerebral cortex prove most crucial for spatial processing. Damage to these regions causes impairment of the ability to find one's way around a site, to recognize faces or scenes, or to notice fine details. . . .

Interpersonal Intelligence

. . . Interpersonal intelligence builds on a core capacity to notice distinctions among others—in particular, contrasts in their moods, temperaments, motivations, and intentions. In more advanced forms, this intelligence permits a skilled adult to read the intentions and desires of others, even when they have been hidden. This skill appears in a highly sophisticated form in religious or political leaders, salespersons, marketers, teachers, therapists, and parents. . . . All indices in brain research suggest that the frontal lobes play a prominent role in interpersonal knowledge. Damage in this area can cause profound personality changes while leaving other forms of problem solving unharmed—after such an injury, a person is often not the "same person." . . .

Biological evidence for interpersonal intelligence encompasses two additional factors often cited as unique to humans. One factor is the prolonged childhood of primates, including the close attachment to the mother. In cases where the mother (or a substitute figure) is not available and engaged, normal interpersonal development is in serious jeopardy. The second factor is the relative importance in humans of social interaction. Skills such as hunting, tracking, and killing in prehistoric societies required the participation and cooperation of large numbers of people. The need for group cohesion, leadership, organization, and solidarity follows naturally from this.

Intrapersonal Intelligence

In an essay called "A Sketch of the Past," written almost as a diary entry, Virginia Woolf discusses the "cotton wool of existence"—the various mundane events of life. She contrasts this cotton wool with three specific and poignant memories from her childhood: a fight with her brother, seeing a particular flower in the garden, and hearing of the suicide of a past visitor:

> These are three instances of exceptional moments. I often tell them over, or rather they come to the surface unexpectedly. But now for the first time I have written them down, and I realize something that I have never realized before. Two of these moments ended in a state of despair. The other ended, on the contrary, in a state of satisfaction. . . . The sense of horror [in hearing of the suicide] held me powerless. But in the case of the flower, I found a reason; and was thus able to deal with the sensation. I was not powerless. . . . Though I still have the peculiarity that I receive these sudden shocks, they are now always welcome; after the first surprise, I always feel instantly that they are particularly valuable. And so I go on to suppose that the shock-receiving capacity is what makes me a writer. I hazard the explanation that a shock is at once in my case followed by the desire to explain it. I feel that I have had a blow; but it is not, as I thought as a child, simply a blow from an enemy hidden behind the cotton wool of daily life; it is or will become a revelation of some order; it is a token of some real thing behind appearances; and I make it real by putting it into words.

This quotation vividly illustrates the intrapersonal intelligence—knowledge of the internal aspects of a person: access to one's own feeling life, one's range of emotions, the capacity to make discriminations among these emotions and eventually to label them and to draw on them as a means of understanding and guiding one's own behavior. A person with good intrapersonal intelligence has a viable and effective model of him- or herself—one consistent with a description constructed by careful observers who know that person intimately. Since this intelligence is the most private, evidence from language, music, or some other more expressive form of intelligence is required if the observer is to detect it at work. In the above quotation, for example, linguistic intelligence serves as a medium in which to observe intrapersonal knowledge in operation.

We see the familiar criteria at work in the intrapersonal intelligence. As with the interpersonal intelligence, the frontal lobes play a central role in personality change. Injury to the lower area of the frontal lobes is likely to produce irritability or euphoria, whereas injury to the higher regions is more likely to produce indifference, listlessness, slowness, and apathy—a kind of depressive personality. In persons with frontal lobe injury, the other cognitive functions often remain preserved. In contrast, among aphasics who have recovered sufficiently to describe their experiences, we find consistent testimony: while there may have been a diminution of general alertness and considerable depression about the condition, the individual in no way felt himself to be a different person. He recognized his own needs, wants, and desires and tried as best he could to achieve them.

The autistic child is a prototypical example of an individual with impaired intrapersonal intelligence; indeed, the child may not even be able to refer to himself. At the same time, such children may exhibit remarkable abilities in the musical, computational, spatial, mechanical, and other nonpersonal realms. . . .

The Unique Contributions of the Theory

As human beings, we all have a repertoire of skills for solving different kinds of problems. My investigation began, therefore, with a consideration of these problems, the contexts in which they are found, and the culturally significant products that are the outcome. I did not approach "intelligence" as a reified human faculty that is brought to bear in literally any problem setting; rather, I began with the problems that human beings solve and the products that they cherish. In a sense I then worked back to the intelligences that must be responsible.

Evidence from brain research, human development, evolution, and cross-cultural comparisons was brought to bear in the search for the relevant human intelligences: a candidate was included only if reasonable evidence to support its membership was found across these diverse fields. Again, this tack differs from the traditional one: since no candidate faculty is necessarily an intelligence, I could make an up-or-down decision on a motivated basis. In the traditional approach to intelligence, there is no opportunity for this type of empirical decision.

My belief is that these multiple human faculties, the intelligences, are to a significant extent independent of one another. Research with brain-damaged adults repeatedly demonstrates that particular faculties can be lost while others are spared. This independence of intelligences implies that a particularly high level of ability in one intelligence, say mathematics, does not require a similarly high level in another, like language or music. This independence of intelligences contrasts sharply with traditional measures of IQ that find high correlations among test scores. I speculate that the usual correlations among subtests of IQ tests come about because all of these tasks in fact measure the ability to respond rapidly to items of a logical-mathematical or linguistic sort; these correlations might be substantially reduced if one were to survey in a contextually appropriate way—what I call "intelligence-fair assessment"—the full range of human problem-solving skills.

Until now, my discussion may appear to suggest that adult roles depend largely on the flowering of a single intelligence. In fact, however, nearly every cultural role of any degree of sophistication requires a combination of intelligences. Thus, even an apparently straightforward role, like playing the violin, transcends a reliance on musical intelligence. To become a successful violinist requires bodily-kinesthetic dexterity and the interpersonal skills of relating to an audience and, in a different way, of choosing a manager; quite possibly it involves an intrapersonal intelligence as well. Dance requires skills in bodily-kinesthetic, musical, interpersonal, and spatial intelligences in varying degrees. Politics requires an interpersonal skill, a linguistic facility, and perhaps some logical aptitude.

Inasmuch as nearly every cultural role requires several intelligences, it becomes important to consider individuals as a collection of aptitudes rather than as having a singular problem-solving faculty that can be measured directly through pencil-and-paper tests. Even given a relatively small number of such intelligences, the diversity of human ability is created through the differences in these profiles. In fact, it may well be that the total is greater than the sum of the parts. An individual may not be particularly gifted in any intelligence, and yet, because of a particular combination or blend of skills, he or she may be able to fill some niche uniquely well. Thus, it is of paramount importance to assess the particular combination of skills that may earmark an individual for a certain vocational or avocational niche.

In brief MI theory leads to three conclusions:

1. All of us have the full range of intelligences; that is what makes us human beings, cognitively speaking.
2. No two individuals—not even identical twins—have exactly the same intellectual profile because, even when the genetic material is identical, individuals have different experiences (and identical twins are often highly motivated to distinguish themselves from one another).
3. Having a strong intelligence does not mean that one necessarily acts intelligently. A person with high mathematical intelligence might use her abilities to carry out important experiments in physics or create powerful new geometric proofs; but she might waste these abilities in playing the lottery all day or multiplying ten-digit numbers in her head.

All of these statements are about the psychology of human intelligence—to which MI theory seeks to make a contribution. But of course they raise powerful educational, political, and cultural questions. Those questions will engage us in later parts of the book.

Conclusion

I believe that in our society we suffer from three biases, which I have nicknamed "Westist," "Testist," and "Bestist." "Westist" involves putting certain Western cultural values, which date back to Socrates, on a pedestal. Logical thinking, for example, is important; rationality is important; but they are not the only virtues. "Testist" suggests a bias towards focusing on those human abilities or approaches that are readily testable. If it can't be tested, it sometimes seems, it is not worth paying attention to. My feeling is that assessment can be much broader, much more humane than it is now and that psychologists should spend less time ranking people and more time trying to help them.

"Bestist" is a thinly veiled reference to David Halberstam's 1972 book *The Best and the Brightest.* Halberstam's title referred ironically to the figures, among them Harvard faculty members, who were brought to Washington to help President John F. Kennedy and in the process launched the Vietnam War. I think any belief that all the answers to a given problem lie in one certain approach, such as logical-mathematical thinking, can be very dangerous. Current views of intellect need to be leavened with other, more comprehensive points of view.

It is of the utmost importance that we recognize and nurture all of the varied human intelligences and all of the combinations of intelligences. We are all so different largely because we have different combinations of intelligences. If we recognize this, I think we will have at least a better chance of dealing appropriately with the many problems that we face in the world. If we can mobilize the spectrum of human abilities, not only will people feel better about themselves and more competent; it is even possible that they will also feel more engaged and better able to join the rest of the world community in working for the broader good. Perhaps if we can mobilize the full range of human intelligences and ally them to an ethical sense, we can help increase the likelihood of our survival on this planet, and perhaps even contribute to our thriving.

John White

Howard Gardner: The Myth of Multiple Intelligences

Introduction

. . . MI theory identifies some eight or nine types of intelligence: not only the logico-mathematical and linguistic kinds measured by IQ, but, also musical, spatial, bodily-kinaesthetic, intrapersonal, interpersonal, to which have now been added naturalist and possibly existential intelligences. My question will be: is there good evidence that these intelligences exist? Or are they a myth?

MI theory is all the rage in school reform across the world. I heard recently from James McAleese of Richard Hale School in Hertford that the Canadian province of Quebec has introduced the idea into all its secondary schools. In Britain many schools are using MI as a basis for a more flexible type of teaching and learning, which acknowledges that children have different preferred "learning styles." Not everyone learns best through traditional methods which draw heavily on linguistic and logical skills. So room is made for children who can bring to bear on their learning their ability in music, say, or their kinaesthetic abilities. In history, for example, pupils' work on the Treaty of Versailles might include a conventional essay for the linguistic children and a rap presentation of the treaty for the musical ones. In many schools children are given questionnaires to profile their intelligences. Some schools give their pupils smart cards—the size of credit cards—inscribed with their preferred intelligences.

And MI does appear to deliver the goods in terms of inclusion and raising self-esteem. Pupils who used to think themselves dim can blossom when they find out how bright they are making music or interacting with people. Kinaesthetic learners can now see themselves as "body smart." The idea that intelligence is not necessarily tied to IQ has been a liberating force.

The educational world, including government agencies as well as schools, has gone for MI in a big way. But for the most part it seems to have taken over the ideas without questioning their credentials. MI theory comes to schools "shrink-wrapped", as one teacher put it to me. This is understandable, since schools do not have the time to investigate all the ideas that come their way that look as if they have some mileage in the classroom.

The idea that children come hard-wired with a whole array of abilities in varying strengths is appealing. But is there any reason to think it true?

Everything turns on the claim that the eight or nine intelligences actually exist. The bare idea that intelligence can take many forms and is not tied

From a Lecture at the Institute of Education, University of London, November 17, 2004. Copyright © 2004 by Institute of Education. Reprinted by permission.

to the abstract reasoning tested by IQ is both welcome and true. But it's hardly news. Many philosophers and psychologists have agreed with common sense that intelligence has a lot to do with being flexible in pursuit of one's goals. You want to buy a washing machine and check things out rather than rush into it. You vary your tactics against your opponent when you are playing tennis. Your child is being bullied at school and you work out what's best to do. There are innumerable forms in which intelligence can be displayed. We don't need a new theory to tell us this. Long ago the philosopher Gilbert Ryle reminded us that 'the boxer, the surgeon, the poet and the salesman' engage in their own kinds of intelligent operation, applying 'their special criteria to the performance of their special tasks." All this is now widely accepted.

This means that there are as many types of human intelligence as there are types of human goals. Gardner has corralled this huge variety into a small number of categories. Is this justified? Is it true that there are just eight or nine intelligences? Or is MI theory a myth? . . .

I'm aware that, if Gardner is right, I'll probably be connecting more with those of you whose preferred learning style is linguistic or logical. But kinaesthetics among you please feel free to walk about the room or express things in mime. Interpersonals are most welcome to discuss the argument with their neighbour as we go along. I thought I'd cracked it for those stronger on the spatial, since I've got some overheads. But then I realized they are mainly filled with words—so I guess the linguistically intelligent will be the winners in this.

How Do You Know When You've Got an Intelligence?

How does Gardner pick out his intelligences? How does he identify them? In Chapter 4 he writes

> First of all, what are the prerequisites for an intelligence: that is, what are the general desiderata to which a set of intellectual skills ought to conform before that set is worth consideration in the master list of intellectual competences? Second, what are the actual criteria by which we can judge whether a candidate competence, which has passed the "first cut," ought to be invited to join our charmed circle of intelligences?

Identifying an intelligence is thus a two-stage process. First, it has to satisfy the prerequisites; and secondly it has to satisfy the criteria.

Prerequisites

The first stage is the more important. If a candidate fails here, it stands no chance. So what Gardner says about prerequisites is crucial. He tells us that

> A human intellectual competence must entail a set of skills of problem-solving . . . and must also entail the potential for finding or creating problems. . . . These prerequisites represent my effort to focus on those intellectual strengths that prove of some importance within a cultural context.

He goes on to say that

> a prerequisite for a theory of multiple intelligences, as a whole, is that it captures a reasonably complete gamut of the kinds of abilities valued by human cultures.

Failing Candidates

Which candidates fail and which pass the test? Among failures, Gardner includes the "ability to recognize faces" because it "does not seem highly valued by cultures."

Is this true? If most of us could not recognize the faces of our relatives, friends, colleagues, or political leaders, it is hard to see how social life would be possible.

Passing Candidates

In Gardner 1983 the passing candidates must include the seven intelligences. They must have all been picked out for their problem-solving and problem-creating skills important in human cultures.

Are we talking about all human cultures, most, or only some of them? Gardner is not clear on this.

Neither is there any evidence that he has surveyed a great number of human societies in order to reach this conclusion.

There is a mystery about this "first cut." How is it that recognizing faces fails, but musical ability passes? Gardner does not give us any clear indication.

What he has in mind, I think, is that the ability to recognize faces is not an *intellectual area* that is culturally valued. It's not like mathematics or music or the visual arts. If this is so—and I give further evidence below that it is—then for something to count as an intelligence it has to be a subdivision of the realm of the intellect. It has to be something like a form of knowledge or understanding in the sense used by Paul Hirst in his well-known theory of "forms of knowledge."

If this is right, then the first thing you have to do to pick out an intelligence—as a prerequisite—has nothing to do with empirical investigations of individuals and seeing how their minds or their brains work. It has all to do with reflecting on the social world—specifically that part of the social world concerned with intellectual activities and achievements. To be an intelligence is—so far—the same as being a separable realm of understanding.

I will come back to the "prerequisites" later. As we shall see, they are of pivotal importance.

Criteria

Once a candidate intelligence has satisfied the prerequisites, it has to meet various criteria. These comprise:

- potential isolation of the area by brain damage
- the existence in it of idiots savants, prodigies and other exceptional individuals

- an identifiable core operation/set of operations
- a distinctive developmental history, along with a definable set of expert "end-state" performances
- an evolutionary history and evolutionary plausibility
- support from experimental psychological tasks
- support from psychometric findings
- susceptibility to encoding in a symbol system.

I examined these problems in a little book I wrote on Gardner's theory in 1998 called *Do Howard Gardner's Multiple Intelligences Add Up?* Here I will simply summarise some main arguments. I begin with specific items. For convenience, I begin with two of them taken together.

"An identifiable core operation/set of operations"

"A distinctive developmental history, along with a definable set of expert 'end-state' performances"

The interconnectedness of these two can be illustrated by linguistic intelligence. This has as its "core operations" a sensitivity to the meaning of words, to the order among words, to the sounds and rhythms of words, and to the different functions of language. These core operations are seen at work "with special clarity" in the work of the poet. Linguistic intelligence also possesses a distinctive developmental history, culminating in expert "end-state" performances like those of the poet. Other intelligences illustrate the same point.

Gardner's theory of intelligence is developmentalist. Developmentalism is the theory that the biological unfolding between two poles from seed through to mature specimen that we find in the physical world is also found in the mental world. In his criteria, Gardner acknowledges the two poles in the mental case. At one end, there are allegedly genetically given capacities. At the other end is the mature state, the "definable set of expert 'end-state' performances". Gardner is interested in the really high fliers in each area—people like famous poets (linguistic); famous mathematicians (logic-mathematical); famous musicians (musical); famous visual artists; famous dancers, mime-artists (bodily/kinaesthetic); famous politicians (interpersonal); writers like Proust (intrapersonal).

Problems in Developmentalism
Gardner's theory faces an objection besetting all forms of developmentalism. This theory is based on the assumption that the unfolding familiar in the biological realm is also found in the mental. There are two problems about this, one for each of the two poles.

i) First the seed, or initial state. Biological seeds, plant or animal, *have within them the power to unfold* into more complex stages, given appropriate environmental conditions. To locate a parallel initial state in the mental case it is not enough to pick out innately given capacities. There is no doubt that such capacities exist. We are all born with the power to see and hear things, to desire food etc. But these do not have within them the power to *unfold* into more complex forms. They do *change* into more sophisticated versions: the desire for food, for instance, becomes differentiated into desires for hamburgers and ice-cream. But it does not unfold into these. The changes are cultural products: people are socialized into them.

ii) Secondly, the mature state—Gardner's "end-state." We understand this notion well enough in physical contexts. A fully-grown human body or delphinium is one which can grow no further. It can certainly go on *changing*, but the changes are to do with maintenance and deterioration, not further growth. If we apply these ideas to the mind, do we want to say that all human beings have mental ceilings—e.g. in each of Gardner's intelligences—beyond which they cannot progress? Psychologists like Cyril Burt have believed this, but the notion is deeply questionable. I can argue this through further if you wish.

There is also a problem about *what counts* as maturity—the end-state—in the case of the intelligences. With the human body, we know through the use of our senses when maturity has occurred: we can *see* that a person is fully grown. What equivalent is there in the mental realm?

We do not just use our senses. We cannot see a person's intellectual maturity as we can see that he or she is physically fully grown. Significantly, ideas about maturity are likely to be controversial. Some people would understand intellectual maturity in quiz show terms, as being able to marshal and remember heaps of facts; others would emphasize depth of understanding, etc. The judgments lack the consensus found in judgments about fully grown pine trees. This is because we are in the realm of value judgments rather than of observable facts.

Gardner's examples of high levels of development in the intelligences reflect his own value judgments. He has in mind the achievements of selected poets, composers, religious leaders, politicians, scientists, novelists and so on. It is Gardner's value judgments, not his empirical discoveries as a scientist, that are his starting point.

I have tried to show that whether we look towards the beginning or towards the end of the development process, we find apparently insuperable problems in identifying mental counterparts to physical growth. Since developmentalist assumptions are central to Gardner's MI theory, the latter is seriously undermined.

"Susceptibility to encoding in a symbol system"

Gardner writes:

following my mentor Nelson Goodman and other authorities, I conceive of a symbol as any entity (material or abstract) that can denote or refer to any other entity. On this definition, words, pictures, diagrams, numbers, and a host of other entities are readily considered symbols.

It is important to see how wide the range of Gardner's symbols is. They include not only obvious ones like words and mathematical symbols, but also paintings, symphonies, plays, dances and poems. It is because works of art are symbols in his view that he can connect many of his intelligences with their own kind of symbolic entities. For instance, it is not only words which are the symbols associated with linguistic intelligence: this also contains such symbols as poems. Symbols in music include musical works; in spatial intelligence paintings and sculptures, in b/k intelligence dances; in intrapersonal intelligence introspective novels like Proust's. But the notion that a work of art is itself a symbol is problematic in aesthetics. The main difficulty is: what is it symbolizing? Take a work of abstract art. Or a poem by Sylvia Plath. What are these symbols of?

The whole theory of symbolization in art from Suzanne Langer to Nelson Goodman is deeply problematic.

We can discuss this further later if you'd like. For the moment my claim is that this criterion **"susceptibility to encoding in a symbol system"** rests on a highly dubious aesthetic theory. It is a long way from empirical science.

Without going through all the other criteria, a word about two of them.

"The potential isolation of the area by brain damage"

I think we can take it that there are localized areas of function within the brain. If one part of the brain is damaged, one's sight is impaired, if another, one's ability to move one's left hand. All this shows is that certain physiological necessary conditions of exercising these capacities are absent. It does not help to indicate the existence of separate "intelligences."

Given his developmentalism, one can understand why Gardner should look to brain localization in order to identify intelligences, for he has to provide an account of the "seed" which is to unfold into its mature form, and this seed has to be part of our original constitution. But the kinds of function picked out by brain localization research do not have the power to *unfold* into maturer versions of themselves.

"The existence, in an area, of idiots savants, prodigies and other exceptional individuals"

Gardner invokes the existence of *idiots savants* to support his theory, but what I know of them does not lead me to think of them as intelligent. What they all have in common is a *mechanical* facility, one which lacks the flexibility of adapting means to ends found in intelligent behaviour.

Prodigies only support Gardner's case if there is good evidence that their talents are innate. But what evidence there is seems to point to acquired abilities.

Conclusion

It would be natural to think that the "criteria" are all straightforwardly applicable. But this is not so. The criteria to do with development and with symbols presuppose the truth of *theories*—one in psychology, the other in aesthetics—which turn out to be untenable. And this undermines the viability of MI theory as a whole. . . .

My main concern is not with MI theory for its own sake but with its present influence in the educational world. If I am right, the eight or nine intelligences have not been shown to exist. If so, what are the implications for the school reforms based on the theory? As things are now, children are being encouraged to see themselves, in PSHE (Personal, Social and Health Education) lessons and elsewhere, as having innately given strengths in certain areas. This is part of their self-understanding. But if the theory is wrong, they may be getting a false picture of themselves. . . .

CHALLENGE QUESTIONS

Is the Theory of Multiple Intelligences Valid?

1. Why might the educational world be drawn toward a theory of multiple intelligences? Support your answer with examples from your own educational experience.
2. What possible dangers could arise from schools applying multiple intelligence theory, especially as described by White?
3. White argues that Gardner's list of intelligences is too restrictive. Can you think of any intelligences that do not appear in Gardner's list? Justify your claim.
4. What is the difference between talent and intelligence? Should intelligence be considered primarily a measure of cognitive and academic abilities? Support your answers.
5. Gardner argues that some intelligences are not covered by IQ tests. How might a psychologist evaluate these intelligences? For example, what kind of test or evaluation would you use to determine an individual's musical intelligence?

Internet References . . .

Mental Health Infosource: Disorders

This no-nonsense page lists links to pages dealing with psychological disorders, including anxiety, panic, phobic disorders, schizophrenia, and violent/self-destructive behaviors.

http://www.mhsource.com/disorders

Wikipedia: The Free Encyclopedia

An online encyclopedia, this site includes information on a variety of topics. This particular link contains information on ADHD and provides a forum for discussion.

http://en.wikipedia.org/wiki/
Attention_deficit_hyperactivity_disorder

Self-Esteem

The self-esteem movement has a substantial following on the Internet, and the National Association of Self-Esteem, one of the leading organizations in the self-esteem movement, hosts this webpage.

http://www.self-esteem-nase.org

Mental Health

A mental disorder is often defined as a pattern of thinking or behavior that is either disruptive to others or harmful to the person with the disorder. This definition seems straightforward, yet there is considerable debate about whether or not some disorders truly exist. For example, does a child's acute disruptive behavior and short attention span unquestionably warrant that he or she be diagnosed with Attention Deficit Hyperactive Disorder (ADHD)? Also, many psychological disorders, including ADHD, are treated with medications, most of which have side effects. Could some of these side effects make certain medications unsafe? Some psychologists claim that antidepressants make patients suicidal, but other psychologists have found it difficult for patients to control their symptoms without the help of antidepressants. What about mental health when a person is not "disordered?" An almost commonsensical notion is that really good mental health requires high self-esteem. Unfortunately, high self-esteem is not always correlated with positive outcomes, and low self-esteem is not always correlated with negative outcomes. What then is the role of self-esteem in mental health?

- Does ADHD Exist?
- Does Taking Antidepressants Lead to Suicide?
- Does Low Self-Esteem Lead to Antisocial Behavior?

ISSUE 12

Does ADHD Exist?

YES: **Russell A. Barkley,** from "International Consensus Statement on ADHD," *Clinical Child and Family Psychology Review* (June 2002)

NO: **Sami Timimi et al.,** from "A Critique of the International Consensus Statement on ADHD," *Clinical Child and Family Psychology Review* (March 2004)

ISSUE SUMMARY

YES: Psychiatry Professor Russell A. Barkley claims that evidence provided by heritability and neuro-imaging studies points unarguably toward ADHD's validity and existence.

NO: Psychiatrist Sami Timimi claims the current ADHD epidemic is the result of unrealistic expectations for today's children and the pharmaceutical companies' desire to sell more drugs.

Over the past several years, the acronym "ADHD" (attention deficit hyperactivity disorder) has almost become a household term. Just about everybody knows someone, usually a child, who has been diagnosed with ADHD. Still, the current popularity and prevalence of ADHD has brought with it a heated controversy over whether the disorder even exists. Because ADHD involves childlike behavior, some people have wondered if this diagnosis is a sign that childishness is no longer tolerated in our culture, even in children. Is ADHD a mental disease or are psychologists and scientists unwittingly trying to purge the childishness out of children?

If ADHD can be shown to have a biological basis, then it would follow that it is more than merely an intolerance of childlike behavior. Many psychologists attribute mental illness today to an irregularity in the physiological make-up of the brain, making the cause of psychological disorders just as biological as heart disease or cancer. This focus on "nature" or biology, rather than "nurture" or environment, has persuaded many psychologists to favor biological explanations for the inattentiveness and hyperactivity of ADHD children. However, these explanations normally mean that the mechanisms of ADHD are outside the control of the children or their parents. The emphasis in treatment then shifts from educating the children to medicating them.

In the *International Consensus Statement on ADHD*, a group of psychologists led by Russell A. Barkley asserts that ADHD does exist in this biological manner. In support of their claim, these psychologists cite studies of genetic heritability, particularly those involving twins, which they believe establishes the heritability of ADHD. They also point toward neuro-imaging studies that show a common structural and chemical irregularity in the brains of many children diagnosed with ADHD. By providing this type of empirical or scientific evidence, these psychologists hope to solidify ADHD's relation to other known biological disorders and thus prove the reality of its existence.

Other psychologists, however, question the biological reality of ADHD. In their critique of the International Consensus Statement on ADHD, Sami Timimi, along with another group of psychologists, claim current scientific evidence does not support ADHD as a neurobiological disorder. They accuse Barkley and his colleagues of trying to close an issue that has yet to be resolved. Timimi and his colleagues attribute the increasing number of ADHD diagnoses in the Western world to a new cultural demand for children to behave more like adults. They also accuse pharmaceutical companies of being too eager to help parents cover up poor childrearing by medicating their kids. In an effort to debunk some of the most popular evidence for the existence of ADHD, Timimi et al. claim that the psychotropic medications used to treat children diagnosed with ADHD have the same effect on "normal" children and might actually cause the apparent brain irregularities depicted in neuro-imaging.

POINT	COUNTERPOINT
• The vast majority of competent scholars agree that ADHD is a valid disorder.	• There is no stable definition for ADHD and, therefore, it is impossible to diagnose correctly.
• Neuro-imaging studies show brain irregularities are common among ADHD children.	• Neuro-imaging studies have not adequately shown that ADHD is a biochemical brain disorder.
• ADHD meets the scientific criteria for a valid psychological disorder.	• The prevalence of ADHD results from unrealistic expectations and pushing medications.
• Twin studies show that ADHD is extremely heritable.	• The idea that ADHD is strongly heritable is open to interpretation.
• Not enough ADHD sufferers are receiving the available medications for treatment.	• ADHD medications have similar effects on non-ADHD children and have dangerous, long-term side effects.

YES

Russell A. Barkley

International Consensus Statement on ADHD January 2002

We, the undersigned consortium of international scientists, are deeply concerned about the periodic inaccurate portrayal of attention deficit hyperactivity disorder (ADHD) in media reports. This is a disorder with which we are all very familiar and toward which many of us have dedicated scientific studies if not entire careers. We fear that inaccurate stories rendering ADHD as myth, fraud, or benign condition may cause thousands of sufferers not to seek treatment for their disorder. It also leaves the public with a general sense that this disorder is not valid or real or consists of a rather trivial affliction.

We have created this consensus statement on ADHD as a reference on the status of the scientific findings concerning this disorder, its validity, and its adverse impact on the lives of those diagnosed with the disorder as of this writing (January 2002).

Occasional coverage of the disorder casts the story in the form of a sporting event with evenly matched competitors. The views of a handful of nonexpert doctors that ADHD does not exist are contrasted against mainstream scientific views that it does, as if both views had equal merit. Such attempts at balance give the public the impression that there is substantial scientific disagreement over whether ADHD is a real medical condition. In fact, there is no such disagreement—at least no more so than there is over whether smoking causes cancer, for example, or whether a virus causes HIV/AIDS.

The U.S. Surgeon General, the American Medical Association, the American Psychiatric Association, the American Academy of Child and Adolescent Psychiatry, the American Psychological Association, and the American Academy of Pediatrics, among others, all recognize ADHD as a valid disorder. Although some of these organizations have issued guidelines for evaluation and management of the disorder for their membership, this is the first consensus statement issued by an independent consortium of leading scientists concerning the status of the disorder. Among scientists who have devoted years, if not entire careers, to the study of this disorder there is no controversy regarding its existence.

From *Clinical Child and Family Psychology Review*, vol. 5, no. 2, June 2002, pp. 89–90. Copyright © 2002 by Springer Journals (Kluwer Academic) via Copyright Clearance Center. Reprinted by permission. References omitted.

ADHD and Science

We cannot overemphasize the point that, as a matter of science, the notion that ADHD does not exist is simply wrong. All of the major medical associations and government health agencies recognize ADHD as a genuine disorder because the scientific evidence indicating it is so overwhelming.

Various approaches have been used to establish whether a condition rises to the level of a valid medical or psychiatric disorder. A very useful one stipulates that there must be scientifically established evidence that those suffering the condition have a serious deficiency in or failure of a physical or psychological mechanism that is universal to humans. That is, all humans normally would be expected, regardless of culture, to have developed that mental ability.

And there must be equally incontrovertible scientific evidence that this serious deficiency leads to harm to the individual. Harm is established through evidence of increased mortality, morbidity, or impairment in the major life activities required of one's developmental stage in life. Major life activities are those domains of functioning such as education, social relationships, family functioning, independence and self-sufficiency, and occupational functioning that all humans of that developmental level are expected to perform.

As attested to by the numerous scientists signing this document, there is no question among the world's leading clinical researchers that ADHD involves a serious deficiency in a set of psychological abilities and that these deficiencies pose serious harm to most individuals possessing the disorder. Current evidence indicates that deficits in behavioral inhibition and sustained attention are central to this disorder—facts demonstrated through hundreds of scientific studies. And there is no doubt that ADHD leads to impairments in major life activities, including social relations, education, family functioning, occupational functioning, self-sufficiency, and adherence to social rules, norms, and laws. Evidence also indicates that those with ADHD are more prone to physical injury and accidental poisonings. This is why no professional medical, psychological, or scientific organization doubts the existence of ADHD as a legitimate disorder.

The central psychological deficits in those with ADHD have now been linked through numerous studies using various scientific methods to several specific brain regions (the frontal lobe, its connections to the basal ganglia, and their relationship to the central aspects of the cerebellum). Most neurological studies find that as a group those with ADHD have less brain electrical activity and show less reactivity to stimulation in one or more of these regions. And neuro-imaging studies of groups of those with ADHD also demonstrate relatively smaller areas of brain matter and less metabolic activity of this brain matter than is the case in control groups used in these studies.

These same psychological deficits in inhibition and attention have been found in numerous studies of identical and fraternal twins conducted across various countries (US, Great Britain, Norway, Australia, etc.) to be primarily inherited. The genetic contribution to these traits is routinely found to be among the highest for any psychiatric disorder (70–95% of trait variation in the population), nearly approaching the genetic contribution to human height. One gene has recently been reliably demonstrated to be associated with this disorder and the search for more is underway by more than 12 different scientific teams worldwide at this time.

Numerous studies of twins demonstrate that family environment makes no significant separate contribution to these traits. This is not to say that the home environment, parental management abilities, stressful life events, or deviant peer relationships are unimportant or have no influence on individuals having this disorder, as they certainly do. Genetic tendencies are expressed in interaction with the environment. Also, those having ADHD often have other associated disorders and problems, some of which are clearly related to their social environments. But it is to say that the underlying psychological deficits that comprise ADHD itself are not solely or primarily the result of these environmental factors.

This is why leading international scientists, such as the signers below, recognize the mounting evidence of neurological and genetic contributions to this disorder. This evidence, coupled with countless studies on the harm posed by the disorder and hundreds of studies on the effectiveness of medication, buttresses the need in many, though by no means all, cases for management of the disorder with multiple therapies. These include medication combined with educational, family, and other social accommodations. This is in striking contrast to the wholly unscientific views of some social critics in periodic media accounts that ADHD constitutes a fraud, that medicating those afflicted is questionable if not reprehensible, and that any behavior problems associated with ADHD are merely the result of problems in the home, excessive viewing of TV or playing of video games, diet, lack of love and attention, or teacher/school intolerance.

ADHD is not a benign disorder. For those it afflicts, ADHD can cause devastating problems. Follow-up studies of clinical samples suggest that sufferers are far more likely than normal people to drop out of school (32–40%), to rarely complete college (5–10%), to have few or no friends (50–70%), to underperform at work (70–80%), to engage in antisocial activities (40–50%), and to use tobacco or illicit drugs more than normal. Moreover, children growing up with ADHD are more likely to experience teen pregnancy (40%) and sexually transmitted diseases (16%), to speed excessively and have multiple car accidents, to experience depression (20–30%) and personality disorders (18–25%) as adults, and in hundreds of other ways mismanage and endanger their lives.

Yet despite these serious consequences, studies indicate that less than half of those with the disorder are receiving treatment. The media can help substantially to improve these circumstances. It can do so by portraying ADHD and the science about it as accurately and responsibly as possible while not purveying the propaganda of some social critics and fringe doctors whose political agenda would have you and the public believe there is no real disorder here. To publish stories that ADHD is a fictitious disorder or merely a conflict between today's Huckleberry Finns and their caregivers is tantamount to declaring the earth flat, the laws of gravity debatable, and the periodic table in chemistry a fraud. ADHD should be depicted in the media as realistically and accurately as it is depicted in science—as a valid disorder having varied and substantial adverse impact on those who may suffer from it through no fault of their own or their parents and teachers . . .

Sami Timimi et al.

A Critique of the International Consensus Statement on ADHD

Why did a group of eminent psychiatrists and psychologists produce a consensus statement that seeks to forestall debate on the merits of the widespread diagnosis and drug treatment of attention deficit hyperactivity disorder (ADHD)? If the evidence is already that good then no statement is needed. However, the reality is that claims about ADHD being a genuine medical disorder and psychotropics being genuine correctives have been shaken by criticism.

Not only is it completely counter to the spirit and practice of science to cease questioning the validity of ADHD as proposed by the consensus statement, there is an ethical and moral responsibility to do so. History teaches us again and again that one generation's most cherished therapeutic ideas and practices, especially when applied on the powerless, are repudiated by the next, but not without leaving countless victims in their wake. Lack of acknowledgement of the subjective nature of our psychiatric practice leaves it wide open to abuse. For these reasons we, another group of academics and practitioners, feel compelled to respond to this statement.

Merits of the ADHD Diagnosis

The evidence does not support the conclusion that ADHD identifies a group of children who suffer from a common and specific neurobiological disorder. There are no cognitive, metabolic, or neurological markers for ADHD and so there is no such thing as a medical test for this diagnosis. There is obvious uncertainty about how to define this disorder, with definitions changing over the past 30 years depending on what the current favourite theory about underlying aetiology is, and with each revision producing a higher number of potential children deemed to have the disorder. It is hardly surprising that epidemiological studies produce hugely differing prevalence rates from 0.5% to 26% of all children.

Despite attempts at standardising criteria, cross-cultural studies on the rating of symptoms of ADHD show major and significant differences between raters from different countries, rating of children from different cultures, and even within cultures (for example, rates of diagnosis of ADHD have been shown to vary by a factor of 10 from county to county within the same state in the United States.

From *Clinical Child and Family Psychology Review*, vol. 7, no. 1, March 2004, pp. 59–63. Copyright © 2004 by Springer Journals (Kluwer Academic) via Copyright Clearance Center. Reprinted by permission. References omitted.

There are high rates of comorbidity between ADHD and conduct, anxiety, depression, and other disorders, with about three quarters of children diagnosed with ADHD also fulfilling criteria for another psychiatric disorder. Such high rates of comorbidity suggest that the concept of ADHD is inadequate to explain clinical reality.

Neuroimaging research is often cited as "proof" of a biological deficit in those with ADHD, however, after almost 25 years and over 30 studies, researchers have yet to do a simple comparison of unmedicated children diagnosed with ADHD with an age matched control group. The studies have shown nonspecific and inconsistent changes in some children in some studies. However, sample sizes have been small and in none of the studies were the brains considered clinically abnormal; nor has any specific abnormality been convincingly demonstrated. Most worryingly, animal studies suggest that any differences observed in these studies could well be due to the effects of medication that most children in these studies had taken. Even a U.S. federal government report on ADHD concluded that there was no compelling evidence to support the claim that ADHD was a biochemical brain disorder. Research on possible environmental causes of ADHD type behaviors has largely been ignored, despite mounting evidence that psychosocial factors such as exposure to trauma and abuse can cause them.

With regards the claim that ADHD is a genetic condition that is strongly heritable, the evidence is open to interpretation. ADHD shares common genetics with conduct disorder and other externalising behaviors, and so if there is a heritable component it is not specific to ADHD.

Efficacy of Drug Treatment

The relentless growth in the practice of diagnosis of childhood and adolescent psychiatric disorders has also led to a relentless increase in the amount of psychotropic medication being prescribed to children and adolescents. The amount of psychotropic medication prescribed to children in the United States increased nearly threefold between 1987 and 1996, with over 6% of boys between the ages of 6 and 14 taking psychostimulants in 1996, a figure that is likely to be much higher now. There has also been a large increase in prescriptions of psychostimulants to preschoolers (aged 2–4 years). One study in Virginia found that in two school districts, 17% of White boys at primary school were taking psychostimulants. Yet in the international consensus statement the authors still believe that less than half of those with ADHD are receiving treatment. Many of the authors of the consensus statement are well-known advocates of drug treatment for children with AHDH and it is notable that in the statement they do not declare their financial interests and/or their links with pharmaceutical companies.

Despite claims for the miraculous effects of stimulants they are not a specific treatment for ADHD, because they are well known to have similar effects on otherwise normal children and other children regardless of diagnosis. A recent meta-analysis of randomised controlled trials of methylphenidate found that the trials were of poor quality, there was strong evidence of publication bias, short-term effects were inconsistent across different rating scales, side effects were frequent and problematic and long-term effects beyond 4 weeks of treatment were not demonstrated.

The authors of the consensus statement claim that untreated ADHD leads to significant impairment and harm for the afflicted individual; not only do the authors conflate a statistical association with cause but other evidence suggests that drug treatment has at best an inconsequential effect on long-term outcome.

The potential long-term adverse effects of giving psychotropic drugs to children need to cause us more concern than the authors of the consensus statement will allow. Stimulants are potentially addictive drugs with cardio-vascular, nervous, digestive, endocrine, and psychiatric side effects. At a psychological level the use of drug treatment scripts a potentially life-long story of disability and deficit that physically healthy children may end up believing. Children may view drug treatment as a punishment for naughty behaviour and may be absorbing the message that they are not able to control or learn to control their own behavior. Drug treatment may also distance all concerned from finding more effective, long-lasting strategies. The children and their carers may be unnecessarily cultured into the attitude of a "pill for life's problems."

A Cultural Perspective on ADHD

Why has ADHD become so popular now resulting in spiralling rates of diagnosis of ADHD and prescription of psychostimulants in the Western world? This question requires us to examine the cultural nature of how we construct what we deem to be normal and abnormal childhoods and child rearing methods. Although the immaturity of children is a biological fact, the ways in which this immaturity is understood and made meaningful is a fact of culture. Differences between cultures and within cultures over time mean that what are considered as desirable practices in one culture are often seen as abusive in another.

In contemporary, Western society children are viewed as individuals who have rights and need to express their opinions as well as being potentially vulnerable and needing protection by the state when parents are deemed not to be adequate. At the same time there has been a growing debate and belief that childhood in modern, Western society has suffered a strange death. Many contemporary observers are concerned about the increase in violence, drug and alcohol abuse, depression, and suicide amongst a generation perceived to have been given the best of everything. Some commentators believe we are witnessing the end of the innocence of childhood, for example, through the greater sexualization and commercialization of childhood interests. It is claimed that childhood is disappearing, through media, such as television, as children have near complete access to the world of adult information leading to a collapse of the moral authority of adults. Coupled with this fear that the boundary between childhood and adulthood is disappearing is a growing sense that children themselves are a risk with some children coming to be viewed as too dangerous for society and needing to be controlled, reshaped and changed.

Thus, in the last few decades of the twentieth century in Western culture, the task of child rearing has become loaded with anxiety. On the one hand, parents and teachers feeling the pressure from the breakdown of adult authority discourse, feel they must act to control unruly children; on the other hand they feel inhibited from doing so for fear of the consequences now that people are aware that families can be ruined and careers destroyed should the state decide to intervene. This cultural anxiety has provided the ideal social context for growth of popularity of the concept of ADHD. The concept of ADHD has helped shift focus away from these social dilemmas and onto the individual child. It has been in the best interests of the pharmaceutical industry to facilitate this change in focus. Drug company strategy for expanding markets for drug treatment of children is not confined to direct drug promotion but includes illness promotion (e.g., funding for parent support groups such as CHADD) and influencing research activities. Thus, the current "epidemic" of ADHD in the West can be understood as a symptom of a profound change in our cultural expectations of children coupled with an unwitting alliance between drug companies and some doctors, that serves to culturally legitimize the practice of dispensing performance enhancing substances in a crude attempt to quell our current anxieties about children's (particularly boys) development.

In their consensus statement, the authors are at pains to point out that it is not the child's, the parent's or the teacher's fault. However, trying to understand the origins and meaning of behaviors labelled, as ADHD does not need to imply blame. What it does require is an attempt to positively engage with the interpersonal realities of human life. This can be done through individualized family counseling and educational approaches, as well as using multiple perspectives to empower children, parents, teachers, and others.

Conclusion

The authors of the consensus statement sell themselves short in stating that questioning the current practice concerning diagnosis and treatment of ADHD is like declaring the earth is flat. It is regrettable that they wish to close down debate prematurely and in a way not becoming of academics. The evidence shows that the debate is far from over.

CHALLENGE QUESTIONS

Does ADHD Exist?

1. What other psychological disorders are commonly treated with medication? Could the existence of these disorders be attributed to the same causes that Timimi and his colleagues attribute to the existence of ADHD? Defend your position.
2. The authors of each selection cannot seem to agree on how to interpret the findings of neuro-imaging studies of ADHD. Look at the available studies yourself and draw your own conclusion.
3. Both selections discuss treating ADHD with medication but only briefly mention other treatments. Research medication treatments for ADHD on your own. Which treatments would you consider to be the most effective? Defend your answer.
4. Find out what the side effects are for current ADHD medications. If you had a particularly hyperactive child who had trouble paying attention, would you medicate him with these drugs? List the pros and cons.
5. If you were a teacher or parent with responsibility for an especially unruly child, how might you help that child change his or her behavior without using medication to alter his or her temperament?

ISSUE 13

Does Taking Antidepressants Lead to Suicide?

YES: David Healy and Chris Whitaker, from "Antidepressants and Suicide: Risk-Benefit Conundrums," *Journal of Psychiatry & Neuroscience* (September 2003)

NO: Yvon D. Lapierre, from "Suicidality with Selective Serotonin Reuptake Inhibitors: Valid Claim?" *Journal of Psychiatry & Neuroscience* (September 2003)

ISSUE SUMMARY

YES: Psychiatrist David Healy and statistician Chris Whitaker argue that psychological research reveals a significant number of suicidal acts by individuals taking antidepressants and, thus, they recommend stricter controls on these drugs.

NO: In response, psychiatrist Yvon D. Lapierre maintains that the research on suicidality and antidepressants is unconvincing, recommending that conclusions from these findings should be severely limited.

Drugs for depression have become so familiar and are used so frequently in our society that their safety has been almost taken for granted. It was surprising, then, when recent research findings seemed to indicate that suicide is a possible effect of a certain class of antidepressants—specifically, selective serotonin reuptake inhibitors, or SSRIs. Almost immediately, the defenders of these drugs offered another explanation: These findings are the result of an increase in the number people with depression and not an effect of anti-depressants. In other words, because suicide is a risk for people with depression, an increase in the number of depressed people accounts for the increase in the number of suicides.

The problem is that the Food and Drug Administration (FDA) does not seem to agree with this explanation. Recently, it ordered manufacturers of all antidepressants, not just SSRIs, to include a "black box" warning on their labels—the most serious caution the government can require. This warning alerts people to the increased risk of suicide among children and adolescents taking antidepressant medication. This move by the FDA means the U.S. government believes that current evidence is sufficient to take serious action. Some health professionals fear that people might misinterpret this serious action and resist seeking treatment for depression altogether.

The first article supports the FDA decision. Looking at figures from randomized controlled trials (RCTs)—the gold-standard of research designs—David Healy and Chris Whitaker found too many suicidal acts among people on antidepressants, especially when compared with people using placebos (drugs that have no treatment effect). While the authors agree these studies show that SSRIs do reduce suicidality in some patients, they argue that there is a net increase in suicidal acts associated with their use. In other words, more people are ultimately harmed than helped. Still, Healy and Whitaker do not recommend that people stop taking antidepressants. They do, however, believe that warnings and monitoring of antidepressants are necessary to reduce the overall risk of suicide.

In response, Yvon D. Lapierre disagrees with Healy and Whitaker's contention that antidepressants increase the risk of suicide. He notes the number of methodological problems and biases with the studies Healy and Whitaker used to support their conclusions. He also points to other studies that just as strongly indicate that suicidal thoughts are lessened by the same drugs. He admits that the research as a whole has yielded mixed findings. Still, this is all the more reason to avoid hastily concluding that antidepressants lead to suicide. The conclusions of Healy and Whitaker, therefore, are premature.

POINT

- Studies show an increase in suicidal acts when people take antidepressants.

- Studies that claim a reduction of suicidality in some patients ignore how the same treatment can produce suicidality in others.

- Clinicians should be more vigilant and restrict treatment for those most at risk for suicide.

- Consumers and clinicians should be warned about the dangers of antidepressants.

COUNTERPOINT

- The inherent biases of these studies decrease the ability to draw valid conclusions.

- Studies strongly suggest that antidepressants decrease suicidal thoughts in some patients.

- Suicide is already recognized among clinicians as a major risk of depression.

- Because results of clinical studies are inconclusive, more research should be conducted before serious action is taken.

YES

**David Healy and
Chris Whitaker**

Antidepressants and Suicide: Risk–Benefit Conundrums

Introduction

. . . The debate regarding selective serotonin reuptake inhibitors (SSRIs) and suicide started in 1990, when Teicher, Glod and Cole described 6 cases in which intense suicidal preoccupation emerged during fluoxetine treatment. This paper was followed by others, which, combined, provided evidence of dose–response, challenge, dechallenge and rechallenge relations, as well as the emergence of an agreed mechanism by which the effects were mediated and demonstrations that interventions in the process could ameliorate the problems. A subsequent series of reports on the effects of sertraline and paroxetine on suicidality and akathisia pointed to SSRI-induced suicidality being a class effect rather than something confined to fluoxetine.

An induction of suicidality by SSRIs, therefore, had apparently been convincingly demonstrated according to conventional criteria for establishing cause and effect relations between drugs and adverse events, as laid out by clinical trial methodologists, company investigators, medico-legal authorities and the federal courts. Far less consistent evidence led the Medicines Control Agency in Britain in 1988 to state unambiguously that benzodiazepines can trigger suicide.

Specifically designed randomized controlled trials (RCTs) on depression-related suicidality at this time would have established the rates at which this seemingly new phenomenon might be happening. However, no such studies have ever been undertaken. This review, therefore, will in lieu cover the RCT data on newly released antidepressants and suicidal acts, the meta-analyses of efficacy studies in depression that have been brought to bear on the question and relevant epidemiological studies.

Efficacy Studies

In lieu of specifically designed RCTs, the RCTs that formed the basis for the licence application for recent antidepressants are one source of data. Khan and colleagues recently analyzed RCT data to assess whether it was ethical to continue using placebos in antidepresant trials. Although the U.S. Food and

From *Journal of Psychiatry & Neuroscience*, vol. 28, no. 5, September 2003, pp. 332–337. Copyright © 2003 by CMA Management. Reprinted by permission. References omitted.

Drug Administration (FDA), in general, recommends that data from clinical trials be analyzed both in terms of absolute numbers and patient exposure years (PEY), given that an assessment of the hazards posed by placebo was the object of this study, the investigators appropriately analyzed the figures in terms of PEY only. Khan et al. found an excess of suicidal acts by individuals taking antidepressants compared with placebo, and this was also replicated in another analysis, but the rates of suicidal acts in patients taking antidepressants and those taking placebo were not significantly different in these analyses. Yet, another study reported that rates of suicidal acts of patients taking antidepressants for longer durations may, in fact, fall relative to placebo, which might be expected because longer term studies will select patients suited to the agent being investigated.

Although an analysis in terms of PEYs may be appropriate for an assessment of the risk of exposure to placebo, it is inappropriate for the assessment of a problem that clinical studies had clearly linked to the first weeks of active therapy. An analysis of suicidal acts on the basis of duration of exposure systematically selects patients who do not have the problem under investigation, because those with the problem often drop out of the trial, whereas others who do well are kept on treatment for months or more on grounds of compassionate use.

The data presented by Khan and colleagues has accordingly been modified here in 4 respects (Table 1). First, suicides and suicidal acts are presented in terms of absolute numbers of patients. Second, on the basis of an FDA paroxetine safety review and FDA statistical reviews on sertraline, it is clear that some of the suicides and suicidal acts categorized as occurring while patients were taking placebo actually occurred during a placebo washout period; placebo and washout suicides are therefore distinguished here. Third, data for citalopram, from another article by Khan et al., are included (although no details about the validity of assignments to placebo are available). Fourth, fluoxetine data from public domain documents are presented, again dividing the data into placebo and washout period suicidal acts, along with data for venlafaxine.

When washout and placebo data are separated and analyzed in terms of suicidal acts per patient (excluding missing bupropion data) using an exact Mantel–Haenszel procedure with a 1-tailed test for significance, the odds ratio of a suicide while taking these new antidepressants as a group compared with placebo is 4.40 (95% confidence interval [CI] 1.32–infinity; $p = 0.0125$). The odds ratio for a suicidal act while taking these antidepressants compared with placebo is 2.39 (95% CI 1.66–infinity; $p \leq 0.0001$). The odds ratio for a completed suicide while taking an SSRI antidepressant (including venlafaxine) compared with placebo is 2.46 (95% CI 0.71–infinity; $p = 0.16$), and the odds ratio for a suicidal act while taking SSRIs compared with placebo is 2.22 (95% CI 1.47–infinity; $p \leq 0.001$).

If washout suicidal acts are included with placebo, as the companies appear to have done, but adjusting the denominator appropriately, the relative risk of suicidal acts while taking sertraline, paroxetine or fluoxetine compared with placebo becomes significant, with figures ranging from 3.0 for sertraline to over 10.0 for fluoxetine.

Table 1

Incidence of Suicides and Suicide Attempts in Antidepressant Trials from Khan et al. and Kirsch et al.

Treatment	No. of Patients	No. of Suicides	No. of Suicide Attempts	Suicides and Attempts, %
Sertraline hydrochloride*	2053	2	7	0.44
Active comparator	595	0	1	0.17
Placebo	786	0	2	0.25
Placebo washout		0	3	
Paroxetine hydrochloride*	2963	5	40	1.52
Active comparator	1151	3	12	1.30
Placebo	554	0	3	0.54
Placebo washout		2	2	
Nefazodone hydrochloride	3496	9	12	0.60
Active comparator	958	0	6	0.63
Placebo	875	0	1	0.11
Mirtazapine	2425	8	29	1.53
Active comparator	977	2	5	0.72
Placebo	494	0	3	0.61
Bupropion hydrochloride	1942	3	—	
Placebo	370	0	—	
Citalopram*	4168	8	91	2.38
Placebo	691	1	10	1.59
Fluoxetine*	1427	1	12	0.91
Placebo	370	0	0	0
Placebo washout		1	0	
Venlafaxine*	3082	7	36	1.40
Placebo	739	1	2	0.41
All investigational drugs	21556	43	232	1.28
All SSRIs*	13693	23	186	1.53
Active comparators	3681	5	24	0.79
Total placebo	4879	2	21	0.47
SSRI trial placebo	3140	2	16	0.57

*SSRI = selective serotonin reuptake inhibitor.

Other data sets yield similar findings. For instance, in Pierre Fabre's clinical trial database of approximately 8000 patients, the rate for suicidal acts by those taking SSRIs appears to be 3 times the rate for other antidepressants. However, these other data sets include a mixture of trials. The current analysis limits the number of studies but ensures that they are roughly comparable, and the selection of studies is based on regulatory requirements rather than individual bias.

Meta- and Other Analyses of SSRIs and Suicidal Acts

In addition to the RCT data indicating an excess of suicidal acts by those taking SSRIs, the clinical trials on zimelidine, the first SSRI, suggested there were more suicide attempts by patients taking it than by those taking comparators, but Montgomery and colleagues reported that although this might be the case, zimelidine appeared to do better than comparators in reducing already existing suicidal thoughts. A similar analysis demonstrated lower suicide attempt rates for those taking fluvoxamine than the comparators in clinical trials. Problems with paroxetine led to similar analyses and similar claims.

The best-known analysis of this type was published by Eli Lilly after the controversy with fluoxetine emerged; from the analysis of pooled data from 17 double-blind clinical trials in patients with major depressive disorder, the authors concluded that "data from these trials do not show that fluoxetine is associated with an increased risk of suicidal acts or emergence of substantial suicidal thoughts among depressed patients." There are a number of methodological problems with Lilly's analysis, however, and these apply to some extent to all other such exercises. First, none of the studies in the analysis were designed to test whether fluoxetine could be associated with the emergence of suicidality. In the case of fluoxetine, all of the studies had been conducted before concerns of suicide induction had arisen. Some of the studies used in the analysis had, in fact, been rejected by the FDA. Second, only 3067 patients of the approximately 26,000 patients entered into clinical trials of fluoxetine were included in this meta-analysis. Third, no mention was made of the fact that benzodiazepines had been coprescribed in the clinical trial program to minimize the agitation that Lilly recognized fluoxetine could cause. Fourth, no reference was made to the 5% of patients who dropped out because of anxiety and agitation. Given that this was arguably the very problem that was at the heart of the issue, the handling of this issue was not reassuring. The 5% dropout rate for agitation or akathisia holds true for other SSRIs as well, and the differences between SSRIs and placebo are statistically significant. Given that the *Diagnostic and Statistical Manual of Mental Disorders, fourth edition, text revision* (DSM-IV-TR) has connected akathisia with suicide risk, this point is of importance.

Finally, this and other analyses depend critically on item 3 (i.e., suicide) of the Hamilton Rating Scale for Depression; this approach to the problem is one that FDA officials, Lilly personnel and Lilly's consultants agreed was methodologically unsatisfactory. The argument in these meta-analyses has, broadly speaking, been that in the randomized trials, the SSRI reduced suicidality on item 3 and that there was no emergence of suicidality, as measured by this item. To claim that the prevention of or reduction of suicidality in some patients in some way means that treatment cannot produce suicidality in others is a logical non sequitur. The argument that item 3 would pick up emergent suicidality in studies run by clinicians who are not aware of this possible adverse effect has no evidence to support it.

Despite these methodological caveats, the claim that SSRIs reduce suicidality in some patients appears strong. However, insofar as SSRIs reduce suicidal acts in some, if there is a net increase in suicidal acts associated with SSRI treatment in these same trials, the extent to which SSRIs cause problems for some patients must be greater than is apparent from considering the raw data.

Epidemiological Studies

Epidemiology traditionally involves the study of representative samples of the population and requires a specification of the methods used to make the sample representative. A series of what have been termed epidemiological studies have been appealed to in this debate. The first is a 1-column letter involving no suicides. The second is a selective retrospective postmarketing chart review involving no suicides, which analyzed by the American College of Neuropsychopharmacology, the FDA and others, shows a 3-fold increased relative risk of emergent suicidality for fluoxetine versus other antidepressants.

A third study was conducted by Warshaw and Keller on patients with anxiety disorder, in which the only suicide was committed by a patient taking fluoxetine. However, only 192 of the 654 patients in this study received fluoxetine. This, therefore, was not a study designed to test fluoxetine's capacity to induce suicidality. In a fourth study of 643 patients, conceived 20 years before fluoxetine was launched and instituted 10 years before launch, only 185 patients received fluoxetine at any point. This was clearly not a study designed to establish whether fluoxetine might induce suicidality. None of these studies fit the definition of epidemiology offered above.

Although not properly epidemiological, 2 post-marketing surveillance studies that compared SSRI with non-SSRI antidepressants found a higher rate of induction of suicidal ideation for those taking SSRIs, although not in the rates of suicidal acts or suicides.

In a more standard epidemiological study of 222 suicides, Donovan et al. reported that 41 of those suicides were committed by people who had been taking an antidepressant in the month before their suicide; there was a statistically significant doubling of the relative risk of suicide in those taking SSRIs compared with tricyclic antidepressants. In a further epidemiological study of 2776 acts of deliberate self-harm, Donovan et al. found a doubling of the risk for deliberate self-harm for those taking SSRIs compared with other antidepressants.

A set of post-marketing surveillance studies carried out in primary care in the United Kingdom by the Drug Safety Research Unit (DSRU) recorded 110 suicides in over 50,000 patients being treated by general practitioners in Britain. The DSRU methodology has since been applied to mirtazapine, where there have been 13 suicides reported in a population of 13,554 patients. This permits the comparisons outlined in Table 2.

A further study from British primary care was undertaken by Jick and colleagues, who investigated the rate and means of suicide among people taking common antidepressants. They reported 143 suicides among 172,580 patients taking antidepressants and found a statistically significant doubling of the relative risk of suicide with fluoxetine compared with the reference antidepressant, dothiepin, when calculated in terms of patient exposure years. Controlling for confounding factors such as age, sex and previous suicide

Table 2

Drug Safety Research Unit Studies of Selective Serotonin Reuptake Inhibitors (SSRIs) and Mirtazapine in Primary Care Practice in the United Kingdom

Drug	No. of Patients	No. of Suicides	Suicides/100,000 Patients (and 95% confidence interval)	
Fluoxetine	12692	31	244	(168–340)
Sertraline	12734	22	173	(110–255)
Paroxetine	13741	37	269	(192–365)
Fluvoxamine	10983	20	182	(114–274)
Total SSRIs	**50150**	**110**	**219**	
Mirtazapine	13554	13	96	(53–158)

attempts left the relative risk at 2.1 times greater for fluoxetine than for dothiepin and greater than any other antidepressant studied, although statistical significance was lost in the process. Of further note are the elevated figures for mianserin and trazodone, which are closely related pharmacologically to mirtazapine and nefazodone. Controlling for confounding factors in the case of mianserin and trazodone, however, led to a reduction in the relative risk of these agents compared with dothiepin.

To provide comparability with other figures, I have recalculated these data in terms of absolute numbers and separated the data for fluoxetine (Table 3). The data in the Jick study, however, only allow comparisons between antidepressants. They shed no light on the differences between treatment with antidepressants and non-treatment or on the efficacy of antidepressants in reducing suicide risk in primary care. The traditional figures with which the DSRU studies and the Jick study might be compared are a 15% lifetime risk for suicide for affective disorders. This would be inappropriate, however, because this 15% figure was derived from patients with melancholic depression in hospital in the pre-antidepressant era.

There are very few empirical figures available for suicide rates in primary care depression, the sample from which the Jick et al. and DSRU data come. One study from Sweden reports a suicide rate of 0 per 100,000 patients in non-hospitalized depression. Another primary care study from the Netherlands gives a suicide rate of 33 per 100,000 patient years. Finally, Simon and VonKorff in a study of suicide mortality among individuals treated for depression in Puget Sound, Wash., reported 36 suicides in 62,159 patient years. The suicide risk per 100,000 patient years was 64 among those who received outpatient specialty mental health treatment, 43 among those treated with antidepressant medications in primary care and 0 among those treated in primary care without antidepressants.

Utilizing a database of 2.5 million person years and 212 suicides from North Staffordshire, Boardman and Healy modeled the rate for suicide in treated or untreated depression and found it to be of the order of 68/100,000

Table 3

Suicides Rates of Patients Taking Antidepressants in Primary Care Settings in the United Kingdom*

Drug	Suicides/100,000 Patients (and 95% CI)		No. Suicides/No. Patients
Dothiepin	70	(53–91)	52/74 340
Lofepramine	26	(8–61)	4/15 177
Amitriptyline	60	(41–84)	29/48 580
Clomipramine	80	(38–144)	9/11 239
Imipramine	47	(20–90)	7/15 009
Doxepin	69	(17–180)	3/4 329
Flupenthixol	78	(43–129)	13/16 599
Trazodone	99	(31–230)	4/4049
Mianserin	166	(86–285)	11/6609
Fluoxetine	93		11/11 860
Total excluding fluoxetine	67		132/195 931

Note: CI = confidence interval.

* From Jick et al.

Table 4

Relative Risk (RR) of Suicide While Taking SSRIs (from DSRU Studies) Compared with General Risk of Suicide in UK Primary Care Primary Affective Disorders and in UK Primary Care Depression Treated with Non-SSRI Antidepressants

Drug	RR from DSRU Sample Compared with Primary Care Sample	RR from DSRU Sample Compared with Primary Care Depression Sample Treated with Non-SSRI Antidepressants
Sertraline	6.4	2.54
Fluoxetine	9.2	3.59
Paroxetine	10.2	3.96
Total SSRI	**8.3**	**3.44**

Note: DSRU = Drug Safety Research Unit.

patient years for all affective disorders. This rate gives an upper limit on the suicide rate in mood disorders that is compatible with observed national rates of suicide in the United Kingdom. Boardman and Healy estimate a rate of 27 suicides per 100,000 patients per annum for primary care primary affective disorders. Possible relative risks for SSRIs from the DSRU studies set against these figures and the findings from the Jick study for all antidepressants excluding fluoxetine are presented in Table 4.

Comparing the figures for SSRIs from Table 2 with those for the non-SSRI antidepressants from the Jick study gives a mean figure for non-SSRI antidepressants of 68 suicides per 100,000 patients exposed compared with a figure of 212 suicides for the SSRI group. Based on an analysis of 249,803 exposures to antidepressants, therefore, the broad relative risk on SSRI antidepressants compared with non-SSRI antidepressants or even non-treatment is 234/68 or 3.44.

There are 2 points of note. First, these low rates for suicide in untreated primary care mood disorder populations are consistent with the rate of 0 suicides in those taking placebo in antidepressant RCTs. Second, correcting the DSRU figures for exposure lengths gives figures for suicides on sertraline and paroxetine comparable to those reported from RCTs by Khan et al.

Conclusion

Since antidepressant drug treatments were introduced, there have been concerns that their use may lead to suicide. Hitherto, there has been a legitimate public health concern that the debate about possible hazards might deter people at risk from suicide from seeking treatment, possibly leading to an increased number of suicides. The data reviewed here, however, suggest that warnings and monitoring are more likely to reduce overall risks or that at least we should adopt a position of clinical equipoise on this issue and resolve it by means of further study rather than on the basis of speculation.

The evidence that antidepressants may reduce suicide risk is strong from both clinical practice and RCTs. An optimal suicide reduction strategy would probably involve the monitored treatment of all patients and some restriction of treatment for those most at risk of suicide. In addition, given evidence that particular personality types suit particular selective agents and that mismatching patients and treatments can cause problems, further exploration of this area would seem called for.

Yvon D. Lapierre

 **NO**

Suicidality with Selective Serotonin Reuptake Inhibitors: Valid Claim?

Introduction

. . . A plethora of new antidepressants followed the introduction of the selective serotonin reuptake inhibitors (SSRIs) with the associated claims of their relative innocuity compared with the previous generation of tricyclics antidepressants (TCAs) and monoamine oxidase inhibitors. These claims seem to have reached their high point, and SSRIs as well as other antidepressants are now undergoing a second phase of critical review. This reappraisal of antidepressants addresses not only the claims of efficacy but also those related to side effects and to the toxicological profiles of the old as well as of the newer products. These have challenged long-held views and have brought to light new findings that would most likely not have come about otherwise. Invariably, in such circumstances, the pendular shift of attitudes can easily lead to exaggerated claims toward the negative and unwanted effects to the point of discarding previously demonstrated positive findings. It is then necessary to have a critical and balanced expression of opinions and analytic reviews of the available data to arrive at a just appraisal of reality.

The risk of suicide has remained at around 15% in patients with mental disorders, with only a marginal decline of suicide rate since the advent of antidepressants. Over 50% of those who commit suicide have an associated mood disorder, which is usually depression. Long-term follow-up shows that this is more pronounced in unipolar depressives and that treatment lessens the risk somewhat, but it still remains above the norm.

One considerably controversial issue has been the risk of suicide in relation to SSRI antidepressants. The issue arose from a series of case reports of patients who developed intense suicidal preoccupations and intense thoughts of self-harm while taking antidepressants. The initial reports implicated fluoxetine, and this was followed by reports suggesting a similar phenomenon with other SSRIs, thus leading to the speculation of a class effect.

Retrospective analyses of some randomized controlled trials (RCTs) on SSRIs suggest that the incidence of suicide may be higher in patients undergoing treatment with this new class of antidepressant, but any conclusion is still

From *Journal of Psychiatry & Neuroscience*, vol. 28, no. 5, September 2003, pp. 340–347. Copyright © 2003 by CMA Management. Reprinted by permission. References omitted.

uncertain. This leads to the purpose of this duo of papers (Healy and Whitaker and this one), where facts may be submitted to different views and interpretation. Healy and Whitaker's contention is that SSRIs are conductive to an increased risk of suicide; this author disagrees.

The first question that arises is whether there is a temporal cause–effect relation between the administration of a specific drug and the development of suicidal ideation and of suicide. The order of such a cause and effect relation may then be examined and attributed, if applicable, as either a primary drug effect, a paradoxical drug effect, an expected side effect of the drug or, finally, an action that may be secondary to a side effect of the compound. A second issue to be addressed is whether this effect is drug specific or class specific. The question of validity of any imputed causality must be critically re-evaluated throughout this process. Once these issues are clarified, strategies that would improve the outcome of treatment for patients with depression may arise.

This paper will address the problem by first looking at issues of efficacy and suicide data and then discussing the case for the alleged link between suicide and SSRI and other antidepressant therapies.

Efficacy Issues

The efficacy of a widely used intervention may be evaluated by assessing its impact on the population at large through epidemiological approaches and then on the experiences obtained from clinical trials and clinical practice.

Epidemiological observations suggest that there has been a gradual increase in the incidence of depression in post-World War II generations. There are indications that this illness will become an ever-increasing burden of disability in Western societies. Given that depression is the predominant risk factor for suicide, one would expect that with the increased numbers of depressed individuals, there would be an increase in suicide rates. Furthermore, if there is validity to the claim that SSRIs play a causative role in suicide, there would be an even greater increase in suicide rates since the advent of these drugs. Although this may not have materialized as such, these speculations are not necessarily dismissed as being completely invalid.

Epidemiological studies on the issue of antidepressant treatment and suicide have been conducted in a number of countries. In Italy, there was found to be a possible relation between increased SSRI use from 1988 to 1996 and suicide rate. There was a slight increase in suicide rates for men but a more pronounced decrease for women; however, these changes were not significant. In Sweden, from 1976 to 1996, increased utilization of antidepressants paralleled a decrease in suicide rates. In Finland, the increased use of SSRIs coincided with a decrease in suicide mortality, as well as with an increase in the incidence of fatal overdoses with TCAs. The tricyclics accounted for 82% of suicides by antidepressant overdose.

In the National Institute of Mental Health Collaborative Depression Study, Leon et al. assessed the possibility of an increased suicidal risk associated with the SSRI fluoxetine. In the 185 patients in follow-up, there was a trend for a decrease in the number of suicide attempts compared with patients receiving other treatments. Although this cohort was at higher risk because of a history of repeated suicide attempts, treatment with fluoxetine resulted in a nonsignificant reduction of attempts in these patients.

The findings of these epidemiological studies do not provide any indication that the use of antidepressants, and more specifically SSRIs, contribute to an increased risk of suicide in population bases or in depressed populations.

The main sources of information on psychopharmacological agents are the data from clinical trials. Then, post-marketing studies are intended to provide the alerts on safety and potentially new indications for the drug. Both of these sources have limitations and biases, however, inevitably adding fuel to the present debate.

Given that RCTs are designed to primarily identify clinical efficacy and acute or short-term safety of antidepressants, there are limitations on the gathering of exhaustive data on unwanted side effects. The selection of patients for an RCT generally excludes those who are considered to be at risk for suicide. This is usually determined clinically, and the judgment is based on clinical indicators that have, in past experience, been associated with increased risk. Up to 80% of depressed patients may experience thoughts of suicide, and there is a greater than 15% risk of suicide with depression, making the elucidation of suicidal thoughts and intent increasingly relevant to a valid assessment of risk.

This rationale is based on the premise that suicidal ideation is the precursor to and is likely to lead to suicidal acting out. Suicidal acts in the recent past, as well as a number of other associated factors, contribute to the evaluation of risk and the decision of inclusion or exclusion. This inevitably leads to a skewed population, where those appearing to be most clearly at risk and those more severely depressed are often excluded.

The experimental design most often used is a single-blind placebo-washout phase followed by a double-blind randomized phase with a placebo control, a standard active treatment control and an experimental treatment arm. Because of the pressures against the use of placebo in RCTs, as well as cost considerations, there is a trend toward having unbalanced groups, with fewer subjects in the placebo and control arms. This results in reduced statistical power and the need for more patients in the studies and has contributed to increasing numbers of multicentre trials to meet these and other exigencies.

The end point of an RCT is time limited, and the criteria of successful outcome are based on clinical evaluations that of necessity are quantified using rating scales and focus on the immediate objective. They then have limited retrospective applicability and intrinsic limitations when explored retroactively for other purposes. This does not necessarily invalidate subsequent retrospective studies, but one must consider that there are limits on conclusions that can be reached because of these limitations and other biases. To mention but a few that may be relevant to the issue at hand, patient selection, diagnostic considerations and statistical limitations come to mind.

A similar pattern of biases occurs in post-marketing surveillance studies. The source of data varies from one jurisdiction to the next, as do the methods and obligations to report adverse events. Clinicians are known to adopt different prescribing patterns for patients presenting more severe states of depression and for those considered to be at greater risk for suicide. The former group are more likely to receive a TCA, whereas the latter are more likely to receive a "safer-in-overdose" SSRI. Thus, a significant bias in patient selection arises in the evaluation of suicidal risk under one form of treatment or another.

Suicidality and suicide should be distinguished. Thoughts of suicide are not uncommon in the general population but become problematic if they are too frequent, intense or commanding and lead to greater risk of acting on the ideation. Most suicides are preceded by increases in suicidal ideation. Thus, this becomes an important consideration in the assessment of suicide risk. On the other hand, suicidal ideation as such cannot be totally equated to suicidal behaviour.

Conditions favourable to acting on the ideation, such as increased impulsivity or a high level of anxiety and agitation, increase the risk of suicide. The suicidal tendencies item of the Hamilton Rating Scale for Depression is the instrument for quantification of suicidality in RCTs. It allows for a certain degree of quantification on the seriousness of suicidal tendencies and emphasizes mainly suicidal ideation as such. It is not meant to clearly discriminate and quantify the nuances of suicidality to allow for definitive conclusions to be drawn on the severity of the suicidal risk. However, it is probably the most widely used rating scale for RCTs on depression and has become the standard instrument for the analysis of the many features of this illness and for assessing change at different intervals during a clinical trial.

Meta-analyses of RCTs have yielded conflicting results. The short duration of RCTs, which are the basis of these meta-analyses, may not provide valid long-term data, but they do contribute to an understanding of acute therapeutic effects. There is an inherent deficiency in meta-analyses because of the intrinsic limitations of post hoc analyses. Nevertheless, a few of these reports suggested that fluoxetine was associated with a greater incidence of suicidal thoughts. This was followed by other reports suggesting that sertraline, fluvoxamine, paroxetine and citalopram produced similar effects. This led to the speculation of a class effect of SSRIs. On the other hand, there are meta-analytic and other types of studies that just as strongly suggest that emergent suicidal ideation was lessened by these same SSRIs. In the Verkes et al. study, the findings are more convincing because of the high-risk population involved. Others have suggested that, not only do SSRIs reduce suicidal ideation, but the symptom is increased in patients taking norepinephrine reuptake inhibitors.

A meta-analytic study of treatment with fluoxetine, tricyclic antidepressants are placebo in large samples of patients with mood disorders ($n = 5655$) and non-mood disorders ($n = 4959$) did not identify satistically significant differences in emergent suicidal thoughts between groups, and there were no suicides in the non-mood disorder group. These data do not support a suicidogenic effect of SSRIs or TCAs.

Firm conclusions on suicidality and SSRIs based on these findings should be guarded at this point. Suffice it to say that the evidence to suggest that SSRIs generally reduce suicidality is more convincing than that supporting the contrary.

Suicide

The risk of a depressed patient committing suicide with prescribed antidepressants has been a long-standing concern of clinicians treating depressed patients. This was particularly significant with the older generation tricyclics and was one reason to advocate the use of the newer agents (because of their reported lower lethal potential in overdose). On the other hand, it is surprisingly rare for patients to use prescribed antidepressants for suicidal purposes. Data on the agents used for suicide from a number of countries suggest that only about 5% of overdoses are with antidepressants (range 1%–8%). An outlier appears to be the United Kingdom, with reports of 14%. Men commit suicide by overdose much less frequently than women. An important finding in these reports is that patients tend to use previously prescribed, undiscarded antidepressants as their drug of choice. This points to the important role of therapeutic failure in a number of patients who commit suicide.

The advent of the SSRIs brought a renewed impetus in physician and public education on depressive disorders to not only raise professional and public awareness of depression but also publicize the profile of the new antidepressants in their treatment. This, in addition to other factors, has led to many of these educational activities being sponsored by the pharmaceutical industry, with the inevitable ensuing risk of bias. These efforts have certainly contributed to a heightened awareness of depression by professionals and to less reluctance in using antidepressants because of improved safety profiles with equivalent efficacy.

Although antidepressants have been pivotal in the treatment of depression for more than 4 decades, a number of unanswered questions remain. The therapeutic superiority of antidepressants has been taken for granted despite the inconsistent robustness in many controlled studies, where their superiority over placebo is not always clearly demonstrated. Recent data on the latest generation of antidepressants, the SSRIs and serotonin–norepinephrine reuptake inhibitors suggest that only 48% of placebo-controlled studies show a consistent statistically significant superiority of the antidepressant over placebo. This figure may be inferior to the generally accepted greater success rate and emphasizes the need for individualized therapeutic strategies. This becomes critical for poor responders, where the limitations of available treatments become obvious. Depression is the main risk factor for suicide, the final and fatal outcome of non-response to treatment. If, as is suggested by some, the risk of suicide is increased by antidepressants, which are considered to be the cornerstone and most widely accepted treatment for depression, the use of such agents would obviously necessitate a critical re-evaluation.

Suicidality and suicidal actions induced de novo by SSRIs was suggested by a few clinical papers that followed Teicher's initial case report. Because of the paradoxical nature of these observations, a number of retrospective analyses of large cohorts were then conducted. The analyses of the US Food and Drug Administration database by Kahn et al. looked at suicidality and suicide rates in a cohort of 23,201 patients participating in clinical trials of antidepressants. Overall suicide rates for patients were 627/100,000 compared with a general population rate of 11/100,000. There were no significant differences between rates for placebo, comparator drugs and new-generation investigational drugs. The mortality rates ranged from 0.19% for placebo to 0.14% for the investigational drugs and 0.11% for the active comparators. There were no significant differences in patient exposure years between these 3 groups, although the numerical values were higher for the antidepressant groups. The attempted suicide rate ranged from 0.66% for the investigational drugs to 1.37% for the comparators to 1.39% for placebo (no significant differences). Patient exposure years also did not differ significantly. These findings do not provide information on the duration of exposure to treatment but include the data on all patients who participated in the trials and are thus quite representative of short-term studies. Patient exposure years, which cumulates the duration of treatment and the number of patients treated, did not show differences either. These data do not support the suggestion that SSRIs add to suicide risk.

A similar study was done in the Netherlands by Storosum et al. on data submitted to the Medicines Evaluation Board of the Netherlands for 12,246 patients treated in short-term (< 8 wk) clinical trials. Attempts at suicide occurred in 0.4% of patients in both placebo and active drug groups. Completed suicide occurred in 0.1% of patients in both placebo and active treatment groups. In longer-term studies (> 8 wk) involving 1949 patients, attempted suicide occurred in 0.7% of patients in both groups, and completed suicides occurred in 0.2% (2 patients) of the active drug group (no significant difference). These results also do not support a suicidogenic effect of these antidepressants.

Donovan et al. reviewed 222 suicides that occurred in a 4-year period in 3 different regions of the United Kingdom. Of these, 83% had been diagnosed with depression in the past and 56% had been prescribed antidepressants in the previous year; 41 had been prescribed a TCA and 13 an SSRI within 1 month of their suicide, and these formed the main cohort of the study. On the basis of the relative proportion of prescriptions in these regions, the authors concluded that the risk of suicide is greater with SSRIs than with TCAs. An important variable that may have skewed these findings is that those taking SSRIs included most of the patients who had a recent history of deliberate self harm, which in itself is recognized as an important predictor of suicide. It is thus difficult to make any definitive conclusions from these findings because the inherent biases in patient selection for treatment force the results and conclusions.

More recently, Oquendo et al. reported on 136 depressed patients who were discharged from hospital after a major depressive episode and were followed in community settings for 24 months; 15% of patients attempted suicide during the 2 years, and 50% of these attempts occurred during the first 5 months of follow-up. Treatment was in a naturalistic setting and was monitored regularly. The medications administered were mainly the new-generation antidepressants. A critical review of the dosage administered considered it to be adequate in only 9 (43%) of the patients at the time of attempted suicide. Four of these patients had relapsed into a recurrence of depression. These findings elicit a number of questions such as the importance of treatment resistance, history of suicide attempts, components of adequate treatment, adequacy of drug treatment and compliance.

The case put forth in the first of this duo of papers is beguiling. It is indeed seductive to use legal precedents and the court of public opinion to evaluate the scientific merit and withdrawal of a therapeutic agent. However, it remains paramount that methodology not be changed to lead to selective data. For this reason, it is not appropriate in these instances to allow the bias introduced by separating placebo washout out of the trial data, especially if "intent to treat" and last observation carried forward data are to serve as the basis of outcome analyses.

It is not appropriate to agree with the statement that clinicians would not be vigilant to the risk of suicide in antidepressant RCTs, because suicide is universally recognized as the major complication of depression. Although antidepressant RCTs are not designed to evaluate suicide risk, disregarding the data generated is as inappropriate as disregarding the data collected for the study's designed purpose.

Discussion

SSRI antidepressants as a class are among the most frequently prescribed drugs in the Western world. Their applications have broadened from their initial indication in depression to a number of other psychiatric conditions such as obsessive–compulsive disorder, generalized anxiety disorder and, more recently, late luteal phase disorder. This provides a wide spectrum of conditions under which the SSRIs are administered and allows for a much broader clinical experience for the appraisal of the drugs in question. There have not been any reports of suicide in patients taking SSRIs for these other conditions.

Suicide is a leading public health problem in all societies. It is estimated that known suicides account for 1 million deaths worldwide annually. Given that depression is a significant factor in nearly 50% of these cases, the treatment of depression merits critical appraisal, especially if this treatment contributes further to suicidal behaviour, as has been suggested. This partly explains the reaction to the initial reports of increased suicidality during treatment with fluoxetine and then with the other SSRIs. These reports have led to a healthy second look at the available data and to the pursuit of additional studies and observations.

Clinical studies and meta-analyses indicate that an overwhelming number of patients experience a decrease in suicidal ideation while taking SSRIs. The fact that these meta-analyses were based on data collected primarily to demonstrate efficacy does not diminish their validity. Although the method of evaluation has been criticized (i.e., a single item on the HAM-D) and the evidence of decreased suicidality admittedly not highly nuanced, the data still reflect the observed clinical reality. A decrease in suicidality must be considered to reflect an improvement in the depressed condition.

Despite the availability of less toxic antidepressant drugs, the increasing use of antidepressants has not consistently been associated with a significant decline in suicide rates. As the SSRIs gain popularity, the use of the older TCAs as instruments of suicide by overdose has decreased. However, other more violent means are resorted to, thus indirectly reducing the positive safety impact of the SSRIs. It would be simplistic to make conclusions on single causality in suicidal behaviour without recognizing the complexities of the behaviour and circumstances that lead to the outcome.

Although evidence from large studies points to a reduction in suicidal ideation, the few reports of the appearance of intense suicidal thoughts in a few patients must not pass unnoticed. There were sporadic reports of suicidality with zimelidine, the first SSRI. This did not hold up to statistical testing and, because the drug was discontinued shortly after being launched, there was no follow-up. There were no major concerns at this time because most patients experienced an improvement in suicidal thoughts. A sporadic paradoxical effect to a psychotropic agent is a well-known phenomenon. It is well documented with antipsychotic agents such as the phenothiazines, where excitement and even worsening of the psychotic disorder have been observed. These are rare events but must be kept in mind so they will be recognized when they do occur. It is also essential to recognize that the emergence of suicidal thoughts may simply be attributable to underlying psychopathology.

Studies of fluoxetine have reported that this drug, in addition to causing some increase in agitation in some patients, may also cause akathisia. High levels of anxiety and agitation are known to accompany increased suicidal behaviour. In such a situation, the behaviour would be secondary to a side effect of the drug, rather than to its primary action.

Post hoc studies have intrinsic limitations but can shed some light on the understanding of this issue. The findings of Donovan and colleagues suggest that the increased risk of suicide is to a great extent explained by patient selection in some clinical studies. They did not factor in deliberate self-harm in the attribution of patients in their study. The increased risk of suicidality in patients with a history of repeated deliberate self-harm is well known. Even if these patients had been screened as not being actively suicidal at the onset of a trial, they were nevertheless still at higher risk subsequently. This type of susceptibility bias was very much present in the Leon et al. study and in that by Donovan et al.

A common deficiency in many studies of the treatment of depression is a consideration of unipolarity or bipolarity. The latter is readily missed for a number of reasons but, because the condition is not uncommon and requires adapted treatment with mood stabilizers, a greater risk of suicide may appear in these patients than in undertreated patients.

Despite anecdotal reports implicating most of the SSRIs, a drug-specific or class effect is not substantiated. Unfortunately, SSRIs have not been compared critically with other classes of antidepressants. On the other hand, the common pharmacological action of serotonin reuptake inhibition does not explain all of the actions of these drugs. A comparison of fluoxetine with its activating properties and citalopram with its more sedating profile illustrates the different effects SSRIs can have. Fluoxetine is known to occasionally cause some agitation. This may be experienced independently from akathisia which may, albeit rarely, also result from fluoxetine. The combination of the 2 (i.e, akathisia and agitation) has been associated with increased suicidal tendencies in depressed patients, but it is unlikely that this would support a class effect or phenomenon. It is more likely a consequence of a rare side effect of the drug.

A pharmacological explanation for a rare event is difficult to establish because it is, by definition, unpredictable. However, it is not beyond the realm of possibility and merits further exploration, although it is unlikely to attract interest simply because of the rarity of the event and the unpredictability of a host of variables.

Conclusion

Any conclusions based on these few reports of sporadic cases of increased suicidality with SSRIs must be limited and highly tentative. The most these cases can suggest is an individual paradoxical effect, and these can be compared with the large number of patients who experience a diminution of suicidality and an improvement in depression. Another significant factor is that as the use of these antidepressants has broadened, the initial reports have not been followed by an increasing number of cases. Results of clinical studies are inconclusive, with some supporting a link and others refuting one. However, the awareness of the possibility of increased suicidality with SSRI treatment must be taken in the context of the risk of suicide in treating depression with any other antidepressant. Suicide is an inherent risk in the context of depression but this should not deter from adequate treatment.

A review of this issue serves as a reminder of the basic principles of good therapeutics that recommend that the complete profile of the drug be taken into account when selecting a pharmacotherapeutic agent. Once the primary (desired) and secondary (unwanted or not) effects have been fully considered, the total profile of the drug can be tailored to the clinical profile of an individual patient.

The newer SSRI antidepressants were never considered to be superior in efficacy to the TCAs, but their entry into the therapeutics of depression has reduced the risk of iatrogenic intoxication and, most likely, the overall risk of suicidal outcome in adequately treated patients. There is, at this time, insufficient evidence to claim that they lead to suicide.

CHALLENGE QUESTIONS

Does Taking Antidepressants
Lead to Suicide?

1. How would you account for the major differences in the results of the studies that Healy/Whitaker and Lapierre present?
2. From the data presented, do you think antidepressants pose a risk for suicide? Support your answer.
3. If you were the parent of a child, under what circumstances would you permit him or her to take antidepressants? Justify your answer with information from the two articles.
4. One of the issues that separates these two sets of authors is whether the data are "sufficient." Interview two faculty members from the psychology department to find out how they would know when the data are sufficient for action, such as the black box warning on antidepressants.
5. There was some discussion about taking SSRI drugs off the market when the potential for suicide was revealed. Why do you think the FDA did not do so? Do you agree? Support your opinion.

ISSUE 14

Does Low Self-Esteem Lead to Antisocial Behavior?

YES: M. B. Donnellan et al., from "Low Self-Esteem Is Related to Aggression, Antisocial Behavior, and Delinquency." *Psychological Science* (April 2005)

NO: Roy F. Baumeister, Jennifer D. Campbell, Joachim I. Krueger, and Kathleen D. Vohs, from "Exploding the Self-Esteem Myth," *Scientific American* (January 2005)

ISSUE SUMMARY

YES: Psychologist M. Brent Donnellan and his colleagues describe empirical investigations that show low self-esteem as highly predictive of many externalizing problems, including antisocial behavior.

NO: Social psychologist Roy Baumeister and his associates review self-esteem studies to argue that low self-esteem generally has little influence on negative outcomes such as antisocial behavior.

Today, the concept of the self is one of Western psychology's central focuses. Contemporary psychologists study self-concept, self-awareness, self-actualization, and self-esteem, to name a few lines of research. Self-help books are bestsellers in today's bookstores, and building self-esteem is often a primary emphasis of these books. Indeed, self-esteem is a major topic not only in psychology but also in our modern society. Part of today's "common sense" is that we should feel good about ourselves in order to be healthy and productive. Also, low self-esteem is frequently proffered as the cause of many societal maladies, such as drug abuse.

Perhaps surprisingly, not all experts agree that enhancing self-esteem is a cure-all or even a partial remedy to individual or societal ills. Some scholars believe that *high* self-esteem (sometimes undistinguished from narcissism) actually leads to more negative behaviors than low self-esteem. However, other researchers agree that there is a higher correlation between undesirable behaviors and *low* self-esteem. The latter position has been the major debate, both historically and currently. If low self-esteem leads to no "bad" behaviors, such as aggressive and antisocial behavior, then the need to emphasize and encourage positive self-esteem is decreased. Indeed, without both positive behavior associated with high self-esteem and negative behavior associated with low self-esteem, the widespread societal and developmental concern for self-esteem is unwarranted.

In the first of the articles, M. B. Donnellan and his colleagues describe three empirical investigations in which they examine the relationship between self-esteem and "externalizing" problems, such as aggression and other antisocial behaviors. They found a consistent "robust relationship between low self-esteem and aggression" across participants of different nationalities and age groups. These findings were also based on multiple sources for self-esteem ratings, and "held both cross-sectionally and longitudinally and after controlling for potential confounding variables." Donnellan and his colleagues also found that "the effect of self-esteem on aggression was independent of narcissism," implying that both low self-esteem *and* narcissistic high self-esteem can lead to problematic externalizing behavior. While not explicitly addressing the issue of causation, they unequivocally conclude that "low self-esteem . . . contribute[s] to externalizing problems."

In the second article, Baumeister and his colleagues report on a two-year literature review they conducted on studies of self-esteem. They studied three main areas of this research: the relation of self-esteem to academic performance, the relation of self-esteem to sexual activity and drug use, and the relation of self-esteem to aggressive behavior. In each of these areas, the authors explore reasons why low self-esteem might contribute to negative behaviors and show how the research does not validate any of these explanations. They also show how high self-esteem could be a more probable reason for many externalizing problems. Their ultimate conclusion is that, while high self-esteem may in some cases be important, the research by no means shows either that low self-esteem causes antisocial behavior or that we should strive to indiscriminately promote self-esteem.

POINT	COUNTERPOINT
• Self-esteem plays an important role in some important psychological outcomes.	• Low self-esteem is not a major cause of social or psychological problems.
• Both low self-esteem and narcissistic self-regard can lead to problems.	• Excessively high self-esteem is more likely to lead to problem behavior than low self-esteem.
• Low self-esteem correlates highly with problematic behavior.	• Correlation never implies causation;
• Self-esteem can be accurately measured and is in many studies.	• Studies usually draw on highly subjective self-report.

YES

M. Brent Donnellan et al.

Low Self-Esteem Is Related to Aggression, Antisocial Behavior, and Delinquency

ABSTRACT—*The present research explored the controversial link between global self-esteem and externalizing problems such as aggression, antisocial behavior, and delinquency. In three studies, we found a robust relation between low self-esteem and externalizing problems. This relation held for measures of self-esteem and externalizing problems based on self-report, teachers' ratings, and parents' ratings, and for participants from different nationalities (United States and New Zealand) and age groups (adolescents and college students). Moreover, this relation held both cross-sectionally and longitudinally and after controlling for potential confounding variables such as supportive parenting, parent-child and peer relationships, achievement-test scores, socioeconomic status, and IQ. In addition, the effect of self-esteem on aggression was independent of narcissism, an important finding given recent claims that individuals who are narcissistic, not low in self-esteem, are aggressive. Discussion focuses on clarifying the relations among self-esteem, narcissism, and externalizing problems.*

The link between global self-esteem and aggression is currently being debated by researchers and in the popular media. Researchers on one side of the debate have argued that individuals with low self-esteem are prone to real-world externalizing problems such as delinquency and antisocial behavior. However, others have questioned this claim, noting that several studies have failed to find a relation between low self-esteem and externalizing problems or between low global self-esteem and laboratory measures of aggression. On the basis of this research, Baumeister, Bushman, and Campbell suggested that "future research can benefit from discarding the obsolete view that low self-esteem causes violence." Instead, Baumeister and his colleagues have posited that any link between self-esteem and aggression probably occurs at the high end of the self-esteem continuum; that is, unrealistically high self-esteem (best captured by measures of narcissism), not low self-esteem, contributes to aggression and crime.

At least three distinct traditions in the social sciences posit a link between low self-esteem and externalizing problems. Rosenberg suggested

From *Psychological Science*, vol. 16, issue 4, April 2005, pp. 328–335. Copyright © 2005 by Association for Psychological Science. Reprinted by permission of Blackwell Publishing, Ltd.

that low self-esteem weakens ties to society; according to social-bonding theory, weaker ties to society decrease conformity to social norms and increase delinquency. Humanistic psychologists such as Rogers have argued that a lack of unconditional positive self-regard is linked to psychological problems, including aggression. Finally, neo-Freudians also posit that low self-regard motivates aggression. For example, Horney and Adler theorized that aggression and antisocial behavior are motivated by feelings of inferiority rooted in early childhood experiences of rejection and humiliation. More specifically, Tracy and Robins suggested that individuals protect themselves against feelings of inferiority and shame by externalizing blame for their failures, which leads to feelings of hostility and anger toward other people. Thus, three separate theoretical perspectives posit that externalizing behaviors are motivated, in part, by low self-esteem.

Despite these theoretical arguments, research on the link between low self-esteem and externalizing problems has failed to produce consistent results. An understanding of the precise nature of this relation has important theoretical implications, as well as practical implications given the media attention surrounding the issue. To bring new data to bear on this controversy, we report results from three studies that extend previous research in several ways. First, we used a multimethod approach to assessing self-esteem and externalizing problems. Previous research has relied almost exclusively on self-report measures, so it is possible that the relations that have been observed are due to shared method variance. Second, we examined several theoretically relevant variables that might account for the effects of self-esteem on externalizing problems, including IQ, academic achievement, socioeconomic status (SES), and the quality of parent-child relationships. Third, we used longitudinal data to test the hypothesis that low self-esteem is related to future externalizing problems (Study 2). Finally, we assessed narcissism to examine the possibility that unrealistically high self-esteem is related to aggression and to determine whether self-esteem and narcissism have independent effects (Study 3).

Study 1

Study 1 investigated the relation between self-reports and teacher ratings of self-esteem and self-reports of delinquency in a sample of 11- and 14-year-olds. We also controlled for two theoretically relevant variables—supportive parenting and academic achievement—that might account for the effects of self-esteem on delinquency.

Method

Participants

The sample included 292 (78% response rate) 11- and 14-year-old participants (mean age = 12.66 years, $SD = 1.57$; 55% female; 56.5% European American, 4.8% Asian American or Pacific Islander, 20.5% Hispanic American, 9.2%

African American, and 9.0% "other" or not reported) from two schools in northern California.

Measures

Self-esteem was measured with the 10-item Rosenberg Self-Esteem Scale (RSE; $\alpha = .81$) and the 6-item Global subscale of the Harter (1985) Self-Perception Profile for Children (SPPC; $\alpha = .75$). Teachers completed a modified teacher version of the SPPC ($\alpha = .88$).

   Delinquency was measured using a 12-item delinquent-behaviors scale adapted from Elliott, Huizinga, and Ageton ($\alpha = .85$).

   Supportive parenting (warmth, monitoring, use of inductive reasoning, and consistent discipline) was measured using a modified scale from the Iowa Youth and Families Project (e.g., $\alpha = .89$).

   Academic achievement was measured by a composite of the Math and Reading percentile scores from the Stanford Achievement Test Battery.

Results and Discussion

Self-esteem was consistently negatively correlated with delinquency, regardless of whether self-esteem was assessed by the RSE ($r = -.35$), the self-report version of the SPPC ($r = -.39$), or the teacher version of the SPPC ($r = -.29$; all $ps < .05$). To explore these effects further, we compared the self-esteem scores of individuals who reported at least one delinquent act (76% of the sample) and those who reported no delinquent acts. The delinquent group had lower self-esteem than the nondeliquent group on all three self-esteem measures (Cohen's $d = 0.48$, 0.63, and 0.35 for the RSE, self-report SPPC, and teacher SPPC, respectively; all $ps < .05$).

   Baumeister et al. focused their critique of the low-self-esteem hypothesis on aggression, and it was possible that our results were due to delinquent behaviors not involving aggression. To address this issue, we divided the delinquency scale into a 2-item aggression scale ("got into a fight," "beat someone up") and a 10-item nonaggression scale (e.g., "lied to parents or teachers," "used drugs or alcohol"). All the effects of self-esteem remained significant for both the aggression scale (rs ranged from $-.17$ to $-.26$, $ps < .05$) and the nonaggression scale (rs ranged from $-.28$ to $-.39$, $ps < .05$).

   To test whether supportive parenting and academic achievement could account for the relation between low self-esteem and delinquency, we used structural equation modeling with latent variables defined by item parcels rather than individual items. Supportive parenting was defined by three parcels of eight items; self-esteem was defined by the RSE and the self- and teacher-based SPPC scales; delinquency was defined by three parcels of four items; and academic achievement was modeled as a manifest variable. An initial base model that included only self-esteem and delinquency had good fit, χ^2 (8) = 9.09, n.s. (comparative fit index, CFI = 1.00; root mean square error of approximation, RMSEA = .02, p close fit = .76), and the path linking self-esteem to delinquency was negative ($\beta = -.52$, $p < .05$). . . . Thus, supportive parenting and academic achievement could not explain the relation between self-esteem and delinquency.

Study 2

The results of Study 1 provided support for the low-self-esteem hypothesis. In Study 2, we extended Study 1 in several ways. First, we used a longitudinal design to examine the prospective relation between self-esteem and externalizing problems. Second, Study 2 included non-self-report measures of externalizing problems, specifically, teacher- and parent-rated antisocial behavior. Third, Study 2 examined additional control variables, including the quality of parent-child and peer relationships, SES, and IQ. Finally, Study 2 was based on data from a representative birth cohort of New Zealanders, so the range of externalizing problems in the sample reflects the variation found in the general population.

Method

Sample
Participants were members of the Dunedin Multidisciplinary Health and Development Study, a longitudinal investigation of a complete cohort of consecutive births between April 1, 1972, and March 31, 1973, in Dunedin, New Zealand. The present study included participants who completed a measure of self-esteem at age 11 ($n = 812$; 48% female; 78% of the initial cohort) or age 13 ($n = 736$; 48% female; 71% of the initial cohort).

Measures
Self-esteem was measured at age 11 and age 13 with the RSE. The use of a yes/no response format resulted in reliabilities that were somewhat lower than usual for the RSE ($\alpha = .64$ at age 11 and .60 at age 13).

    Externalizing problems were assessed using the Rutter Child Scale (RCS) and the Revised Behavior Problem Checklist (RBPC). Teachers completed the RCS when the participants were ages 11 and 13; parents completed the RCS when the participants were age 11 and the RBPC when they were age 13. Information about the reliability and validity of these measures is provided by Moffitt et al.

    Relationship with parents and peers was assessed at age 13 using the Inventory of Parent Attachment ($\alpha = .77$) and the Inventory of Peer Attachment ($\alpha = .80$). These scales measure the degree to which adolescents feel they can trust, communicate with, and are not alienated from their parents or peers.

    IQ was assessed using the mean of each participant's scores on the Wechsler Intelligence Scale for Children–Revised at ages 7, 9, 11, and 13.

    SES was calculated as the average social class of each participant's family from birth to age 15. Scores at each assessment ranged from 1 (parents are unskilled laborers) to 6 (parents are professionals).

Results and Discussion

Relation Between Self-Esteem and Externalizing Problems
Results were consistent with those of Study 1: Self-esteem was negatively correlated with parent reports of externalizing problems ($r = -.18$ at age 11 and

$r = -.27$ at age 13, $ps < .05$) and with teacher reports of externalizing problems ($r = -.16$ at age 11 and $r = -.18$ at age 13, $ps < .05$). Moreover, self-esteem at age 11 was prospectively related to both parent and teacher reports of externalizing problems at age 13 (both $rs = -.20$, $ps < .05$). As in Study 1, the cross-method effects were significant; individuals with low self-esteem were more likely to engage in antisocial behaviors as reported by their parents and teachers. We divided the items on the antisocial-behavior scales according to whether they involved aggressive (e.g., fighting, bullying) or nonaggressive (e.g., lying, disobedient) behaviors, and the effects of self-esteem remained significant for both the aggression items (rs ranged from $-.13$ to $-.26$, $ps < .05$) and the nonaggression items (rs ranged from $-.18$ to $-.21$, $ps < .05$).

We next tested whether theoretically relevant third variables could account for the relation between low self-esteem and delinquency. The base model of self-esteem and externalizing problems had good fit, $\chi^2(1) = 3.61$, n.s. (CFI = .99; RMSEA = .06, p close fit = .32), and the path linking self-esteem to externalizing problems was negative ($\beta = -.49$, $p < .05$). . . . Thus, parent and peer relationships, IQ, and SES could not explain the relation between self-esteem and delinquency.

Cross-Lagged Relations Between Self-Esteem and Externalizing Problems

To examine the effect of self-esteem at age 11 on externalizing problems at age 13, we conducted cross-lagged analyses controlling for prior levels of externalizing problems. Although these analyses do not establish causal direction, they help rule out alternative causal interpretations related to temporal sequence. We created latent measures of self-esteem at ages 11 and 13 using five two-item parcels of RSE items, and latent measures of externalizing problems at ages 11 and 13 using an indicator of aggressive behaviors (a standardized composite of parent and teacher reports) and an indicator of nonaggressive behaviors (a standardized composite of parent and teacher reports). To improve model fit, we allowed the errors for the indicators at age 11 to correlate with the same errors at age 13. . . . This model had good fit, $\chi^2(64) = 116.06$, $p < .05$ (CFI = .99; RMSEA = .03, p close fit = 1.00), and self-esteem was concurrently related to externalizing problems at age 11 ($r = -.31$, $p < .05$) and age 13 ($r = -.25$, $p < .05$). The path linking self-esteem at age 11 to externalizing problems at age 13 was negative and significant ($\beta = -.15$, $p < .05$), whereas the path linking externalizing problems at age 11 to self-esteem at age 13 was negative but not statistically significant ($\beta = -.08$, $p = .11$). These results are consistent with the claim that low self-esteem leads to increases in externalizing problems. However, given the magnitude of the effect and the nonexperimental design, we are hesitant to conclude that self-esteem causes future externalizing problems.

Study 3

The results of Studies 1 and 2 support the low-self-esteem hypothesis. In Study 3, we tested the hypothesis that unrealistically high, not low, self-esteem predicts aggression by assessing both self-esteem and narcissism and examining their relations with reports of real-world aggression. Previous research on narcissism has used laboratory measures of aggression, and it is not clear whether the findings generalize to real-world aggression.

Method

Sample
The sample consisted of 3,143 undergraduate students (68.3% female; mean age = 19.6 years, SD = 1.6) from a large research university in northern California. They participated in exchange for course credit.

Measures
Self-esteem was measured with the RSE (α = .90). *Narcissism* was measured by the 40-item Narcissistic Personality Inventory (α = .84). *Aggression* was assessed using the 29-item Buss-Perry Aggression Questionnaire (AQ). The AQ includes a Total Aggression scale (α = .90) and four subscales: Physical Aggression (α = .83), Verbal Aggression (α = .76), Anger (α = .81), and Hostility (α = .84).

Results and Discussion

. . . Results were consistent with the findings of Studies 1 and 2: Self-esteem was negatively correlated with the Total Aggression scale of the AQ (r = −.30, p < .05) and with all of the subscales except Verbal Aggression. Note that self-esteem was related to the Physical Aggression subscale, which has been linked to real-world displays of violence. In contrast, narcissism was positively correlated with the Total Aggression scale (r = .18, p < .05) and with all of the subscales except Hostility. Thus, we found support for the claim that narcissistic individuals are prone to aggression.

Self-esteem and narcissism were moderately related (r = .32, p < .05), so we conducted multiple regression analyses to test whether they had independent effects on aggression. In general, the effect sizes increased in the multiple regression analyses (e.g., the zero-order relation between self-esteem and Total Aggression was −.30, whereas the regression coefficient controlling for narcissism was −.39). We conducted Sobel tests to determine if these apparent suppression effects were statistically significant. For the total AQ scale and all four subscales, the effects of self-esteem were significantly stronger when narcissism was included in the equation than when it was not included (all zs > −4.90, ps < .05), and, similarly, all of the effects of narcissism were significantly stronger when self-esteem was included in the equations (all zs > 6.28, ps < .05). Thus, low self-esteem and narcissism contribute independently to aggressive thoughts, feelings, and behaviors, and in fact serve as mutual suppressors.

General Discussion

In three studies, we found a robust relation between low self-esteem and externalizing problems. This relation held for different age groups, different nationalities, and multiple methods of assessing self-esteem and externalizing problems; after controlling for potential confounding variables; and when we delved beneath the broad construct of externalizing problems and examined specific aggressive thoughts, feelings, and behaviors. Moreover, our results indicate that self-esteem may foretell future externalizing problems; 11-year-olds with low self-esteem tended to increase in aggression by age 13. Finally, the effect of low self-esteem on aggression was independent of narcissism; in fact, when healthy self-regard was disentangled from narcissistic self-perceptions, the relation between low self-esteem and aggression became even stronger. Thus, our results support the concern about the dangers of narcissism but do not support the conclusion that low self-esteem is unrelated to externalizing problems. In this section, we discuss conceptual and methodological issues that may help explain the inconsistencies in the literature on the association between low self-esteem and externalizing problems.

Baumeister et al. suggested that inflated high self-esteem (as captured by measures of narcissism) is a better predictor of aggression than low self-esteem. This suggestion seems to be based on the assumption that low self-esteem and narcissism are opposite ends of the same continuum (self-hate vs. self-love). For example, Baumeister et al. noted that "an effective and valid [self-esteem] scale would identify the arrogant, conceited narcissist just as well as the person who holds an unbiased appreciation of his or her own well-recognized good qualities." Accepting this view may result in the need to pit the low-self-esteem hypothesis against the narcissism hypothesis; that is, antisocial individuals have either low self-esteem or its antithesis, narcissism. Moreover, conceptualizing low self-esteem and narcissism as opposite ends of the same continuum leads to the concern that "the societal pursuit of high self-esteem for everyone may literally end up doing considerable harm."

However, this concern may not be warranted because it is possible to draw a distinction between healthy self-regard and narcissistic self-views. For example, Rosenberg noted that "when we deal with self-esteem, we are asking whether the individual considers himself adequate—a person of worth—not whether he considers himself superior to others." In contrast, narcissists describe themselves as special, extraordinary people who are better and more deserving than others. Empirically, measures of self-esteem and narcissism typically correlate only in the .20s to low .30s, which is far below the level of convergent validity one would expect between two self-report measures of the same construct. Thus, the precise relation between self-esteem and narcissism remains an open question.

Several conceptualizations are currently being debated in the self-esteem literature, including whether narcissism is an exaggerated form of high self-esteem, a particular facet of self-esteem, a highly contingent and unstable form of self-esteem, a need to feel superior to others, or a defensive shell of inflated self-esteem that compensates for unconscious feelings of inadequacy. Although resolving this issue is beyond the scope of this article, our results indicate that self-esteem and narcissism have independent effects on externalizing problems, thus demonstrating their discriminant validity. Moreover, when narcissism is partialed out of self-esteem, the regression coefficient for self-esteem more closely captures Rosenberg's conceptualization of self-esteem and provides clear support for the low-self-esteem hypothesis.

Another way to reconcile the inconsistent results in the literature is to consider methodological differences between our work and previous laboratory research on self-esteem and aggression. Although experimental measures of aggression have a great deal of external validity, they do not necessarily have the same correlates as measures of real-world aggression and antisocial behavior. In fact, in their review of the literature, Anderson and Bushman noted that lab and real-world studies sometimes produce discrepant results, and suggested that "rather than take the perspective that one 'side' or the other is wrong, it may be more prudent to try to locate the source of the discrepancies in psychological processes that may differ in the two settings."

There are several possible sources of the discrepancy between our findings and those of the previous lab studies. First, lab studies typically examine a specific form of aggression, namely, aggression provoked by a competitive task in which self-evaluative processes have been activated. In contrast, real-world externalizing problems occur in a wide range of contexts, and these other forms of aggression may have distinct correlates.

Second, aggressive behavior in the lab does not lead to any serious harm to the other person, whereas real-world aggression often does; blasting someone with white noise does not have the same consequences as hitting someone. The correlates of milder forms of aggression, particularly those that have no clear negative repercussions, may differ from the correlates of other forms of aggression.

Third, aggressive behaviors occurring in the lab are not antisocial to the same extent as real-world aggression. One could argue that it is socially appropriate to blast one's opponent with white noise in the context of an experiment that has been sanctioned by the university. In contrast, the externalizing behaviors assessed in the present research are explicitly socially undesirable, antisocial, and in most cases illegal. Thus, the discrepancy between our findings and those of previous lab studies may reflect the fact that individuals with narcissistically high self-esteem are more likely to be aggressive when it is socially desirable (e.g., lab paradigms for assessing aggression, athletic events, some corporate settings), whereas individuals with low self-esteem are more likely to be aggressive when it is socially undesirable and contrary to social norms. Future research should examine the specific motivational processes underlying different forms of aggressive behavior in individuals with low versus high self-esteem.

Finally, the relation between low self-esteem and aggression was generally small to moderate in the present studies. This result might provide the simplest explanation for inconsistencies in the literature. If the true effect size is small, then it is not surprising that some studies have reported null findings because of lack of power and fluctuations in observed effect sizes across samples due to systematic and random factors. Moreover, from a meta-analytic perspective, variation in effect sizes across studies indicates the presence of moderator variables. Thus, researchers need to develop theoretical models that generate testable predictions about the boundary conditions on the effect of low self-esteem.

Although much work on these exciting and controversial topics remains to be completed, we believe it is reasonable to conclude that both low self-esteem and narcissism contribute to externalizing problems. Our findings provide strong support for a replicable link between low self-esteem and externalizing problems, and we recommend that the low-self-esteem hypothesis not be discarded prematurely. . . .

Roy F. Baumeister, Jennifer D. Campbell,
Joachim I. Krueger, and Kathleen D. Vohs  **NO**

Exploding the Self-Esteem Myth

People intuitively recognize the importance of self-esteem to their psychological health, so it isn't particularly remarkable that most of us try to protect and enhance it in ourselves whenever possible. What *is* remarkable is that attention to self-esteem has become a communal concern, at least for Americans, who see a favorable opinion of oneself as the central psychological source from which all manner of positive outcomes spring. The corollary, that low self-esteem lies at the root of individual and thus societal problems and dysfunctions, has sustained an ambitious social agenda for decades. Indeed, campaigns to raise people's sense of self-worth abound.

Consider what transpired in California in the late 1980s. Prodded by State Assemblyman John Vasconcellos, Governor George Deukmejian set up a task force on self-esteem and personal and social responsibility. Vasconcellos argued that raising self-esteem in young people would reduce crime, teen pregnancy, drug abuse, school underachievement and pollution. At one point, he even expressed the hope that these efforts would one day help balance the state budget, a prospect predicated on the observation that people with high self-regard earn more than others and thus pay more in taxes. Along with its other activities, the task force assembled a team of scholars to survey the relevant literature. The results appeared in a 1989 volume entitled *The Social Importance of Self-Esteem* (University of California Press, 1989), which stated that "many, if not most, of the major problems plaguing society have roots in the low self-esteem of many of the people who make up society." In reality, the report contained little to support that assertion. The California task force disbanded in 1995, but a nonprofit organization called the National Association for Self-Esteem (NASE) has picked up its mantle. Vasconcellos, until recently a California state senator, is on the advisory board.

Was it reasonable for leaders in California to start fashioning therapies and social policies without supportive data? Perhaps, given that they had problems to address. But one can draw on many more studies now than was the case 15 years ago, enough to assess the value of self-esteem in several spheres. Regrettably, those who have been pursuing self-esteem-boosting programs, including the leaders of NASE, have not shown a desire to examine the new work, which is why the four of us recently came together under the aegis of the American Psychological Society to review the scientific literature.

In the Eye of the Beholder

Gauging the value of self-esteem requires, first of all, a sensible way to measure it. Most investigators just ask people what they think of themselves. Naturally enough, the answers are often colored by the common tendency to want to make oneself look good. Unfortunately, psychologists lack good methods to judge self-esteem.

Consider, for instance, research on the relation between self-esteem and physical attractiveness. Several studies have generally found clear positive links when people rate themselves on both properties. It seems plausible that physically attractive people would end up with high self-esteem because they are treated more favorably than unattractive ones—being more popular, more sought after, more valued by lovers and friends, and so forth. But it could just as well be that those who score highly on self-esteem scales by claiming to be wonderful people all around also boast of being physically attractive.

In 1995 Edward F. Diener and Brian Wolsic of the University of Illinois and Frank Fujita of Indiana University South Bend examined this possibility. They obtained self-esteem scores from a broad sample of the population and then photographed everybody, presenting these pictures to a panel of judges, who evaluated the subjects for attractiveness. Ratings based on full-length photographs showed no significant correlation with self-esteem. When the judges were shown pictures of just the participants' unadorned faces, the correlation between attractiveness and self-esteem was once again zero. In that same investigation, however, self-reported physical attractiveness was found to have a strong correlation with self-esteem. Clearly, those with high self-esteem are gorgeous in their own eyes but not necessarily to others.

This discrepancy should be sobering. What seemed at first to be a strong link between physical good looks and high self-esteem turned out to be nothing more than a pattern of consistency in how favorably people rate themselves. A parallel phenomenon affects those with low self-esteem, who are prone to floccinaucinihilipilification, a highfalutin word (among the longest in the Oxford English Dictionary) but one that we can't resist using here, it being defined as "the action or habit of estimating as worthless." That is, people with low self-esteem are not merely down on themselves; they are negative about everything.

This tendency has certainly distorted some assessments. For example, psychologists once thought that people with low self-esteem were especially prejudiced. But thoughtful scholars, such as Jennifer Crocker of the University of Michigan at Ann Arbor, questioned this conclusion. After all, if people rate themselves negatively, it is hard to label them as prejudiced for rating people not like themselves similarly. When one uses the difference between the subjects' assessments of their own group and their ratings of other groups as the yardstick for bias, the findings are reversed: people with *high* self-esteem appear to be more prejudiced. Floccinaucinihilipilification also raises the danger that those who describe themselves disparagingly may describe their lives similarly, thus furnishing the appearance that low self-esteem has unpleasant outcomes.

Given the often misleading nature of self-reports, we set up our review to emphasize objective measures wherever possible—a requirement that greatly reduced the number of relevant studies (from more than 15,000 to about 200). We were also mindful to avoid another fallacy: the assumption that a correlation between self-esteem and some desired behavior establishes causality. Indeed, the question of causality goes to the heart of the debate. If high self-esteem brings about certain positive outcomes, it may well be worth the effort and expense of trying to instill this feeling. But if the correlations mean simply that a positive self-image is a result of success or good behavior—which is certainly plausible—there is little to be gained by raising self-esteem alone. We began our two-year effort by reviewing studies relating self-esteem to academic performance.

School Daze

At the outset, we had every reason to hope that boosting self-esteem would be a potent tool for helping students. Logic suggests that having a good dollop of self-esteem would enhance striving and persistence in school, while making a student less likely to succumb to paralyzing feelings of incompetence or self-doubt. Modern studies have, however, cast doubt on the idea that higher self-esteem actually induces students to do better.

Such inferences about causality are possible when the subjects are examined at two different times, as was the case in 1986 when Sheila M. Pottebaum and her colleagues at the University of Iowa, tested more than 23,000 high school students, first in the 10th and again in the 12th grade. They found that self-esteem in 10th grade is only weakly predictive of academic achievement in 12th grade. Academic achievement in 10th grade correlates with self-esteem in 12th grade only trivially better. Such results, which are now available from multiple studies, certainly do not indicate that raising self-esteem offers students much benefit. Some findings even suggest that artificially boosting self-esteem may lower subsequent performance.

Even if raising self-esteem does not foster academic progress, might it serve some purpose later, say, on the job? Apparently not. Studies of possible links between workers' self-regard and job performance echo what has been found with schoolwork: the simple search for correlations yields some suggestive results, but these do not show whether a good self-image leads to occupational success, or vice versa. In any case, the link is not particularly strong.

The failure to contribute significantly at school or at the office would be easily offset if a heightened sense of self-worth helped someone to get along better with others. Having a good self-image might make someone more likable insofar as people prefer to associate with confident, positive individuals and generally avoid those who suffer from self-doubts and insecurities.

People who regard themselves highly generally state that they are popular and rate their friendships as being of superior quality to those described by people with low self-esteem, who report more negative interactions and less social support. But as Julia Bishop and Heidi M. Inderbitzen-Nolan of the University of Nebraska–Lincoln showed in 1995, these assertions do not reflect reality.

The investigators asked 542 ninth-grade students to nominate their most-liked and least-liked peers, and the resulting rankings displayed no correlation whatsoever with self-esteem scores.

A few other methodologically sound studies have found that the same is true for adults. In one of these investigations, conducted in the late 1980s, Duane P. Buhrmester, now at the University of Texas at Dallas, and three colleagues reported that college students with high levels of self-regard claimed to be substantially better at initiating relationships, disclosing things about themselves, asserting themselves in response to objectionable behaviors by others, providing emotional support and even managing interpersonal conflicts. Their roommates' ratings, however, told a different story. For four of the five interpersonal skills surveyed, the correlation with self-esteem dropped to near zero. The only one that remained statistically significant was with the subjects' ability to initiate new social contacts and friendships. This does seem to be one sphere in which confidence indeed matters: people who think that they are desirable and attractive should be adept at striking up conversations with strangers, whereas those with low self-esteem presumably shy away from initiating such contacts, fearing rejection.

One can imagine that such differences might influence a person's love life, too. In 2002 Sandra L. Murray of the University at Buffalo found that people low in self-esteem tend to distrust their partners' expressions of love and support, acting as though they are constantly expecting rejection. Thus far, however, investigators have not produced evidence that such relationships are especially prone to dissolve. In fact, high self-esteem may be the bigger threat: as Caryl E. Rusbult of the University of Kentucky showed back in 1987, those who think highly of themselves are more likely than others to respond to problems by severing relations and seeking other partners.

Sex, Drugs, Rock 'n' Roll

How about teenagers? How does self-esteem, or the lack thereof, influence their love life, in particular their sexual activity? Investigators have examined this subject extensively. All in all, the results do not support the idea that low self-esteem predisposes young people to more or earlier sexual activity. If anything, those with high self-esteem are less inhibited, more willing to disregard risks and more prone to engage in sex. At the same time, bad sexual experiences and unwanted pregnancies appear to lower self-esteem.

If not sex, then how about alcohol or illicit drugs? Abuse of these substances is one of the most worrisome behaviors among young people, and many psychologists once believed that boosting self-esteem would prevent such problems. The thought was that people with low self-esteem turn to drinking or drugs for solace. The data, however, do not consistently show that low adolescent self-esteem causes or even correlates with the abuse of alcohol or other drugs. In particular, in a large-scale study in 2000, Rob McGee and Sheila M. Williams of the Dunedin School of Medicine at the University of Otago in New Zealand found no correlation between self-esteem measured between ages nine and 13 and drinking or drug use at age 15. Even when findings do show links between alcohol use and self-esteem, they are mixed and inconclusive. We did find, however, some evidence that low self-esteem contributes to illicit drug use. In particular, Judy A. Andrews and Susan C. Duncan of the Oregon Research Institute found in 1997 that declining levels of academic motivation (the main focus of their study) caused self-esteem to drop, which in turn led to marijuana use, although the connection was weak.

Interpretation of the findings on drinking and drug abuse is probably complicated by the fact that some people approach the experience out of curiosity or thrill seeking, whereas others may use it to cope with or escape from chronic unhappiness. The overall result is that no categorical statements can be made. The same is true for tobacco use, where our study-by-study review uncovered a preponderance of results that show no influence. The few positive findings we unearthed could conceivably reflect nothing more than self-report bias.

Another complication that also clouds these studies is that the category of people with high self-esteem contains individuals whose self-opinions differ in important ways. Yet in most analyses, people with a healthy sense of self-respect are, for example, lumped with those feigning higher self-esteem than they really feel or who are narcissistic. Not surprisingly, the results of such investigations may produce weak or contradictory findings.

Bully for You

For decades, psychologists believed that low self-esteem was an important cause of aggression. One of us (Baumeister) challenged that notion in 1996, when he reviewed assorted studies and concluded that perpetrators of aggression generally hold favorable and perhaps even inflated views of themselves.

Take the bullying that goes on among children, a common form of aggression. Dan Olweus of the University of Bergen was one of the first to dispute the notion that under their tough exteriors, bullies suffer from insecurities and self-doubts. Although Olweus did not measure self-esteem directly, he showed that bullies reported less anxiety and were more sure of themselves than other children. Apparently the same applies to violent adults.

After coming to the conclusion that high self-esteem does not lessen a tendency toward violence, that it does not deter adolescents from turning to alcohol, tobacco, drugs and sex, and that it fails to improve academic or job performance, we got a boost when we looked into how self-esteem relates to happiness. The consistent finding is that people with high self-esteem are significantly happier than others. They are also less likely to be depressed.

One especially compelling study was published in 1995, after Diener and his daughter Marissa, now a psychologist at the University of Utah, surveyed more than 13,000 college students, and high self-esteem emerged as the strongest factor in overall life satisfaction. In 2004 Sonja Lyubomirsky, Christopher Tkach and M. Robin DiMatteo of the University of California, Riverside, reported data from more than 600 adults ranging in age from 51 to 95. Once again, happiness and self-esteem proved to be closely tied. Before it is safe to conclude that high self-esteem leads to happiness, however, further research must address the shortcomings of the work that has been done so far.

First, causation needs to be established. It seems possible that high self-esteem brings about happiness, but no research has shown this outcome. The strong correlation between self-esteem and happiness is just that—a correlation. It is plausible that occupational, academic or interpersonal successes cause both happiness and high self-esteem and that corresponding failures cause both unhappiness and low self-esteem. It is even possible that happiness, in the sense of a temperament or disposition to feel good, induces high self-esteem.

Second, it must be recognized that happiness (and its opposite, depression) has been studied mainly by means of self-report, and the tendency of some people toward negativity may produce both their low opinions of themselves and unfavorable evaluations of other aspects of life. Yet it is not clear what could replace such assessments. An investigator would indeed be hard-pressed to demonstrate convincingly that a person was less (or more) happy than he or she supposed. Clearly, objective measures of happiness and depression are going to be difficult if not impossible to obtain, but that does not mean self-reports should be accepted uncritically.

What then should we do? Should parents, teachers and therapists seek to boost self-esteem wherever possible? In the course of our literature review, we found some indications that self-esteem is a helpful attribute. It improves persistence in the face of failure. And individuals with high self-esteem sometimes perform better in groups than do those with low self-esteem. Also, a poor self-image is a risk factor for certain eating disorders, especially bulimia—a connection one of us (Vohs) and her colleagues documented in 1999. Other effects are harder to demonstrate with objective evidence, although we are inclined to accept the subjective evidence that self-esteem goes hand in hand with happiness.

So we can certainly understand how an injection of self-esteem might be valuable to the individual. But imagine if a heightened sense of self-worth prompted some people to demand preferential treatment or to exploit their fellows. Such tendencies would entail considerable social costs. And we have found little to indicate that indiscriminately promoting self-esteem in today's children or adults, just for being themselves, offers society any compensatory benefits beyond the seductive pleasure it brings to those engaged in the exercise.

CHALLENGE QUESTIONS

Does Low Self-Esteem Lead to Antisocial Behavior?

1. Why do you think there is so much focus on the self in contemporary psychology? What alternatives to this emphasis on the self can you think of?
2. Is there a difference between high self-esteem and narcissism? What is the difference, and how can we distinguish between the two?
3. How does self-esteem influence your own behavior? Are you more prone to act in a negative way when you are feeling really good or really bad about yourself?
4. Why is it that correlational evidence cannot specify causal conclusions, and why does this distinction have practical significance in the case of self-esteem?
5. Baumeister and his colleagues claim that self-esteem is difficult to operationalize. Why might they make this claim, and how should this difficulty, if true, affect our interpretation of self-esteem research?

Internet References . . .

PrescribingPsychologist.com

PrescribingPsychologist.com provides information and links regarding the prescription privilege debate.

http://www.prescribingpsychologist.com

Psychotherapy Links

This directory of psychotherapy websites is sponsored by the University of Western Ontario Department of Psychiatry.

http://www.aboutpsychotherapy.com/

Association for Gay, Lesbian, and Bisexual Issues in Counseling

This is the website of the Association for Gay, Lesbian, and Bisexual Issues in Counseling, a division of the American Counseling Association that works toward educating mental health service providers about issues faced by gay, lesbian, bisexual, and transgendered individuals.

http://www.aglbic.org

Psychological Treatment

*P*sychologists have a long history of formulating and testing treatments for psychological, emotional, and social ills. Unfortunately, drugs are increasingly being used to treat traditionally psychological disorders, and most psychologists are not permitted to prescribe drugs. Should psychologists, given the proper training, be allowed to prescribe drugs related to mental disorders? Many psychologists feel that the move to gain prescription privileges fundamentally changes the nature of psychology. Others believe that psychology must change in accord with the most effective treatments. Otherwise, psychology will die. What about treating something that is not currently considered a psychological illness or disorder? Many psychologists argue that homosexuality is not an illness, so there is no need to treat or change it. Indeed, homosexuality is not included in the classification of mental illness in the DSM-IV. Yet other psychologists insist that some homosexuals desire a change. If such a change is possible, should psychologists attempt to accommodate these desires? Who decides what should be changed in psychological treatment?

- Should Psychologists Be Able to Prescribe Drugs?
- Is Treating Homosexuality Ethical?

ISSUE 15

Should Psychologists Be Able to Prescribe Drugs?

YES: Patrick H. DeLeon and Debra Lina Dunivin, from "The Tide Rises," *Clinical Psychology: Science and Practice* (Fall 2002)

NO: William N. Robiner et al., from "Prescriptive Authority for Psychologists: A Looming Health Hazard?" *Clinical Psychology: Science and Practice* (Fall 2002)

ISSUE SUMMARY

YES: Psychologists Patrick H. DeLeon and Debra Lina Dunivin assert that granting prescription authority to psychologists will improve the quality of psychological care because they will be able to treat a patient's mind and body.

NO: Psychologist William Robiner and his colleagues object to the idea of giving psychologists prescription privileges because psychologists do not receive the same rigorous medical training as those who can prescribe medicine.

While medication has long been a primary treatment for physical health, it has quickly become a primary treatment for mental health as well. One difficulty is that medication for mental disorders cannot currently be prescribed by the traditional experts on mental health—psychologists. The privilege of writing prescriptions has traditionally been assigned solely to medical personnel. Should psychologists be able to prescribe medication as well? Some see definitive benefits while others see blatant dangers.

A legitimate concern of those who oppose such privileges is that psychologists do not have the necessary training in physiology and chemistry to competently prescribe medication to patients. Those who advocate prescription privileges for psychologists have attempted to address this concern by requiring extensive training for those who would like to prescribe medication. Many, however, in the medical establishment argue that psychologists are overstepping their bounds. Interestingly, this argument is not unique to medical professionals. Many psychologists themselves are opposed to the prescription movement.

As proponents of the prescription movement, psychologists Patrick H. DeLeon and Debra Line Dunivin strongly believe that granting psychologists prescription authority will benefit society. They argue that many controversial issues in psychology have met with initial resistance only to be widely accepted with time. They attempt to show that the issue of prescription privileges, though not part of psychology's tradition, will nevertheless become an obvious and necessary part of psychological treatment. DeLeon and Dunivin are confident that knowledge of psychopharmacology will enhance a psychologist's ability to provide the highest possible quality of care. They support this assertion by describing several psychologists who have gone through the necessary training and are now functionally prescribing medications.

Psychologist William Robiner and his colleagues disagree with the prescription movement even though Robiner himself is a psychologist. They express concern about the fact that most psychologists lack the broad medical training required of those who are given prescription privileges. Because medical personnel are more familiar with anatomy and physiology in general, Robiner and his colleagues argue that those with medical training are better suited to understand the effects of medication on the *entire* health of the person and not just on a patient's *mental* health. They further contend that patients will not be disadvantaged because psychiatrists and psychologists can easily collaborate and consult on the use of psychopharmacology in the psychologist's practice.

POINT

- Psychologist have a responsibility to society to provide high-quality health care. Not having prescription privileges limits their ability to do so.

- The U.S. Department of Defense showed that psychologists can be successfully trained to prescribe medication.

- Psychology is a growing profession that should not be afraid to modify itself when the modification benefits clients.

- Objective studies have shown that nonphysicians can safely utilize medicine.

COUNTERPOINT

- Psychologists and psychiatrists can work together to make sure that a psychologist's patients are receiving the most comprehensive care available.

- The results of the Department of Defense study cannot be generalized because those involved in the study had received specialized treatment not available to most psychologists.

- Prescription authority will fundamentally alter the field of psychology—not just modify it.

- Specific studies need to be conducted on whether nonphysicians can safely use psychoactive drugs, an especially volatile type of medication.

YES

Patrick H. DeLeon and
Debra Lina Dunivin

The Tide Rises

... **W**e must admit that we have genuinely enjoyed watching the maturation of professional psychology's prescriptive authority (RxP-) agenda since U.S. Senator Daniel K. Inouye first raised this issue at the Hawaii Psychological Association annual meeting in November 1984. We say this because in our judgment, the essence of the RxP-movement is providing high quality health care to as many Americans as possible. Psychology is one of the learned professions and, as such, has a societal responsibility to provide proactive vision and programmatic leadership. Since the release of *Healthy People* by the Carter Administration, there has been steadily growing clinical and scientific evidence that the behavioral, environmental, and psychosocial (e.g., psychological) aspects of health care are absolutely critical on both an individual case basis and across populations. As we enter the twenty-first century, it is clear to us that our nation's health care system is embarking upon an era of unprecedented change: educated consumers, the extraordinary impact of technological advances, systemic reliance upon interdisciplinary health care, and growing institutional appreciation for objective (e.g., data-based) practice protocols. We are, of course, acutely aware that change in the status quo is always unsettling and that the specifics of change can never be predicted with any assurance of accuracy.

We maintain that the present prescription privileges movement parallels the professional school movement of 30 years ago. What was then a contentious issue within the profession has now become mainstream. What was then considered by its opponents as a misguided new direction has now become a valuable part of the profession. We fully expect that the same will become true for this new direction taken by proponents of prescriptive authority for psychologists. Other examples of this same phenomenon exist from the beginning of psychology as a discipline—expanding beyond scientific theory into clinical practice, for example, and branching from psychological assessment to psychotherapy. In this brief commentary, we take a closer look at the most recent of these phenomena: the professional school movement and the actual data that have accumulated when members of our profession have incorporated the practice of pharmacotherapy into psychological practice. Taken together, these make the conclusion inevitable. We must take into account the history of our profession, its tendency to grow and

From *Clinical Psychology: Science and Practice,* vol. 9, no. 3, Fall 2002, pp. 249–255. Copyright © 2002 by Oxford University Press Journals. Reprinted by permission.

develop in new directions, to incorporate new knowledge and skills into our professional practice, sometimes taking what seems at the time to be a dramatic shift, but always doing it with the highest standards. This is an essential component of what psychology is—a viable, growing profession that isn't afraid to change when it's good for us and the people we serve.

A Historical Perspective

If one reflects upon the history of professional psychology, it soon becomes evident that at every stage in the profession's maturation, psychologists and nonpsychologists expressed grave concern. This was true for the profession's initial efforts to independently diagnose and treat, to be reimbursed for providing clinical services, to administer mental health clinics, to obtain membership on hospital medical staff, and so on. Those who opposed these expansions in psychology's scope of practice frequently expressed the view that these functions were solely reserved for graduates of another profession (i.e., they were medicine's turf). If one wanted to provide care within a hospital ward or be the administrator of a clinic, one should first go to medical school.

Since the establishment of the Task Force on Psychopharmacology by the APA Council of Representatives at the Boston convention, by the overwhelming vote of 118 to 2, in August 1990, the underlying policy issue of psychology prescribing has been thoroughly debated throughout the APA governance. At Council's August 1995 meeting in New York City, obtaining prescriptive privileges for appropriately trained psychologists became formal APA policy. The following year in Toronto, Council adopted a model prescription bill and a model training curriculum. To our knowledge, this is the only time in APA's history that the association's highest elected body (e.g., the Council of Representatives) had ever deemed it appropriate to endorse a particular clinical modality. Accordingly, we were not surprised when in 1997, the American Psychological Association of Graduate Students (APAGS) adopted a formal "resolution of support" for RxP-. It is their future that the RxP- agenda contemplates.

Although the discipline of psychology dates back to the founding of Wundt's laboratory in 1879, on September 21, 1970, classes began at the first independent professional school of psychology: the California School of Professional Psychological (CSPP). This was to become the era of the Doctor of Psychology degree (PsyD), the first program being launched in the Department of Psychology at the University of Illinois at Champaign-Urbana in 1968. There can be little disagreement that the paradigm shift from the traditional research-oriented PhD degree to the professional-oriented PsyD degree represented a fundamental change in psychology's self image and underlying mission, a change that will never be reversed. Today there are 48 accredited PsyD programs, most of which are within professional schools that graduate 58% of all clinical students.

Over the past several decades, professional psychology has done very well in advancing its legislative and administrative agendas. Psychology's clinicians are independently recognized under all federal and private health care (e.g., insurance) programs; psychological expertise is readily utilized throughout the judiciary; and individual psychologists have served at the highest levels of clinical and public policy responsibility. During the 107th Congress, for example, three psychologists were elected to serve in the U.S. House of Representatives. Today there are 155,000 members and affiliates of the American Psychological Association (APA), with APAGS possessing 59,700 members. These are very impressive numbers and they speak well for the future.

The Opposition

If one reflects on the arguments promulgated by those who have consistently opposed psychology obtaining prescriptive authority, they generally fall into several discrete categories. Within the profession, there is a somewhat vocal minority that, from our perspective, may also fundamentally disagree with the underlying tenets of the professional school movement. These are generally academic-based colleagues, housed within traditional social science and educational structures. Some train clinical psychologists. It would admittedly be very difficult for their programs to expand to include psychopharmacology, given the traditional academic pressures involved in allocating constrained teaching resources. The RxP-agenda began with the practitioner community (as, we would note, did the professional school movement). At times, the opposition's apparent lack of respect for those teaching and participating in postdoctoral psychopharmacology training modules seems puzzling at best. They seem to be asserting that psychology's graduates are incapable of learning new materials. Clearly this assertion that psychologists can't learn is contrary to the data: these professionals have spent over two decades in educational pursuit and obtained a least one advanced degree at the doctoral level. Certainly one must conclude that psychologists are not only capable of, but committed to, learning.

Another distinct category of opposition postulates the alleged "public health hazard" argument. These individuals seem to genuinely believe that when psychology's practitioners obtain prescriptive authority, they will affirmatively harm their patients. Over the years, variations on this fundamental theme have been emotionally employed by medical colleagues in efforts to protect their self-proclaimed turf. It has been interesting to observe over the years that organized medicine has used this scare tactic in their efforts to limit consumer access to dental surgery and chiropractic care. Most recently, the anaesthesiologists have questioned the clinical competence of certified nurse anaesthetists in the popular media; notwithstanding the excellent track record of nursing throughout rural American and within federal installations. These physician versus nonphysician battles have been well documented in numerous national health policy reports. Clinical pharmacists, nurse practitioners, optometrists, and podiatrists have had to overcome this scurrilous argument, as they have legislatively succeeded in obtaining prescriptive authority in the various state legislatures and federal agencies. Objective studies over the years demonstrating that nonphysicians (often with considerably less training than psychologists) can safely and cost-effectively utilize medications do not deter these opponents. Nor does the reality that countless psychologists, without any formal psychopharmacology training, have functionally prescribed without adverse consequences under a wide range of conditions.

Accountability to the Public

Traditionally, psychology's practicing clinicians are expected to live up to the standard of functioning within one's scope of competence and keeping up with scientific advances. In addition to this ethical requirement for competent practice, psychologists are also held accountable for competence by state statutes. Under our nation's form of elected constitutional government, it is the fundamental responsibility of the states to establish public agencies (e.g., licensing boards) to protect the public from incompetent or disreputable practitioners. Although there have been increasing calls for national licensure standards over the past several years, with some professions (e.g., professional nursing) rapidly moving toward that objective, within the profession of psychology this responsibility remains at the individual state level. We would remind the readership that within the federal and state systems, professional licensure is generally required, with the specific facility at which the practitioner is employed determining scope of practice issues (within broad agency guidelines). The facility also institutionally provides quality of care oversight, generally through an active peer review process. Similarly, over the years, our nation's educational institutions have established their own formal review procedures for authorizing the establishment of new courses and degrees. Ultimately, the institution's Board of Regents retains final responsibility.

This comprehensive regulatory framework possesses a long and honorable tradition, stretching back over hundreds of years of public disclosure and dialogue. There is every indication that society has been well served by this approach. Accordingly, the efforts of those opposing psychology obtaining prescriptive authority to "debate" the specifics of course content, public licensure board competency, and details of acceptable supervision are not central to this issue. The agencies involved have long demonstrated their competency to resolve these types of matters, changing requirements over time based on practical experiences, and are well-suited to continue in this capacity. One could even suggest that in some instances, the underlying tenor of some of the opponents' arguments are fundamentally anti-intellectual.

The Twenty-First Century

The twenty-first century will be an era of extraordinary reliance on objective, data-driven decision-making processes within the health care arena. Numerous health policy experts have commented on the extent to which, in their judgment, the health care segment of our economy has not yet institutionally incorporated information technological advances. The number of Americans who use the Internet to retrieve health-related information is estimated to be approximately 70–100 million. Currently over half of American homes possess computers, and while information presently doubles every 5 years, it will soon double every 17 days, with traffic on the Web already doubling every 100 days.

At the same time, from a public policy perspective, one can see the process evolving whereby those who are systematically exploring changing definitions of "Quality of Care" are increasingly raising fundamental questions about today's practices. The Institute of Medicine (IOM) was chartered in 1970 by the National Academy of Sciences, acting under the Academy's 1863 congressional charter responsibility to be an advisor to the federal government. The IOM serves as a highly respected health policy think tank for the Congress and various Administrations. In 1999, the IOM released a highly controversial report that found that each year, between 44,000 and 98,000 Americans died in hospitals as a result of medical errors. The report noted that medications are the most frequent medical intervention. Encouraging interdisciplinary collaboration, the report further described how merely by having clinical pharmacists participate during daily hospital rounds, the rate of preventable adverse drug events relating to prescribing decreased significantly (66%) within major teaching facilities. Another IOM report addressed the extent to which the current American health care system lags significantly behind other segments of the economy in utilizing advances in relevant technology and in ensuring that scientific advances are employed in a timely fashion. The American health care delivery system is in need of fundamental change. Americans should be able to count on receiving care that meets their needs and is based on the best scientific knowledge. Yet there is strong evidence that this frequently is not the case. The lag between the discovery of more efficacious forms of treatment and their incorporation into routine patient care is unnecessarily long, in the range of about 15 to 20 years. Even then, adherence of clinical practice to the evidence is highly uneven.

To suggest, as those who employ the fundamental "public health hazard" argument overtly do, that psychology's practitioners will affirmatively harm their patients by prescribing is to ignore not only the realities of today's health care system but also to ignore the data on prescribing psychologists, as discussed in the next section. We are confident that by providing doctoral level psychologists with targeted postdoctoral psychopharmacological training, a highly competent new breed of practitioner will evolve. These will be practitioners who will see their patients in a different (e.g., psychological and holistic) light and who have been extensively trained to value and utilize scientific principles and knowledge in their clinical practices.

Similarly, from an educational perspective, the underlying question should be: what didactic content (that might presently be taught by medicine, nursing, or pharmacy) would effectively complement the extensive psychological knowledge base our colleagues already possess? To draw a visual analogy, the first author's teenage daughter does not need an engineering or computer science degree to effectively utilize the most up-to-date computer software available off the shelf. She does not have to design and build her own computer in order to conduct highly advanced statistical analyses for her high school presentations. Competent educators *can* teach outstanding students; desktop computers *will* provide practitioners of all disciplines (and educated consumers) with helpful input, designed specifically for diagnostic symptom relief. The time has long passed for individual patients to be given a psychiatric diagnosis and placed on a medication for years at a time, without constant monitoring and exploration of a less invasive alternative treatment approach.

A Fundamental Public Health Approach

If one reflects on the psychological or public health literature published over the past decade, there is scarcely any specific subpopulation of patients for which a highly reputable source has not proclaimed that its members have been inappropriately medicated. This would include ethnic minority individuals, women, those with serious mental illnesses, those residing in rural America, the elderly, and those residing in long-term care facilities and nursing homes. During the first author's presidency, the APA actively participated in several White House conferences regarding the alleged excessive reliance on medication by those licensed clinicians treating our nation's children. The critical key to effectively utilizing psychotropic medication is, and always has been, an accurate assessment and diagnosis and developing a therapeutic alliance. This has always been the strength of professional psychology.

Psychopharmacology Training Modules

Several different training models in psychopharmacology for psychologists have emerged around the country. Most of these training programs result in enhanced consultation between psychologists and their medical colleagues around the prescription of medications for their mutual patients. In the absence of state laws permitting prescribing of medications by psychologists, those trained in these postdoctoral programs have put their knowledge of psychopharmacology to use in collaborative practice. For some, participation in other training modules results in the practice of clinical psychopharmacology by virtue of another license, for example, prescribing as a nurse practitioner after completing a degree in advanced practice nursing. And participation in one of these programs, the Department of Defense (DoD) Psychopharmacology Demonstration Project (PDP), has resulted in the practice of pharmacotherapy by psychologists *as* psychologists.

In all cases, it is our collective judgment that participation in any one of these programs has resulted in an enhanced scope of clinical competence and practice whether or not that practice includes pharmacotherapy. The Department of Psychology at Eisenhower Army Medical Center (where the second author was stationed) conducted a customer satisfaction survey of all patients seen by her, during her first year after graduation from the DoD psychopharmacology training program. The results indicated "a high level of overall satisfaction with the services she provided. The most common answer to questions regarding satisfaction with Dr. Dunivin, desire to work with her in the future, and willingness to refer a friend to Dr. Dunivin is 'Strongly Agree.' The percentage of those who agree or strongly agree on these three areas are 94%, 88%, and 86%, respectively."

Although highly visible, the DoD program is not the only one of the training models in clinical psychopharmacology for psychologists that has emerged. Over the past several years, the first author has had the pleasure of serving as the commencement speaker for three separate university-based psychopharmacology postdoctoral training graduations. The graduates have been licensed clinicians (often rather senior) who have subsequently obtained specialized masters degrees, fulfilling the APA model didactic curriculum through special executive track programs targeted toward full-time clinicians. Although clearly considered highly competent professionals by their peers prior to enrolling in the psychopharmacology training, the graduates spoke profusely about how this additional knowledge had subsequently enhanced their clinical skills. They were outstanding clinicians. Now they had become even better with a value-added component. They now tend to gravitate toward different types of patients and to engage in more extensive collaborative practices with relevant medical specialists. Simply stated, they are a new breed of clinicians and still clearly psychologists. Their enthusiasm and successes have become the catalyst for additional training modules (some Web based) to flourish.

The Data on Prescribing Psychologists

A substantial body of data has emerged during the past decade about the practice of pharmacotherapy by psychologists. The conclusions drawn from this data are unequivocal: appropriately trained psychologists can and do provide excellent, high quality psychopharmacological care to their patients. There are dozens of anecdotal reports of psychologists prescribing medications in military and public health service facilities. However, the most extensively evaluated practice of pharmacotherapy by psychologists has occurred within the DoD Psychopharmacology Demonstration Project (PDP). The first two psychopharmacology Fellow psychologists graduated from this program on June 17, 1994, and a total of 10 psychologists have now graduated. Seven of the 10 graduates are still practicing pharmacotherapy within the military health care system. Collectively, they have treated thousands of patients with high quality care. Performance of the Fellows has been subjected to intense evaluation, not only within the military systems in which they worked but also by several outside evaluations over a 7-year period. However, RxP-opponents seem largely to ignore this data. It thus seems appropriate to remind the readership of these findings.

Each of the evaluation reports concluded that the DoD Fellows had been trained to safely and effectively prescribe psychotropic and adjunctive medications through the 2-year postdoctoral fellowship. The investigative arm of the Congress, the General Accounting Office (GAO), surveyed performance of each of the Fellows at their duty stations and concluded that the quality of care provided by them to their patients was well regarded by both their supervisors and other health care providers. The supervisors consistently rated their quality of care as "good to excellent" and had found no evidence of quality problems or adverse outcomes. The GAO further noted that nearly all of the physicians and others interviewed were convinced by the Fellows' performance that they were well trained and knowledgeable, despite the fact that some of the graduates had experienced early resistance at their work sites, particularly among military psychiatrists. The GAO specifically noted that "several physicians also told us that they came to rely on the graduates for information about psychotropic medications."

With respect to the clinical supervision of the Fellows by psychiatrists, the GAO reported: "Without exception, these supervisors—all psychiatrists— stated that the graduates' quality of care was good." Additionally, the report stated: "One supervisor, for example, noted that each of the graduate's patients had improved as a result of the graduate's treatment; another supervisor referred to the quality of care provided by the graduate as 'phenomenal'. The supervisors noted that the graduates are aware of their limitations. . . . Further, the supervisors noted that no adverse patient outcomes have been associated with the treatment provided by the graduates."

By far, the most comprehensive study of the DoD program was the ongoing evaluation performed by the American College of Neuropsychopharmacology, a well-respected professional association of clinical and basic science researchers from the fields of neurology, psychiatry, psychology, and pharmacology. Between 1991 and 1998, the ACNP was contracted to provide DoD with an independent assessment of the psychopharmacology training curriculum and to monitor the ongoing progress of the program's participants, during their fellowship and after graduation. The evaluation process included site visits several times each year; interviews of the participants, their clinical and administrative supervisors, as well as other health care providers; review of clinical records; and conducting written and oral examinations. Despite some early reservations about the feasibility of the project, the final report of the ACNP evaluation panel contained many positive findings, among them the observation that the graduates "filled critical needs, and performed with excellence wherever they served." The ACNP reported that eight of the ten graduates were serving as clinic chiefs or assistant chiefs, and noted that the graduates made valuable contributions to the continuing education of psychologists as well as physicians. As would be expected, the medical knowledge of the graduates was not judged to be comparable to that of psychiatrists; however, as we already noted, it was reported that no adverse effects were associated with the practices of the graduates. Furthermore, they were found to be "medically safe," again providing direct evidence contrary to the public health hazard argument against prescription privileges for appropriately trained psychologists.

Perhaps most important, in our opinion, is the conclusion of the ACNP that those participating in the DoD psychopharmacology program had maintained their professional identities as psychologists, that the program had not produced "mini-psychiatrists" or "psychiatrist-extenders," but rather "extended psychologists with a value added component prescriptive authority provides. They continued to function very much in the traditions of clinical psychology (psychometric tests, psychological therapies) but a body of knowledge and experience was added that extended their range of competence."

The ACNP concluded their executive summary of their final report with what must be considered a ringing endorsement:

> The PDP graduates have performed and are performing safely and effectively as prescribing psychologists. Without commenting on the social, economic, and political issues of whether a program such as the PDP should be continued or expanded, it seems clear to the evaluation panel that a 2-year program—one year didactic, one year clinical practicum that includes at least a 6 month inpatient rotation—can transform licensed clinical psychologists into prescribing psychologists who can function effectively and safely in the military setting to expand the delivery of mental health treatment to a variety of patients and clients in a cost effective way. We have been impressed with the work of the graduates, their acceptance by psychiatrists (even while they may have disagreed with the concept of prescribing psychologists), and their contribution to the military readiness of the groups they have been assigned to serve. We have been impressed with the commitment and involvement of these prescribing psychologists to their role, their patients, and the military establishment. We are not clear about what functions the individuals can play in the future, but we are convinced that their present roles meet a unique, very professional need of the DoD. As such, we are in agreement that the Psychopharmacology Demonstration Project is a job well done.

Throughout the course of the DoD Psychopharmacology Fellowship training program, the participants provided regular updates at the APA annual conventions. What comes through in listening to their collective reflections is how differently they view their primary care patients. They approach their patients from a fundamentally psychological orientation, not from an illness-oriented model. They report that there is a real qualitative difference. Patient satisfaction and clinic administration confidence in the DoD Fellows remains high.

Final Comments

We would suggest from our public policy perspective that in the same manner that the establishment of the professional school movement in the 1970s has had a profound impact on all of psychology, the twenty-first century evolution toward prescriptive authority will have a similarly beneficial and monumental impact on the profession and our nation. To conclude otherwise is to ignore the data and professional psychology's history.

William N. Robiner et al.

Prescriptive Authority for Psychologists: A Looming Health Hazard?

Advances in neuroscience, the development of safer, efficacious drugs such as the SSRIs, and changing realities in health care economics are transforming the delivery of mental health services. As these unfold, and as the use of psychotropics increases (Pincus et al., 1998), psychologists' interest in obtaining prescriptive authority for psychotropic medication has also increased (Ax, Forbes, & Thompson, 1997; Brentar & McNamara, 1991a, 1991b; Burns, DeLeon, Chemtob, Welch, & Samuels, 1988; Cullen & Newman, 1997; DeLeon, Folen, Jennings, Wilkis, & Wright, 1991; DeLeon, Fox, & Graham, 1991; DeLeon & Wiggins, 1996; Fox, 1988; Sammons, 1994). In this article we address a range of issues related to prescriptive authority for psychologists, including training, accreditation, regulation, and other topics raised by proponents of the prescriptive agenda, and discuss our concerns about it. . . .

Department of Defense Psychopharmacology Project

The controversy surrounding psychologists' prescription privileges was heightened by the Department of Defense (DoD) Psychopharmacology Demonstration Project (PDP). The PDP ultimately trained ten psychologists to prescribe in military health care settings (U.S. General Accounting Office, 1999). The initial PDP participants undertook some preparation in chemistry and biochemistry before completing a majority of first-year medical school courses. During their first full-time year at the Uniformed Services University of the Health Sciences, they worked with the Psychiatry-Liaison service and assumed night call with second-year psychiatry residents. In the second full-time year, they completed core basic science courses and continued psychopharmacology training and clinical work. After 2-day written and oral examinations, they had a third year of supervised clinical work at Walter Reed Army Medical Center or Malcolm Grow Medical Center. The PDP curriculum underwent subsequent iterations, streamlining training to 1 year of coursework and a year of supervised clinical practice (Sammons & Brown, 1997; Sammons, Sexton, & Meredith, 1996). For example, the didactic hours decreased by 48% in the second iteration. Most PDP graduates have functioned as prescribing psychologists in branches of the military. One graduate went on to medical school.

The PDP was discontinued after the first few years. Advocates of psychologist prescription privileges argue that the successes of the small sample of PDP participants justify extending prescriptive authority to other psychologists who undergo training consistent with the American Psychological Association (APA) (Council of Representatives [COR], 1996) model, even though that training model and the likely resources available for the training differ substantially from the PDP. It is not known how well the successes of the 10 PDP psychologists, who were trained within a military medical school and military hospital settings, and whose care was confined to a patient population largely screened for health and other factors, would generalize to the potentially thousands of psychologists who might wish to obtain psychopharmacology training and to practice independently across the spectrum of clinical or counseling settings with diverse populations (Bieliauskas, 1992a; Kennedy, 1998). If the clinical psychopharmacology training psychologists obtain elsewhere is less rigorous or is based on more limited access to medical populations than the PDP, the outcomes of the PDP potentially would overestimate outcomes of such training.

Additional skepticism seems warranted especially in light of the concerns about certain limitations of the PDP fellows' clinical proficiencies, such as in treating medically complex patients (Kennedy, 1998). The Final Report of the American College of Neuropsychopharmacology (1998) on the PDP assessed graduates as weaker medically and psychiatrically than psychiatrists. The report indicated that graduates only saw patients ages 18–65, some had limited formularies, and some continued to have dependent prescriptive practice (i.e., supervised by a physician). Moreover, the PDP graduates advised against "short-cut" programs and considered that a year of intensive full-time clinical experience, including inpatient care, was essential. Some of the program's psychiatrists, physicians, and graduates expressed doubts about the safety and effectiveness of psychologists prescribing independently outside of the interdisciplinary team of the military context. This latter concern has been echoed in a survey of military psychiatrists, nonpsychiatric physicians, and social workers (Klusman, 1998). Given the likelihood that other programs would lack some of the advantages of the PDP, and would provide less training than some of the PDP graduates received, we question how well the conditions of the PDP would be duplicated. Despite the positive experiences of PDP graduates, these concerns justify wariness about prescribing psychologists relative to other prescribers, especially for populations not included or emphasized in the PDP. We believe that more complete disclosure and consideration of the limitations and problems noted in the PDP are needed, both in the dialogue within the profession as well as in terms of public policy reviews of the prescriptive agenda. . . .

Quality of Care: The Central Concern about Psychologist Prescribing

Our primary concern is the risk of suboptimal care if psychologists undertake prescribing that could arise from their limited breadth and depth of knowledge about human physiology, medicine, and related areas. This risk would be compounded by psychologists' limited supervised physical clinical training experiences. Such knowledge and skills are fundamental to competent prescribing but have been limited or absent in training professional (i.e., clinical, counseling, school) psychologists. In one survey, more than two thirds of psychologists in independent practice described their training related to psychopharmacological issues as poor (APA, 1992b, p. 50). This is not surprising given the limited psychopharmacology training in doctoral programs and psychology internships (APA, 1992b).

Although advocates of prescription privileges readily acknowledge that additional training is needed to prepare psychologists to prescribe, the central questions are these. How much training is needed? Is it possible to attain adequate knowledge and skill through abbreviated training, such as proposed in models by the APA (CoR, 1996) or the California Psychological Association-California School of Professional Psychology Blue Ribbon Panel (1995)? How would psychologists who undergo the proposed training measure up to other prescribers? The concern is that abbreviated "crash courses" are inadequate to make up for psychologists' deficits in medical education (Bieliauskas, 1992a; Bütz, 1994).

At times, advocates for psychologist prescription privileges gloss over the complexity of knowledge sets inherent in competent prescribing (Kennedy, 1998; Kingsbury, 1992; Pies; 1991). For example, Patrick DeLeon, PhD, JD, Past President of the APA, contends that "prescription privileges is no big deal. It's like learning how to use a desk-top computer" (Roan, 1993). Related speculation that technological advances, such as computer-assisted learning (DeLeon & Wiggins, 1996), or prescriptive algorithms, could abbreviate the education necessary to prescribe competently strikes even proponents of prescription privileges as naïve (Pachman, 1996). Similarly, it seems unlikely that relying on more active roles of pharmacists or computerized systems for administration of drugs would compensate adequately for gaps in prescribers' medical knowledge. Ultimately, competence in prescribing demands adequate understanding not just of psychology and psychopharmacology but also of other domains of medical knowledge (e.g., human physiology, pathophysiology, biochemistry, clinical medicine) and clinical proficiencies (e.g., physical examination, interpretation of laboratory data) that historically have been excluded from the education and training of psychologists. More specifically, thorough understanding and proficiency related to two broad medical domains are required: understanding patients' medical status prior to and concurrent with prescribing and their medical status during and after treatment (i.e., their physiological responses to prescribed medications) (Pies, 1991; Robiner, 1999; see Table 1).

There are scant data regarding how well prepared psychologists are to prescribe. Anecdotally, psychologists' confidence in diagnosing patients and

Table 1

Knowledge Base and Clinical Proficiencies Required for Prescribing

Psychopathology and Psychological Issues	Medical Status Prior to Prescribing	Response to Treatments
Primary psychiatric conditions	Comorbid medical conditions	Knowledge of adverse reactions 1. Side effects 2. Toxic effects
Comorbid psychiatric conditions Prevalence and course of psychiatric conditions	Contraindications Medical effects of concurrent treatments 1. Drug interactions 2. Other treatments (e.g., dialysis, plasmaphoresis)	Ability to recognize, diagnose, and treat adverse reactions Ability to differentiate between physical and psychiatric effects of psychoactive agents and concurrent medications
Knowledge of nonpharmacologic treatment options	Long-term effects of medications History of medication use	Other issues related to monitoring, titrating, or discontinuing prescribed medications

Note: The education of psychologists typically addresses column 1, but neglects columns 2 and 3.

providing other types of psychological treatment, combined with limited psychopharmacology training and informal exposure to medications, may provide some sense that they have much of the knowledge related to prescribing. Thus far, however, little is known about how well the combination of doctoral training in psychology and relatively brief, focused training in psychopharmacology would develop psychologists' knowledge base and clinical proficiency for managing patients' medications, especially long-term and in diverse settings. Noteworthy differences exist between pharmacotherapy and current aspects of psychologists' clinical practice. As one psychologist turned psychiatrist observes:

> The effects of medications on the kidney, the heart, and so forth is important for the use of many medications. Managing these effects is often crucial and has more to do with biochemistry and physiology than with psychology. I was surprised to discover how little about medication use has to do with psychological principles and how much of it is just medical. (Kingsbury, 1992, p. 5)

Training for Prescribing

Proponents have construed prescriptive authority for psychologists as an "evolutionary" or "logical" step (DeLeon, Folen, et al., 1991; Fox, 1988) or even a "right" (Brentar & McNamara, 1991a) that is consistent with the trend in other health care disciplines towards broadened scopes of professional practice, including prescribing.

The first premise is debatable, especially given its fundamental departure from psychology's historic training paradigms and conceptualizations of psychopathology and intervention. The education and training for a doctoral degree in psychology largely neglects key topics relevant to prescribing (i.e., the biological and physical sciences, physical examination). Also, psychology historically has questioned, de-emphasized, or even eschewed the "medical model" (Matthews, 1998; May & Belsky, 1992). Pursuing prescriptive authority reflects a profound change in the direction toward embracing the medical model. Adding prescribing to psychology's scope of practice might more realistically be characterized as "revolutionary" or "radical," requiring major shifts in focus; marked expansions of training and continuing education in key areas; reformulation of accreditation criteria; modification of regulatory structure, domains, and processes; expanded ethical guidelines; and uniform requirements that at least part of psychologists' training occur within health care settings.

The second premise, that psychologists' scope of practice should broaden because some nonphysicians such as physician assistants (PAs) and advanced practice nurses (APNs) prescribe also is dubious. This seems to be based on the notion that the overall length of doctoral training that psychologists undergo might justify prescribing despite the limited relevance to prescribing of much of their actual training. Disparities in training between psychology and other professions with prescriptive authority challenge the notion that those professions' scopes of practice justify expanding psychologists' scope of practice to incorporate prescription privileges. Other professions' training models are much closer to that of physicians than to that of psychologists, and their clinical practice is more focused on physical functioning, including medication effects. Comparing the boundaries of other professions' scope of practice with psychology's is inappropriate given the differences in training between those other disciplines and psychology. . . .

The comparisons that advocates draw between psychology's and other disciplines' scope of practice compel closer inspection of the entry requirements and training models for psychology and other prescribing disciplines (McCabe & Grover, 1999). As outlined below, the differences in emphasis and structure are noteworthy. Since prescribing psychologists would probably be compared most closely with psychiatrists, our emphasis is on these two groups.

Undergraduate Training

The APA task force (Smyer et al., 1993) noted that other health professions (e.g., nursing, allied health professions) require undergraduate preparation in anatomy, biology, inorganic and organic chemistry, pharmacology, human physiology, (and some require physics); undergraduate psychology degrees and admission to psychology graduate school do not. The biological sciences and related course work is the educational foundation for knowledge and conceptual understanding related to prescribing safely. Hence, the APA task force envisioned that students with strong undergraduate, postbaccalaureate, or early graduate biological backgrounds would be admitted to psychopharmacology training (Smyer et al., 1993). The problem is that such backgrounds are rare. A survey of psychology graduate students revealed that only 27% thought they had the undergraduate preparation to undertake training to prescribe (Tatman et al., 1997). Only 7% had completed the recommended undergraduate biology and chemistry prerequisites (APA, 1992b; Smyer et al., 1993). Robiner et al. (2001) found that psychologists generally had taken fewer than five courses in the biological and physical sciences during their undergraduate and graduate education. . . .

Unlike medical school applicants and medical students, whose mastery of these areas is reflected through a competitive selection process (e.g., based on grades in biological and physical science courses, MCAT scores) and screened again in objective measures (i.e., national board scores such as steps one, two, and three of the United States Medical Licensing Examination [USMLE]; specialty board examinations following residency), entry into proposed psychopharmacology training programs for psychologists would not require standardized, objective indices of applicants' understanding of the biological and physical sciences. It is not known whether competitive performance in biological and physical science courses with laboratory prerequisites would play any role in determining eligibility for psychologists' psychopharmacology training. In summary, the discrepancies between physicians' and psychologists' education in the biological and physical sciences, and objective mechanisms verifying that general scientific knowledge has been acquired (i.e., psychology has none), begin at the undergraduate level.

The APA College of Professional Psychology in conjunction with Professional Examination Services developed an examination for psychologists who have undergone training in clinical psychopharmacology, the Psychopharmacology Examination for Psychologists (PEP). Other groups have developed other tests (e.g., Veritas Assessment Systems). Within the APA (1996) model, psychologists seeking prescription privileges would be expected to pass one of these written tests. Such testing is an important safeguard, but may be limited, especially in an era when commercial courses have been designed to prepare individuals for tests. Whereas proponents would argue that passage of that examination demonstrates adequate knowledge for prescribing, it seems questionable that a single 3-hour, 150-item test on psychopharmacology could assure adequate knowledge of the broad spectrum of medical issues beyond clinical psychopharmacology per se that are relevant to prescribing safely or knowledge and clinical skill sets comparable to that of other prescribers (e.g., physicians, nurse practitioners).

Graduate Training

Educational discrepancies between psychologists and physicians widen at the graduate level. The training of physicians and other doctoral providers (e.g., dentists) entails coursework in anatomy, biochemistry, cell biology, immunology, microbiology, pathology, pharmacology, physiology, as well as laboratory experiences in the biological and physical sciences and physical, clinical training. Doctoral-level psychology education never has (see APA Office of Program Consultation and Accreditation, 1996). Rather, graduate education in psychology has been characterized as comprising "vastly differing models of study and practice" with "no effort to standardize the training of psychologists" (Klein, 1996). Programs vary in how much training is provided in the biological and physical sciences (Sammons et al., 1996), but it is generally quite limited for degrees in professional psychology. Some types of psychology degrees, (e.g., school psychology) have relatively limited exposure to psychopathology and psychological treatments, let alone the physical sciences (DeMers, 1994; Moyer, 1995) or medical environments. . . .

Surveys suggest that only 25% of psychology graduate students had courses in psychopharmacology (Tatman et al., 1997) and 36% of licensed psychologists indicated that their graduate programs offered psychopharmacology courses (Ferguson, 1997). Presumably fewer had courses in pharmacology or pathophysiology, which are intrinsic to prescribing safely (i.e., due to potential interactions and adverse effects). These limitations are of greater concern than the limitations identified in medical students' psychiatric training (Zimmerman & Wienckowski, 1991) or estimates that medical school students receive only approximately 100 hours of pharmacology instruction (Association for Medical School Pharmacology [1990] cited by the APA Task Force [APA, 1992b]); physicians' other didactics are relevant to prescribing and their lengthy supervised training across a continuum of settings and supervisors includes wide exposure to related topics and patient populations.

By the time psychologists obtain doctorates, most have obtained relatively little training that overlaps with that of physicians or other prescribers. Moreover, there are no objective quality assurance processes to ensure that the biological and physical sciences are well understood by entrants to psychology graduate school or by entrants to proposed postdoctoral psychopharmacology training programs. Even the Examination for the Professional Practice of Psychology (EPPP), the written test required for licensure in psychology, minimally queries knowledge of the biological and physical sciences (e.g., biochemistry) (Association of State and Provincial Psychology Boards, 2000).

Proposed Postdoctoral Level Psychopharmacology Training

. . . The APA (CoR, 1996) emphasizes that the proposed training is "unique to the needs of the practicing psychologist, and does not simply follow traditional medical practices." We question whether such condensed training overcomes current shortcomings to achieve knowledge and clinical proficiency equivalent to that of other prescribers, especially psychiatrists, and ensure competent prescribing that the public should reasonably expect of its doctors. Furthermore, it seems incumbent upon proponents of the prescriptive agenda to fully inform legislators and the public precisely how the psychopharmacology training proposed by the APA differs from "traditional medical practices." . . .

Proponents of prescription privileges recognize that the supervised practice in proposed psychopharmacology training "essential for effective, safe, ethical and practical incorporation of drugs into a psychological practice . . . is a substantive matter" (Fox et al., 1992, p. 218). Curiously, despite recognition of this substantiveness, the scope and requirements for supervised pharmacotherapeutic practice are not fully delineated in the APA model, so it is not possible to evaluate how adequate the supervised practice would be. Consistent with the APA model, training programs are designed for trainees to see a series of patients (e.g., ≥ 100) for psychopharmacologic management. The APA model fails to specify minimal criteria for (a) the breadth of patients' mental health conditions; (b) the duration of treatment (i.e., to allow for adequate monitoring and feedback) or requirements for outpatient or inpatient experiences; (c) exposure to adverse medication effects; or (d) exposure to patients with comorbid medical conditions and complex drug regimens. Also, the qualifications for supervisors are vague. Whereas the CPA-CSPP Panel (1995) recommended an 18-month practicum, the APA model does not specify any length. That the didactic and practical training would be abbreviated relative to the PDP, and less likely to occur in organized, academic health care settings with lengthy track records of providing medical or psychiatric training, raises questions about how comparable such programs would be to the PDP.

We doubt that the proposed models of training in psychopharmacology for psychologists (APA, 1996; CPA/CSPP, 1995; Fox et al., 1992) would prepare them to provide care equivalent to that provided by psychiatrists or other health professionals. Not only would they obtain less didactics in relevant areas, but the supervised pharmacologic care of patients would be considerably less comprehensive and less well organized than training within psychiatric residencies. . . .

Regulatory and Legal Issues

. . . A number of legal issues also would arise if psychologists were granted prescriptive authority. This includes the level of independence versus dependence of this authority, potential restrictions on their prescriptive practices (e.g., limited formulary and duration of treatment; specific settings), and the most appropriate standard of care to which psychologists would be held. Would psychologists be compared with other "reasonably prudent" psychologists who have undergone the proposed psychopharmacology training, or with other prescribers, such as psychiatrists, who have greater training and experience related to medication management and who have set the standard for prescribing psychoactive medications thus far? From the consumer's perspective, it seems likely that a standard of care closer to that provided by psychiatrists would promote accountability and afford greater protections and legal remedies than an unknown, less stringent, evolving standard based on psychologists who might gain prescriptive authority based on training that is less intensive than that of other prescribers. In addition, formulation of ethical guidelines relevant to prescribing, which are beyond the current APA (1992a) Ethical Principles of Psychologists and Code of Conduct, would be needed (Buelow & Chafetz, 1996) to address a range of ethical challenges associated with prescribing (Heiby, 1998).

Proponents' Focus on Peripheral Issues

In essentially waging a campaign for prescriptive authority, proponents tend to focus on certain provocative issues to promote their cause and divert attention away from the inadequacies in psychologists' education, knowledge, and skills in areas critical to prescribing. For example, DeLeon and Wiggins (1996) decry problems of current prescribers as if psychologists (who would have less extensive physical science backgrounds and more limited supervised prescriptive practical training) would avoid developing problematic patterns if they prescribe. Alternative strategies, such as enhancing the ability of current prescribers through such means as education and redesign of prescribing systems (Lesar, Briceland, & Stein, 1997), or enhancing psychologists' collaborative practices, as proposed in the APA task force's (Smyer et al., 1993) Level 2 training, might address such problems without requiring that psychologists prescribe.

Similarly, underserved populations (e.g., rural populations, the seriously and persistently mentally ill [SPMI], the elderly) have been invoked to frame prescriptive authority as a policy response to meet pressing societal needs (DeLeon, Sammons, & Sexton, 1995; Hanson et al., 1999). This line of reasoning is flawed in failing to consider the similar access patterns to psychologists and psychiatrists across the urban-rural continuum (Hendryx, Borders, & Johnson, 1995; Holzer, Goldsmith, & Ciarlo, 1998) and the APA task force's expectation that only "a small . . . minority of psychologists" (APA, 1992b, p. 106) would seek Level 3 psychopharmacology training. Such data and predictions, along with the virtual absence of any concrete plan to redistribute prescribing psychologists to meet the actual needs of underserved populations (May & Belsky, 1992), render broadening psychologists' scope of practice to include prescriptive authority an indirect, needlessly risky, and highly inefficient public policy response to rural areas' shortage of psychopharmacologic prescribers. . . .

Ultimately, there is little reason to assume that psychologists with prescriptive authority actually would relocate to areas lacking other prescribers, or would focus their practices to address the needs of other types of underserved populations (Adams & Bieliauskas, 1994; Bieliauskas, 1992a, 1992b). Even some proponents of prescriptive privileges concede that psychologists may not be more inclined than psychiatrists to work with underserved groups (Hanson et al., 1999).

Attempts to garner support for the prescriptive agenda on the basis of underserved populations also ignores efforts by the American Psychiatric Association to enhance psychiatric consultation to primary care providers ("APA board takes action," 1998) and the potential benefits of expanded use of telehealth technology to supplement the expertise of primary care practitioners in areas underserved by psychiatrists. Similarly, it ignores data that psychiatrists see significantly more SPMI and socially disadvantaged patients than do psychologists (Olfson & Pincus, 1996), which brings into question whether prescriptive authority would have a major impact in expanding care to SPMI populations. Pursuing prescriptive authority may distract focus from important opportunities for psychologists to improve their collaborations with primary care providers to collectively address needs as suggested by groups such as the National Depressive and Manic-Depressive Association (Hirschfeld et al., 1977) or the National Alliance for the Mentally Ill (NAMI). . . .

Another rationale of proponents of prescription privileges is that many mental health services, including prescriptions of psychotropic medications, are provided by nonpsychiatric physicians who have little psychiatric training (DeLeon & Wiggins, 1996). Indeed, the general medical sector is an essential component of the mental health system, serving an estimated 40–50% of people with mental disorders according to the utilization data of the Epidemiologic Catchment Area (ECA) study (Narrow, Regier, Rae, Manderscheid, & Locke, 1993). Similarly, data from the National Ambulatory Medicare Care Survey (NAMCS) reveal that outpatient appointments with primary care physicians and medical specialists account respectively for 48% and 19% of all appointments involving psychoactive prescription drugs: More than the appointments with psychiatrists (33%) (Pincus et al., 1998). General physicians provide somewhat more of the nation's outpatient mental health services (35%) than either psychologists (31%) or psychiatrists (27%) (Olfson & Pincus, 1996).

According to DeLeon and Wiggins (1996), an estimated 135.8 million prescriptions for psychoactive medications were written in 1991, of which only 17.3% were by psychiatrists. Such statistics, albeit interesting, do *not* indicate how many of these physician interactions for prescriptions are enhanced by consultations involving psychiatrists, psychologists, or other mental health professionals, or how many truly need mental health consultation. There are no benchmarks for how many prescriptions nonpsychiatric physicians should write or what percentage of them ought to be informed by collaborations with mental health professionals. It is possible that the large number of prescriptions written by nonpsychiatric physicians reflect that consultation with mental health professionals may be necessary only for subgroups of patients, or that adequate consultation already occurs related to many patients who might need medication. Moreover, despite focus on such patterns (DeLeon & Wiggins, 1996), the numbers neither reveal anything about problematic patterns of prescribing by physicians nor do they persuade that psychologists should prescribe. They probably do reflect several factors, such as (1) some people are more comfortable seeing their primary care physician than a mental health professional (Geller & Muus, 1997; Murstein & Fontaine, 1993), and (2) managed care organizations and capitated systems encourage primary care physicians to treat mental disorders rather than refer to specialist mental health professionals (Pincus et al., 1998). Such systems of health care delivery are similar to the service delivery models in other countries (e.g., Great Britain), where lower per capita rates of psychiatrists reflect psychiatrists' roles as specialist consultants to nonpsychiatric physicians who play primary roles in the psychopharmacological management of most patients' care (Scully, 1999).

The widespread prescription of psychoactive agents by nonpsychiatrist physicians reflects the significant opportunities for psychiatrists and psychologists (especially those with Level 2 training) to collaborate and consult about psychopharmacology. The data confirm the importance of continuing the ongoing efforts to enhance psychopharmacology training of nonpsychiatric physicians and other prescribers. Such trends do not, however, indicate a need or justification for psychologists to prescribe.

Medication Adverse Effects and Errors

Prescribers even of limited formularies necessarily assume some responsibility for the broader health status of their patients (Heiby, 1998; Kingsbury, 1992). Psychoactive medications have been described as presenting more complex drug interactions and adverse effects than any other class of drug (Hayes, 1998). Many people who take psychoactive medications also take other medications that complicate their care. Fewer than 30% who take an antidepressant take no other medications, so it is important to understand the comorbid conditions and other medications that patients concurrently experience (Preskorn, 1999). In primary care and psychiatric settings, more than 70% of patients prescribed an antidepressant take at least one other drug and a third take at least three other drugs (Preskorn, 1999). Polypharmacy rates are often higher with the elderly and medically ill, and in more specialized clinics (e.g., HIV). . . .

The timing of the intensification of psychologists' lobbying for prescriptive authority is ironic in light of growing national concern about errors in prescribing medication (Classen, Pestotnik, Evans, Lloyd, & Burke, 1997). Nationally, medication errors are estimated to lead to as many as 7,000 deaths annually (Phillips, Christenfeld, & Glynn, 1998). The Federal Drug Administration currently receives 235,000 reports per year about adverse drug events (Institute of Medicine Committee on Quality of Health Care in America, 1999). This could increase as medication options expand, requiring constant upgrades in knowledge of the entire pharmaceutical spectrum. In 1998, the FDA approved 90 new drugs, 30 new molecular entities, 124 new or expanded use of agents, and 344 generic drugs, not counting over the counter and orphan drugs (FDA, 1999). That nearly half of the drugs currently marketed have become available in the last decade (Shatin, Gardner, & Stergachis, 1999) suggests that the knowledge base for prescribing is becoming even more complex, requiring yet more extensive scientific understanding. Between 1970 and 1997, the annual number of publications on drug-drug interactions increased fivefold (Preskorn, 1999), reflecting factors such as increased use of medications for chronic conditions and an aging society with more medical problems and more complex medication regimens. Such trends underscore the need for strong basic education in medicine and pharmacology to prepare prescribers to understand medical conditions in integrating pharmacologic developments into their practice.

Among the many contributing factors to medication errors are *inadequate knowledge* and use of knowledge regarding drug therapy and *Inadequate recognition* of important patient factors (e.g., impaired renal function, drug allergies) (Lesar et al., 1997). The influence of other factors that require more sophisticated scientific understanding, such as genetic variation in drug metabolism and uptake, is increasingly likely to affect prescribing. Along with other recommendations, Lesar et al. (1997) recommended *improved prescriber education.* There have not been calls from outside of psychology to create a new category of prescribers with relatively *less* training (as psychologist prescribers would be).

Given the paucity of education and training directly related to prescribing throughout undergraduate and graduate training in psychology

(Robiner et al., 2001), the scant data about psychologists' proficiency in managing medications, which is limited to relatively few individuals, as well as inadequacies in psychologists' knowledge related to psychopharmacology (Robiner et al., 2001), we doubt that abbreviated psychopharmacology training for psychologists would be sufficient to ensure adequate competence in prescribing. Moreover, we are concerned that psychologists would lack the medical expertise to recognize, assess (e.g., all relevant hematological assays), and understand adverse effects and initiate proper medical care.

Short cuts in education seem likely to undermine patient care and contribute to medication errors along the patterns outlined by Lesar et al. (1997). Such training, especially if paired with independent prescriptive authority, risks generating a wave of suboptimal medication management and potentially avoidable adverse drug events. In addition to potentially hazardous consequences for patients, problems associated with psychologist prescribing would present regulatory conundrums, provide a new basis for litigation, and ultimately could detract from the public's esteem of psychologists in general.

Closing Considerations

We appreciate the important roles psychologists play within the delivery of health care broadly and mental health care in particular. Our findings and conclusions in no way belittle psychologists' knowledge or proficiencies in other areas. We agree with the APA task force (APA, 1992b) that it would be beneficial to promote psychologists' psychopharmacology knowledge so as to inform and enhance their collaborations with primary care providers and psychiatrists in providing care to patients who need medications. However, achieving the APA task force's goals for enhancing the care of patients needing medications does not require prescriptive authority for psychologists. Instead, we recommend that the APA refocus its energies to better educate psychologists about psychopharmacology to enhance the psychological services that psychologists provide and their collaborations with prescribers. This is a type of training that most psychology graduate students need and would welcome (Tatman et al., 1997). Also, survey data suggest that most (90%) licensed psychologists feel that psychologists should pursue a minimum of the collaborative practice level of training and most (79%) would be personally willing to pursue it (Ferguson, 1997). Moreover, most (85%) applied psychologists already consult regularly with physicians, so such training would enhance services that already are provided (Barkley, 1991).

Unfortunately, if psychologists prescribe, medically complex patients (e.g., older patients taking multiple medications) would probably be most vulnerable to the adverse consequences that potentially could derive from shortcomings in psychologists' scientific and medical training (Hayes & Heiby, 1996; Klein, 1996). Promoting psychologists' collaborative practices with prescribers rather than psychologists' prescription privileges would preclude new risks to patients associated with a potentially suboptimal level of care. Collaboration would avoid further confusion about psychologists' identities (Ax et al., 1997), skills, scope of practice, and the differentiation between psychology and psychiatry (Murstein & Fontaine, 1993; Wood, Jones, & Benjamin, 1986). . . .

As psychologists, educators of psychologists, and related health professionals, the authors have actively supported psychology's many other advances (e.g., Medicare reimbursement, licensure, provision of nonpharmacologic interventions), including appropriate, innovative roles of psychologists in health care (Schofield, 1969). We caution against framing the debate about prescription privileges as a chapter in the saga of struggles between psychology and psychiatry (DeLeon & Wiggins, 1996). Rather, at its core it is a controversy about the education and training necessary to promote safe and effective treatment that limits unnecessary risks to patients.

We have doubts that the shortcomings in psychologists' education and knowledge related to prescribing can be surmounted through abbreviated training, such as that currently advocated by the APA. Our skepticism that these gaps can be overcome within such a shorter time frame than is involved in the training of other prescribers leads us to urge psychologists to resist the temptation to venture into aspects of health care (i.e., prescribing and its related clinical activities) for which they would not be well-prepared. As legislators and regulators are lobbied about psychologists prescriptive privileges agenda, they need to weigh judiciously any hoped-for benefits against the potential risks associated with the inadequacies in psychologists' preparation to prescribe, even after they may have obtained the psychopharmacology training in accordance with the model recommended by the APA (CoR, 1996).

Acknowledgment

The authors appreciatively acknowledge the editorial guidance and other contributions of William Schofield, PhD, and Irving I. Gottesman, PhD, in the preparation of this article.

References

Adams, K. M., & Bieliauskas, L. A. (1994). On perhaps becoming what you had previously despised: Psychologists as prescribers of medication. *Journal of Clinical Psychology in Medical Settings, 1,* 189–197.

American College of Neuropsychopharmacology. (1998, May). *Final report: DoD prescribing psychologists: External analysis, monitoring, and evaluation of the program and its participants.* Nashville, TN: Author.

American Psychological Association. (1992a). Ethical principles of psychologists and code of conduct. *American Psychologist, 47,* 1597–1611.

American Psychological Association (1992b). *Report of the ad hoc task force on psychopharmacology.* Washington, DC: Author.

American Psychological Association. (1996). *Model legislation for prescriptive authority.* Washington, DC: Author.

APA board takes action to provide consult services in certain areas. (1998, April 17). *Psychiatric News,* 2.

Association for Medical School Pharmacology. (1990, October). *Knowledge objectives in medical pharmacology* (2nd edition). Author.

Association of State and Provincial Psychology Boards. (2000). Psychology Licensure Exam (EPPP). Available online at . . .

Ax, R. K., Forbes, M. R., & Thompson, D. D. (1997). Prescription privileges for psychologists: A survey of predoctoral interns and directors of training. *Professional Psychology: Research and Practice, 28,* 509–513.

Barkley, R. A. (1991, Spring). Health Services Committee: Prescribing privileges for health psychologists: Implications from the Clinical Child Psychology Task Force. *Health Psychologist, 13*(1), 2.

Bieliauskas, L. A. (1992a). Prescription privileges for psychologists? Reality orientation for proponents. *Physical Medicine and Rehabilitation: State of the Art Reviews, 6,* 587–595.

Bieliauskas, L. A. (1992b). Rebuttal of Dr. Frank's position. *Physical Medicine and Rehabilitation: State of the Art Reviews, 6,* 584.

Brentar, J., & McNamara, J. R. (1991a). Prescription privileges for psychology: The next step in its evolution as a profession. *Professional Psychology: Research and Practice, 22,* 194–195.

Brentar, J., & McNamara, J. R. (1991b). The right to prescribe medication: Considerations for professional psychology. *Professional Psychology: Research and Practice, 22,* 179–187.

Buelow, G. D., & Chafetz, M. D. (1996). Proposed ethical practice guidelines for clinical pharmacopsychology: Sharpening a new focus in psychology. *Professional Psychology: Research and Practice, 27,* 53–58.

Burns, S. M., DeLeon, P. H., Chemtob, C. M., Welch, B. L., & Samuels, R. M. (1988). Psychotropic medication: A new technique for psychology? *Psychotherapy, 25,* 508–515.

Bütz, M. R. (1994). Psychopharmacology: Psychology's Jurassic Park? *Psychotherapy, 31,* 692–699.

California Psychological Association, Professional Education Task Force, California School of Professional Psychology. (1995, January). *Report of the Blue Ribbon Panel.* Los Angeles: Author.

Classen, D. C., Pestotnik, S. L., Evans, S., Lloyd, J. F., & Burke, J. P. (1997). Adverse drug events in hospitalized patients: Excess length of stay, extra costs, and attributable mortality. *Journal of the American Medical Association, 277,* 301–306.

Council of Representatives, American Psychological Association. (1996). *Recommended postdoctoral training in psychopharmacology for prescription privileges.* Washington, DC: Author.

Cullen, E. A., & Newman, R. (1997). In pursuit of prescription privileges. *Professional Psychology: Research and Practice, 28,* 101–106.

DeLeon, P. H., Folen, R. A., Jennings, F. L., Wilkis, D. J., & Wright, R. H. (1991). The case for prescription privileges: A logical evolution of professional practice. *Journal of Clinical Child Psychology, 20,* 254–267.

DeLeon, P. H., Fox, R. E., & Graham, S. R. (1991). Prescription privileges: Psychology's next frontier? *American Psychologist, 46,* 384–393.

DeLeon, P. H., Sammons, M. T., & Sexton, J. L. (1995). Focusing on society's real needs: Responsibility and prescription privileges? *American Psychologist, 50,* 1022–1032.

DeLeon, P. H., & Wiggins, J. (1996). Prescription privileges for psychologists. *American Psychologist, 51,* 225–229.

DeMers, S. (1994). Legal and ethical issues in school psychologists' participation in psychopharmacological interventions with children. *School Psychology Quarterly, 9,* 41–52.

Ferguson, V. V. (1997). *Prescription privileges for psychologists: A study of rural and urban licensed psychologists' opinions*. Unpublished doctoral dissertation, University of South Dakota, Vermillion, SD.

Food and Drug Administration. (1999, May). *Managing the risks from medical product use, Creating a risk management framework*. Report to the FDA Commissioner from the Task Force on Risk Management, U.S. Department of Health and Human Services. Washington, DC: Author.

Fox, R. E. (1988). Prescription privileges: Their implications for the practice of psychology. *Psychotherapy, 25,* 501–507.

Fox, R. E., Schwelitz, F. D., & Barclay, A. G. (1992). A proposed curriculum for psychopharmacology training for professional psychologists. *Professional Psychology: Research and Practice, 23,* 216–219.

Geller, J. M., & Muus, K. J. (1997). *The role of rural primary care physicians in the provision of mental health services* (Letter to the Field No. 5). Frontier Mental Health Services Resource Network. Available online at . . .

Hanson, K. M., Louie, C. E., Van Male, L. M., Pugh, A. O., Karl, C., Muhlenbrook, L., Lilly, R. L., & Hagglund, K. J. (1999). Involving the future: The need to consider the views of psychologists-in-training regarding prescription privileges for psychologists. *Professional Psychology: Research and Practice, 30,* 203–208.

Hayes, G. J. (1998). Diving into the chemical soup. In S. C. Hayes & E. M. Heiby (Eds.), *Prescription privileges for psychologists: A critical appraisal*. Reno, NV: Context Press.

Hayes, S. C., & Heiby, E. (1996). Psychology's drug problem: Do we need a fix or should we just say no? *American Psychologist, 51,* 198–206.

Heiby, E. (1998). The case against prescription privileges for psychologists: An overview. In S. C. Hayes & E. M. Heiby (Eds.), *Prescription privileges for psychologists: A critical appraisal*. Reno, NV: Context Press.

Hendryx, M. S., Borders, T., & Johnson, T. (1995). The distribution of mental health providers in a rural state. *Administration and Policy in Mental Health, 23,* 153–155.

Hirschfeld, R. M., Keller, M. B., Panico, S., Arons, B. S., Barlow, D., Davidoff, F., Endicott, J., Froom, J., Goldstein, M., Gorman, J. M., Guthrie, D., Marek, R. G., Maurer, T. A., Meyer, R., Phillips, K., Ross, J., Schwenk, T. L., Sharfstein, S. S., Thase, M. E., & Wyatt, R. J. (1997): The National Depressive and Manic-Depressive Association consensus statement on the undertreatment of depression. *Journal of the American Medical Association, 277,* 333–340.

Holzer, C. E., III, Goldsmith, H. F., & Ciarlo, J. A. (1998). Effects of rural-urban county type on the availability of health and mental health care providers. In R. W. Manderscheid & M. J. Henderson (Eds.), *Mental health, United States* (pp. 204–213). Rockville, MD: U.S. Department of Health and Human Services.

Institute of Medicine Committee on Quality of Health Care in America. (1999). In L. T. Kohn, J. M. Corrigan, & M. S. Donaldson (Eds.), *To err is human: Building a safer health system*. Washington, DC: National Academy Press.

Kennedy, J. (1998, April 3). Prescription privileges for psychologists: A view from the field. *Psychiatric News, 33*(7), 26.

Kingsbury, S. J. (1992). Some effects of prescribing privileges. *Professional Psychology: Research and Practice, 23,* 3–5.

Klein, R. (1996). Comments on expanding the clinical role of psychologists. *American Psychologist, 5,* 216–218.

Klusman, L. E. (1998). Military health care providers' views on prescribing privileges for psychologists. *Professional Psychology: Research and Practice, 29,* 223–229.

Lesar, T. S., Briceland, L., & Stein, D. S. (1997). Factors related to errors in medication prescribing. *Journal of the American Medical Association, 277,* 312–317.

Matthews, W. J. (1998, March 23). In opposition to prescription privileges for psychologists. GO Inside. Available online at . . .

May, W. T., & Belsky, J. (1992). Response to "Prescription privileges: Psychology's next frontier?" or the siren call: Should psychologists medicate? *American Psychologist, 47,* 427.

Moyer, D. (1995). An opposing view on prescription privileges for psychologists. *Professional Psychology: Research and Practice, 26,* 586–590.

Murstein, B. I., & Fontaine P. A. (1993). The public's knowledge about psychologists and other mental health professionals. *American Psychologist, 7,* 838–845.

Narrow, W. E., Regier, D. A., Rae, D. S., Manderscheid, R. W., & Locke, B. Z. (1993). Use of services by persons with mental and addictive disorders: Findings from the National Institute of Mental Health Epidemiologic Catchment Area Program. *Archives of General Psychiatry, 50,* 95–107.

Office of Program Consultation and Accreditation, American Psychological Association. (1996). *Book 1: Guidelines and principles for accreditation of programs in professional psychology.* Washington, DC: Author.

Olfson, M., & Pincus, H. A. (1996). Outpatient mental health care in nonhospital settings: Distribution of patients across provider groups. *American Journal of Psychiatry, 153,* 1353–1356.

Pachman, J. S. (1996). The dawn of a revolution in mental health. *American Psychologist, 51,* 213–215.

Phillips, D. P., Christenfeld, N., & Glynn, L. M. (1998). Increase in US medication-error deaths between 1983 and 1993. *Lancet, 351,* 643–644.

Pies, R. W. (1991). The "deep structure" of clinical medicine and prescribing privileges for psychologists. *Journal of Clinical Psychiatry, 52,* 4–8.

Pincus, H. A., Tanielian, T. L., Marcus, S. C., Olfson, M., Zarin, D. A., Thompson, J., & Zito, J. M. (1998). Prescribing trends in psychotropic medications: Primary care, psychiatry, and other medical specialties. *Journal of the American Medical Association, 279,* 526–531.

Preskorn, S. H. (1999). *Outpatient management of depression: A guide for the practitioner* (2nd ed.). Caddo, OK: Professional Communications, Inc.

Roan, S. (1993, September 7). Tug-of-war over prescription powers; health: Pharmacists, nurses and other non-doctors want the authority to prescribe drugs. Others insist only physicians have the training to do so safely. *Los Angeles Times,* Part E, 1, 6.

Robiner, W. N. (1999, May). Why psychologists should not pursue prescription privileges. In J. Boyd, M. Chesney, R. Kollmorgen, J. L. Raymond, W. Robiner, & J. Boller, *Prescriptive authority for psychologists: Pros and cons.* Annual Meeting of the Minnesota Psychological Association, Minneapolis.

Robiner, W. N., Bearman, D. L., Berman, M., Grove, W., Colön, E., Armstrong, J., Mareck, S., & Tanenbaum, R. (2001). *Prescriptive authority for psychologists: Despite deficits in education and knowledge?* Manuscript submitted for publication.

Sammons, M. T. (1994). Prescription privileges and psychology: A reply to Adams and Bieliauskas. *Journal of Clinical Psychology in Medical Settings, 1,* 199–207.

Sammons, M. T., & Brown, A. B. (1997). The Department of Defense Psychopharmacology Demonstration Project: An evolving program for postdoctoral education in psychology. *Professional Psychology: Research and Practice, 28,* 107–112.

Sammons, M. T., Sexton, J. L., & Meredith, J. M. (1996). Basic science training in psychopharmacology: How much is enough? *American Psychologist, 51,* 230–234.

Schofield, W. (1969). The role of psychology in the delivery of health services. *American Psychologist, 24,* 565–584.

Scully, J. H., Jr. (1999). The psychiatric workforce. In S. Weissman, M. Sabshin, & H. Eist (Eds.), *Psychiatry in the new millennium* (pp. 273–283). Washington, DC: American Psychiatric Press.

Shatin, D., Gardner, J., & Stergachis, A. (1999). Letter. *Journal of the American Medical Association, 281*(4), 319–320.

Smyer, M. A., Balster, R. L., Egli, D., Johnson, D. L., Kilbey, M. M., Leith, N. J., & Puente, A. E. (1993). Summary of the report of the Ad Hoc Task Force on Psychopharmacology of the American Psychological Association. *Professional Psychology: Research and Practice, 24,* 394–403.

Tatman, S. M., Peters, D. B., Greene, A. L., & Bongar, B. (1997). Graduate students' attitudes toward prescription privileges training. *Professional Psychology: Research and Practice, 28,* 515–517.

U.S. General Accounting Office. (1999). *Prescribing psychologists: DOD demonstration participants perform well but have little effect on readiness or costs: Report to the Chairman and Ranking Minority Member, Committee on Armed Services, U.S. Senate.* Washington, DC: Author.

Wood, W., Jones, M., & Benjamin, L. T., Jr. (1986). Surveying psychology's public image. *American Psychologist, 41,* 947–953.

Zimmerman, M. A., & Wienckowski, L. A. (1991). Revisiting health and mental health linkages: A policy whose time has come . . . again. *Journal of Public Health Policy, 12,* 510–524.

CHALLENGE QUESTIONS

Should Psychologists Be Able to Prescribe Drugs?

1. DeLeon and Dunivin assert that prescriptive authority will improve a therapist's ability to treat a client. Do you agree? Support your answer.
2. Would you want your therapist to have the ability to prescribe medicines? Why or why not?
3. Find an article on the new prescription privileges in New Mexico and describe how successful this "experiment" seems to be.
4. Robiner et al. argue that the Department of Defense study should not be used as evidence that nonphysicians can safely use medicine. Examine this study yourself and decide if they are justified in their claim. Support your answer.
5. Collaboration between psychologists and psychiatrists was suggested by Robiner and his colleagues as a possible solution to the issue. What advantages or disadvantages do you see in their suggestion?

ISSUE 16

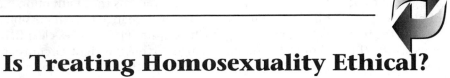

Is Treating Homosexuality Ethical?

YES: Christopher H. Rosik, from "Motivational, Ethical, and Epistemological Foundations in the Treatment of Unwanted Homoerotic Attraction," *Journal of Marital and Family Therapy* (January 2003)

NO: Robert-Jay Green, from "When Therapists Do Not Want Their Clients to Be Homosexual: A Response to Rosik's Article," *Journal of Marital and Family Therapy* (January 2003)

ISSUE SUMMARY

YES: Psychologist Christopher Rosik affirms that a therapist can ethically assist a patient in changing their sexual orientation as long as it is the patient's desire to do so.

NO: Psychologist Robert-Jay Green voices concern with sexual orientation therapy on the grounds that any attempt to sexually reorient a patient implies a moral disapproval of homosexuality.

Perhaps no issue in psychology has provoked more intense debate in the popular culture than that of homosexuality. For nearly 30 years, the governing associations of psychology, psychiatry, and counseling have worked to remove the pathological label from the lifestyles of gay and lesbian individuals. Many professionals assume that empirical research has demonstrated the biological underpinnings of sexual orientation, so many psychologists have chosen to view homosexuality as a normal alternative lifestyle. Other professionals, however, view these efforts as politically motivated and threatening to traditional religious and moral beliefs. Still others professionals resonate with psychology's support of homosexuality as an important protection of minority rights, regardless of the possible moral issues at play.

One facet of this ongoing "culture war" is the treatment of individuals who are dissatisfied with their sexual orientation. Reorientation or conversion therapy, as it is sometimes called, was regularly practiced before the 1970s. However, many psychologists currently believe that this "therapy" is an unethical and unproven brand of treatment. They argue that gay individuals can too easily internalize society's fear of homosexuals, and thus express the desire to leave the homosexual lifestyle. Others counter that no one should stand in the way of an individual's desire and that psychotherapists have an obligation to honor this desire. Another issue concerns the assumption made in honoring this desire—the assumption that such change is even possible.

In the first selection, psychologist Christopher Rosik makes clear that he agrees with the potential for such a change, given the right circumstances and aid. Moreover, he believes it is completely ethical to engage in sexual orientation therapy *if* certain conditions are met. Foremost, the instigation of such therapy needs to come from the individual seeking treatment and not from the therapist. No therapist with a "moral agenda" should advocate this change. Second, there ought to be no coercion involved at all. Caregivers of all varieties should accede to the wishes of their clients, even if they personally might have problems with reorientation treatment. Still, with these conditions in place, Rosik believes that there are valid reasons for pursuing reorientation, including religious conflicts, a desire to remain married, dissatisfaction with sexual nonmonogamy, and concern about HIV infection.

Robert-Jay Green expresses his concern about sexual orientation therapy in the second selection. He argues that even though Rosik tries to take an unbiased stance toward homosexuality, Rosik's disapproval of homosexuality nevertheless shines through. Green argues that such a bias is inappropriate— especially in trying to help people make sense of their own sexuality. Sexual orientation, in his view, is much more than a person's conscious decision to prefer one sex over another; sexual orientation is a complex set of feelings and desires that are formed from birth. Green critiques Rosik's claim that homosexuality leads to a higher rate of psychiatric illness and causes depression. Instead, he cites evidence that external discrimination (e.g., homophobia) is a strong predictor of depression among homosexuals. Lastly, Green challenges sexual orientation therapy itself, describing how data show its high failure rate.

POINT

- Homosexual clients have valid reasons for wanting to change their sexual orientation.

- Those who engage in homosexual behavior are at higher risk for depression, anxiety, and suicide.

- Sexual orientation therapy is ethical if initiated by the patient.

- Research suggests that increasing "heterosexual potential" is possible.

COUNTERPOINT

- Societal discrimination leads clients to want change.

- These Increased risks are the result of external discrimination, not homosexuality.

- Patients may be misled by cultural homophobia.

- Research shows the immutability of sexual orientation.

YES

Christopher H. Rosik

Motivational, Ethical, and Epistemological Foundations in the Treatment of Unwanted Homoerotic Attraction

A recent special section of the *Journal of Marital and Family Therapy* (October, 2000) focusing on the mental health needs of gay, lesbian, and bisexual individuals neglected to address the clinical needs of homosexual persons who desire to increase their heterosexual potential. This article attempts to correct this omission by outlining common motivations for pursuing change, updating the current state of knowledge regarding the effectiveness of change efforts, and providing some ethical guidelines when therapists encounter clients who present with unwanted homoerotic attraction. Finally, to assist marriage and family therapists (MFTs) in more deeply understanding divergent perspectives about reorientation treatments, an examination of the role of moral epistemology is presented and some examples of its potential influence are described. MFTs are encouraged to recognize and accept, rather than ignore or deny the valid needs of clients who seek to modify their same-sex attraction.

There is a growing body of clinical literature that is designed to assist therapists in understanding and addressing the needs of gay, lesbian, and bisexual (GLB) clients. A recent issue of *Journal of Marital and Family Therapy* (October, 2000) dealt specifically with these issues. However, the series of articles failed to recognize an important subgroup of homosexual clients, namely those individuals who present for treatment with unwanted same-sex attractions. Understanding these individuals is an important step in being able to provide treatment that respects their cultural and religious values. Typically what little scholarly literature that exists on these men and women is presented within an evaluative framework that is far removed from how they actually perceive their circumstances. By examining these individuals within a more conservative value schema, MFTs can come to a greater appreciation of the worldview of these clients. This, in turn, can enable a greater tolerance of values and beliefs that are normative within this subgroup but may be foreign or disagreeable to the clinician.

From *Journal of Marital and Family Therapy*, vol. 29, issue 1, January 2003, pp. 13–28. Copyright © 2003 by Blackwell Publishing, Ltd. via the Copyright Clearance Center. Reprinted by permission.

Such analysis is vital for many reasons. Redding (2001) has noted that conservatives and conservative views are vastly underrepresented in mental health professions, and presumably MFT. He contends that without sociopolitical diversity, the therapeutic community undermines its credibility in several ways. Research hypotheses or interpretations from a conservative viewpoint go unasked or unrepresented. Scientific findings are rendered suspect or disregarded altogether among a large portion of society, seen only as the product of liberally dominated mental health guilds. A lack of conservative representation may also impede the ability of therapists to serve conservative clients and communities, as in the present case of homosexual persons who do not wish to self-identify as gay, lesbian, or bisexual.

This article will attempt to provide insight into clients who request treatment to further develop their heterosexual potential. Several motivations that lead individuals to seek such therapeutic goals will be presented and evidence will be outlined that appears to lend validity to these concerns. The issue of increasing heterosexual potential will be addressed and some guidelines for ethically conducting such treatment will be suggested. Finally, an analysis will be offered that makes sense of the controversies in this area of practice as representing a difference in moral epistemologies.

It should be mentioned at the outset that an increasingly vocal number of mental health professionals are on the record as favoring a complete prohibition of any therapeutic attempts to increase a client's heterosexual potential (Davison, 2001; Murphy, 1992). The perspective taken in this analysis is naturally more sympathetic to such a goal, provided that the therapy is conducted in accordance with well-recognized ethical standards. Ignoring the values and beliefs of these clients by prohibiting change-oriented therapies may lead these individuals to avoid the mental health system altogether. Time will tell as to whether our profession will risk precipitating such a large-scale form of client discrimination and abandonment.

Motivations for Pursuing Greater Heterosexual Potential

The limited studies of clients who seek therapeutic assistance in increasing heterosexual potential generally seem to converge around several motivational themes. As summarized most recently by Spitzer (2001a), these themes involve religious conflict, a desire to remain married, dissatisfaction with sexual nonmonogamy, and concern about HIV infection.

Religious/Moral Conflict

It appears that a significant majority of individuals with unwanted homoerotic attraction and who attempt to increase their heterosexual potential come from conservative religious backgrounds (Nicolosi, Byrd, & Potts, 2000; Schaeffer, Hyde, Kroencke, McCormick, & Nottebaum, 2000; Schaeffer, Nottebaum, Dech, & Drawczyk, 2000; Spitzer, 2001a). Spitzer (2001a) found that 79% of his sample of 200 men and women who claimed to have changed their sexual orientation were motivated by their religious beliefs. Moreover, 93% of the sample indicated that religion is "extremely" or "very" important in their lives. Many such individuals are well aware of efforts to revise their religious traditions in gay-affirmative ways, but they nonetheless maintain the conviction that their homoerotic feelings are not a part of who God created them to be. They instead see their homosexual behavior as falling short of the ideals for sexual conduct reflected in the sacred texts of their faith communities. Other individuals may seek to change same-sex attraction because of their moral beliefs and cultural values, which may or may not be connected to a religious worldview.

These concerns are aptly captured in the description of one client's statements about his choice to pursue change-oriented treatment:

> As a foster child, I was developing a coping mechanism of masturbation during which I fantasized about punishing men by beating them. I virtually had no male affirmation as a child. As an adult, I began to develop good relationships with men, which I did not have as a child. Later, under stress of the job and not dealing with my past, I allowed deep yearnings for affirmation from men to become mixed in with lust and finally immorality. It is my sincere desire to break with my sinful behavior and begin a process of healing and restoration.

Opportunity for or Maintenance of Marriage and Family

The desire to have or keep a traditional marriage and family is another powerful impetus for individuals to seek out therapy for unwanted homoerotic feelings. What few empirical studies that assessed this area found high levels of endorsement, especially for men. Spitzer (2001a) reported that 67% of men cited this reason as well as 35% of women. Nicolosi et al. (2000) indicated that 32% of their sample was married. Given the religiously conservative nature of these samples, it is not unexpected that the participants would desire to explore their heterosexual potential and, if possible, move toward the theologically sanctioned context for sexual expression within their faith community.

Marriage and family therapists have a particular expertise in addressing client concerns in a systemic context and should understand the validity of a values-based decision to attempt to increase heterosexual potential to maintain the integrity of a marriage and family. For example, one male client indicated that he sought treatment in order to "deal with my painful past properly and engage in a process of restoration in which I rebuild trust with my wife and family and a firm ability not to go back to my former sinful behaviors." Similarly, a young woman described the struggle between her values and her feelings:

> The big thing right now is my marriage. Am I happy? Why did I have an affair—and with a woman for god's sake? And how do I get over that. I feel so strongly about my lover—I feel like we have a connection that my husband and I never had—like we're soul mates. I want to do the right thing and stay in my marriage and not hurt my husband or my family—but I question—am I sacrificing my chance at true happiness?

Nonmonagomy

According to Spitzer (2001a), many individuals (especially men) who desire to modify homoerotic attraction strongly value monogamy and are motivated by dissatisfaction with their experience of a more sexually open homosexual culture. Statistics generally tend to confirm this, suggesting much higher levels of nonmonogamy and sexual partners, particularly as concerns gay and bisexual male couples in comparison to lesbian and heterosexual couples (Bepko & Johnson, 2000; Dworkin, 2001; Markowitz, 1993; Rust, 2001; Shernoff, 1999). More representative national studies appear to confirm this trend and achieve findings consistent with the research using less stringent sampling techniques (Gilman, Cochran, Mays, Hughes, Ostrow, & Kessler, 2001; Lauman, Gagnon, Michael, & Michaels, 1994). Even for self-identified closed-coupled gay men, nonmonogamy appears to be a frequent occurrence, possibly reflecting a tendency to define commitment in emotional rather than sexual terms (Appleby, Miller, & Rothspan, 1999; Blumstein & Schwartz, 1995; Bringle, 1995).

From the perspective of many GLB writers, failure to morally equate "polyamorous" or "polyfidelous" relationships with monogamous heterosexual ideals constitutes a heterosexist and sex-negative belief system (Dworkin, 2001, p. 674). Bepko and Johnson (2000) caution that it is important to avoid pathologizing what may be normative behavior for couples in the gay and lesbian community. This is equally valid advice for working with individuals who seek to increase their heterosexual potential and may have their normative religious values interpreted pathologically as internalized homophobia. One male client alluded to despondency over his homosexual behavior in his decision to pursue change.

> I was living a complete double life. Happy husband and father, church-goer and successful professional on the outside, rabid homosexual sex addict on the inside. While dating men, adopting a gay identity, and throwing myself into the gay lifestyle had been exhilarating at first, it had soon felt like it was killing my spirit, alienating myself from my goals in life, from God and a sense of higher purpose. I had realized then that I didn't want to be affirmed as gay; I wanted to be affirmed as a man.

Risky Sexual Behavior and Concern about HIV Infection

Some gay or bisexual men who seek change-oriented therapy are motivated in part out of a concern that risky sexual behavior may lead to HIV infection. Unprotected anal intercourse has been a particular focus in the medical literature, and recent studies suggest an upward trend in this practice, especially among young gay men (Catania et al., 2001; Ekstrand, Stall, Paul, Osmond, & Coates, 1999; Graham, Kirscht, Kessler, & Graham, 1998; Mansergh et al., 2001; Suarez & Miller, 2001; Wolitski, Valdiserri, Denning, & Levine, 2001). This practice raises the very real potential for HIV infection among these men. Wolitski et al. report that 260,000 American men who have sex with men (MSM) have died of AIDS, a total that is greater than for all other risk groups combined. They further estimate that 365,000-535,000 MSM in the United

States are infected with HIV, representing more than one-half of those who live with HIV and 70% of HIV-infected men. Wolitski, et al. (2001) concluded that, "Given that only 5% to 7% of American men have sex with another man during adulthood, these figures are overwhelming" (p. 883). In the mid-1990s one epidemiological analysis reported that 30% of all 20-year-old homosexual males would be dead by the time they reached 30 years of age (Goldman, 1994). More recently, Strathdee et al. (2001) found that men who reported recently engaging in homosexual activity were four times more likely to become infected with HIV. In another recent nationally representative sample, Gilman et al. (2001) reported HIV positive prevalence rates to be 2.3% in their same-sex sexual partner subsample and 0.2% in the opposite-sex subsample. Similarly, Wolitski et al. found that 18% of MSM participants compared to less than 1% of the overall population reported being HIV positive.

Fortunately, the advent of highly active antiretroviral therapy (HAART) has improved the lives and decreased the mortality of HIV positive individuals in recent years. This wonderful advancement in medical treatment is not, however, without a significant downside (Catania et al., 2001; Wolitski et al., 2001). Highly active antiretroviral therapy typically has multiple unpleasant side effects and can lead to drug-resistant strains of HIV that can be transmitted to others. In addition, this treatment is costly, lifelong, and medical compliance is difficult to maintain. In fact, one study found that one-third of HIV cases had foregone medical care because they could not afford the time or the expense (Landsberg, 1999). Even under the best conditions, data suggest that nearly 25% of newly infected individuals are resistant to all three current classes of medications, and nearly 80% display resistance to at least one class of antiretrovirals (Voelker, 2000). This appears to place significant limits on current and future treatment options. Preventive measures such as safer sex practices are also a necessary component of combating HIV, although rates of condom failure with anal sexual activity appear to be alarmingly high (Kalichman, Kelly, & Rompa, 1997; Rosser, Metz, Bockting, & Buroker, 1996).

Researchers have suggested many reasons for the apparent increases in risk behavior (Appleby, Miller, & Rothspan, 1999; Dilley, Woods, & McFarland, 1997; Vanable, Ostrow, McKirnan, Taywaditep, & Hope, 2000; Wolitski, et al., 2001). In spite of its limitations, improved medical management of HIV through HAART has caused many gay men to reevaluate their adherence to safer sex practices. The eroticism of HIV, fed by images of persons living with the virus as healthy, virile, and physically fit, may also change perceptions of risk and lead to increasing risk behavior. Years of coping with HIV, changing desired sexual behavior patterns, and exposure to prevention messages may result in "AIDS burnout." Young MSM may feel pessimistic about aging as gay men, and may view HIV as a means to escape a dreaded future. Finally, for some gay men risky sex may be seen as symbolizing trust, love, and commitment. It appears reasonable that some individuals involved in such practices, particularly those with emergent health concerns and newly found or rediscovered traditional religious faith, may grow dissatisfied with their circumstances and desire to increase their heterosexual potential. Such was the case with one religiously oriented male client involved in change-oriented intervention. He decided not to go further into the gay lifestyle after watching his brother die from AIDS and later mistaking as his own HIV infection what eventually was diagnosed to be the symptoms of chronic fatigue syndrome.

The Possibility of Increasing Heterosexual Potential

To evaluate the ethics of therapeutic attempts to assist clients toward greater heterosexual functioning, evidence suggesting that change is possible for at least some people needs to be presented. In spite of a sociopolitical climate that is generally hostile to such analyses, some of the relevant research is indirectly supportive, whereas a few more recent studies have looked directly at the outcomes of change efforts.

Indirect support can be found in the literature concerning Gender Identity Disorder (GID), defined in the DSM-IV as involving "a strong and persistent cross-gender identification" accompanied by the child's "persistent discomfort with his or her sex or sense of inappropriateness in the gender role of that sex" (American Psychiatric Association, 1994). This diagnosis is increasingly coming under attack, in large part because a significant number of adult homosexual men and women report histories of early cross-gender behavior that would fall within the description of GID (Bradley & Zucker, 1997, 1998). An inherent tension thus exists in the DSM, as GID is a childhood mental disorder that is often a developmental precursor to a sexual orientation declassified for adults. Consequently, there is mounting sociopolitical pressure to remove GID in the next DSM revision (Isay, 1997).

In spite of this, research on GID does suggest a developmental factor in the etiology of homosexuality and indirectly supports the potential for increasing heterosexual potential (Bradley & Zucker, 1997; Zucker et al., 1999). Bradley and Zucker (1997) indicate that therapy can be effective in modifying cross-gender feelings. They also describe treatment for GID as involving the discouragement of cross-gender behavior and increasing opportunities to develop same-sex skills and friendships, interventions not unlike those reported as helpful by adults who claim to have changed homoerotic attraction (Spitzer, 2001a).

Another indirect indicator of the potential for development of heterosexual potential is found in the literature on the relative malleability of erotic attraction for lesbians (Baumeister, 2000; Diamond, 1998; Dworkin, 2001; Peplau & Garnets, 2000; Venigas & Conley, 2000). Studies have reported 31% to 50% of lesbians sampled consider their sexual orientation to be the result of a conscious, deliberate choice (Rosenbluth, 1997; Whisman, 1996). The findings that 25%–50% of lesbians report previous heterosexual marriage and that 77% have had one or more long-term male sexual partners also suggest some degree of malleability (Bridges & Croeau, 1994; Diamant, Schuster, McGuigan, & Lever, 1999). Moreover, religious beliefs appear to be an important element in maintaining or returning to heterosexual functioning (Baumeister, 2000; Rosenbluth, 1997). Baumeister's fascinating account posits a brief period of plasticity in childhood for males followed by a relatively more fixed orientation, whereas females retain plasticity throughout adulthood. Overall, these data suggest that increasing heterosexual potential may take less effort for lesbians and bisexual women than for gay and bisexual men.

The limited number of recent studies on change of homosexual feelings and behavior are consistent with the potential for increasing heterosexual functioning. Self-report information by clients and their therapists strongly suggest that some individuals can and do make significant modifications in their homoerotic attractions (Macintosh, 1994; Throckmorton, 1998).

Research by Schaeffer, Hyde, Kroencke, McCormick, and Nottebaum (2000; Schaeffer, Nottebaum et al., 2000) examined religiously motivated attempts to change sexual orientation. They described a sample of 248 adults surveyed at a conference of Exodus International, a religiously oriented organization that assists individuals with unwanted homoerotic attraction. These participants reported experiencing significantly more heterosexuality than they recalled experiencing at age 18. At a 1-year follow-up, 140 of these subjects were reinterviewed and 60.8% of males and 71.1% of females indicated behavioral success, defined as abstaining from homosexual contact. These results did not support the short-term benefit of change-oriented therapy and speak more to modification of homosexual behavior, rather than feelings. However, they did indicate that even when some level of homoerotic attraction persists, change efforts could promote positive mental health and religious experience.

Nicolosi, Byrd, and Potts (2000) surveyed 882 individuals who underwent psychological treatment, in the form of conversion therapy and self-help groups, to modify same-sex attraction. Of the 318 clients who rated themselves as having exclusively same-gender sexual orientation prior to treatment, posttreatment results indicated that 18% rated themselves as exclusively heterosexual, and 17% felt almost entirely heterosexual. Individual pastoral and professional counseling, group therapy, and personal spirituality and faith were identified as key ingredients in the process of change. Self-report information revealed significant improvement in self acceptance, emotional stability, depression, and spirituality. Finally, 30–4% of the respondents spontaneously reported frustration with previous therapists who had dismissed their desire to change homoerotic feelings and had attempted to impose gay-affirmative therapy on them.

Spitzer's (2001a) study marked an improvement over previous research in that he carefully assessed for the affective components of homosexual experience (e.g., subjective ratings of sexual attraction, and sexual fantasies during masturbation and heterosexual sex) and limited his subject pool to individuals reporting at least 5 years of sustained change from a homosexual to a heterosexual orientation. Using reasonably stringent criteria, Spitzer found that 66% of male participants and 44% of female subjects had achieved good heterosexual functioning. Of the 33 men who rated most extreme on the homosexual indicators, a surprising 67% achieved good heterosexual functioning. Although 20% of the sample reported being heterosexually married prior to change attempts, 76% of the men and 47% of the women reported being married at the time of the interview. Even though 42% of the men and 46% of the women reported their sexual attraction to be exclusively homosexual before change attempts, 17% of the men and 55% of the women indicated exclusive heterosexual attraction upon interview. Depression was indicated as a problem prior to change efforts by 43% of the men and 47% of the women, whereas these statistics had fallen to posttreatment levels of 1% and 4%, respectively.

Most of Spitzer's subjects reported a gradual diminution of homosexual feelings and a gradual emerging or intensification of heterosexual feelings, with the completion of the change effort occurring after approximately 5 years. This is consistent with other studies that suggest the benefits of change-oriented therapies may be most fully experienced well into the treatment process (Nicolosi et al., 2000; Schaeffer, Nottebaum et al., 2000). Spitzer excluded 74 subjects from his study because they only reported change in their identity or overt homosexual behavior. However, even these individuals experienced their degree of change as substantially improved, albeit less than desired. Finally, Spitzer also documented reports of earlier change efforts that were not helpful, including many involving therapists who told clients that they had no choice but to accept their homosexuality. Spitzer concludes from his research that change for some individuals is possible along a multidimensional continuum.

Spitzer's (2001a) study has sparked a heated and overdue debate about the possibility of changing homoerotic attraction, especially in light of the fact that he was a primary architect of the 1973 decision to remove homosexuality from the DSM. Much of the criticism has focused on the issue of sample bias, as most of the participants were religiously conservative and were often referred from organizations known to promote and assist in change efforts (Ritter, 2001). However, in actuality this is a strength of the research, given that the vast majority of studies relevant to the issue of change have utilized convenience samples solicited through GLB-affirmative organizations, support groups, and media. This suggests the presence of skew in the existing literature as a whole, the degree of which can only be determined through a closer examination of individuals such as those in Spitzer's study.

In the short term, the more strident elements on both sides of this debate are likely to continue with opposing anecdotal horror stories. However, it appears increasingly certain that at least some highly motivated individuals can significantly increase their heterosexual potential. If the sociopolitical pressures to prohibit such treatment can be withstood, a growing recognition of the possibility for change will hopefully lead to more collaborative research endeavors that can identify criteria associated with the success or failure of reorientation treatments.

Ethical Considerations for Working with Clients Pursuing Change

When a client who experiences unwanted homoerotic attraction first presents to the MFT, the controversial nature of the presenting problem mandates extra care to insure ethical practice. Some therapists, such as Murphy (1992), who view the practice of therapy to increase heterosexual potential (sometimes referred to as reorientation or conversion therapy) as inherently unethical, will need to avoid involvement altogether. However, MFTs who assume a less extreme stance will have to consider several ethical guidelines, including consent, nonexploitation, and respecting client autonomy and diversity.

Consent

The American Association for Marriage and Family Therapy code of ethics (AAMFT; 2001) is clear about the need for informed consent (1.2). In the context of a client requesting assistance for change in homoerotic feelings, some specific areas need to be addressed. The client needs to be informed about the different types of treatment related to sexual orientation that exist along with the potential risks and benefits of each (Yarhouse, 1998a, 1998b). Broadly speaking, the client can be informed that some professionals provide gay-affirmative therapy with the goal of acceptance of a GLB identity, whereas others provide reorientation therapies that assist in increasing heterosexual potential. Assuming the client wishes to pursue change-oriented treatment, several potential risks and benefits can be discussed consistent with the research outlined above. Potential risks include the very real possibility of no change in homoerotic feelings and accompanying religious distress, disappointment with the degree of change achieved, and the likelihood of any change being a slow and gradual experience over a prolonged period of time. Benefits may include increased ability to live within normative religious sexual ideals, subsequently enhanced spiritual and emotional functioning, a decrease in certain health risks, and an increased ability to have or maintain heterosexual marriage and family.

It is wise for the clinician to have clients seeking change articulate what criteria for success they envision. This can allow for identification of unrealistic expectations, education regarding potential outcomes (e.g., behavioral and/or affectional change), and discussion of how failure to achieve the desired degree of change would be experienced. An acknowledgement of the experimental nature of reorientation therapy is also in order, in that a large body of rigorous empirical studies confirming treatment efficacy does not yet exist. Criticisms of reorientation therapies on these grounds have been widely aired, often with the recommendation to refrain from such interventions until supportive research is available (American Psychiatric Association, 2000; Haldeman, 1994). However, these position statements and resolutions, often drafted by GLB committees (American Psychiatric Association, 1999, 2000; American Psychological Association, 2000), risk being perceived as somewhat self serving unless they are also willing to call for funding to support collaborative outcome research among opponents and proponents of change efforts.

Noncoercion

It is essential that MFTs assess the extent to which a client presenting for change-oriented treatment may be motivated by some degree of coercion from others and thus insure that an autonomous decision is being made (AAMFT Code of Ethics, 2001, 1.2, 1.8). This is especially important when adolescent clients are referred by their parents. Great caution must be exercised to avoid exploitation of the client's vulnerability (AAMFT, 2001, 1.3, 3.9).

Therapists need to guard against any impulse to exert pressure on clients to continue in a therapy they no longer wish to pursue. Marriage and family therapists who engage in reorientation treatment must respect a client's decision to leave treatment and pursue gay-affirmative therapy, just as MFTs who operate from a gay-affirmative approach must allow a client who becomes dissatisfied with the gay lifestyle to seek change-oriented intervention. When MFTs feel unable clinically, ethically, or morally to provide either one of these treatments, they should provide referral sources that can assist clients accordingly (AAMFT, Code of Ethics, 2001, 1.10, 3.4, 3.11; Bernstein, 2000; Yarhouse, 1998b). . . . A more exhaustive description and listing of such resources has been published quite recently (Yarhouse, Burkett, & Kreeft, 2002).

Some professionals have claimed that the decision to attempt to increase heterosexual potential can never be ultimately volitional because of societal homophobia (Haldeman, 1994). This hypothesis is stated in such extreme terms as to make it scientifically untestable and classifiable as ideological posturing (Yarhouse, 1998a). It appears to reflect a perspective that assumes personal identity will always be fundamentally organized around sexual feelings. However, for many people, religious belief forms the primary organizing principle of personal identity and, in the case of conservative religious sentiment, a desire to increase heterosexual potential can legitimately result from such self-identification.

Respecting Client Autonomy and Diversity

Assuming clients are provided with informed consent in a noncoercive environment, the recognition that some individuals with homoerotic attraction will still want to pursue change-oriented therapy upholds the ethical assumption that clients make autonomous choices that MFTs must respect (AAMFT Code of Ethics, 2001, 1.8). In addition, because many of these clients are motivated to attempt change because of deeply held religious convictions, allowing them to pursue such therapy supports the AAMFT (Code of Ethics, 2001, 1.1) ethical pledge not to discriminate on the basis of religion, respecting religious diversity even when members may hold different moral beliefs regarding homosexual behavior and sexual identity (Rosik, 2001; Yarhouse, 1998b; Yarhouse & VanOrman, 1999). As Dworkin (2001) affirmed, "Sexual identity is defined by the client, and it is important for therapists to respect that" (p. 674). Similarly, Bernstein (2000) rightly contended, "it is vital that therapists defer to clients in defining their therapeutic goals" (p. 452).

Bernstein (2000) offered many important considerations for straight therapists who work with GLB clients. Primary among them was the need for MFTs to understand cultural backgrounds different from their own. Given that a generally liberal sociopolitical frame of reference dominates the mental health field (Redding, 2001), it may be even more pressing for MFTs to educate themselves about the cultural background, heritage, and normative belief systems of religious conservatives (Yarhouse & VanOrman, 1999). Applying Bernstein's suggestions to this population of clients, MFTs from different cultural backgrounds are encouraged to develop personal relationships with religiously conservative acquaintances, colleagues, and students. Visiting a conservative church, synagogue, or mosque would also provide important insights into the normative beliefs and practices of this population. Such efforts can greatly assist MFTs in examining and challenging their religious prejudices and enable therapeutic sensitivity with religiously conservative clients who present for therapy with the goal of increasing heterosexual potential (Gartner, 1985, 1986). Akin to the need for awareness of heterocentric bias, MFTs working with religious clients should examine their value assumptions regarding sexual behavior and determine whether they can comfortably assist clients whose conservative moral perspective may motivate the pursuit of change in homoerotic attraction.

In fact, it may well be that differences in underlying moral visions provide a framework for understanding the tensions that often arise over attempts to change unwanted homoerotic attraction both within the therapeutic relationship and the mental health profession at large. What follows is an examination of the potential impact of moral epistemology in this arena intended to assist MFTs in the generally accepted mandate to know their own biases (Bernstein, 2000). . . .

Homophobia

Homophobia has generally been defined to denote any negative belief, attitude, or behavior toward gay and lesbian persons (Bernat, Calhoun, Adams, & Zeichner, 2001; O'Donohue & Caselles, 1993; Sanders & Kroll, 2000). More recently, the term biphobia has been coined with reference negative views of bisexuality (Dworkin, 2001; Mohr & Rochlen, 1999). In an important contribution to this literature, O'Donohue and Caselles observe that homophobia has been operationalized using many scale items referring to debatable value positions and moral judgments. Moral disapproval and avoidance may not be irrational or phobic within a specific religious or ideological subculture, and this distinction needs to be taken into account. O'Donahue and Caselles suggest that a valid use of the term homophobia would only refer to the emotional reaction of fear, plus the behavioral reaction of avoidance, in the absence of negative moral or aesthetic arguments. The authors thus contend that, "there are certain value, moral, aesthetic, and political questions and positions that, in a free society, should not be closed and suppressed by mental-health professionals and behavioral science research, and the moral status of homosexuality is one of these" (p. 190).

Recent research suggests the legitimacy and utility of distinguishing between religious belief that is homonegative in evaluating the moral status of homosexual behavior but homopositive in affirming the value of GLB persons versus religious belief that is uniformly homonegative (Bassett, Baldwin, et al, 2001; Bassett, Hodak, et al., 2000; Fulton, Gorsuch, & Maynard, 1999). Such nuances are important to consider when assessing religiously conservative clients who request assistance in increasing heterosexual potential; yet, our current scales of homophobia and biphobia (including internalized versions) are simply unable to take them into account (e.g., Johnson, Brems, & Alford-Keating, 1997). This, in turn, may compromise the usefulness and validity of these terms when applied to this population.

Examining these concerns through the lens of Haidt and Hersh's (2001) findings, it appears that homophobia, biphobia, and related terms (such as heterosexism) derive from and make perfect sense within the EOA adopted by liberalism. The trouble lies in attempts to carry this understanding into conservative groups that do not define their moral domain primarily in terms of autonomy, but also maintain social and religious concerns found in the EOC and EOD. Conservatives within the broader moral domain may thus experience their being labeled homophobic as an attempt to force them to embrace an alien evaluative framework. Indeed, O'Donahue and Caselles (1993) warn that the ambiguity surrounding the construct of homophobia may allow it to be used as a means of influencing individuals to react differently toward homosexuals and homosexuality by condemning certain sets of negative reactions.

Marriage and family therapists who encounter conservative religious individuals struggling with homoerotic attractions need to be very cautious about applying value-laden terms, such as homophobia, to these individuals or their families and support networks. In fact, an uncritical use these terms may actually risk increasing homonegative sentiment should conservatively religious clients and their families perceive their normative beliefs about sexual morality to be globally characterized as homophobic.

Given all the aforementioned considerations, it seems advisable for MFTs dealing with religiously conservative clients to limit the use of the term homophobia to individuals whose moral disapproval of homosexuality is expressed in a way that is inconsistent with the well-accepted values of traditional religious ideology. Thus, incivility, demeaning speech, and any type of aggression toward GLB persons are likely to be forms of behavior for which the term homophobic would be widely endorsed within religious communities and not perceived in an antagonistic manner. Forms of disapproval that appear consistent with the normative values of the religious subculture might preferably be characterized as stemming from a "nonequivalency" position that does not view sexual behavior outside of heterosexual marriage as the moral equivalent of sexual activity within such bounds. This would be a much less pejorative and value-laden term that could facilitate more meaningful dialogue and understanding about reorientation treatment for therapists and clients who operate out of different moral domains.

Causal Attributions for Psychopathology

There is a growing consensus that same-sex behavior is associated with elevated risk of certain forms of psychiatric disorder and with suicide when compared to heterosexual samples (Cochran, 2001; Cochran & Mays, 2000a, 2000b; Diamant, Wold, Spritzer, & Gelberg, 2000; Gilman et al., 2001; Herrell et al., 1999; Hughes & Eliason, 2002; Sandfort, de Graaf, Biji, & Schnabel, 2001; Valanis, Bowen, Bassford, Whitlock, Charney, & Carter, 2000). . . .

Hypothesized biological factors are more commonly minimized or interpreted as signaling constitutional malfunction. This undergirds both the viability of change-oriented therapy and the suspicion that there is something unnatural or sinful in homosexual or bisexual sexual activity.

Conservatives are thus more skeptical of the benefits of normalizing homo-sexual and bisexual sexual behavior in reducing psychological distress. They may point to studies in regions with considerably long histories of tolerance, such as San Francisco or the Netherlands, where elevated emotional and behavioral health risks for GLB individuals persist (Page-Shafer et al., 1999; Sandfort et al., 2001).

The differing emphases in moral vision suggest that both conservative and liberal MFTs may need to look beyond the boundaries of their immediate evaluative frameworks to maintain a balanced attributional perspective. On the one hand, conservative therapists may not sufficiently recognize the impact of stigmatization and discrimination experiences on the psychological distress of GLB clients (Mays & Cochran, 2001). On the other hand, liberally oriented clinicians may be inclined to underestimate or overlook the etiological significance of developmental experience for GLB identity and sexual behavior, such as childhood sexual abuse (Doll et al., 1992; Paul, Catania, Pollack, & Stall, 2001; Tomeo, Templer, Anderson, & Kotler, 2001). . . .

Conclusions

The clinical treatment of unwanted homoerotic attraction continues to be a controversial practice. It is important that MFTs educate themselves on this subject in a manner that includes information and perspectives sensitive to clients who seek such care, the majority of whom have conservative religious backgrounds. This analysis has attempted to provide an initial foray into the issue, utilizing a conservative evaluative framework that is likely to resonate with many of these clients. As such, evidence for the validity of their motivations and efforts toward increasing heterosexual potential has been presented, along with some guidelines for ethical practice that allow for change efforts. Finally, by digging deeper into the divergent moral epistemologies likely to be covertly fueling the debate, it is hoped that the viewpoints of both proponents as well as opponents of reorientation treatment will be regarded as having something important to contribute. Surely, clients who seek to change unwanted homoerotic attraction deserve to have scholarly representation that reflects their experiences, interests, and aspirations. Without this input, the authoritative conclusions about change efforts put forth by mental health associations may merely reflect suppression, rather than consensus, of opinion among therapists and their clients.

References

American Psychiatric Association (1994). Diagnostic and statistical manual of mental disorders. Washington, DC: Author. American Psychiatric Association (1999). Position statement on psychiatric treatment and sexual orientation. *American Journal of Psychiatry, 156,* 1131.

American Psychiatric Association (2000). Position statement on therapies focused on attempts to change sexual orientation (reparative or conversion therapies). *American Journal of Psychiatry, 157,* 1710–1721.

American Psychological Association (2000). Guidelines for psychotherapy with lesbian, gay, and bisexual clients. *American Psychologist, 55,* 1440–1451.

Appleby, P. R., Miller, L. C., & Rothspan, S. (1999). The paradox of trust for male couples: When risking is a part of living. *Personal Relationships, 6,* 81–93.

Bassett, R. L., Baldwin, D., Tammaro, J., Mackmer, D., Mundig, C.,Wareing, A., & Tschorke, E. (2001). Reconsidering intrinsic religion as a source of universal compassion. *Journal of Psychology and Theology, 30,* 131–143.

Bassett, R. L., Hodak, E., Allen, J., Bartos, D., Grastorf, J., Sittig, L., & Strong, J. (2000). Homonegative Christians: Loving the sinner but hating the sin. *Journal of Psychology and Christianity, 19,* 258–269.

Baumeister, R. F (2000). Gender differences in erotic plasticity: The female sex drive as socially flexible and responsive. *Psychological Bulletin, 126,* 347–374.

Bepko, C., & Johnson, T. (2000). Gay and lesbian couples in therapy: Perspectives for the contemporary family therapist. *Journal of Marital and Family Therapy, 26,* 409–419.

Bernstein, A. C. (2000). Straight therapists working with lesbians and gays in family therapy. *Journal of Marital and Family Therapy, 26,* 443–454.

Bernat, J. A., Calhoun, K. S., Adams, H. E., & Zeichner, A. (2001). Homophobia and physical aggression toward homosexual and heterosexual individuals. *Journal of Abnormal Psychology, 110,* 179–187.

Blumstein, P, & Schwartz, P. (1990). Intimate relationships and the creation of sexuality. In D. P. McWirter, S. A. Sanders & J. M. Reinisch (Eds.), *Homosexuality/heterosexuality: Concepts of sexual orientation* (pp. 307–320). New York: Oxford University Press.

Bradley, S. J., & Zucker, K. J. (1997). Gender identity disorder: A review of the past 10 years. *Journal of the American Academy of Child and Adolescent Psychiatry, 36,* 872–880.

Bradley, S. J., & Zucker, K. J. (1998). [Letter to the Editor]. *Journal of the American Academy of Child and Adolescent Psychiatry, 37,* 244–245.

Bridges, K. L., & Croteau, J. M. (1994). Once-married lesbians: Facilitating changing life patterns. *Journal of Counseling and Development, 73,* 134–140.

Bringle, R. G. (1995). Sexual jealousy in the relationships of homosexual and heterosexual men: 1980 and 1992. *Personal Relationships, 2,* 313–325.

Catania, J. A., Osmond, D., Staff, R. D., Pollack, L., Paul, J. P., Blower, S., Binson, D., Canchola, J. A., Mills, T. C., Fisher, L., Choi, K., Porco, T., Turner, C., Blair, J., Henne, J., Bye, L. L., & Coates, T. J. (2001). The continuing HIV epidemic among men who have sex with men. *American Journal of Public Health, 91,* 907–914.

Cochran, S. D. (2001). Emerging issues in research on lesbians' and gay men's mental health: Does sexual orientation really matter? *American Psychologist, 56,* 931–947.

Cochran, S. D., & Mays, V. M. (2000a). Relation between psychiatric syndromes and behaviorally defined sexual orientation in a sample of the U.S. population. *American Journal of Epidemiology, 151,* 516–523.

Cochran, S. D., & Mays, V. M. (2000b). Lifetime prevalence of suicidal symptoms and affective disorders among men reporting same-sex sexual partners: Results from NHANES Ill. *American Journal of Public Health, 90,* 573–578.

Davison, G. C. (2001). Conceptual and ethical issues in therapy for the psychological problems of gay men, lesbians, and bisexuals. *Journal of Clinical Psychology, 57,* 695–704.

Diamant, A. L., Schuster, M. A., McGigan, K., & Lever, J. (1999). Lesbians' sexual history with men. *Archives of Internal Medicine, 159,* 2730–2736.

Diamant, A. L., Wold, C., Spritzer, K., & Gelberg, L. (2000). Health behaviors, health status, and access to health care: A population-based study of lesbian, bisexual, and heterosexual women. *Archives of Family Medicine, 9,* 1043–1051.

Diamond, L. M. (1998). Development of sexual orientation among adolescent and young adult women. *Developmental Psychology, 34,* 1085–1095.

Dilley, J. W., Woods, W. J., & McFarland, W. (1997). Are advances in treatment changing views about high-risk sex? *New England Journal of Medicine, 337,* 501–502.

Doll, L. S., Joy, D., Bartholow, B. N., Bolan, G., Douglas, J. M., Saltzman, L. E., Moss, P. M., & Delgado, W. (1992). Selfreported childhood and adolescent sexual abuse among adult homosexual and bisexual men. *Child Abuse and Neglect, 16,* 855–864.

Dworkin, S. H. (2001). Treating the bisexual client. *Journal of Clinical Psychology, 57,* 671–680.

Ekstrand, M. L., Stall, R. S., Paul, J. P., Osmond, D. H., & Coates, T. J. (1999). Gay men report high rates of unprotected anal sex with partners of unknown or discordant HIV status. *AIDS, 13,* 1525–1533.

Fulton, A. S., Gorsuch, R. L., & Maynard, E. A. (1999). Religious orientation, anti-homosexual sentiment, and fundamentalism among Christians. *Journal for the Scientific Study of Religion, 38,* 14–22.

Gartner, J. D. (1985). Religious prejudice in psychology: Theories of its cause and cure. *Journal of Psychology and Christianity, 4,* 16–23.

Gartner, J. D. (1986). Antireligious prejudice in admissions to doctoral programs in clinical psychology. *Professional Psychology: Research and Practice, 17,* 473–475.

Gilman, S. E., Cochran, S. D., Mays, V. M., Hughes, M., Ostrow, D., & Kessler, R. C. (2001). Risk of psychiatric disorders among individuals reporting same-sex sexual partners in the national comorbidity survey. *American Journal of Public Health, 91,* 933–939.

Goldman, E. L. (1994, October). Psychological factors generate HIV resurgence in young gay men. *Clinical Psychiatry News, 29,* 5.

Graham, R. P, Kirscht, J. P, Kessler, R. C., & Graham, S. (1998). Longitudinal study of relapse from AIDS-preventive behavior among homosexual men. *Health Education and Behavior, 25,* 625–639.

Haidt, J., & Hersh, M. A. (2001). Sexual morality: The cultures and emotions of conservatives and liberals. *Journal of Applied Social Psychology, 31,* 191–221.

Haldeman, D. C. (1994). The practice and ethics of sexual orientation conversion therapy. *Journal of Consulting and Clinical Psychology, 62,* 221–227.

Herrell, R., Goldberg, J., True, W. R., Ramakrishnan, V, Lyons, M., Eisen, S., & Tsuang, M. T. (1999). Sexual orientation and suicidality. A co-twin control study in adult men. *Archives of General Psychiatry, 56,* 867–874.

Hughes, T. L., & Eliason, M. (2002). Substance use and abuse in lesbian, gay, bisexual, and transgender populations. *Journal of Primary Prevention, 22,* 263–298.

Isay, R. A. (1997). Remove gender identity disorder in DSM. *Psychiatric News, 32,* 13.

Johnson, M. E., Brems, C., & Alford-Keating, P. (1997). Personality correlates of homophobia. *Journal of Homosexuality, 34,* 57–69.

Kalichman, S. C., Kelly, J. A., & Rompa, D. (1997). Continued high-risk sex among HIV seropositive gay and bisexual men seeking HIV prevention services. *Health Psychology, 16,* 369–373.

Lauman, E. O., Gagnon, J. H., Michael, T., & Michaels, S. (1994). *The social organization of sexuality.* Chicago: University of Chicago Press.

Mansergh G., Colfax, G. N., Marks, G., Rader, M., Guzman, R., & Bookbinder, S. (2001). The circuit party men's health survey: Findings and implications for gay and bisexual men. *American Journal of Public Health, 91,* 953–958.

Macintosh, H. (1994). Attitudes and experiences of psychoanalysts in analyzing homosexual patients. *Journal of the American Psychoanalytic Association, 42,* 1183–1205.

Markowitz, L. M. (1993, March/April). Understanding the differences: Demystifying gay and lesbian sex. *Family Networker, 17,* 50–59.

Mays, V. M., & Cochran, S. D. (2001). Mental health correlates of perceived discrimination among lesbian, gay, and bisexual adults in the United States. *American Journal of Public Health, 91,* 1869–1876.

Mohr, J. J., & Rochlen, A. B. (1999). Measuring attitudes regarding bisexuality in lesbian, gay male, and heterosexual populations. *Journal of Counseling Psychology, 46,* 353–369.

Murphy, T. F (1992). Redirecting sexual orientation: Techniques and justifications. *Journal of Sex Research, 29,* 501–523.

Nicolosi, J., Byrd, A. D., & Potts, R. W. (2000). Retrospective self-reports of changes in homosexual orientation: A consumer survey of conversion therapy clients. *Psychological Reports, 86,* 1071–1088.

O'Donohue, W., & Caselles, C. E. (1993). Homophobia: Conceptual, definitional, and value issues. *Journal of Psychopathology and Behavioral Assessment, 15,* 177–195.

Page-Shafer, K. A., McFarland, W., Kohn, R., Klausner, J., Katz, M. H., Wohlfeiler, D., & Gibson, S. (1999). Increases in unsafe sex and rectal gonorrhea among men who have sex with men—San Francisco, California, 1994–1997. *Journal of the American Medical Association, 281,* 696–697.

Paul, J. P., Catania, J., Pollack, L., & Stall, R. (2001). Understanding childhood sexual abuse as a predictor of sexual risk-taking among men who have sex with men: The urban men's health study. *Child Abuse and Neglect, 25,* 557–584.

Peplau, L. A., & Garnets, L. D. (2000). A new paradigm for understanding women's sexuality and sexual orientation. *Journal of Social Issues, 56,* 267–282.

Redding, R. E. (2001). Sociopolitical diversity in psychology. *American Psychologist, 56,* 205–215.

Ritter, M. (2001, May 9). Study: Some gays can go straight. *Washington Post.* Retrieved on 5/12/01 from . . .

Rosenbluth, S. (1997). Is sexual orientation a matter of choice? *Psychology of Women Quarterly, 21,* 595–610.

Rosik, C. H. (2001). Conversion therapy revisited: Parameters and rationale for ethical care. *Journal of Pastoral Care, 55,* 47–69.

Rosser, B. R. S., Metz, M. E., Bockting, W. O., & Buroker, T. (1996). Sexual differences, concerns, and satisfaction in homosexual men: An empirical study with implications for HIV prevention. *Journal of Sex and Marital Therapy, 23,* 61–73.

Rust, P. (2001). Two many and not enough: The meanings of bisexual identity. *Journal of Bisexuality, 1,* 31–68.

Sanders, G. L., & Kroll, I. T (2000). Generating stories of resilience: Helping gay and lesbian youth and their families. *Journal of Marital and Family Therapy, 26,* 433–442.

Sandfort, T. G., de Graaf, R., Bijl, R. B., & Schnabel, P. (2001). Same-sex sexual behavior and psychiatric disorders. *Archives of General Psychiatry, 58,* 85–91.

Schaeffer, K. W., Hyde, R. A., Kroencke, T., McCormick, B., & Nottebaum, L. (2000). Religiously-motivated sexual orientation change. *Journal of Psychology and Christianity, 19,* 61–70.

Schaeffer, K. W., Nottebaum, L., Dech, P., & Drawczyk, J. (2000). Religiously-motivated sexual orientation change: A followup study. *Journal of Psychology and Theology, 27,* 329–337.

Shernoff, M. (1999, March/April). Monogamy and gay men. *Family Networker, 23,* 63–71.

Spitzer, R. L. (2001a). 200 subjects who claim to have changed their sexual orientation from homosexual to heterosexual. Paper presented at the meeting of the American Psychiatric Association, New Orleans, LA.

Spitzer, R. L. (2001b, May 23). Psychiatry and homosexuality. *The Wall Street Journal,* A26.

Strathdee, S. A., Galai, N., Safaiean, M., Celentano, D. D., Vlahov, D., Johnson, L., & Nelson, K. E. (2001). Sex differences in risk factors for HIV seroconversion among injection drug users. *Archives of Internal Medicine, 161,* 1281–1288.

Suarez, T., & Miller, J. (2001). Negotiating risks in context: A perspective on unprotected anal intercourse and barebacking among men who have sex with men—where do we go from here. *Archives of Sexual Behavior, 30,* 287–300.

Temeo, M. E., Templer, D. L, Anderson, S., & Kotler, D. (2001). Comparative data of childhood and adolescence molestation in heterosexual and homosexual persons. *Archives of Sexual Behavior, 30,* 535–541.

Throckmorton, W. (1998). Efforts to modify sexual orientation: A review of outcome literature and ethical issues. *Journal of Mental Health Counseling, 20,* 283–304.

Valanis, B. G., Bowen, D. J., Bassford, T., Whitlock, E., Chamey, P., & Carter, R. A. (2000). Sexual orientation and health: Comparisons in the Women's Health Initiative sample. *Archives of Family Medicine, 9,* 843–853.

Vanable, P. A., Ostrow, D. G., McKirnan, D. J., Taywaditep, K. J., & Hope, B. A. (2000). Impact of combination therapies on HIV risk perceptions and sexual risk among HIV-positive and HIV-negative gay and bisexual men. *Health Psychology, 19,* 134–145.

Venigas, R. C., & Conley, T. D. (2000). Biological research on women's sexual orientation: Evaluating the scientific evidence. *Journal of Social Issues, 56,* 267–282.

Voelker, R. (2000). HIV drug resistance. *Journal of the American Medical Association, 12,* 169.

Whisman, V. (1996). *Queer by choice: Lesbians, gay men, and the politics of identity.* New York: Routledge.

Wolitski, R. J., Valdiserri, R. O., Denning, R. H., & Levine, W. C. (2001). Are we headed for a resurgence of the HIV epidemic among men who have sex with men? *American Journal of Public Health, 91,* 883–888.

Yarhouse, M. A. (1998a). When clients seek treatment for same-sex attraction: Ethical issues in the "right to choose" debate. *Psychotherapy, 35,* 248–259.

Yarhouse, M. A. (1998b). When families present with concerns about an adolescent's experience of same-sex attraction. *American Journal of Family Therapy, 36,* 321–330.

Yarhouse, M. A., Burkett, L. A., & Kreeft, E. M. (2002). Paraprofessional Christian ministries for sexual behavior and same-sex identity concerns. *Journal of Psychology and Theology, 30,* 208–227.

Yarhouse, M. A., & VanOrman, B. T. (1999). When psychologists work with religious clients: Applications of the general principles of ethical conduct. *Professional Psychology: Research and Practice, 30,* 557–562.

Zucker, K. J., Bradley, S. J., Kuksis, M., Pecore, K., Birkenfeld-Adams, Doering, R. W., Mitchell, J. N., & Wild, J. (1999). Gender constancy judgments in children with gender identity disorder: Evidence for a developmental lag. *Archives of Sexual Behavior, 28,* 475–502.

Robert-Jay Green

 **NO**

When Therapists Do Not Want Their Clients to Be Homosexual: A Response to Rosik's Article

This commentary is a response to Rosik's "Motivational, Ethical, and Epistemological Foundations in the Treatment of Unwanted Homoerotic Attraction" (this issue). Such treatment raises complex questions that cannot be resolved by focusing on the therapist's conservative versus liberal values. Most such clients are deeply ambivalent about their homosexual attractions. The degree to which their homosexuality is "unwanted" is highly variable among them and sometimes within them over time. Clients who are exclusively homosexual are very unlikely to be able to change their sexual attractions, whereas some clients who are bisexual may be more able to "manage" their homoerotic attractions (acting only on their heterosexual feelings). Marriage and family therapists should be able to support a client along whatever sexual orientation path the client ultimately takes, and the client's sense of integrity and interpersonal relatedness are the most important goals of all.

Although the value of therapeutic "neutrality" has been challenged in the field of family therapy, it is preferable to strive toward neutrality rather than take a partisan position when it comes to the treatment of unwanted homosexuality. If a therapist is not able to support a client's explorations and decisions initially or over the course of treatment to live as heterosexual, homosexual, or bisexual, then I believe that the therapist should excuse her/himself from treating such clients. In contrast to the frame Rosik (this issue) suggests, the treatment of clients' "unwanted homosexuality" should not be approached as mostly a matter of therapists' politics with equal pro and con (liberal vs. conservative) positions or reduced to a matter of religious debate.

There is a crucial difference between religious exhortation/proselytizing and psychotherapy, and that difference lies primarily in whose needs and beliefs are at the center of attention. I do not believe that clients can resolve any major internal conflict in therapy when the continuation of treatment is contingent on the client accepting the therapist's preferred resolution. For example, although he does not state so explicitly, Rosik seems to believe (based on his personal interpretation of the Bible) that homosexuality is a sin, and he seems willing to agree with clients who assert that homosexuality is a sin. Thus, it is unclear how he would treat clients who decided over the course

From *Journal of Marital and Family Therapy*, vol. 29, issue 1, 2003, pp. 29–38. Copyright © 2003 by Blackwell Publishing, Ltd. Reprinted by permission.

of treatment that they wanted to embrace their homosexuality, as many clients seeking reorientation therapy later do (Shidlo & Schroeder, 2001). Would Rosik reject these clients and refer them elsewhere at such a juncture? Or do these clients leave treatment without explanation, sensing that he would be unable to support their new direction?

Although Rosik (this issue)—in one of the more inflammatory remarks in his article—accuses our profession of risking "a large scale form of client discrimination and abandonment" (p. 14) toward gay or bisexual clients who wish to become heterosexual, this claim is unjustified. Gay-affirmative couple and family therapists such as myself (Green & Mitchell, 2002; Laird & Green, 1996) believe just as strongly that clients should set the goals of their treatment. For example, in my practice, I personally have helped lesbian/gay clients stay in heterosexual marriages, and I am comfortable with this goal if clients approach it with integrity (i.e., honesty with their spouse, rather than deception). Also, more than half of my clients at any given time tend to be heterosexuals, and I fully support their being so. In contrast, Rosik seems not to feel that homosexuality is a legitimate moral choice and presumably would have a hard time or find it impossible to work with clients who start out and wish to remain lesbian or gay or wish to increase their self-acceptance. Ironically (borrowing his words), it seems that Rosik and other conversion therapists advocate "discrimination and abandonment" of gay/lesbian clients who wish to remain gay-identified.

Thus, although Rosik would have us believe that his approach is the moral or political equivalent of a "prochoice" position, he is actually communicating a rather confusing double message. If he views the choice of homosexuality as a sin and believes that homosexuality can only to lead to unhappiness and a morally inferior life, it becomes impossible to accept his claim of giving clients any "choice" in therapy other than to adopt his views of homosexuality if they wish to remain in therapy with him. He states, for example: "MFTs who engage in reorientation therapy must respect a client's decision to leave treatment and pursue gay-affirmative therapy" (p. 19). Clearly, the implication of the phrase "leave treatment" is that such clients would be terminated and have to seek treatment elsewhere. Presumably this is because Rosik believes there is only one mentally healthy choice that could bring happiness and ethical fulfillment: heterosexuality.

Despite his pronouncements to that effect, the research literature on lesbian/gay psychology shows clearly that acceptance of one's sexual orientation and finding social support within the lesbian/gay community are the strongest predictors of mental health (Diplacido, 1998; Herek, 1998; Meyer & Dean, 1998). The majority of lesbian/gay people are as happy and mentally healthy as heterosexuals, even if the overall group means differ slightly in large population rates of substance use, depression, and attempted suicide (Bell & Weinberg, 1978; Cochran, 2001; Gonsiorek, 1991). The researchers attribute these small (but statistically significant) differences in group averages to the greater minority stress experienced by lesbian/gay people in society, whereas Rosik implies that these differences are endemic to homosexual orientation itself. If the latter were true, however, how would he explain that the vast majority of lesbian/gay people do not differ from the majority of heterosexuals in terms of substance abuse and mental health? In light of this research, it seems highly inappropriate for a therapist to support a client's jaundiced view that homosexuality is antithetical to psychological well-being and happiness, which is exactly what Rosik appears to do in his article.

Motivations for Seeking Conversion Therapy

The notion of "unwanted homoerotic attraction" is much more complex than Rosik implies in his article, particularly in his section on "motivations for pursuing greater heterosexual potential" (p. 14). Clients with these concerns run the gamut from having no same-sex experiences at all to having exclusive same-sex experiences over many years. In addition, many such clients are bisexual in attractions and/or behavior (Fox, 1996; Klein, 1993). Some of these "bisexual" clients fantasize only homosexual activity even when they are having heterosexual sex.

Many clients who are seeking treatment for unwanted homoerotic attraction are actually rather ambivalent about it. They say they do not want to be homosexual, yet they continue homosexual behavior and do not show serious intent to change. Others seem to be saying something like "I'm okay with being homosexual, but I'm afraid my parents, employers, children, or friends will find out and reject or discriminate against me." It is essential to help clients examine what is motivating their desire to change at the time treatment is started and whether their motivation is externalized or internalized, temporary in response to some precipitating event (e.g., a breakup of a same-sex relationship, or an attempt to appease a heterosexual spouse who discovered an affair), or persistent over time. As every therapist knows, almost no presenting problem or treatment is quite as simple and straightforward as it might appear to be at the outset, and many attempts to change that are begun "under duress" (due to external pressures) meet with initial success but are not sustained over time.

There are many minority human traits that may be "unwanted" by their holders in our society (e.g., ethnic appearance, body shapes that do not match the cultural ideal, foreign accents), but these attributes are undesired because someone (or some group) defines them as undesirable, not because they are problematic in and of themselves (Green, 1998). In addition to facing external prejudice and discrimination, members of minority groups frequently internalize society's irrational views of their group traits and suffer various levels of psychological distress as a result (DiPlacido, 1998; Meyer & Dean, 1998). However, often their internalization of society's prejudice is highly conflicted because they simultaneously understand that prejudice is arbitrary, irrational, and can be resisted. Although some of these minority group traits might be changeable (e.g., plastic surgery to reshape a nose, or surgery to remove epicanthic folds in eyelids), it is valuable to inquire what motivates such clients to seek change, whether change in that trait is possible, what obstacles exist to accepting one's "differentness," rather than trying to eliminate it, and what advantages/disadvantages might follow from embracing one's individuality and minority status versus trying to conform to the dominant social norms of the majority group.

Clearly, there are some therapeutic goals (for example, an anorectic's goal to become even thinner; an abusive husband's desire to increase his dominance over his wife) that therapists may not be able to support because the achievement of those goals would severely threaten the well being of the client or another family member. For these reasons, the first steps in the treatment of "unwanted homoerotic attraction" should include efforts to understand with the client why he/she does not want homoerotic attraction. I do not mean that one should dismiss or refute the client's stated goals. Rather, that it is important to try to understand the basis of the client's motivation to change and whether it is internalized and stable (versus externalized and ambivalent) or based on negative stereotypes about homosexuality (such as the false ideas that gay people are invariably unhappy, lonely in old age, promiscuous, unable to establish lasting relationships, afflicted with HIV, etc.), some of which Rosik actually endorses in his article.

For example, Rosik suggests in his "motivations" section that many male clients justifiably want to rid themselves of homoerotic desire because of the heightened risk of contracting HIV in sex with gay men. However, most of the people in the world with AIDS now are heterosexuals (in Africa), and lesbians have the lowest rates of HIV infection. By using Rosik's logic (that homosexual clients should seek to become heterosexual to lessen their risks of contracting HIV), one could argue just as easily that heterosexual women should be encouraged to become lesbians to reduce their chances of contracting HIV. The fact is that homosexuality does not cause AIDS. Unsafe sex with HIV-positive partners (heterosexual or homosexual) causes AIDS. Obviously, the solution in HIV prevention is safer sex, not sexual orientation conversion therapy for heterosexual women and gay men.

Likewise, the solution to the unique mental health stresses faced by lesbians and gay men is a reduction in the prejudice to which they are subjected. Research shows quite clearly that external discrimination (homophobia) and internalized homophobia (Malyon, 1982; Shidlo, 1994) are strong predictors of depression, suicidality, and HIV-risk behaviors among gay, lesbian, and bisexual persons. Lesbians and gay men who are more self accepting of their sexual orientations, who receive more acceptance of their sexual orientation from family, friends, or coworkers, and who are more involved in the gay community have lower rates of mental health problems and HIV risk behaviors than do lesbians/gay men who are less self accepting and less identified with the gay community (Green & Mitchell, 2002; Herek, 1998; Meyer & Dean, 1998). Rosik seems to have gotten these results backwards in his "motivations" section. He seems to be arguing that gay/lesbian persons who accept and live out their sexual orientations will have greater mental health problems, but the research shows the opposite to be true.

The Possibility of Eliminating Homoerotic and Increasing Heteroerotic Potential

At the outset, we need to clarify that the terms heterosexual, bisexual, and homosexual are much more complicated than their casual usage by Rosik and most authors writing on these topics imply. As readers may know, Kinsey (Kinsey, Pomeroy, & Martin, 1948; Kinsey, Pomeroy, Martin, & Gebhard, 1953) counterpoised heterosexuality and homosexuality on a single bipolar continuum, which ranged from exclusive heterosexuality (0) to exclusive homosexuality (6):

0 = Exclusively heterosexual

1 = Predominantly heterosexual, only incidentally homosexual

2 = Predominantly heterosexual, but more than incidentally homosexual

3 = Equally heterosexual and homosexual

4 = Predominantly homosexual, but more than incidentally heterosexual

5 = Predominantly homosexual, only incidentally heterosexual

6 = Exclusively homosexual

However, in this rating system, Kinsey did not distinguish the person's overt sexual behavior from underlying feelings, attractions, or fantasies, nor did he distinguish either of these dimensions from the person's self-labeling or presentation to others (as heterosexual, bisexual, or gay/lesbian). By putting heterosexuality and homosexuality on a single bipolar continuum, Kinsey created a kind of "zero sum game," in which it was assumed that the more one was heterosexual, the less one was homosexual, and vice versa.

More recently, theorists such as Klein (1993) have suggested that several other theoretical continua are needed to understand a person's sexual orientation. Revising Klein's framework, I would suggest that it is most important to take into account the person's attractions, behavior, self-identification, and self-presentation, as follows:

1. Degree of heterosexual attractions (from high to low)
2. Degree of heterosexual behavior (from high to low)
3. Degree of homosexual attractions (from high to low)
4. Degree of homosexual behavior (from high to low)
5. Self-identity (self-labeling) as heterosexual, bisexual, or gay/lesbian
6. Self-presentation to others as heterosexual, bisexual, or gay/lesbian

In contrast to Kinsey, there is no reason to believe that the strength of one's heterosexual attractions diminishes one's homosexual attractions or vice-versa. That is, one may have a high degree of attraction to persons of both sexes; or a low degree of attraction to persons of both sexes; or be highly attracted to one sex and not to the other at all; or have all other possible combinations of levels of attractions to males and females. Likewise, for behavior, some people are high in heterosexual activity and simultaneously high in homosexual activity and others are low in both, with most people higher in heterosexual attractions and behavior.

In this framework, sexual orientation can best be conceptualized as encompassing several dimensions, and the person's functioning across those dimensions may or may not be consistent. For example, Ms. Smith may be strongly attracted to women but only have sex with men (while fantasizing only about women); and she may inwardly label herself as "bisexual" but present herself to others as exclusively heterosexual. In general, greater levels of incongruity among the dimensions are associated with greater levels of internal conflict, relationship dissatisfaction, and potential dissolution of relationships over time.

It is not clear whether Rosik believes that all clients seeking treatment for unwanted homoerotic attraction stand an equal chance of success at conversion. For example, in his review of the developmental research, Rosik erroneously stated that the link between gender nonconformity in childhood and homosexual orientation in adulthood "indirectly supports the potential for increasing heterosexual potential" (p. 16). However, this whole line of scientific evidence actually does the opposite. It shows that sexual orientation in these cases is part of a continuous developmental process that begins quite early in life, manifesting as cross-gender behavior during childhood and manifesting as homosexual orientation later, in adulthood (Bailey & Zucker, 1995; Bell, Weinberg, & Hammersmith, 1981; D'Augelli & Patterson, 1995; Green, Bettinger, & Zacks, 1996). Most researchers interpret this finding as evidence for the immutability of sexual orientation, concluding that it must be highly resistant to change, given the enormous social sanctions that gender nonconforming children and lesbian/gay adults encounter throughout life.

Thus, most sexologists tend to believe that sexual attractions are relatively fixed early in life, whereas sexual behavior, self labeling, and self presentation can vary dramatically according to situational and personality factors. Some of the sex therapy literature indicates that clients who start out as truly bisexual in their attractions may be able to suppress their homosexual activity and increase their heterosexual activity at least temporarily during the treatment period or beyond (Masters & Johnson, 1979). However, clients who are exclusively homosexual (in terms of attractions) are very unlikely to succeed in developing enduring heterosexual attractions. Some proportion of the latter clients may be able to engage in temporary heterosexual behavior while utilizing homosexual fantasies. However, most of them would not find this mode of sexual expression sufficiently fulfilling emotionally over the long term. As one might imagine, the maintenance of changes after treatment in these different subgroups of clients may be quite variable depending on their degree of initial bisexual versus homosexual attractions.

Lastly, it is worth noting that women seem to be somewhat more fluid in their sexual orientation than are men, and the reasons for this difference are not entirely known (Peplau & Garnets, 2000). One may speculate, however, than women are aroused sexually more by emotional and interactional aspects of a romantic relationship, whereas men are more aroused by visual stimuli alone. Also, for obvious anatomical reasons, men require a relatively higher degree of attraction and physical arousal to participate in sexual intercourse, whereas woman can often participate at much lower levels of arousal or in its absence. This enables women to move more easily from heterosexual to lesbian relationships or vice-versa, regardless of their degree of sexual arousal in those relationships.

Research on Conversion Therapy

Rosik's entire article seems based on the premise that unwanted homoerotic attraction could be eliminated and heterosexual responsiveness developed through reorientation therapy. To support this contention, he presents a selective review of the research on this topic, emphasizing studies conducted by religiously based researchers whose findings are consistent with his point of view, while omitting the most significant research (e.g., Shidlo & Schroeder, 2001) that throws those findings into question. However, even the research he emphasizes shows that a majority of participants in conversion therapies fail to attain their goals.

For example, Rosik cites the survey by Nicolosi, Byrd, and Potts (2000) showing that 18% of participants in conversion therapy changed to becoming exclusively heterosexual and 17% almost entirely heterosexual. But this leaves two-thirds of clients who failed to attain or nearly attain the sought-after changes. Rosik also touts research by Shaeffer, Hyde, Kroencke, McCormick, and Nottebaum (2000) but then advises that: "These results did not support the short-term benefit of change-oriented therapy and speak more to modification of homosexual behavior rather than feelings" (p. 17).

With more fanfare, Rosik then presents the results of a recent study by Spitzer (2001a), who specifically sought research subjects who claimed to have changed their sexual orientations as a result of conversion therapy. This research design cannot yield information on what percentage of attempters succeed or fail to convert. Rather, it reveals only what self-described converters have to say about their experiences. Many, if not most, of Spitzer's research participants were religious conservatives and were referred by religious ex-gay groups. Although Rosik selectively reports some of Spitzer's data to buttress his contention that lesbian/gays can change their sexual orientations, it is interesting that Spitzer (2001b) himself draws a much more cautious conclusion from the study:

> Complete change was uncommon. . . . In reality, change should be seen as complex and on a continuum. Some homosexuals appear able to change self-identity and behavior, but not arousal and fantasies; others can change only self-identity; and only a very few, I suspect, can substantially change all four. Change in all four is probably less frequent than claimed by therapists who do this kind of work; in fact, I suspect the vast majority of gay people would be unable to alter by much a firmly established homosexual orientation (Spitzer, 2001b).

Furthermore, there is reason to doubt the veracity of research participants who were referred by religion-oriented conversion treatment programs (as was the case in the studies by Shaeffer et al., 2000; Nicolosi et al., 2001; and Spitzer, 2001a). For example, Exodus (which is listed in the appendix to

Rosik's article and is the largest of the ex-gay religious groups) was founded in 1976 by Michael Bussee, Gary Cooper, and others. Bussee became one of Exodus's main leaders and spokespersons. However, even as they claimed to be ex-gays and worked to convert others to heterosexuality, Bussee and Cooper secretly were involved with each other romantically and sexually, and they subsequently left Exodus together in 1979. In interviews later, Bussee stated:

> "The desires never go away. . . . The confrontations begin and the guilt gets worse and worse." Bussee recalled that some people who went through the Exodus program had breakdowns or committed suicide. "One man slashed his genitals with a razor and poured Drano on his wounds. Another man impulsively underwent an incomplete sex-change operation because he believed his sexual desires might receive divine approval were he biologically a woman." After dealing with hundreds of people, Bussee concluded that he and his partner had not "met one who went from gay to straight. Even if you manage to alter someone's sexual behavior, you cannot change their true sexual orientation. . . . If you got them away from the Christian limelight... and asked them, 'Honestly now, are you saying that you are no longer homosexual and you are now heterosexually oriented?' . . . not one person said, 'Yes, I am actually now heterosexual.'" (Mills, 1999).

More recently, John Paulk, a gay man who undertook conversion therapy with Exodus and claimed to have converted to heterosexuality, was appointed Chairman of the Board of Exodus North America. He married an "ex-lesbian" and frequently was described at the time as the "poster child" of the ex-gay movement, becoming its main public spokesman and appearing very frequently on television and other news media. However, in September 2000, Paulk was spotted in a gay bar in Washington, DC. He claimed initially that he did not realize that he had walked into and was sitting in a gay bar. However, he later recanted this story and was put on probation by the Exodus North America board of directors for what the board described as Paulk's "lapse" in judgment (Exodus North America, 2000).

These episodes among the leaders of Exodus throw into serious doubt the statements religious "ex-gays" make about their sexual orientations to the media and to researchers. For obvious reasons, members of fundamentalist religious groups have very strong incentives to be in denial or to hide their sexual orientations from researchers who are studying their group's treatment outcomes. Spitzer's follow-back sample of ex-gays was made up mainly of such persons. Given the history of duplicity among the leadership of Exodus as described above, it is difficult to determine whether self-reports given over the telephone by religious "ex-gay" research participants in the studies cited by Rosik were valid.

In contrast to Spitzer's (2001a) study of self-described "ex-gays," Shidlo and Schroeder (2001) undertook a survey of all clients who had attempted sexual orientation conversion treatment, regardless of whether or not they had succeeded in changing their sexual orientation. These authors found that the attempt to convert was itself severely damaging psychologically to many clients; that it reflected and contributed to their self-hatred; and that it delayed the ultimate acceptance of their sexual orientation later in life. Furthermore, Shidlo and Schroeder found that many clients involved in such treatments had lied to their therapists about continuing homosexual activity. Their conversion therapists never learned of the longer-term outcomes, which usually involved more therapy later on and ultimate acceptance of homosexuality.

Of the 202 participants in Shidlo and Schroeder's (2001) study who had participated in some form of conversion therapy, only eight participants (about 4%) reported having achieved the goal of being in a heterosexual relationship and not struggling with homoerotic desires/behavior. Of these eight participants, seven provided ex-gay counseling, and four of the seven had paid positions as ex-gay or conversion counselors. In other words, this shift in sexual orientation may have been sustained partially by work involvements as well as by participation in treatment. But even if these eight successful cases (out of 202 attempts) are genuine and permanent conversions, the generally high failure rate of conversion therapy (96%) found by Shidlo and Schroeder has to be addressed in terms of the ethical implications for clients who are seeking to eliminate homoerotic attractions.

Given the above studies, it is probably fair to conclude from the existing research that only a very small percentage of exclusively gay/lesbian people could undertake a significant degree of heterosexual involvement and feel reasonably content in doing so. Mostly, the changes that could be achieved would be behavioral and in terms of identity, rather than in terms of underlying attractions. These "ex-gays" could engage in heterosexual relationships and present themselves as heterosexual despite predominant homosexual attractions and despite using homosexual fantasies during heterosexual encounters. For some strongly religious clients or clients with few relationship alternatives, this adaptation may be adequately satisfying and workable, especially if their partner/spouse were aware and willing to accommodate the situation, as is sometimes the case.

However, for most other predominantly homosexual clients, the large discrepancy between their attractions and their behavior would become intolerable over time, and they would feel that a deeper love and emotional fulfillment was missing in their lives. The fact remains that most homosexual (as opposed to bisexual) clients seeking conversion therapy are simply unable to make a sustained shift to heterosexuality, especially in underlying attractions, rather than in overt behavior or self-presentation. Many of these clients continue to engage in homosexual activity during and/or after treatment, and the vast majority of them are likely to accept a lesbian/gay identity later in their lives, after conversion therapy ends (see Duberman, 2002, and Moor, 2001, for very poignant case examples).

Ethical Issues

Given the high likelihood of failure in the treatment of unwanted homoerotic attraction, serious ethical issues arise regarding informed consent and the possibility that such failed therapy will be harmful to clients. If, as even the religion-motivated research cited by Rosik shows, the vast majority of clients who undertake conversion therapy do not succeed at suppressing their homosexuality and converting to heterosexuality, then therapists have an ethical obligation to so inform clients at the outset of treatment.

In addition, there is much documentation of the destructive effects that certain sexual orientation conversion treatments have had on lesbian/gay/bisexual people. These treatments often exacerbate internalized homophobia and all of its correlates, such as self-hatred, depression, suicidality, drug abuse, and HIV-risk behaviors (Garnets, Hancock, Cochran, Godchilds, & Peplau, 1991; Schroeder & Shidlo, 2001; Shidlo, Schroeder, & Drescher, 2001). Clients need to be informed of these risks at the start of therapy and advised to discuss with their therapists any signs that the therapy is making things worse, rather than better.

Obviously, no psychotherapeutic treatments are 100% successful. However, conversion therapy appears to fail such a significant amount of the time and to be harmful such a large proportion of the time that this issue of informed consent seems essential to raise with a client. The most ethical stance is to: (a) present the information on conversion therapy outcomes as it currently exists in the scientific literature as summarized above; (b) inform the client that this literature is still not definitive; (c) indicate one's willingness to continually review the client's progress toward goals as therapy progresses and to stop therapy if it is unhelpful or harmful; (d) indicate that the continuation of therapy is not contingent on the client selecting any particular sexual orientation; and (e) emphasize that the main concern of therapy will be the client living his or her life with the greatest degree of interpersonal relatedness (connection and compassion) and with integrity (differentiation of a "whole self" based on lived experience, rather than a "pseudo-self"). This stance allows the client to fully utilize his/her religious values in deciding whether and how to express sexuality with integrity. It also leaves the client free to attempt heterosexuality and still provides a safety net and psychological help if the client does not achieve that goal or changes goals along the way.

What Is Rosik's "Treatment of Unwanted Homoerotic Attraction?"

Although the title of Rosik's article refers to a "treatment," it is noteworthy that there is almost no description of that treatment. Instead, the author focuses almost exclusively on the polemics of liberal versus conservative therapists' acceptance of the client's initial goal to become heterosexual. In addition, while claiming that his approach is grounded in religion, Rosik overlooks other religious perspectives and interpretations of the Bible that help clients incorporate their religious beliefs into a positive gay identity (see the website of PFLAG—Parents, Families, & Friends of Lesbians and Gays—for a continually updated reading list on "Homosexuality and Religion," www.pflag.org). Thus, Rosik's article remains rather abstract throughout, tending toward caricatures of liberal and conservative therapists, but avoiding the nitty-gritty information about how to conduct this treatment with real people.

For example, Rosik states: "Conservatives, in contrast, tend to grapple with a broader and more multifaceted moral domain that extends beyond the EOA to include two other influential dimensions in their evaluative framework: the ethics of community (EOC), and the ethics of divinity (EOD)" (p. 20). He then explains that this larger domain goes beyond the "ethics of autonomy (EOA)" (which are supposedly the only ethics embraced by liberal therapists) to include the "ethics of community (EOC)" and the "ethics of divinity (EOD)," the latter referring to Biblical and other religious precepts. However, it is completely arbitrary to state that liberal therapists are concerned only with the ethics of autonomy and not with the ethics of community or divinity, and to anoint conservative therapists the keepers of a "larger" (presumably superior) morality compared to the rest of the professional and academic community. There simply is no basis for claiming that the bulk of therapists are dealing with a smaller moral domain than conservative therapists or for assuming that conservative religious therapists' applications of the Bible are superior to those of other, less conservative therapists with religious affiliations. Yet this is the kind of ad hoc reasoning that makes much of Rosik's writing about moral epistemology so polemical at the core.

The omission of a treatment method description is quite worrisome, because many religious conversion programs seem to use techniques that are ethically questionable from the standpoint of mainstream psychological treatments. In addition, readers are unable to evaluate the merits of Rosik's treatment techniques even on theoretical or logical grounds, because these techniques were never described. For example, does Rosik engage in various combinations of Biblical study, prayer groups, and pastoral counseling? Exorcisms or other rituals based on a sin-based conception of homosexuality? Aversion therapy to decrease homosexual attractions, or classical conditioning techniques to increase heterosexual attractions? Does the treatment use fear-based tactics with references to Satan and punishment in the afterlife?

Frequently, conversion therapists authoritatively attribute the cause of homosexuality to factors that research has shown are completely unrelated to the development of sexual orientation. Such attributions seem unethical in light of the existing research. For example, that old psychodynamic saw of blaming "overinvolved mothers and/or distant fathers" for a child's homosexual orientation (and for almost every other psychological problem) is still frequently used by conversion therapists, even though research findings have long since put that notion to rest (Bell et al., 1981). In fact, no family patterns have been found to bear a causal relationship to the development of homosexuality. Nor has child physical or sexual abuse been found to bear a relationship with homosexuality. No longitudinal studies on this question have been conducted, and some studies show that the rates of such prior abuse are identical for heterosexual and lesbian women (Herman, 1992), yet this is another frequent interpretation offered to clients by conversion therapists.

Because he does not give us specifics, we are left with many more questions than answers when it comes to understanding Rosik's clinical treatment for unwanted homoerotic attraction. I invite Dr. Rosik to provide in his rejoinder a more tangible description of the treatment, however briefly. We need to know what sorts of interpretations, homework assignments, suggestions, adjunctive treatments, referrals, religious activities, and sequences of interventions are typically used in his method of therapy. We need to know what information about sexual orientation the clients are advised to disclose to their spouses or dating partners, and whether and how spouses or partners are involved in the treatment. We also need to know how therapists working in Rosik's framework would respond if a client changed goals and decided to try to accept his/her homosexuality during the course of treatment. Lacking such basic information, it is impossible for readers to adequately evaluate Rosik's treatment methods or his ethics.

References

Bailey, J. M, & Zucker, K. J. (1995). Childhood sex-typed behavior and sexual orientation: A conceptual analysis and quantitative review. *Developmental Psychology, 31,* 43–55.

Bell, A. P, & Weinberg, M. (1978). *Homosexualities: A study of diversity among men and women.* New York: Simon and Schuster.

Bell, A. P, Weinberg, M. S., & Hammersmith, S. K. (1981). *Sexual preference: Its development in men and women.* Bloomington, IN: Indiana University Press.

Cochran, S. D. (2001). Emerging issues in research on lesbians' and gay men's mental health: Does sexual orientation really matter? *American Psychologist, 56,* 931–947.

D'Augelli, A. R., & Patterson, C. J. (Eds.). (1995). *Lesbian, gay, and bisexual identities over the lifespan: Psychological perspectives.* New York: Oxford University Press.

DiPlacido, J. (1998). Minority stress among lesbians, gay men and bisexuals. In G. M. Herek (Ed.), *Stigma and sexual orientation: Understanding prejudice against lesbians, gay men, and bisexuals* (pp. 138–159). Thousand Oaks, CA: Sage.

Duberman, M. J. (2002). *Cures: A gay man's odyssey* (10th anniversary ed.). Boulder, CO: Westview Press.

Exodus North America (October 3, 2000). Chairman Disciplined for Gay Bar Visit (Press release). Retrieved July 31, 2002, from . . .

Fox, R. (1996). Bisexuality in perspective: A review of theory and research. In B. Firestein (Ed.), *Bisexuality: The psychology and politics of an invisible minority* (pp. 3–50). Thousand Oaks, CA: Sage.

Garnets, L., Hancock, K. A., Cochran, S. D., Godchilds, J., & Peplau, L. A. (1991). Issues in psychotherapy with lesbians and gay men: A survey of psychologists. *American Psychologist, 46,* 964–972.

Gonsiorek, J. C. (1991). The empirical basis for the demise of the illness model of homosexuality. In J. C. Gonsiorek & J. D. Weinrich, J. D. (Eds.), *Homosexuality: Research implications for public policy* (pp. 115–136). Thousand Oaks, CA: Sage.

Green, R.-J., (1998a). Race and the field of family therapy. In M. McGoldrick (Ed.), *Revisioning family therapy: Race, culture, and gender in clinical practice* (pp. 93–110). New York: Guilford Press.

Green, R.-J., Bettinger, M., & Zacks, E. (1996). Are lesbian couples fused and gay male couples disengaged? Questioning gender straightjackets. In J. Laird & R.-J. Green (Eds.), *Lesbians and gays in couples and families: A handbook for therapists* (pp. 185–230). San Francisco: Jossey-Bass.

Green, R.-J., & Mitchell, V. (2002). Gay and lesbian couples in therapy: Homophobia, relational ambiguity, and social support. In A. S. Gurman & N. S. Jacobson, (Eds.), *Clinical handbook of couple therapy* (3rd ed., pp. 546-568). New York: Guilford Press.

Herek, G. M. (Ed.) (1998). *Stigma and sexual orientation: Understanding prejudice against lesbians, gay men, and bisexuals.* Thousand Oaks, CA: Sage.

Herman, J. L. (1992). *Trauma and recovery.* New York: Basic Books.

Klein, E (1993). *The bisexual option.* New York: Haworth Press.

Kinsey, A. C., Pomeroy, W. B., & Martin, C. E. (1948). *Sexual behavior in the human male.* Philadelphia: W. B. Saunders.

Kinsey, A. C., Pomeroy, W. B., Martin, C. E., & Gebhard, P. H. (1953). *Sexual behavior in the human female.* Philadelphia: W. B. Saunders.

Laird, J., & Green, R.-J. (Eds.). (1996). *Lesbians and gays in couples and families: A handbook for therapists.* San Francisco: Jossey-Bass.

Malyon, A. K. (1982). Psychotherapeutic implications of internalized homophobia in gay men. In J. Gonsiorek (Ed.), *Homosexuality and psychotherapy: A practitioner's handbook of affirmative models* (pp. 59-69). New York: Haworth Press.

Masters, W., & Johnson, V. (1979). *Homosexuality in perspective.* Boston: Little, Brown.

Meyer, I. H., & Dean, L. (1998) Internalized homophobia, intimacy, and sexual behavior among gay and bisexual men. In G. M. Herek (Ed.), *Stigma and sexual orientation: Understanding prejudice against lesbians, gay men, and bisexuals* (pp. 160–186). Thousand Oaks, CA: Sage.

Mills, K. I. (February, 1999). Mission impossible: Why reparative therapy and ex-gay ministries fail. Retrieved July 31, 2002 from: . . .

Moor, P. (2001). The view from Irving Bieber's couch: "Heads I win, tails you lose." In A. Shidlo, M. Schroeder, & J. Drescher (Eds.), *Sexual conversion therapy: Ethical, clinical, and research perspectives* (pp. 25–36). New York: Haworth Press.

Nicolosi, J., Byrd, A. D., & Potts, R. W. (2000). Retrospective self-reports of changes in homosexual orientation: A consumer survey of conversion therapy clients. *Psychological Reports, 86,* 1071–1088.

Peplau, L. A., & Garnets, L. D. (2000). A new paradigm for understanding women's sexuality and sexual orientation. *Journal of Social Issues, 56,* 267–282.

Rosik, C. H. (2002). Motivational, ethical, and epistemological foundations in the treatment of unwanted homoerotic attraction. *Journal of Marital & Family Therapy, 29,* pp. 13–28.

Schaeffer, K. W., Hyde, R. A., Kroencke, T., McCormick, B., & Nottebaum, L. (2000). Religiously-motivated sexual orientation change. *Journal of Psychology & Christianity, 19,* 61–70.

Schroeder, M., & Shidlo, A. (2002). Ethical issues in sexual orientation conversion therapies. In A. Shidlo, M. Schroeder, & J. Drescher (Eds.), *Sexual conversion therapy: Ethical, clinical, and research perspectives* (pp. 131–166). New York: Haworth Press.

Shidlo, A. (1994). Internalized homophobia: Conceptual and empirical issues in measurement. In B. Greene & G. Herek (Eds.), *Lesbian and gay psychology: Theory, research, and clinical applications* (pp. 176–205). Thousand Oaks, CA: Sage.

Shidlo, A., & Schroeder, M. (2001). Conversion therapy: A consumers report. *Professional Psychology: Research & Practice, 33,* 249–259.

Shidlo, A., Schroeder, M., & Drescher, J. (2001). (Eds.). *Sexual conversion therapy: Ethical, clinical, and research perspectives.* New York: Haworth Press.

Spitzer, R. L. (2001a). Two hundred subjects who claim to have changed their sexual orientation from homosexual to heterosexual. Paper presented at the meeting of the American Psychiatric Association, New Orleans, LA.

Spitzer, R. L. (May 23, 20016). Commentary: Psychiatry and Homosexuality. *Wall Street Journal.* Retrieved July 31, 2002 from . . .

CHALLENGE QUESTIONS

Is Treating Homosexuality Ethical?

1. Is homosexuality a product of nature or nurture? Support your claims with research evidence.
2. Does a patient's request to engage in sexual orientation therapy make the therapist's choice to do so ethical?
3. Should homophobia be considered treatable? Support your answer.
4. Both Rosik and Green point to gender identity disorder as support for their claims. Whose position do you think gender identity disorder better supports? Justify and support your answer.
5. Which, if any, motivations for participating in sexual orientation therapy do you find valid? Why?

Internet References . . .

Libertus.net: Studies & Research

This Libertus.net page contains links to studies and research on the effects of portrayals of violence in the electronic media, as well as reviews, analysis, and commentaries on that research.

`http://libertus.net/censor/studies.html`

Journal of Personality and Social Psychology

This site contains a description of the *Journal of Personality and Social Psychology*, the current issue's table of contents (with abstracts), past tables of contents, and selected online articles from the journal. Looking over the table of contents should provide you with an overview of current topics of interest to social psychologists.

`http://www.apa.org/journals/psp.html`

The Society for the Psychological Study of Social Issues

This homepage of the Society for the Psychological Study of Social Issues (SPSSI) provides information about current research in social psychology as well as abstracts of issues of the *Journal of Social Issues*.

`http://www.spssi.org`

Sexhelp.com

This is Dr. Patrick Carnes's website, through which he extends hope and comfort to many who are struggling with sexual addiction. This site has links to other readings and materials as well as the selection included in this volume.

`http://www.sexhelp.com/index.cfm`

Google.com

Simply Google "sexual addiction" (with SafeSearch ON) and you will be given thousands of links to sex addiction information and recovery sites.

Social Psychology

Social psychology is the study of humans in their social environments. A central concern of social psychologists is how aspects of society affect the individual. For example, does the "social environment" of media violence, such as video games, harm children or adults? Does playing a violent video game make children more prone to aggressive behavior? What about relatively recent changes in our social environment? Some psychologists have pointed to the recent upsurge of sexually explicit "societal and cultural messages" on the Internet and other media. Could this upsurge lead to problems such as pornography addiction and sexual addictions in general? Do such addictions even exist? If so, can they best be treated with addiction treatments, such as the 12-step model?

- Do Video Games Lead to Violence?

- Can Sex Be Addictive?

ISSUE 17

Do Video Games Lead to Violence?

YES: Douglas A. Gentile and Craig A. Anderson, from "Violent Video Games: The Newest Media Violence Hazard," in Douglas A. Gentile, ed., *Media Violence and Children: A Complete Guide for Parents and Professionals* (Praeger, 2003)

NO: Cheryl K. Olson, from "Media Violence Research and Youth Violence Data: Why Do They Conflict?" *Academic Psychiatry* (Summer 2004)

ISSUE SUMMARY

YES: Developmental psychologist Douglas A. Gentile and department of psychology chair Craig A. Anderson assert that violent video games cause several physiological and psychological changes in children that lead to aggressive and violent behavior.

NO: Cheryl K. Olson, a professor of psychiatry, contends that further research is needed because there is so little current evidence of a substantial connection between exposure to violent video games and serious real-life violence.

T he nation was horrified when Eric Harris and Dylan Klebold brutally murdered 13 students and a teacher at their high school in Littleton, Colorado. What could have caused these teenagers to commit such merciless acts of violence? As authorities investigated, they discovered that Harris and Klebold spent much of their time playing violent video games. Could exposure to such games lead to this kind of violent behavior?

Almost 30 years have past since the first violent video game was released. Debate about the effects of violent games on children's behavior has filled the last 20 of those 30 years. Many scholars have concluded from this debate that playing violent video games increases a child's violent behavior. They contend that by being involved in this kind of interactive, violent stimuli, children essentially train themselves to act in violent ways. This is especially true of those children who are notably aggressive prior to their experience with violent games. As graphics improve and game-play becomes more and more realistic, these scholars and some parents worry that these unhealthy effects will only increase.

In the first selection, Douglas A. Gentile and Craig A. Anderson address what they feel recent research has made very clear: playing violent video games leads to violent behavior. Gentile and Anderson claim that several things happen while a child is playing violent video games: an increase in physiological arousal, aggressive cognitions and emotions, aggressive behaviors, and decreased prosocial behaviors. These researchers also take on some of the more popular criticisms facing video game research. For instance, some say violent video games affect only a select few who are already abnormally aggressive. However, Gentile and Anderson argue that this criticism is illegitimate because no group has ever been discovered to be totally immune to the effects of violent video games.

In the second selection, Cheryl K. Olson suggests there might not be as strong a connection between violent video games and violent behavior as researchers like Gentile and Anderson depict. She points to a lack of definitive consensus on what is meant by "violence" and "aggression." How can we be so sure about these findings, Olson seems to say, when we cannot even define the main concepts involved? Moreover, she insists violent behavior and playing violent video games are not as connected as the popular media likes to portray. While she does not deny the possibility that violent video games could affect kids in some way, Olson feels current research is inadequate and cannot be generalized to situations outside a laboratory setting due to small, nonrandom, and unrepresentative sampling.

POINT

- Research shows that playing violent video games increases aggressive thoughts and emotions.

- Experiments with violent video games demonstrate increases in aggressive behaviors.

- The validity and generalization of these studies are widely acknowledged.

- More realistic video games increases physiological arousal.

- Because violent video games are interactive, what children learn comes quickly and is deeply absorbed.

COUNTERPOINT

- Vague definitions of aggression and violence undermine the credibility of such studies.

- There is little evidence of a substantial link between exposure to violent video games and serious, real-life violence.

- Test conditions are difficult to generalize to the real world and the results are often erroneously interpreted.

- National data show no correlation between the recent rise in violent video game usage and violent juvenile crime.

- Researchers have not considered video game violence alongside recognized causes of violent behavior.

YES

Douglas A. Gentile and
Craig A. Anderson

Violent Video Games: The Newest Media Violence Hazard

... Time Spent with Video Games

Video games have become one of the dominant entertainment media for children in a very short time. In the mid-1980s, children averaged about four hours a week playing video games, including time spent playing at home and in arcades. By the early 1990s, home video game use had increased and arcade play had decreased. The average amount was still fairly low, averaging about two hours of home play per week for girls, and about four hours of home play per week for boys. By the mid 1990s, home use had increased for fourth grade girls to 4.5 hours per week, and to 7.1 hours per week for fourth grade boys. In recent national surveys of parents, school-age children (boys and girls combined) devote an average of about seven hours per week playing video games. In a recent survey of over 600 eighth and ninth grade students, children averaged 9 hours per week of video game play overall, with boys averaging 13 hours per week and girls averaging 5 hours per week. Thus, while sex-correlated differences in the amount of time committed to playing video games continue to exist, the rising tide has floated all boats.

Even very young children are playing video games. Gentile & Walsh found that children aged two to seven play an average of 43 minutes per day (by parent report), and Woodard and Gridina found that even preschoolers aged two to five average 28 minutes of video game play per day. Although few studies have documented how the amount of time devoted to playing video games changes with development, some studies have suggested that video game play may peak in early school-age children. Buchman & Funk found the amount of time was highest for fourth grade children and decreased steadily through eighth grade. Others have suggested that play is highest between ages 9 and 12, decreases between ages 12 and 14, and increases again between ages 15 and 18. Surprisingly, the amount of time children devote to television has remained remarkably stable even as the amount of time devoted to video and computer games has increased.

Although the research evidence is still limited, amount of video game play has been linked with a number of risk factors for maladaptive development, including smoking, obesity, and poorer academic performance.

From *Media Violence and Children: A Complete Guide for Parents and Professionsals,* 2003, pp. 131–133, 135–136, 139–140, 141–142, 147–150. Copyright © 2003 by Greenwood Publishing Group, Inc., Westport, CT. Reprinted by permission.

These results parallel those showing that greater use of television is correlated with poorer grades in school. . . .

Preferences for Violent Video Games

Although video games are designed to be entertaining, challenging, and sometimes educational, most include violent content. Recent content analyses of video games show that as many as 89 percent of games contain some violent content, and that about half of the games include violent content toward other game characters that would result in serious injuries or death.

Many children prefer to play violent games. Of course, what constitutes a "violent" game varies depending upon who is classifying them. The video game industry and its ratings board (Entertainment Software Rating Board) claim to see much less violence in their games than do parents and other researchers. Even within the research community there is some inconsistency in definition of what constitutes a violent video game. Generally, however, researchers consider as "violent" those games in which the player can harm other characters in the game. In many popular video games, harming other characters is the main activity. It is these games, in which killing occurs at a high rate, that are of most concern to media violence researchers, child advocacy groups, and parents. . . . In studies of fourth through eighth grade children, more than half of the children state preferences for games in which the main action is predominantly human violence or fantasy violence. In surveys of children and their parents, about two-thirds of children named violent games as their favorites. Only about one-third of parents were able to correctly name their child's favorite game, and in 70 percent of the incorrect matches, children described their favorite game as violent. A preference for violent games has been linked with hostile attribution biases, increased arguments with teachers, lower self-perceptions of behavioral conduct, and increased physical fights. . . .

Why Violent Video Games May Have a Greater Effect Than Violent TV

The public health community has concluded from the preponderance of evidence that violent television leads to "increases in aggressive attitudes, values, and behavior, particularly in children." Although the research on violent video games is still growing, there are at least six reasons why we should expect violent video games to have an even greater impact than violent television. These reasons are based on what we already know from the television and educational literatures.

1. *Identification with an aggressor increases imitation of the aggressor.* It is known from research on violent television that children will imitate aggressive actions more readily if they identify with an aggressive character in some way. On television, it is hard to predict with which characters, if any, a person will identify. One might identify

most closely with the victim, in which case the viewer would be less likely to be aggressive after watching. In many violent video games, however, one is required to take the point of view of one particular character. This is most noticeable in "first-person shooter" games, in which the players "see" what their character would see as if they were inside the video game. Thus, the player is forced to identify with a violent character. In fact, in many games, players have a choice of characters to play and can upload photographs of their faces onto their character. This identification with the aggressive character is likely to increase the likelihood of imitating the aggressive acts.

2. *Active participation increases learning.* Research on learning shows that when one becomes actively involved in something, one learns much more than if one only watches it. This is one reason computer technology in the classroom has been considered to be educationally beneficial. Educational video games are theorized to be effective partly because they require active participation. With regard to violent entertainment, viewers of violent content on television are passive observers of the aggressive acts. In contrast, violent video games by their very nature require active participation in the violent acts.

3. *Practicing an entire behavioral sequence is more effective than practicing only a part.* If one wanted to learn how to kill someone, one would quickly realize that there are many steps involved. At a minimum, one needs to decide whom to kill, get a weapon, get ammunition, load the weapon, stalk the victim, aim the weapon, and pull the trigger. It is rare for television shows or movies to display all of these steps. Yet, violent video games regularly require players to practice each of these steps repeatedly. This helps teach the necessary steps to commit a successful act of aggression. In fact, some video games are so successful at training whole sequences of aggressive behaviors that the U.S. Army has licensed them to train their forces. For example, the popular violent video game series *Rainbow Six* is so good at teaching all of the steps necessary to plan and conduct a successful special operations mission that the U.S. Army has licensed the game engine to train their special operations soldiers. Furthermore, the U.S. Army has created their own violent video game as a recruitment tool.

4. *Violence is continuous.* Research with violent television and movies has shown that the effects on viewers are greater if the violence is unrelieved and uninterrupted. However, in both television programs and movies, violent content is rarely sustained for more than a few minutes before changing pace, changing scenes, or going to commercials. In contrast, the violence in violent video games is often continuous. Players must constantly be alert for hostile enemies, and must constantly choose and enact aggressive behaviors. These behaviors expose players to a continual stream of violent (and often gory) scenes accompanied by screams of pain and suffering in a context that is incompatible with feelings of empathy or guilt.

5. *Repetition increases learning.* If one wishes to learn a new phone number by memory, one often will repeat it over and over to aid memory. This simple mnemonic device has been shown to be an

effective learning technique. With few exceptions (e.g., *Blue's Clues*), children rarely see the same television shows over and over. In a violent video game, however, players often spend a great deal of time doing the same aggressive actions (e.g., shooting things) over and over. Furthermore, the games are usually played repeatedly, thus giving a great deal of practice repeating the violent game actions. This increases the odds that not only will children learn from them, but they will make these actions habitual to the point of automaticity.

6. *Rewards increase imitation.* There are at least three different processes involved. First, rewarding aggressive behavior in a video game (e.g., winning extra points and lives) increases the frequency of behaving aggressively in that game (see number 5, above). Second, rewarding aggressive behavior in a video game teaches more positive attitudes toward the use of force as a means of solving conflicts. Television programs rarely provide a reward structure for the viewer, and it would be rarer still to have those rewards dependent on violent acts. In contrast, video games often reward players for participating. Third, the reward patterns involved in video games increase the player's motivation to persist at the game. Interestingly, all three of these processes help educational games be more effective. The last process can make the games somewhat addictive.

The Effects of Violent Video Games

Over the past 20 years, a number of scholars have expressed concern over the potential negative impact of exposing youth to violent video games. . . .

Meta-Analytic Summary of Violent Video Game Effects

Narrative reviews of a research literature, such as that by Dill and Dill, are very useful ways of examining prior studies. Typically, the researchers try to find an organizing scheme that makes sense of the varied results that typically occur in any research domain. However, as useful as such reviews of the literature are, meta-analyses (studies of studies) are a much more powerful technique to find the common effects of violent video games across multiple studies. Specifically, a meta-analysis uses statistical techniques to combine the results of various studies of the same basic hypothesis, and provides an objective answer to the questions of whether or not the key independent variable has a reliable effect on the key dependent variable, and if so, what the magnitude of that effect is. Only recently have there been enough studies on violent video games to make meta-analysis a useful technique. In 2001, the first comprehensive meta-analysis of the effects of violent video games was conducted. A more recent update to that meta-analysis produced the same basic findings. A consistent pattern of the effects of playing violent games was documented in five areas.

1. *Playing violent video games increases physiological arousal.* Studies measuring the effects of playing violent video games tend to show

larger increases in heart rate and systolic and diastolic blood pressure compared to playing nonviolent video games. The average effect size across studies between violent game play and physiological arousal was 0.22.[1] For example, Ballard and West showed that a violent game (*Mortal Kombat* with the blood "turned on") resulted in higher systolic blood pressure responses than either a nonviolent game or a less graphically violent game (*Mortal Kombat* with the blood "turned off"). . . .

2. *Playing violent video games increases aggressive cognitions.* Studies measuring cognitive responses to playing violent video games have shown that aggressive thoughts are increased compared to playing nonviolent video games. The average effect size across studies between violent game play and aggressive cognitions was 0.27. These effects have been found in children and adults, in males and females, and in experimental and nonexperimental studies. . . .

3. *Playing violent video games increases aggressive emotions.* Studies measuring emotional responses to playing violent video games have shown that aggressive emotions are increased compared to playing nonviolent video games. The average effect size across studies between violent game play and aggressive emotions was 0.18. These effects have been found in children and adults, in males and females, and in experimental and nonexperimental studies. In one study, adults' state hostility and anxiety levels were increased after playing a violent game compared to controls. In a study of third through fifth grade children, playing a violent game increased frustration levels more than playing a nonviolent game.

4. *Playing violent video games increases aggressive behaviors.* Studies measuring aggressive behaviors after playing violent video games have shown that aggressive behaviors are increased compared to playing nonviolent video games. The average effect size across studies between violent game play and aggressive behaviors was 0.19. These effects have been found in children and adults, in males and females, and in experimental and nonexperimental studies. . . .

5. *Playing violent video games decreases prosocial behaviors.* Studies measuring responses to playing violent video games have shown that prosocial behaviors are decreased compared to playing nonviolent video games. The average effect size across studies between violent game play and prosocial behaviors was -0.16. These effects have been found in both experimental and nonexperimental studies. In one study of 278 seventh and eighth graders, children who named violent games as their favorite games to play were rated by their peers as exhibiting fewer prosocial behaviors and more aggressive behaviors in the classroom. . . .

Critiques of the Video Game Research Literature

Any new research domain has strengths and weaknesses. If all goes well, over time the researchers identify the weaknesses and address them in a variety of ways. When the new research domain appears to threaten the profits of some large industry, there is a tendency for that industry to deny the threatening research and to mount campaigns designed to highlight the weaknesses, obfuscate the legitimate findings, and cast doubt on the quality of the research. The history of the tobacco industry's attempt to ridicule, deny, and obfuscate research linking smoking to lung cancer is the prototype of such efforts. The TV and movie industries have had considerable success in their 40-year campaign against the media violence research community. The same type of effort has now been mounted by the video game industry. We do not claim that there are no weaknesses in the video game research literature. Indeed, we have highlighted some of them in our own prior writings. In this final section, we focus on two types of criticisms, legitimate ones (usually raised by researchers) and illegitimate ones (usually raised by the video game industry and their supporters in the scholarly community).

Illegitimate Criticisms

1. *There are too few studies to warrant any conclusions about possible negative effects.*

This can be a legitimate concern if the small number of studies yields a lack of power to detect small effects. However, it is an illegitimate argument when it is used to claim that the current set of video game studies do not warrant serious concern about exposure to violent video games. If anything, it is remarkable that such reliable effects have emerged from such a relatively small number of studies (compared to TV and movie violence studies), and that the studies that vary so much in method, sample population, and video game stimuli.

2. *There are problems with the external validity of lab experiments due to demand characteristics, participant suspicion and compliance problems, trivial measures, artificial settings, and unrepresentative participants.*

These old arguments against laboratory studies in the behavioral sciences have been successfully debunked many times, in many contexts, and in several different ways. Both logical and empirical analyses of such broad-based attacks on lab experiments have found little cause for concern. Furthermore, more specific examination of these issues in the aggression domain have consistently found evidence of high external validity, and have done so in several very different ways.

3. *Complete dismissal of correlational studies: "Correlation is not causation."*

This is an overly simplistic view of how modern science is conducted. Psychology instructors teach this mantra to introductory psychology students, and hope that they will gain a much more sophisticated view of methods and scientific inference by the time they are seniors. Whole fields of science are based on correlational data (e.g., astronomy). Correlational studies are used to test causal theories, and thus provide falsification opportunities. A well-conducted correlational design, one which attempts to control for likely "third variable" factors, can provide much useful information. To be sure, correlational studies are generally (but not always) less informative about causality than experimental ones. What is most important is the whole pattern of results across studies that differ in design, procedure, and measures. And the existing research on violent video games yields consistent results.

4. *Arousal accounts for all video game effects on aggressive behavior.*

Physiological arousal dissipates fairly quickly. Therefore, the arousal claim does not apply to studies that measure aggressive behavior more than 30 minutes after game play has occurred, or studies in which aggression is measured by a retrospective report. For example, this criticism generally doesn't apply to correlational studies, but correlational studies show a significant link between violent video game exposure and aggression. Furthermore, there are a few experimental studies in which the violent and nonviolent game conditions were equated on arousal, and significant violent-content effects still occurred.

5. *There are no studies linking violent video game play to "serious" or actual aggression.*

This criticism is simply not true. A number of correlational studies have linked repeated violent video game play to serious aggression. For example, Anderson and Dill showed that college-student reports of violent video game play in prior years were positively related to aggression that would be considered criminal (e.g., assault, robbery) if known to police. Similarly, Gentile et al. found significant links between violent game play and physical fights.

6. *Violent media affect only a few who are already disturbed.*

As discussed earlier, there are reasons (some theoretical, some empirical) to believe that some populations will be more negatively affected than others. However, no totally "immune" population has ever been identified, and populations sometimes thought to be at low risk have nonetheless yielded significant violent video game exposure effects.

7. *Effects of media violence are trivially small.*

Once again, this is simply not true. Violent video game effects are bigger than: (a) effects of passive tobacco smoke and lung cancer; (b) exposure to lead and IQ scores in children; (c) calcium intake and bone mass.

Note that the critics use these seven illegitimate criticisms to basically dismiss all research on violent video games. Once one has dismissed all correlational studies (number 3, above) and all experiments that use laboratory or other "trivial" measures of aggression (number 2, above), the only potential type of study left is clearly unethical: an experimental field study in which violent crime is the measure of aggression. Such a study would require randomly assigning children to high versus low video game violence conditions for a period of years and then following up on their rates of violent criminal activity over the course of their lives. It is not an accident that all ethically feasible types of studies are dismissed by the industry and its supporters.

Legitimate Criticisms

1. *Sample sizes tend to be too small in many studies.*

If the average effect size is about $r = 0.20$, then N (the number of study participants) should be at least 200 for 0.80 power (power is the likelihood of being able to find a legitimate difference between groups). When N is too small, individual studies will *appear* inconsistent even if they are all accurate samples of the true $r = 0.20$ effect. For this reason, the best way of summarizing the results of a set of too-small studies is to combine the results via meta-analysis, rather than using the more traditional narrative review. When this is done, we see that the video game studies yield consistent results.

2. *Some studies do not have "violent" and "nonviolent" games that are sufficiently different in actual violent content.*

This problem was noted earlier in this chapter in the discussion of how early studies might find weaker effects because the "violent" video games in the early years were not very violent by contemporary standards. . . . Future studies need to do a better job of assessing the violent content of the video games being compared.

3. *Some experimental studies have used a "control" or "nonviolent game" condition that was more boring, annoying, or frustrating than the violent game.*

The obvious solution for future studies is to do more pilot testing or manipulation checks on such aggression-relevant dimensions. In trying to summarize past research, one can sometimes find a more appropriate comparison condition within the same experiment.

4. *Some studies did not report sufficient results to enable calculation of an effect size for participants who actually played a video game.*

This problem arose in several cases in which half of the participants played a video game while the other half merely observed. Reported means then collapsed across this play versus observe dimension. Future reports should include the individual means.

5. *Some studies that purportedly study aggressive behavior have used dependent variables that are not true aggressive behavior.*

A surprising number of past studies have used trait or personality aggression scales as measures of aggressive behavior in short-term experiments. This is a problem because there is no way that a short-term manipulation of exposure to violent versus nonviolent video games (e.g., 20 minutes) can influence one's past frequency of aggression. In this short-term context, such a trait measure might possibly be conceived as a measure of cognitive priming, but clearly it is not a measure of aggressive behavior.

A related problem is that some studies have included hitting an inanimate object as a measure of aggressive behavior. Most modern definitions of aggression restrict its application to behaviors that are intended to harm another person.

The obvious solution for future studies is to use better measures of aggression. In the analysis of past research one can sometimes disaggregate the reported composite measure to get a cleaner measure of aggression.

> 6. *There are no longitudinal studies.*

This is true. Major funding is needed to conduct a large-scale longitudinal study of video game effects. To date, such funding has not been forthcoming. Thus, one must rely on longitudinal studies in the TV/movie violence domain to get a reasonable guess as to the likely long-term effects. . . .

Summary

Although there is less research on the effects of violent video games than there is on television and movies, the preponderance of evidence looks very similar to the research on violent television. In particular, violent video games appear to increase aggressive thoughts and feelings, physiological arousal, and aggressive behaviors, as well as to decrease prosocial behaviors. There are many theoretical reasons why one would expect violent video games to have a greater effect than violent television, and most of the reasons why one would expect them to have a lesser effect are no longer true because violent video games have become so realistic, particularly since the late 1990s. . . .

Note

1. All effect sizes reported in the chapter are scaled as correlation coefficients, regardless of whether the study was experimental or correlational in design. . . .

Cheryl K. Olson

 **NO**

Media Violence Research and Youth Violence Data: Why Do They Conflict?

. . . **I**t's almost an American tradition to blame the corruption of youth on violent mass media, from the lurid "half-dime" novels of the 19th century to 1930s gangster films and 1950s horror/crime comics. In 1972, a report to the U.S. Surgeon General addressed then-growing concerns about violent television. Its authors pondered how television content and programming practices could be changed to reduce the risk of increasing aggression without causing other social harms. They concluded: "The state of present knowledge does not permit an agreed answer."

Violent video games are the most recent medium to be decried by researchers, politicians, and the popular press as contributing to society's ills. In particular, they were implicated in a series of notorious shootings:

> Although it is impossible to know exactly what caused these teens to attack their own classmates and teachers . . . one possible contributing factor is violent video games. Harris and Klebold enjoyed playing the bloody, shoot-'em-up video game *Doom,* a game licensed by the U.S. Army to train soldiers to effectively kill.

(Anderson and Dill did not cite a source for the use of *Doom* by the military. However, according to the web site of the U.S. Army Corps of Engineers Topographic Engineering Center, *Doom II* was indeed licensed in 1996 and transformed into *Marine Doom,* which "teaches concepts such as mutual fire team support, protection of the automatic rifleman, proper sequencing of an attack, ammunition discipline and succession of command" [see . . .]).

> "We've been seeing a whole rash of shootings throughout this country and in Europe that relate back to kids who obsessively play violent video games. The kids involved as shooters in Columbine were obsessively playing violent video games. We know after the Beltway sniper incident where

From *Academic Psychiatry*, Summer 2004, pp. 144–149. Copyright © 2004 by American Psychiatric Publishing via the Copyright Clearance Center. Reprinted by permission.

the 17-year-old was a fairly good shot, but Mr. Muhammad, the police tell us, got him to practice on an ultra-violent video game in sniper mode to break down his hesitancy to kill."

—Washington State Rep. Mary Lou Dickerson, on *The NewsHour with Jim Lehrer,* July 7, 2003. (She co-sponsored legislation to ban the sale or rental of games that portray violence against police to children under 17.)

The series of random shootings by Lee Malvo and John Muhammad created panic in the Washington, D.C. area. News headlines repeated claims by Malvo's defense team that the youth had been brainwashed and trained to kill while playing video games with sniper shooting modes such as *Halo, Tom Clancy's Ghost Recon,* and *Tom Clancy's Rainbow Six: Covert Ops.* The jury was shown clips of these games and of the film *The Matrix.* A psychologist testified that exposure to this kind of entertainment makes violence seem more acceptable and promotes violent thoughts and actions. In response, the prosecutor simply asked, "What about the millions and millions of young American males who play video games and don't go out and kill random people on the street?"

Certainly, the stealing, beating, strangling, and hacking depicted in games such as *Grand Theft Auto III, Manhunt,* and *Mortal Kombat: Deadly Alliance* are shocking to many adults. It seems reasonable to assume that wielding virtual guns and chainsaws must be bad for our children. However, the potential of gangster movies to trigger violence or teach criminal methods to the young seemed just as real to previous generations. Local censorship boards in New York and Chicago edited out hundreds of scenes that "glorified gangsters or outlaws" or "showed disrespect for law enforcement."

In that place and time, it's possible that cinema criminals such as James Cagney and Edward G. Robinson were bad influences on some young people. This can't be proved or disproved. Today, however, most of us view these films as quaint entertainment classics. Before we make sweeping assumptions about the effects of media content, we must examine the data.

School Shootings and Video Games

In response to the outcry that followed deadly shootings in Colorado, Oregon, Kentucky, and Arkansas, the U.S. Secret Service and the U.S. Department of Education began a study called the Safe School Initiative. This involved an intensive review of the 37 incidents of "targeted" school violence, aimed at a specific person, group, type (such as "jocks" or "geeks"), or at an entire school, that took place between 1974 and 2000. The goal was to look for commonalities and create a profile of potential attackers in order to prevent future tragedies.

The conclusion: There was no useful profile. Along with male gender, the most common shared trait was a history of suicide attempts or suicidal thoughts, often with a documented history of extreme depressed feelings. If all schools instituted programs to identify and refer depressed and suicidal youth, more would receive treatment and promising futures could be saved.

But using those methods to detect potential killers would result in overwhelming numbers of false positives and the stigmatization of thousands.

Moreover, there is no evidence that targeted violence has increased in America's schools. While such attacks have occurred in the past, they were and are extremely rare events. The odds that a child will die in school through murder or suicide are less than one in one million. What *has* dramatically increased is our exposure to local and national news about the "recent trend" in school shootings. Research has shown that crime-saturated local and national television news reports increase viewers' perception of both personal and societal risk, regardless of actual danger.

Constant news coverage leaves the impression that youthful crime is increasing. Some have referred to a "wave of violence gripping America's youth," fueled by exposure to violent media. Using data supplied to the FBI by local law enforcement agencies, the U.S. Office of Juvenile Justice and Delinquency Prevention reported that the rate of juvenile arrests increased in the late 1980s, peaking in 1994. At the time, this seemed to be a worrisome trend, but it proved to be an anomaly. Juvenile arrests declined in each of the next 7 years. Between 1994 and 2001, arrests for murder, forcible rape, robbery, and aggravated assaults fell 44%, resulting in the lowest juvenile arrest rate for violent crimes since 1983. Murder arrests, which reached a high of 3,800 in 1993, fell to 1,400 in 2001.

Interestingly, the sharp temporary rise in juvenile murders from 1983 to 1993 has been attributed to a rapid rise in gun use, concentrated among black male adolescents. We have no evidence that black male adolescents' use of violent media differed significantly from that of other young people, though there is ample evidence that as a group, they have greater exposure to other risk factors for violence. And what of juvenile arrests for property crimes? In 2001, these achieved their lowest level in over 30 years. In other words, there's no indication that violence rose in lockstep with the spread of violent games. Of course, this is not proof of lack of harm.

Could violent media have played some role in the rare but horrifying mass murders in our schools? This can't be ruled out, but evidence is scant. According to the Secret Service review, one in eight perpetrators showed some interest in violent video games, one-fourth in violent movies, and one-fourth in violent books, but there was no obvious pattern. Instead of interactive games, their interactive medium of choice was pen and paper. Thirty seven percent expressed violent thoughts and imagery through poems, essays, and journal entries.

Trends in Violent Game Use

The rapid spread of video games among the young, including violent games, has surprised and unnerved many parents. Games with violent content and "Mature" ratings are available for computers, all three major game consoles (PlayStation 2, Xbox, and GameCube), and portable handhelds such as Game Boy.

According to a 1999 survey by the Kaiser Family Foundation, 83% of children ages 8 to 18 reported having at least one video game console in their home, and 45% had one in their bedroom. In addition, 74% have at least one computer at home. Fifty-five percent of boys and 23% of girls said they played video games on a typical day, with nearly 20%, primarily boys, playing an "action or combat [game], (i.e., *Duke Nukem, Doom*)."

These figures have probably increased since that time. According to the Entertainment Software Association (formerly called the Interactive Digital Software Association), sales of video and computer games in the United States have grown steadily, from $3.2 billion in 1995 to $7 billion in 2003. The industry group is coy about how many children are actually playing, stating only that among the "most frequent" computer and video game players, 30% and 38%, respectively, are under age 18. Citing market research data from 2000, an IDSA report states that 61% of game users are 18 or older (suggesting that 39% are *under* 18).

Violent games are also widely sold. It is possible to find even gore-laden games such as *BloodRayne* (named for its bustier-clad vampire spy heroine and described on the maker's web site as "an intense third-person action/horror experience") at child-friendly outlets such as Toys R Us. Similar to R-rated movie restrictions, retailers are supposed to prevent sales of M-rated games to youth under age 17. However, "mystery shopper" studies by the U.S. Federal Trade Commission found that young teens ages 13 to 16 were able to purchase M-rated games 85% of the time. This number declined to 69% in a follow-up survey released in October 2003. In sum, playing video and computer games—including games with violent content—is now a routine activity for American youth, particularly boys.

Video Game Research and Public Policy

How has this spurt in electronic game play affected our youth? Along with the Washington, D.C. snipers and school shooters, several academic studies (primarily experiments) have received broad coverage in the popular media and are cited by the press and some advocacy groups as evidence that video games create dangerous, aggressive thoughts, feelings, and behaviors. Local, state, and federal legislation, including criminal penalties for selling or renting certain games to minors, have been introduced based on these studies, as have private lawsuits.

Many of these studies provide useful insights into the potential for harm (and sometimes benefit) from violent interactive games. But problems arise when the customary discussion of limitations falls by the wayside. Ideas are taken out of context and repeated in the media echo chamber, creating a false sense of certainty. Here are some of the limitations of current studies as a basis for policy making, with illustrative examples.

Vague Definitions of Aggression

Some researchers use "aggression" and "violence" almost interchangeably, implying that one inevitably leads to the other. Aggressive play that follows exposure to games or cartoons containing violence is not distinguished from aggressive behavior intended to harm. Aggressive thoughts, feelings, and behaviors may be presented as equivalent in importance and treated as valid surrogates for real-life violence, with the assumption that reducing these factors will reduce harm. The muddled terminology and unspoken assumptions can undermine the credibility of studies. After all, most parents of whining toddlers have occasional aggressive thoughts and feelings, but that's a far cry from actual child abuse.

Use of Violent Media Is Not Put into Context with Other Known Contributors to Aggression or Violence

Lee Malvo, for example, had a history of antisocial and criminal behavior. He reportedly hunted and killed perhaps 20 cats with a slingshot and marbles. Compared to playing violent video games, animal torture is both more unusual and directly related to harming humans. According to public health and juvenile justice research, the strongest childhood predictors of youth violence are involvement in crime (not necessarily violent crime), male gender, illegal substance use, physical aggressiveness, family poverty, and antisocial parents. As children grow older, peer relationships become important predictors: associating with antisocial or delinquent peers, gang membership, and lack of ties with prosocial peers and groups.

A final problem with using aggression as a surrogate for violence is that most children who are aggressive or engage in antisocial behavior do not grow up to be violent adolescents or adults, and most violent adolescents were not notably aggressive as children.

Test Conditions That Are Difficult to Generalize to the Real World

Experimental settings are not only artificial, but turn game play into game "work." Subjects may have only 10 minutes to learn and play a game before results are measured and cannot choose when to start or stop playing. Most experiments involve a single game exposure, which cannot reasonably represent the effects of playing an array of games in real life. Additionally, young people commonly play games with others. In the Kaiser Family Foundation survey, virtually all children played their video games with friends, siblings, or other relatives. (By contrast, the majority of computer games were played alone, although some children played with a friend in the room or with someone over the Internet.) Effects of the social context of games, be they positive or negative, have received little attention to date.

Small, Nonrandom, or Nonrepresentative Samples

This is another barrier to broad generalization of research results. While it is not uncommon to recruit college undergraduates in psychology courses for experimental studies, those students differ in numerous ways from the typical young American teen—the population of greatest interest to most researchers and policy makers. Other studies use samples that are very narrow in age or geography (e.g., 10- and 11-year-old Flemish children).

A Blinkered View of Causality

Some (but not all) experimental studies have found that aggressive thoughts or behavior increase after playing a particular video game. It has been postulated that experimental studies prove causality by ruling out other plausible explanations. In the real world, however, this could be a very complex relationship. That is, aggressive children may seek out violent games, and violent games may reinforce aggressive behavior. This may be a two-way relationship or the result of other factors such as lack of parental supervision or connection. Additionally, effects of moderating variables, such as the nature and context of violence in a given game, or subject age or developmental stage are often not considered.

Study Findings Are Combined in Ways Not Appropriate for Policy Use

"Meta-analysis" and related techniques, for example, may be used to merge study findings for a more robust result. A 2004 meta-analysis of the effects of playing violent video games combined studies with subjects of varying age and gender who were exposed to different types and amounts of game violence in a variety of environments (experiments and correlational studies), with varying outcomes—a range of behavioral, cognitive, affective, and arousal measures. Results were represented only in terms of average effect size. Given the different study types, exposures, populations, and outcome measures, this goes well beyond the prohibition against "comparing apples and oranges" in meta-analyses.

Again, however, the primary problem is the way these findings are interpreted. The size and representativeness of study samples were not considered in assessing study quality, and the outcome of concern—real-world violence or related harm—was never directly studied. Despite this, the results were viewed as important evidence that violent game exposure leads to major societal harm.

Current Thinking on Game Violence Effects

The research community is sharply divided on whether violent games are harmful, and if so, for whom and to what degree. Several well-regarded reviews have concluded that the current body of research is unable to support the argument that the fantasy violence of games leads to real-life violence—although this could change as evidence accumulates or games become more realistic.

In an appendix to its chapter on risk factors, the Surgeon General's 2001 report on youth violence reviewed effects of exposure to violent media. The report noted that there is evidence for a small to moderate short-term increase in physically and verbally aggressive behavior. However, the sum of findings from cross-sectional, experimental, and longitudinal studies "suggest that media violence has a relatively small impact on violence" and that "the impact of video games on violent behavior remains to be determined."

Potential Effects of Games on "Below the Radar" Violence

This does not mean that we should put research on media violence on the back burner. Instead, we need to put it in context. First, many known risk factors for violence aren't amenable to change, while exposure to media (content and dose) is potentially alterable. Second, while they may not play a starring role in headline-grabbing crimes, video games and other violent media could have less visible but significant harmful effects on children's lives. For example, it's feasible that certain types or amounts of video game play could affect emotions, cognitions, perceptions, and behaviors in ways that promote bullying and victimization.

In recent years, we have become increasingly aware of bullying as a threat to healthy development and well being. A large United States survey of children in grades 6 through 10 found that nearly 30% reported occasional or frequent (at least once a week) involvement as a bully, victim, or both. The most recent government report on school crime and safety found that the percentage of children ages 12 to 18 who reported being bullied increased from 1999 (5%) to 2001 (8%). According to the latest National Youth Risk Behavior Survey, the percentage of high school students who felt too unsafe to go to school at least once in the previous 30 days increased significantly from 1997 to 2001 (from 4% to 6.6%). In 2001, fewer adolescents reported carrying weapons on school property (which could reflect aggressive intent or a fear-based need for self-protection), but the risk of being threatened or injured with a gun, club, or knife on school property has not decreased, as 8.9% of students reported this had happened to them at least once in the previous 12 months.

Suggestions for Future Research

In summary, it's very difficult to document whether and how violent video and computer games contribute to serious violence such as criminal assault or murder. (Practically speaking, this would require a massive and expensive study because game playing is common, and murder is rare.) It is feasible, however, to study how violent games may contribute to some types of every-day violence and aggression and to the beliefs, attitudes, and interpretations of behavior that support them. For example, are heavy players of violent games more likely to view aggression as a first-choice solution to problems instead of a last resort (e.g., instead of talking or seeking mediation first), to see violence as easily justified, to feel less empathy for others, or to interpret ambiguous behavior (e.g., a bump in the school hallway) as deliberately hostile, threatening, or disrespectful? Another issue is whether and how the effects of video game violence might be compounded by exposure to violence in other media. Cautious interpretation is necessary, since there is always the risk of confusing cause and effect or correlation with causation.

To make intervention efforts more effective and cost-efficient, it's important to focus on which children are at risk. Risk factors for violence tend to occur in clusters. Violent game play may disproportionately affect children who lack protective factors such as a nurturing relationship with at least one adult and connection to and relative success in school. A child's stage of emotional or cognitive development may also be important.

The amount of time spent playing games is also worthy of study. Given the ubiquity of violent game play among boys, we might see a J-shaped curve, similar to common findings in research on adult alcohol use: a little is healthy, but a lot becomes a health risk. In other words, a moderate amount of interactive game play may be associated with a healthier social life, while increasing amounts of play (or solitary play) may correlate with poor adjustment or emotional difficulties.

Few researchers have asked children *why* they play games and what meaning games have for them. While most probably play for fun or sociability, some children seem to use games to vent anger or distract themselves from problems. This could be functional or unhealthy, depending on the child's mental health and the amount and type of game play. We know almost nothing about the differential effects of games on depressed or anxious children or those with attention deficit-hyperactivity disorder.

There is also a need for research on the effects of different types of games, going beyond the gore level. Does violence that serves a worthy end (e.g., a SWAT team rescuing hostages) or violence that is ultimately punished (e.g., a criminal protagonist ends up dead or in jail) have different effects than violence that is rewarded, even if the games are equally bloody? Do children who enjoy violent games with story lines differ from those who prefer bouts of fighting? Do violent games that make use of irony and sarcasm, such as *Grand Theft Auto: Vice City,* have differential effects on children who are not cognitively able to detect that irony and sarcasm?

We need to learn more about what activities are displaced by game play. A teenager who spends hours playing games over the Internet might miss key opportunities to build social skills with real people or lose opportunities for healthy physical activity.

Finally, researchers must acknowledge that electronic games are a moving target. The technology is constantly advancing. Studies conducted 5 or even 2 years ago may have limited relevance given improvements in graphics, the rise of Internet gaming, the introduction of games controlled by voice of body movements, and the potential for increased tactile feedback via "haptics" technology to create the sense of immersion in a virtual world.

We might take a lesson from America's history of media hysteria. It's time to move beyond blanket condemnations and frightening anecdotes and focus on developing targeted educational and policy interventions based on solid data. As with the entertainment media of earlier generations, we may look back on some of today's games with nostalgia, and our grandchildren may wonder what the fuss was about.

CHALLENGE QUESTIONS

Do Video Games Lead to Violence?

1. Is Olson's criticism of the research on video game violence—that the test conditions are difficult to generalize to real-world settings—a criticism that could be made of other areas of psychological research? If so, describe one such area.
2. Gentile and Anderson list several reasons why violent video games may have a greater effect on kids than violent television. Which do you think has the greater effect? Defend your position.
3. What is the difference between correlation and causation? How does this difference pertain to Olson's critique of violent video game research?
4. Based on what you have learned from the two selections, what kinds of restrictions, if any, do you think parents should place on their children's exposure to violent video games? Defend your answer with information from both selections.
5. Olson cites a Web site where she learned of the U.S. Army's use of violent video games to train its troops. Find examples of other organizations that use video games to educate their personnel. Are they using violent video games? Why or why not?

ISSUE 18

Can Sex Be Addictive?

YES: Patrick J. Carnes, from "Sexual Addiction Q&A," http://www.sexhelp.com/sa_q_and_a.cfm (November 11, 2006)

NO: Lawrence A. Siegel and Richard M. Siegel, from "Sex Addiction: Recovering from a Shady Concept," An Original Essay Written for *Taking Sides: Human Sexuality, 10th edition* (2007)

ISSUE SUMMARY

YES: Sexual addiction expert Patrick J. Carnes argues not only that sex can be addictive but that sex can be as addictive as drugs, alcohol, or any other chemical substance.

NO: Sex therapists Lawrence A. Siegel and Richard M. Siegel believe that while some sexual behaviors might be dysfunctional, calling those behaviors "addictive" confuses a moralistic ideology with a scientific fact.

Addiction has become a pervasive feature of modern societies. Of the $666 billion spent for health care in the United States, 25% was spent on health-care problems related to addiction (Kinney, 2003; American Medical Association, 2003). Of the 11 million victims of the violent crimes that are committed each year in the United States, nearly 3 million reported that the offender had been drinking prior to the crime (Greenfield, 1998). Research also suggests that between 6 and 15 million Americans have compulsive shopping behaviors that result in unmanageable debt, bankruptcy, and damaged relationships (Stanford University, 2005). These varied examples demonstrate not only the damage addiction does but also the widely varying meanings it has—from drug addiction to shopping addiction.

Should we add "sex addiction" to the list? Few would dispute that certain chemicals, such as cocaine and even alcohol, merit the addiction label, but is considering sexual dysfunction an addiction taking this label too far? The term "addiction" is thought to be derived from the Latin word *addicere*, meaning to adore or to surrender oneself to a master (White, 1998). From this perspective, the term seems to fit, because some people appear to "surrender" themselves to the "master" of sexual games, sexual banter, and sexual intercourse. Indeed, sexuality seems to consume our popular culture.

On the other hand, would not many adolescent boys be considered "addicts" in this sense? What meaning does addiction have if everyone is addicted? Would not everyone be addicted to food in the same sense? Obviously, such questions have great importance for whether something should be treated in psychotherapy.

Widely regarded as an expert on sexual addiction, Patrick J. Carnes has been at the forefront of sexual addiction therapy. Carnes firmly believes that sex can be addictive and sexual dysfunction ought to be treated as any other physical or chemical addiction. In fact, on Carnes's website www.sexhelp.com, he promotes the use of the 12-step program of Alcoholics Anonymous for help in overcoming sex addiction. He justifies this parallel with chemical dependency and chemical dependency treatment because sexual intercourse itself has a clear physiological component—sexual pleasure. Carnes claims that sexual stimulation releases chemicals into the body that are just as potent as any chemical, including heroin or morphine—substances that few dispute as being addictive in nature.

Sex therapists Lawrence A. Siegel and Richard M. Siegel disagree sharply with Carnes's position. In the second article they argue that those who want to call sex addictive have a hidden agenda. Their agenda is to extend society's fairly clear moral condemnation of drug abuse to sexual behaviors. The Siegels ask whether sexual behaviors are not in a different category altogether than drug abuse. If they are, then the unacceptability of drug-related abuse should not be extended to sexual behaviors, at least not in the same way. The Siegels go on to argue that the term "addiction" itself has difficulties. They contend that psychology cannot decide what it means either to be addicted to something or to have an addictive nature. They conclude by reviewing some of Carnes's early work in sexual addiction and then respond to it by attempting to show his moral bias toward any sexual practice other than monogamous intimacy in marriage.

POINT	COUNTERPOINT
• Sex can be addictive.	• Addiction is merely a term for any behavior that falls outside of social norms.
• Sex can produce a dependency that is just as strong as alcohol or drugs.	• Chemical dependence should not be confused with the mechanisms that drive one's sexual appetite.
• Many deviant sexual behaviors fit the definition of what makes something addictive.	• A consistent clinical definition of "addiction" has not been agreed upon.
• Sex addicts, like alcohol and drug addicts, cannot control their self-destructive behavior.	• Sexual behavior is an issue of personal responsibility, not physiology.

YES

Patrick J. Carnes

Sex Addiction Q & A

"Like an alcoholic unable to stop drinking, sexual addicts are unable to stop their self-destructive sexual behavior. Family breakups, financial disaster, loss of jobs, and risk to life are the painful themes of their stories.

Sex addicts come from all walks of life—they may be ministers, physicians, homemakers, factory workers, salespersons, secretaries, clerks, accountants, therapists, dentists, politicians, or executives, to name just a few examples. Most were abused as children—sexually, physically, and/or emotionally. The majority grew up in families in which addiction already flourished, including alcoholism, compulsive eating, and compulsive gambling. Most grapple with other addictions as well, but they find sex addiction the most difficult to stop.

Much hope nevertheless exists for these addicts and their families. Sex addicts have shown an ability to transform a life of self-destruction into a life of self-care, a life in chaos and despair into one of confidence and peace."

Sexual Dependency: What It Is

Sexual addiction is defined as any sexually-related, compulsive behavior which interferes with normal living and causes severe stress on family friends, loved ones, and one's work environment.

Sexual addiction has been called sexual dependency and sexual compulsivity. By any name, it is a compulsive behavior that completely dominates the addict's life. Sexual addicts make sex a priority more important than family, friends, and work. Sex becomes the organizing principle of addicts' lives. They are willing to sacrifice what they cherish most in order to preserve and continue their unhealthy behavior.

No single behavior pattern defines sexual addiction. These behaviors, when they have taken control of addicts' lives and become unmanageable, include: compulsive masturbation, compulsive heterosexual and homosexual relationships, pornography, prostitution, exhibitionism, voyeurism, indecent phone calls, child molesting, incest, rape, and violence. Even the healthiest forms of human sexual expression can turn into self-defeating behaviors.

Recognition of Sexual Addiction by the Professional Health Care Community

Sexual addiction was first brought to the forefront in Dr. Patrick Carnes' 1983 book, *Out of the Shadows: Understanding Sexual Addiction* (CompCare Publishers). Since then, thousands of people have come forward seeking help, and more and more professionals are being trained to identify and treat sexual addiction.

The National Council on Sexual Addiction (NCSA) was created in 1987 to serve as an independent clearing house for information on sexual addiction and treatment options. One of NCSA's missions is to decrease the stigma surrounding sexual addiction problems and treatment. They may be contacted at:

NATIONAL COUNCIL ON SEXUAL ADDICTION/COMPULSIVITY
1090 Northchase Parkway, Suite 100 South
Marietta, Georgia 30067, 1-770-989-9754

Sexual Dependency and Other Addictions

Sexual addiction can be understood by comparing it to other types of addictions. Individuals addicted to alcohol or other drugs, for example, develop a relationship with their "chemical(s) of choice"—a relationship that takes precedence over any and all other aspects of their lives. Addicts find they need drugs merely to feel *normal.*

In sexual addiction, a parallel situation exists. Sex—like food or drugs in other addictions—provides the "high" and addicts become dependent on this sexual high to feel normal. They substitute unhealthy relationships for healthy ones. They opt for temporary pleasure rather than the deeper qualities of "normal" intimate relationships.

Sexual addiction follows the same progressive nature of other addictions. Sexual addicts struggle to control their behaviors, and experience despair over their constant failure to do so. Their loss of self-esteem grows, fueling the need to escape even further into their addictive behaviors. A sense of powerlessness pervades the lives of addicts.

How Many People Are Affected by Sexual Addiction?

Estimates range from three to six percent of the population.

Multiple Addictions

National surveys revealed that most sexual addicts come from severely dysfunctional families. Usually at least one other member of these families has another addiction (87%).

Dual addictions include sexual addiction and:

- Chemical dependency 42%
- Eating disorder 38%
- Compulsive working 28%
- Compulsive spending 26%
- Compulsive gambling 5%

Sexual Addiction and Abuse

Research has shown that a very high correlation exists between childhood abuse and sexual addiction in adulthood.

Sexual addicts who have reported experiencing:

- Emotional abuse 97%
- Sexual abuse 83%
- Physical abuse 71%

Sexual Addicts: Male and Female

It remains unclear whether one gender has a higher incidence of sexual addiction than the other. Research by Dr. Carnes shows that approximately 20% of all patients seeking help for sexual dependency are women. (This same male-female ratio is found among those recovering from alcohol addiction.)

As once was the case with alcohol addiction, many people cannot accept the reality that women can become sexual addicts. One of the greatest problems facing female sexual addicts is convincing others that they have a legitimate problem.

Why Sexual Addicts Don't "Just Stop" Their Destructive Behavior

Sexual addicts feel tremendous guilt and shame about their out-of-control behavior, and they live in constant fear of discovery. Yet addicts will often act out sexually in an attempt to block out the very pain of their addiction. This is part of what drives the addictive cycle. We say that they are addicts because they are out of control and unable to stop their behaviors *despite* their self-destructive nature and potentially devastating consequences. Years of treating chemically dependent individuals have shown that successful intervention with an addict's extensive denial and repression system often requires professional help.

AIDS and the Sexual Addict

As a function of their denial system, sexual addicts often ignore the severe emotional, interpersonal, and physical consequences of their behavior. Addicts are so entrenched in maintaining their behaviors that environmental cues which would signal caution and danger to most non-addicted people are lost to them. Such has been the case with the HIV virus and other dangerous, sexually transmitted diseases (STDs).

Sexual addicts are focused on getting a sexual 'fix.' They may occasionally consider the possible consequences of their activities, but in the throes of the addictive cycle, rational thinking is seldom, if ever, present. Often dismissing the potential danger of their behavior, addicts will embrace an anxiety-laden situation to enhance their sexual high. Avoiding reality and disregarding personal safety and health are typical symptoms of sexual addiction, and they put sexual addicts at grave risk for contracting one of the many disabling STDS, including HIV.

Fear of being infected with the HIV virus and developing AIDS is not enough to stop an addict intent on being anonymously sexual, picking up prostitutes, or having multiple affairs with unsafe sex partners. Even the potential of infecting a loved one with an STD is often not enough to stop addicts from acting out. In fact, sexual addicts may find ways to act out even more intensely after such sexual practices in order to help drown out the shame and guilt of an overloaded and repressed emotional life.

Despite the frequency and range of their acting-out experiences, sexual addicts are often poorly informed about sexuality in general. An important part of their recovery process is learning about healthy sexual practices: behaviors which are connecting and affirming rather than shaming and guilt inducing. In addition, sexual addicts often need to be taught about safe sexual practices, basic self-care, and health concerns.

Diagnosing Sexual Addiction

Often sexual addicts don't know what is wrong with them. They may suffer from clinical depression or have suicidal tendencies. They may even think they are losing their minds.

There are, however, recognizable behavior patterns which indicate the presence of sexual addiction. Diagnosis should be done by a mental health professional trained in carrying out such diagnoses.

To help professionals determine whether a sexual addiction is present, Dr. Carnes has developed the Sexual Addiction Screening Test (SAST), an assessment tool specially designed for this purpose.

Behavior Patterns Which May Indicate Sexual Addiction

While an actual diagnosis for sexual addiction should be carried out by a mental health professional, the following behavior patterns can indicate the presence of sexual addiction. Individuals who see any of these patterns in their own life, or in the life of someone they care about, should seek professional help.

1. Acting Out, a Pattern of Out-of-Control Sexual Behavior
Examples may include:

- Compulsive masturbation
- Indulging in pornography
- Having chronic affairs
- Exhibitionism
- Dangerous sexual practices
- Prostitution
- Anonymous sex
- Compulsive sexual episodes
- Voyeurism

2. Experiencing Severe Consequences Due to Sexual Behavior, and an Inability to Stop Despite These Adverse Consequences
Some of the losses reported by sexual addicts include:

- Loss of partner or spouse 40%
- Severe marital or relationship problems 70%
- Loss of career opportunities 27%
- Unwanted pregnancies 40%
- Abortions 36%
- Suicidal obsession 72%
- Suicide attempts 17%
- Exposure to AIDS and venereal disease 68%
- Legal risks from nuisance offenses to rape 58%

3. Persistent Pursuit of Self-Destructive Behavior
Even understanding that the consequences of their actions will be painful or have dire consequences does not stop addicts from acting out. They often seem to have a willfulness about their actions, and an attitude that says, "I'll deal with the consequences when they come."

4. Ongoing Desire or Effort to Limit Sexual Behavior
Addicts often try to control their behavior by creating external barriers to it. For example, some move to a new neighborhood or city, hoping that a new environment removed from old affairs will help. Some think marriage will keep them from acting out. An exposer may buy a car in which it's difficult to act out while driving.

Others seeking control over their behavior try to immerse themselves in religion, only to find out that while religious compulsion may soothe their shame, it does not end their acting out.

Many go through periods of sexual anorexia during which they allow themselves no sexual expression at all. Such efforts, however, only fuel the addiction.

5. Sexual Obsession and Fantasy as a Primary Coping Strategy
Though acting out sexually can temporarily relieve addicts' anxieties, they still find themselves spending inordinate amounts of time in obsession and

fantasy. By fantasizing, the addict can maintain an almost constant level of arousal. Together with obsessing, the two behaviors can create a kind of analgesic "fix." Just as our bodies generate endorphins, natural antide-pressants, during vigorous exercise, our bodies naturally release peptides when sexually aroused. The molecular construction of these peptides par-allels that of opiates like heroin or morphine, but are many times more powerful.

6. Regularly Increasing the Amount of Sexual Experience Because the Current Level of Activity Is No Longer Sufficiently Satisfying

Sexual addiction is often progressive. While addicts may be able to control themselves for a time, inevitably their addictive behaviors will return and quickly escalate to previous levels and beyond. Some addicts begin adding additional acting out behaviors. Usually addicts will have three or more behaviors which play a key role in their addiction—masturbation, affairs, and anonymous sex, for instance.

In addition, 89% of addicts reported regularly "bingeing" to the point of emotional exhaustion. The emotional pain of withdrawal for sexual addicts can parallel the physical pain experienced by those withdrawing from opiate addiction.

7. Severe Mood Changes Related to Sexual Activity

Addicts experience intense mood shifts, often due to the despair and shame of having unwanted sex. Sexual addicts are caught in a crushing cycle of shame-driven and shame-creating behavior. While shame drives the sexual addicts' actions, it also becomes the unwanted consequence of a few moments of euphoric escape into sex.

8. Inordinate Amounts of Time Spent Obtaining Sex, Being Sexual, and Recovering from Sexual Experiences

Two sets of activities organize sexual addicts' days. One involves obsessing about sex, time devoted to initiating sex, and actually being sexual. The second involves time spent dealing with the consequences of their acting out: lying, covering up, shortages of money, problems with their spouse, trouble at work, neglected children, and so on.

9. Neglect of Important Social, Occupational, or Recreational Activities Because of Sexual Behavior

As more and more of addicts' energy becomes focused on relationships which have sexual potential, other relationships and activities—family, friends, work, talents and values—suffer and atrophy from neglect. Long-term relationships are stormy and often unsuccessful. Because of sexual over-extension and intimacy avoidance, short-term relationships become the norm.

Sometimes, however, the desire to preserve an important long-term rela-tionship with spouse or children, for instance, can act as the catalyst for addicts to admit their problem and seek help.

Getting Help: The First Step

The first step in seeking help is to admit to the problem. Though marital, professional, and societal consequences may follow, admission of the problems must come, no matter the cost. Fear of these consequences unfortunately keeps many sexual addicts from seeking help.

Many sources of help are available to provide information, support, and assistance for sexual addicts trying to regain control of their lives. These include inpatient and outpatient treatment, professional associations, self-help groups, and aftercare support groups.

Treating Sexual Addiction

Treatment programs for sexual addiction include patient, outpatient, and aftercare support, and self-help groups. Treatment programs also offer family counseling programs, support groups, and educational workshops for addicts and their families to help them understand the facets of belief and family life that are part of the addiction.

Unlike recovering alcoholics who must abstain from drinking for life, sexual addicts are led back into a normal, healthy sex life much in the way those suffering from eating disorders must relearn healthy eating patterns.

Dr. Carnes' program is based on the spiritual principals of the Twelve Step program of Alcoholics Anonymous, and it incorporates the expertise of the most knowledgeable health care professionals in the field of sexual addiction.

Recovery from sexual addiction is a lifelong journey. Dr. Carnes' program is designed to set addicts on the road to recovery, to provide relapse prevention techniques, and to help them stay in recovery with the help of aftercare and Twelve Step recovery support groups.

Are Sexual Addicts Ever Cured?

Like other types of addicts, some sexual addicts may never be "cured." Sexual addicts achieve a state of recovery, but maintaining that recovery can be a lifelong, day-by-day process. The Twelve Step treatment approach teaches addicts to take their recovery "one day at a time"—concentrating on the present, not the future.

Sexual Codependency—The Co-Addict

Partners of sexual addicts, like partners of alcoholics, can also benefit from counseling and support groups. Normally these partners are codependents, and they, too, suffer from the extreme adverse effects of the addiction. Inpatient and outpatient programs, counseling, and support groups are all available to help them regain control of their lives and support the recovery of their partner.

**Lawrence A. Siegel and
Richard M. Siegel**

 **NO**

Sex Addiction: Recovering from a Shady Concept

It seems, more than ever, that many Americans are more comfortable keeping sex in the dark or, as sex addiction advocates might actually prefer, *in* the shadows. We seem to have gotten no further than the Puritan claims of sex being evil and pleasure being threatening. "The Devil made me do it" seems to be something of a battle cry, especially when someone gets caught cheating on their spouse, having inappropriate dalliances with congressional pages, or visiting prostitutes. Even those not in relationships are easily targeted. We constantly hear about the "dangers" of internet porn and how every internet chat room is just teeming with predators just waiting to devour our children. Daily masturbation is considered by these folks as being unhealthy and a marked pathology. As a society, we seem able to be comfortable with sex only as long as we make it uncomfortable. As one of the leading sexologists, Marty Klein, once wrote:

> "If mass murderer Ted Bundy had announced that watching Cosby Show reruns had motivated his awful crimes, he would have been dismissed as a deranged sociopath. Instead, Bundy proclaimed that his 'pornography addiction' made him do it, and many Right-wing feminists and conservatives treated this as the conclusion of a thoughtful social scientist. Why?"[1]

The whole idea of "sex addiction" is borne out of a moralistic ideology masquerading as science. It is a concept that seems to serve no other purpose than to relegate sexual expression to the level of shameful acts, except within the extremely narrow and myopic scope of a monogamous, heterosexual marriage. Sexual diversity? Interests in unusual forms or frequency of sexual expression? Choosing not to be monogamous? Advocates of "sex addiction" would likely see these as the uncontrollable acts of a sexually pathological individual; one who needs curing.

To be clear, we do not deny the fact that, for some people, sexual behavior can become problematic, even dysfunctional or unmanageable. Our objection is with the use of the term "sexual addiction" to describe a virtually unlimited array of—in fact, practically ANY—aspect of sexual expression that falls outside of the typically Christian view of marriage. We believe that the term contributes to a generally sex-negative, pleasure-phobic tone in American society, and it also tends to "pathologize" most forms of sexual expression that fall outside of a narrow view of what "normal" sex is supposed to look like. This is a point made clear by sex addiction advocates" own rhetoric. Three of the guiding principles of Sexaholics Anonymous include the notion that (1) sex is most healthy in the context of a monogamous, heterosexual relationship; (2) sexual expression has "obvious" limits; and (3) it is unhealthy to engage in any sexual activity for the sole purpose of feeling better, either emotionally or to escape one's problems. These principles do not represent either science or most people's experience. They, in fact, represent a restrictive and repressive view of sex and sexuality and reflect an arrogance that sex addiction proponents are the keepers of the scepter of morality and normalcy. Moreover, the concept of "sex addiction" comes out of a shame-based, arbitrarily judgmental addiction model and does not speak to the wide range of sexual diversity; both in and outside the context of a committed relationship.

A primary objection to the use of the term "sex addiction," an objection shared with regard to other supposed behavioral "addictions," is that the term *addiction* has long ago been discredited. Back in 1964, the World Health Organization (WHO) declared the term "addiction" to be clinically invalid and recommended in favor of dependence, which can exist in varying degrees of severity, as opposed to an all-or-nothing disease entity (as it is still commonly perceived).[2] This is when we began to see the terms *chemical dependency* and *substance abuse,* terms considered to be much more appropriate and clinically useful. This, however, did not sit well with the addiction industry. Another objection to the concept of "sex addiction" is that it is a misnomer whose very foundation as a clinically significant diagnosis is built on flawed and faulty premises. For example, a common assertion put forth by proponents of sex addiction states that the chemical actions in the brain during sexual activity are the same as the chemical activity involved in alcohol and drug use. They, therefore, claim that both sexual activity and substance abuse share reward and reinforcement mechanisms that produce the "craving" and "addictive" behaviors. This assertion is flawed on several levels, not the least of which is that it is based on drawing conclusions from brain scan imaging that are devoid of any real interpretive foundation; a "leap of faith," so to speak. Furthermore, it is somewhat of a stretch to equate the neurophysiological mechanisms which underlie chemical dependency, tolerance, and withdrawal with the underlying mechanisms of what is most often obsessive-compulsive or anxiety-reducing behaviors like gambling, shopping, and sex. Another example often cited by sex addiction proponents is the assertion that, like alcohol and drugs, the "sex addict" is completely incapable of controlling his or her self-destructive behavior. Of course, this begs the question of how, then, can one change behavior they are incapable of controlling? More importantly, however, is the unique excuse this "disease" model provides for abdicating personal responsibility. "It's not my fault, I have a disease." Finally, a major assertion put out by sex addiction advocates is that anyone who is hypersexual in any way (e.g., frequent masturbation, anonymous "hook ups," infidelity, and cybersex) must have been abused as children or adolescents. Again, the

flaws here are obvious and serve to continue to relegate any type of frequent sexual engagement to the pathological and unseemly.

Every clinician knows that "addiction" is not a word that appears anywhere in the Diagnostic and Statistical Manual, or "DSM," the diagnostic
guidebook used by psychiatrists and psychologists to make any psychopatho-
logical diagnosis. Nor does it appear in any of the International Classification
of Diseases (ICD-10), codes used for classifying medical diagnoses. "Abuse"
and "dependence" do appear in the DSM, relevant only to substance use patterns, but "addiction" does not. Similarly, there is an ICD-10 code for "substance dependence," but not addiction. Why? Perhaps because the word
means different things to different people, especially when used in so many
different contexts. Even without acknowledging the many trivial uses of the
addiction concept, such as bumper stickers that proclaim, *"addicted to sports,
not drugs,"* cookies that claim to be *"deliciously addicting,"* Garfield coffee
mugs that warn *"don't talk to me until after my first cup,"* or T-shirts that say
"chocoholic," there aren't even consistent *clinical* definitions for the concept of
addiction. A 1993 study, published in the American Journal of Drug and Alcohol
Abuse, compared the diagnostic criteria for substance abuse and dependence
between the DSM and ICD-10. The results showed very little agreement
between the two.[3]

Pharmacologists, researchers who study the effects of drugs, define
addiction primarily based on the presence of tolerance and withdrawal. Both
of these phenomena are based on pharmacological and toxicological concepts
of "cellular adaptation," wherein the body, at the very cellular level, becomes
accustomed to the constant presence of a substance, and readjusts for "normal"
function; in other words, whatever the "normal" response was before regular
use of the substance began returns. This adaptation first accounts for tolerance, wherein an increasing dose of the substance to which the system has
adapted is needed to maintain the same level of "normal." Then it results in
withdrawal, wherein any discontinuation of the substance disrupts the "new"
equilibrium the system has achieved and symptoms of "withdrawal sickness"
ensue. This is probably most often attributed to addiction to opiates, such as
heroin, because of its comparison to "having a monkey on one's back," with a
constantly growing appetite, and its notorious "cold turkey" withdrawal. But
perhaps it is most commonly observed with the chronic use of drugs with less
sinister reputations, such as caffeine, nicotine or alcohol.

Traditional psychotherapists may typically define addiction as a faulty
coping mechanism, or more accurately, the *result* of using a faulty coping
mechanism to deal with some underlying issue. Another way to consider this
is to see addiction as the symptom, rather than the disease, which is why the
traditional therapist, of any theoretical orientation, is likely to want to find
the causative issue or issues, and either teach the patient more effective coping mechanisms or resolve the unresolved issue(s) altogether.

Another definition of addiction has emerged, and seems to have taken
center-stage, since the development of a pseudo-medical specialty known as
"addictionology" within the last twenty or so years. Made up primarily of
physicians, but including a variety of "addiction professionals," this field has

helped to forge a treatment industry based on the disease model of addiction that is at the core of 12-Step "fellowships," such as Alcoholics Anonymous and Narcotics Anonymous. Ironically, despite the resistance to medical or psychiatric treatment historically expressed in AA or NA, their philosophy has become the mainstay of the addictionological paradigm.

If the concept of chemical addictions, which have a neurophysiological basis that can be measured and observed, yields no clinical consensus, how, then, can we legitimize the much vaguer notion that individuals can be "addicted" to behavior, people, emotions, or even one's own brain chemistry? Other than to undermine responsibility and self-determination, we really can't. It does a tremendous disservice to our clients and patients to brand them with a label so full of judgment, arbitrary opinion, and fatuous science. It robs individuals of the ability to find their own levels of comfort and, ultimately, be the determining force in directing their own lives. There is a significant and qualitative difference between the person who acts because he or she can't (not a choice, but a position of default) and the person who is empowered to choose not to. As clinicians, we should be loathe to send our clients and patients down such a fearful, shameful road.

In 1989, Patrick Carnes, founder of the sex addiction movement, wrote a book entitled "Contrary to Love." The book is rife with rhetoric and personal ideology that reveals Carnes's lack of training, knowledge, and understanding of sexuality and sexual expression; not surprising for someone whose background is solely in the disease model of alcoholism. This, while seemingly a harsh judgment, is clearly reflected in his Sex Addiction Screening Test (SAST). Even a cursory glance at the items on the SAST show a deep-seeded bias against most forms of sexual expression. Unlike other legitimate screening and assessment tools, there is no scientific foundation that would show this tool to be credible (i.e., tests of reliability and validity). Instead, Carnes developed this "test" by simply culling his own ideas from his book. Annie Sprinkle, America's first adult-film-star-turned-PhD-Sexologist, has written a very good web article on the myth of sex addiction. In it, she also describes some of the shortcomings of the SAST. While not describing the complete test here, a listing of some of the assessment questions are listed below, along with commentary.[4]

1. *Have you subscribed to sexually explicit magazines like Playboy or Penthouse?* This question is based on the assumption that it is unhealthy to view images of naked bodies. Does that mean that the millions of people who subscribe to or buy adult magazines are sex addicts? Are adolescent boys who look at the Sports Illustrated Swim Suit edition budding sex addicts? By extension, if looking at Playboy or Penthouse is unhealthy and pathological, then those millions of people who look at hardcore magazines or Internet porn should be hospitalized!

2. *Do you often find yourself preoccupied with sexual thoughts?* This is totally nebulous. What does "preoccupied" mean? How often does one have to think about sex in order to constitute preoccupation? Research has shown that men, on average, think about sex every eight seconds; does that mean that men are inherently sex addicts?

3. *Do you feel that your sexual behavior is not normal?* What is normal? What do they use as a comparison? As sexologists, we can state unequivocally that the majority of people's sexual concerns relate, in one way or another, to the question "Am I normal?" This is incredibly vague, nebulous, and laughably unscientific.

4. *Are any of your sexual activities against the law?* This question is also steeped in a bias that there is only a narrowly acceptable realm of sexual expression. It assumes that any sexual behavior that is against the law is bad. Is being or engaging a prostitute a sign of pathology? What about the fact that oral sex, anal sex, and woman on top are illegal in several states?

5. *Have you ever felt degraded by your sexual behavior?* Again, there is a serious lack of quantification here. Does regretting a sexual encounter constitute feeling degraded? Does performing oral sex for your partner, even though you think it's degrading, constitute a pathology or compromise? What if one's partner does something during sex play that is unexpected and perceived as degrading (like ejaculating on someone's face or body)? What if someone enjoys feeling degraded? This question pathologizes at least half of the S/M and B/D communities. Moreover, anyone who has had a long and active sexual life may likely, at one point, have felt degraded. It is important to note that this question does not ask if one consistently puts oneself in a position of being degraded but, rather, have you ever felt degraded. We suspect that most people can lay claim to that.

6. *Has sex been a way for you to escape your problems?* Is there a better way to escape one's problems temporarily? This is a common bias used against both sex and alcohol use: using sex or alcohol to provide relief from anxieties or problems is inherently problematic. It also begs the question: why are things like sex and alcohol not appropriate to change how one is feeling but Zoloft, Paxil, Xanax, and Klonopin are? The truth of the matter is that sex is often an excellent and healthy way to occasionally experience relief from life's stressors and problems.

7. *When you have sex, do you feel depressed afterwards?* Sex is often a great way to get in touch with one's feelings. Oftentimes, people do feel depressed after a sexual experience, for any number of reasons. Furthermore, this doesn't mean that sex was the depressing part! Perhaps people feel depressed because they had dashed expectations of the person they were involved with. Unfulfilled expectations, lack of communication, and inattentiveness to one's needs and desires often result in post-coital feelings of sadness and disappointment. In addition, asking someone if they "feel depressed" is arbitrary, subjective, and clinically invalid.

8. *Do you feel controlled by your sexual desire?* Again, we are being asked to make an arbitrary, subjective, and clinically invalid assessment. There is an undercurrent here that seems to imply that a strong sexual desire is somehow not normal. Human beings are biologically programmed to strongly desire sex. Our clients and patients might be better served if we addressed not their desires, but how and when they act upon them.

Again, it needs noting that the concept of "sex addiction" is one with very little clinical relevance or usefulness, despite it's popularity. Healthy sexual expression encompasses a wide array of forms, functions, and frequency, as well as myriad emotional dynamics and personal experiences. Healthy behavior, in general, and sexual behavior, in particular, exists on a continuum rather than a quantifiable point. Using the addiction model to describe sexual behavior simply adds to the shame and stigma that is already too often attached to various forms of sexual expression. Can sexual behaviors become problematic? Most certainly. However, we must be careful to not overpathologize even problematic sexual behaviors because, most often, they are symptomatic expressions rather than primary problems.

For many years, sexologists have described compulsive sexual behavior, where sexual obsessions and compulsions are recurrent, distressing, and interfere with daily functioning. The actual number of people suffering from this type of sexual problem is relatively small. Compulsive sexual behaviors are generally divided into two broad categories: *paraphilic* and *non-paraphilic.*[5] Paraphilias are defined as recurrent, intensely arousing fantasies, sexual urges, or behaviors involving non-human objects, pain and humiliation, or children.[6] Paraphilic behaviors are usually non-conventional forms of sexual expression that, in the extreme, can be harmful to relationships and individuals. Some examples of paraphilias listed in the DSM are pedophilia (sexual attraction to children), exhibitionism (exposing one's genitals in public), voyeurism (sexual excitement from watching an unsuspecting person), sexual sadism (sexual excitement from dominating or inflicting pain), sexual masochism (sexual excitement from being dominated or receiving pain), transvestic fetishism (sexual excitement from wearing clothes of the other sex), and frotteurism (sexual excitement from rubbing up against or fondling an unsuspecting person). All of these behaviors exist on a continuum of healthy fantasy play to dangerous, abusive, and illegal acts. A sexologist is able to view these behaviors in varying degrees, knowing the difference between teacher-student fantasy role play and cruising a playground for victims; between provocative exhibitionist displays (including public displays of affection) and illegal, abusive public exposure. For those with a "sex addiction" perspective, simply having paraphilic thoughts or desires of any kind is reason to brand the individual a "sex addict."

The other category of compulsive sexual behavior is non-paraphilic, and generally involves more conventional sexual behaviors which, when taken to the extreme, cause marked distress and interference with daily functioning. This category includes a fixation on an unattainable partner, compulsive masturbation, compulsive love relationships, and compulsive sexuality in a relationship. The most vocal criticism of the idea of compulsive sexual behavior as a clinical disorder appears to center on the overpathologizing of these behaviors. Unless specifically trained in sexuality, most clinicians are either uncomfortable or unfamiliar with the wide range of "normal" sexual behavior and fail to distinguish between individuals who experience conflict between their values and sexual behavior, and those with obsessive sexual behavior.[7] When diagnosing compulsive sexual behavior overall, there is little consensus even among sexologists. However, it still provides a more useful clinical framework for the professional trained in sexuality and sexual health.

To recognize that sexual behavior can be problematic is not the same as labeling the behaviors as "sexually compulsive" or "sexual addiction." The reality is that sexual problems are quite common and are usually due to non-pathological factors. Quite simply, people make mistakes (some more than others). People also act impulsively. People don't always make good sexual choices. When people do make mistakes, act impulsively, and make bad decisions, it often negatively impacts their relationships; sometimes even their lives. Moreover, people do often use sex as a coping mechanism or, to borrow from addiction language, medicating behavior that can become problematic. However, this is qualitatively different from the concept that problematic sexual behavior means the individual is a "sexual addict" with uncontrollable urges and potentially dangerous intent. Most problematic sexual behavior can be effectively redirected (and cured) through psycho-sexual education, counseling, and experience. According to proponents of "sex addiction," problematic sexual behavior cannot be cured. Rather, the "sex addict" is destined for a life of maintaining a constant vigil to prevent the behavior from reoccurring, often to the point of obsession, and will be engaged in a lifelong process of recovery. Unfortunately, this view often causes people to live in fear of the "demon" lurking around every corner: themselves.

References

1. Klein M. The myth of sex addiction. Sexual Intelligence: An Electronic Newsletter (Issue #1). March, 2000. . . .

2. Center for Substance Abuse Treatment (CSAT) and Substance Abuse and Mental Health Services Administration (SAMHSA). Substance use disorders: A guide to the use of language. 2004.

3. Rappaport M., Tipp J., Schuckit M. A comparison of ICD-10 and DSM-III criteria for substance abuse and dependence. American Journal of Drug and Alcohol Abuse. June, 1993.

4. Sprinkle, A. Sex addiction. Online article. . . .

5. Coleman E. What sexual scientists know about compulsive sexual behavior. Electronic series of the Society for the Scientific Study of Sexuality (SSSS). Vol 2(1). 1996. . . .

6. American Psychiatric Association. Diagnostic and Statistical Manual of Mental Disorders. 4th edition, TR. Washington: American Psychiatric Publishing. June, 2000.

7. Coleman E. What sexual scientists know about compulsive sexual behavior. Electronic series of the Society for the Scientific Study of Sexuality (SSSS). Vol 2(1). 1996. . . .

CHALLENGE QUESTIONS

Can Sex Be Addictive?

1. The Siegels seem to see the "diagnosis" of sexual addiction as having a moral basis. Are there other, more conventional diagnoses in the DSM-IV that might also be viewed in this manner? If so, what implications would this have for these diagnoses?
2. Become familiar with several definitions of "addiction." According to those definitions, can sex be addictive? Support your answer.
3. Imagine you are working with a couple in therapy where the husband frequently indulges in pornography. What possible dangers could his behavior present? Should his habit be considered a sexual addiction? Support your answer.
4. Become familiar with Alcoholics Anonymous's 12-Step program. In your opinion, can this program be successfully revised to help those trying to overcome sexual dysfunction? What similarities do you see between alcoholism and compulsive sexual dysfunction?
5. Compare and contrast the physiological mechanisms underlying chemical addiction with the physiological mechanisms underlying sexual stimulation. Are they similar, as Carnes suggests?

Contributors to This Volume

EDITOR

DR. BRENT SLIFE is currently professor of psychology at Brigham Young University, where he chairs the doctoral program in theoretical and philosophical psychology and serves as a member of the doctoral program in clinical psychology. He has been honored recently with several awards for his scholarship and teaching, including the Eliza R. Snow Award (for research on the interface of science and religion), the Karl G. Maeser Award (top researcher at BYU), Circle of Honor Award (Student Honor Association), and both Teacher of the Year by the university and Most Outstanding Professor by the psychology student honorary, Psi Chi.

Professor Slife moved from Baylor University where he served as director of clinical training for many years and was honored there as Outstanding Research Professor. He also received the Circle of Achievement award for his teaching. The recipient of numerous grants (e.g., NSF, NEH), he is also listed in *Who's Who in the World, America, Science and Engineering,* and *Health and Medicine.* As a fellow of several professional organizations, including the American Psychological Association, he recently served as the president of the Society of Theoretical and Philosophical Psychology and serves currently on the editorial boards of six journals: *Journal of Mind and Behavior, Journal of Theoretical and Philosophical Psychology, Humanistic Psychologist, Qualitative Research in Psychology, International Journal of Existential Psychology and Psychotherapy,* and *Terrorism Research.*

He has authored over 120 articles and six books, including *Taking Sides: Clashing Views on Psychological Issues* (2008, McGraw-Hill), *Critical Thinking About Psychology: Hidden Assumptions and Plausible Alternatives* (2005, APA Books), *Critical Issues in Psychotherapy: Translating New Ideas into Practice* (2001, Sage Publications), *What's Behind the Research? Hidden Assumptions in the Behavioral Sciences* (1995, Sage Publications), and *Time and Psychological Explanation* (1993, SUNY Press). Dr. Slife also continues his psychotherapy practice of over 25 years, where he specializes in marital and family therapies. Please check his website, www.brentdslife.com, for downloadable articles and links to his books.

AUTHORS

CRAIG A. ANDERSON received his Ph.D. in psychology from Stanford University and is currently a professor and chair of the Department of Psychology at Iowa State University.

PHILIP ASPDEN is executive director of the Center for Research on the Information Society (CRIS) in Pennington, New Jersey. He has consulted in telecommunications and technology-based economic development for a wide range of high-tech firms, public bodies, and foundations in both the United States and Europe. He has also been a research scholar at the International Institute for Applied Systems Analysis.

HOWARD E. BARBAREE is clinical director of the Law and Mental Health Program at the Centre for Addiction and Mental Health and a professor in the Department of Psychiatry at the University of Toronto. He is also founding director of the Warkworth Sexual Behaviour Clinic, a Canadian Federal Penitentiary treatment program for sex offenders. Dr. Barbaree has published numerous journal articles and book chapters on the topic, and he is coeditor, with William L. Marshall and Stephen M. Hudson, of *The Juvenile Sex Offender* (Guilford, 1993).

JOHN A. BARGH is a professor of psychology at Yale University. In 1989, he received the American Psychological Association (APA) Early Career Award for contributions to psychology. His research interests include attitudes; close relationships; ethics and morality; motivation and goal setting; person perception; prejudice and stereotyping; and social cognition.

RUSSELL A. BARKLEY is currently professor of psychiatry at the Medical University of South Carolina. The recipient of numerous awards for his research on ADHD, Dr. Barkley has authored, co-authored, or co-edited 15 books and clinical manuals and has published more than 170 scientific articles and book chapters on ADHD and related disorders.

ROY F. BAUMEISTER is a professor of psychology and the Francis Eppes Eminent Scholar at Florida State University. He is the author of sixteen books and dozens of journal articles and book chapters. His current research interests include the psychology of self control, self-destructive behavior, and the need to belong.

DIANA BAUMRIND is a research psychologist and the principal investigator for the Family Socialization and Developmental Competence Project of the University of California's Institute for Human Development in Berkeley, California. She has contributed numerous articles to professional journals and books, and she is on the editorial board of *Developmental Psychology*. She is also the author of *Child Maltreatment and Optimal Caregiving in Social Contexts* (Garland, 1995).

JOSEPH BIEDERMAN is chief of the Joint Program in Pediatric Psychopharmacology at the Massachusetts General and McLean Hospitals in Boston, Massachusetts, and a professor of psychiatry at Harvard Medical School. He is board certified in general and child psychiatry. His clinical program treats more than 2,000 children, adolescents, and adults, and evaluates more than 300 new patients every year. Dr. Biederman's research focus is on attention deficit hyperactivity disorder, juvenile mood and anxiety disorders, and studies of children at risk.

ARTHUR C. BOHART is a professor of psychology at California State University in Dominguez Hills. He is also affiliated with Saybrook Graduate School and Research Center in San Francisco, CA. He has published extensively on the client's active role in psychotherapy. He is the author of several books, including *How Clients Make Therapy Work: The Process of Active Self-Healing* (with Karen Tallman; APA, 1999) and *Foundations of Clinical and Counseling Psychology* (with Judith Todd; Waveland Press, 3rd edition, 2002).

JEANNE BROOKS-GUNN is the Virginia and Leonard Marx Professor of Child Development and Education at Teacher's College, Columbia University. She assesses parental contributions to cognitive development and studies the impact of poverty on child outcomes. She earned her Ed.M. from Harvard University and her Ph.D. from the University of Pennsylvania. She has published over 300 articles and 15 books, including *Conflict and Cohesion in Families: Causes and Consequences,* coedited with Martha J. Cox (Lawrence Erlbaum, 1999).

PATRICK J. CARNES is a nationally known speaker and pioneer in the field of sexual addiction. His work has brought hope and understanding to millions of people seeking to overcome the power of their addictions. An award-winning author, his work has been described as "simply the best available on addiction and its consequences." Dr. Carnes is the primary architect of the Gentle Path clinical program and is the executive director of the Gentle Path program at Pine Grove, located in Hattiesburg, MS.

GRACE CHANG is currently a doctoral student in the clinical psychology program at the University of Nebraska.

TANYA L. CHARTRAND is an associate professor of marketing and psychology in the Fuqua School of Business at Duke University. Her research interests include consumer behavior, social psychology, social cognition, automaticity and nonconscious processes, and research methods.

GERALD COLES is an educational psychologist who focuses mainly on literacy and learning disabilities. He is the author of *Reading the Naked Truth: Literacy, Legislation, and Lies* (Heinemann, 2003) and *Misreading Reading: The Bad Science that Hurts Children* (Heinemann, 2000). He was formerly a professor at the Robert Wood Johnson Medical School and the University of Rochester.

PATRICK H. DELEON is a former president of the American Psychological Association. He received a Ph.D. in Clinical Psychology at Purdue University, a Master of Public Health at the University of Hawaii, and a JD at the Columbus School of Law. He is currently using his training and skills as a clinical psychologist by working on Capital Hill. He helps shape policy and legislation that best reflects both the science and application of clinical psychology.

M. B. DONNELLAN is an assistant professor in the Department of Psychology at Michigan State University. He actively conducts research on several topics related to personality traits, self-esteem, and personality development. He also has interests in psychological assessment and longitudinal research.

DEBRA LINA DUNIVIN was a 1992–1994 APA Congressional Fellow. Currently, she is a major in the U.S. Army and is a Department of Defense Psychopharmacology Fellow in Washington, D.C.

PAUL R. EHRLICH is a professor in the Department of Biological Sciences at Stanford University. He is also the president of the Center for Conservation Biology at Stanford. He is a fellow of the American Association for the Advancement of Science, the American Academy of Arts and Sciences, and the American Philosophical Society, and a member of the National Academy of Sciences.

STEPHEN V. FARAONE, a clinical psychologist, is an associate professor in the Department of Psychiatry at Harvard Medical School at the Massachusetts Mental Health Center and director of Pediatric Psychopharmacology Research at Massachusetts General Hospital. He is coeditor of the journal *Neuropsychiatric Genetics* and statistical section editor of the *Journal of Child and Adolescent Psychopharmacology*. The author or coauthor of over 300 journal articles, editorials, chapters, and books, he was the eighth highest producer of high-impact papers in psychiatry from 1990 to 1999, as determined by the Institute for Scientific Information.

MARCUS W. FELDMAN is a professor in the Department of Biological Sciences and director of the Morrison Institute for Population and Resource Studies at Stanford University. He uses applied mathematics and computer modeling to simulate the process of evolution. He is managing editor of *Theoretical Population Biology* and associate editor of the journals *Genetics, Complexity,* the *Annals of Human Genetics, Human Genomics,* and the *Annals of Human Biology*. He is a former editor of *The American Naturalist*.

R. G. FREY, a professor of philosophy at Bowling Green State University, is a senior research fellow of the Social Philosophy and Policy Center in Bowling Green, of the Kennedy Institute of Ethics, and of the Westminster Institute of Ethics and Public Policy at the University of Ontario, Canada. He is the author of numerous articles and books on ethical theory, applied ethics, the history of ethics, and social/political theory. And he is coauthor, with Gerald Dworkin and Sissela Bok, of *Euthanasia and Physician-Assisted Suicide* (Cambridge University Press, 1988).

HOWARD GARDNER is the John H. and Elisabeth A. Hobbs Professor in Cognition and Education at the Harvard Graduate School of Education. He also holds positions as adjunct professor of psychology at Harvard, adjunct professor of neurology at the Boston University School of Medicine, and codirector of Harvard Project Zero. He is the author of several hundred articles and 18 books, including *Extraordinary Minds* (Basic

Books, 1997) and *The Disciplined Mind: What All Students Should Understand* (Simon & Schuster, 1999).

DOUGLAS A. GENTILE received his doctorate in child psychology from the Institute of Child Development at the University of Minnesota. He is a developmental psychologist and the director of research for the National Institute on Media and the Family. He is currently a member of the psychology department faculty at Iowa State University.

LINDA S. GOTTFREDSON is a professor of educational studies at the University of Delaware, where she has been teaching since 1986, and codirector of the Delaware–Johns Hopkins Project for the Study of Intelligence and Society. She earned her Ph.D. in sociology from the Johns Hopkins University in 1977 and won the Mensa Research Foundation Award for Excellence in Research, 1999–2000. Her research interests include intelligence and social inequality, employment testing and job aptitude demands, and affirmative action and multicultural diversity.

ROBERT-JAY GREEN is a distinguished professor and associate director of the clinical psychology Ph.D. program at the California School of Professional Psychology. He has written over 70 publications on topics that include multicultural couple and family therapy, male gender roles, and gay and lesbian couples in family relationships. Green is the winner of the 2001 Award for Distinguished Contributions to Family Systems Research, American Family Therapy Academy.

WEN-JUI HAN is an assistant professor of social work in the School of Social Work at Columbia University. Her professional interests include social welfare policy, with an emphasis on children and families, and child care issues facing immigrant families. She earned her M.S.W. from the University of California, Los Angeles, and her Ph.D. from Columbia University.

STEVEN C. HAYES is a professor in the Department of Psychology at the University of Nevada. An author of 25 books and 340 scientific articles, his career has focused on an analysis of the nature of human language and cognition and the application of this to the understanding and alleviation of human suffering. In 1992, the Institute for Scientific Information listed him as the 30th "highest impact" psychologist in the world during 1986–1990. Dr. Hayes has also been President of Division 25 of the American Psychological Association, of the American Association of Applied and Preventive Psychology, and of the Association for Advancement of Behavior Therapy.

DAVID HEALY is a psychiatrist at Cardiff University in Wales. He has authored 13 books on various aspects of psychopharmaceuticals as well as 110 peer-reviewed papers and approximately 100 other publications. Nine of these books are on the area of the history of psychopharmacology, for which Healy has a leading role worldwide. His other research interests include cognitive functioning in affective disorders and psychoses, and circadian rhythms in affective disorders.

E. MAVIS HETHERINGTON is an emeritus professor in the Department of Psychology at the University of Virginia. She is also a former president of Division 7, the Developmental Psychology Division of the American Psychological Association, and of the Society for Research in Child Development in Adolescence. She has authored and edited many books in the area of child development, including *Child Psychology: A Contemporary Viewpoint,* updated 5th ed., coauthored with Virginia Otis Locke and Ross D. Parke (McGraw-Hill, 2002). She earned her Ph.D. in psychology from the University of California, Berkeley.

GAIL E. JOSEPH is an assistant professor in educational psychology at the University of Colorado at Denver. She has been involved in national projects designed to help professionals work with children who have challenging behaviors.

JAY JOSEPH is a registered clinical psychologist doing a postdoctoral internship at a psychotherapy clinic.

JAMES E. KATZ is a professor of communication at Rutgers University and a senior scientist at Bellcore (Bell Communications Research) in New Jersey. He has examined a variety of issues concerning the Internet and its societal consequences, and he is an expert in privacy policy. He has also been involved in the World Wide Web Consortium and U.S. National Science Foundation planning exercises for research on knowledge networks.

JOHN KELLY is a freelance journalist and coauthor of a number of books, including *Stepfamilies: Love, Marriage, and Parenting in the First Decade* (Broadway Books, 1999).

ALFIE KOHN is a popular lecturer and the author of several books on education and human behavior. He is often viewed as the leading critic of competition and his works fly in the face of traditional wisdom about motivation and compensation. Kohn was educated at Brown University and the University of Chicago.

ROBERT KRAUT is a professor of social psychology and human computer interaction at Carnegie Mellon University, with joint appointments in the Department of Social and Decision Sciences, the Human Computer Interaction Institute, and the Graduate School of Industrial Administration. His current research focuses on the design and social impacts of information technologies in small groups, in the home, and between organizations. He is coauthor of *Research Recommendations to Facilitate Distributed Work* (National Academy Press, 1994).

GEORGIOS K. LAMPROPOULOS has a Master's Degree in Clinical Psychology and is currently a Ph.D. candidate in Counseling Psychology at Ball State University. He is also a practitioner and a clinical researcher with primary interests in the process and outcome of psychotherapy. He has guest-edited three special issues in psychology journals (e.g., *Journal of Clinical Psychology*) and has published over 20 peer-reviewed journal articles on psychotherapy practice, research, and training.

YVON D. LAPIERRE is the founder and former director general of the University of Ottawa Institute of Mental Health Research and is an internationally recognized clinical researcher in biological psychiatry and psychopharmacology. He has collaborated with the pharmaceutical industry in the development of new therapeutic agents for the treatment of major mental disorders, and with other leading investigators in the study of the relationship between pharmacologic treatment options and clinical response. His expertise has placed him in high demand as a consultant for many other national and international organizations. Dr. Lapierre has also authored or co-authored over 300 scientific publications.

JULIA M. LEWIS is a professor of psychology at San Francisco State University. Her area of expertise is divorce and its effect on children, and she hold a Ph.D. in psychology from the University of California, Los Angeles.

GARY F. MARCUS is a professor of psychology at New York University and director of the NYU Infant Language Learning Center. Among others, he is the author of *The Birth of the Mind: How a Tiny Number of Genes Creates the Complexities of Human Thought* (Basic Books, 2004) and *The Algebraic Mind: Integrating Connectionism and Cognitive Science* (The MIT Press, 2003).

ALEXANDRA MARIC is affiliated with the Forensic Division of the Clarke Institute of Psychiatry, which is part of the University of Toronto's Centre for Addiction and Mental Health.

STANLEY MILGRAM (1933–1984) was an experimental social psychologist and a professor of psychology at the Graduate School and University Center of the City University of New York. He is especially well known for his series of controversial investigations regarding obedience to authority, which were performed at Yale University from 1960 to 1963. His publications include *Obedience to Authority: An Experimental View* (Harper & Row, 1975).

CHERYL K. OLSON is a professor of psychiatry at the Harvard Medical School Center for Mental Health and Media and has been recognized nationally as an expert in health communications and behavior change.

ELLEN C. PERRIN is a professor of pediatrics at Tufts-New England Medical Center. She is the author of *Sexual Orientation in Child and Adolescent Health Care* (Springer, 2002).

WILLIAM N. ROBINER is currently at the University of Minnesota, where he teaches in the Department of Neurology. He is a diplomate in Health Psychology through the American Board of Professional Psychology and is former chair of the Psychology Standards Committee of the University of Minnesota Hospital. Dr. Robiner's clinical and research interests include AIDS, anxiety disorders, sexuality, and psychotherapy.

CHRISTOPHER H. ROSIK is a psychologist who has written extensively on the subject of homosexuality and therapy. He is a past president of the Christian Association for Psychological Studies, Inc., and a member of the National Association for Research and Therapy of Homosexuality.

DONALD L. RUBIN is a professor in both the Department of Speech Communication and the Department of Language Education at the University of Georgia. His long list of awards includes receiving the "Top Paper in Health Communication" from the International Communication Association in 2001 and the "Top Paper in Language and Social Interaction" from the Speech Communication Association in 2003.

DIANA E. H. RUSSELL is a professor emeritus of sociology at Mills College in Oakland, California. A leading authority on sexual violence against women and girls, she has performed research and written articles and books on rape, incest, the misogynist murder of women, and pornography for 25 years. Her publications include *Against Pornography: The Evidence of Harm* (Russell, 1994) and *Making Violence Sexy: Feminist Views on Pornography* (Teachers College Press, 1993).

JEFFREY A. SCHALER has been a psychologist and therapist in private practice since 1973. He is also an adjunct professor of justice, law, and society at American University's School of Public Affairs, where he has taught courses on drugs, psychiatry, liberty, justice, law, and public policy since 1990. He writes a regular column for *The Interpsych Newsletter,* and he is the author of *Smoking: Who Has the Right?* (Prometheus Books, 1998).

BARRY A. SCHREIER is coordinator of training for Counseling and Psychological Services at Purdue University in West Lafayette, Indiana. His areas of interest include gay, lesbian, bisexual, and transgendered issues; interpersonal supervision and training; and clinical ethics. He earned his Ph.D. in counseling psychology from the University of Missouri at Kansas City.

MICHAEL C. SETO is a research psychologist in the Law and Mental health Program at the Centre for Addiction and Mental Health in Toronto, Ontario, Canada. He earned his Ph.D. from Queen's University in 1997.

SALLY SHAYWITZ is a professor of pediatrics and child study at the Yale University School of Medicine. Her duties there include co-directing the Yale Center for the Study of Learning and Attention. She was recognized as both "One of the Best Doctors in America" and "One of America's Top Doctors" in 2002.

BENNETT A. SHAYWITZ is a professor of pediatrics and neurology at the Yale University School of Medicine. He is also the chief of pediatric neurology there. His honors include being elected to membership in the Institute of Medicine of the National Academy of Sciences, and receiving the Sidney Berman Award for the Study and Treatment of Learning Disabilities.

LAWRENCE A. SIEGEL is a certified clinical sexologist and associate fellow in the American Academy of Clinical Sexologists. He has served on faculty at several local colleges and universities, as well as other national health and teaching institutions, and currently serves as the health promotions coordinator for the Sexual Health Programs at Florida Atlantic University. He has been a private consultant for over 15 years and is the President/CEO of the Sage Institute for Family Development.

RICHARD M. SIEGEL is a Certified Addictions Professional and Certified Sex Therapist, as well as a sexuality educator certified by the American Association of Sex Educators, Counselors and Therapists. He is a seasoned educator and trainer for Planned Parenthood of South Palm Beach & Broward Counties, Palm Beach Community College, and serves as director of continuing education for the Sage Institute for Family Development.

PETER SINGER is the DeCamp Professor of Bioethics in the University Center for Human Values at Princeton University. He was foundation president of the International Association of Bioethics, and he is currently a member of its board of directors. He is coeditor of the journal *Bioethics,* and he is the author of *One World: The Ethics of Globalization* (Yale University Press, 2002).

BRENT D. SLIFE is currently a professor of psychology at Brigham Young University, where he chairs the doctoral program in theoretical and philosophical psychology and serves as a member of the doctoral program in clinical psychology. He has authored over 120 articles and six books, and currently serves on the editorial boards of six scholarly journals.

AMY FISHER SMITH is an assistant professor of psychology at the University of Dallas. She is a licensed clinical psychologist, and her most current research interests include the role and management of values—particularly therapist values—in psychotherapy.

PHILLIP S. STRAIN is a professor in educational psychology at the University of Colorado at Denver. Some of his work includes the development of comprehensive early-intervention programs for children with autism or severe problem behaviors.

ROBERT W. SUSSMAN is a professor of physical anthropology at Washington University in St. Louis, Missouri, and editor emeritus of *American Anthropologist.* He is the author of *The Biological Basis of Human Behavior: A Critical Review,* 2d ed. (Prentice Hall, 1998) and *Primate Ecology and Social Structure, Vol. 2: New World Monkeys,* 2d ed. (Pearson Higher Education, 2003). He earned his Ph.D. from Duke University in 1972.

WARREN THROCKMORTON is director of College Counseling and an associate professor of psychology at Grove City College in Grove City, Pennsylvania. He holds an M.A. from Central Michigan University and a Ph.D. from Ohio University.

SAMI TIMIMI is a consultant child and adolescent psychiatrist who works for the National Health Service in the United Kingdom. Timimi has published on several topics, including cross-cultural psychiatry, psychotherapy, eating disorders, and Attention Deficit Hyperactivity Disorder (ADHD).

THOMAS M. VANDER VEN is an assistant professor in the Department of Sociology and Anthropology at Ohio University. His areas of specialization include crime and delinquency and links between work, family, and crime. His articles have appeared in such journals as *Criminology* and *Social Problems,* and he is the author of *Working Mothers and Juvenile Delinquency* (LFB Scholarly Pub LLC, 2003).

JANE WALDFOGEL is a professor of social work in the School of Social Work at Columbia University. Her professional interests focus on social policy, including the impact of public policies on child and family well-being, Comparative Social Welfare policy, and child protective services and child welfare policy. She earned her M.Ed. and Ph.D. from Harvard University, and she is coeditor, with Sheldon Danziger, of *Securing the Future: Investing in Children From Birth to Adulthood* (Russell Sage Foundation, 2000).

JUDITH S. WALLERSTEIN is an internationally recognized authority on the effects of divorce on children and their parents. She has been executive director of the Center for the Family in Transition and a senior lecturer in the School of Social Welfare at the University of California, Berkeley. She is the author of *The Good Marriage: How and Why Love Lasts* (Warner Books, 1996) and coauthor, with Sandra Blakeslee, of *What About the Kids? Raising Your Children Before, During, and After Divorce* (Hyperion Press, 2003).

DENNIS C. WENDT is a graduate student at Brigham Young University's Department of Psychology, where he specializes in philosophical and theoretical issues regarding evidence-based practice and the therapeutic relationship in clinical psychology.

CHRIS WHITAKER is a statistician in the department of psychology at the University of Wales, Bangor.

JOHN WHITE is an emeritus professor of philosophy of education in the School of Educational Foundations and Policy Studies at the Institute of Education, University of London. His interests are in interrelationships among educational aims and applications to school curricula. His particular interest is in the concept of personal well-being and its educational importance. He has published many papers in the area of intelligence and is the author of *Do Howard Gardner's Multiple Intelligences Add Up?* (Institute of Education, 1998).

ERIN L. WILLIAMS is a researcher and Ph.D. candidate in psychology at Yale University.

RICHARD N. WILLIAMS is a researcher, statistician, theoretical psychologist, and professor of psychology at Brigham Young University. He currently serves as the assistant to the associate academic vice president of the university. He is one of the editors of the book, *Psychology for the Other: Levinas, Ethics and the Practice* of Psychology (Duquesne University Press, 2002), and has published numerous papers evaluating and critiquing psychological research.

MICHAEL L. WILSON has been studying primates in East Africa since 1992, starting with baboons in Kenya (1992–1993) and continuing with chimpanzees in Uganda (1996–1998) and Tanzania (2001–present). He received his Ph.D. in anthropology at Harvard University and is currently the director of field research for Gombe Stream Research Centre, Jane Goodall Institute–Tanzania.

LAURA L. WINN is an assistant professor in the Department of Communication at the Wayne State University. Her research interests include the effect that gender and class have on personal relationships.

JULIA T. WOOD is a professor of communication studies at the University of North Carolina at Chapel Hill. Her areas of specialization are gender, culture and communication, feminist theories, and personal relationships. Among many other publications, she is the editor of *Gender and Communication Research* (with Bonnie Dow, Sage Publications, 2006) and author of *Gendered Lives, Seventh edition* (Thomson/Wadsworth, 2006).

RICHARD WRANGHAM is a professor of anthropology at Harvard University. His main research interests are primate behavioral ecology and human evolutionary ecology. He earned his Ph.D. in zoology from Cambridge University in 1975, and he is coeditor of *Chimpanzee Cultures* (Harvard University Press, 1994).

ALICE M. YOUNG is a professor of psychology and of psychiatry and behavioral neurosciences at Wayne State University, where she also serves as associate dean of the College of Science. Her research interests include behavioral and brain processes involved in opioid tolerance and dependence.